THE UNIVERSITY IN SOCIETY

Written under the auspices of the
Shelby Cullom Davis Center for Historical Studies,
Princeton University

THE
UNIVERSITY IN SOCIETY

VOLUME II

*Europe, Scotland, and the United States from
the 16th to the 20th Century*

CONTRIBUTORS

Richard L. Kagan   Nicholas Phillipson

James McLachlan   R. Steven Turner

Konrad H. Jarausch   Robert L. Church

James M. McPherson

Edited by Lawrence Stone

PRINCETON UNIVERSITY PRESS

Library of Congress Cataloguing in Publication Data will be found
on the last printed page of this book.
Publication of this book has been aided by the Whitney Darrow
Publication Reserve Fund of Princeton University Press
and by the Shelby Cullom Davis Center for
Historical Studies, Princeton University.

This book has been composed in Linotype Janson.

Printed in the United States of America by
Princeton University Press,
Princeton, New Jersey

Introduction to Vols. I & II

When in 1969 the Shelby Cullom Davis Center for Historical Studies was established at Princeton University, it was decided to allocate part of the funds to the support of a research seminar. The purpose of the seminar is to bring together a group of scholars who are all working on a single theme, although their particular interests may be widely scattered in area, time, and even discipline. The theme of the seminar changes every four years or so, and is chosen on the basis of its intrinsic importance, its relative underdevelopment in the historical literature, and its interest to a core of members of the History Department at Princeton. The history of education fulfilled all three of these criteria, and it was therefore chosen as the theme for the first four years. This book of essays is the product of the first two years, 1969-71, all the contributors being participating members of the seminar, either as Visiting Fellows of the Center, as faculty at Princeton, or as graduate students.

Not all the contributors to this volume are concerned with identical problems in the history of higher education. But in one way or another they are all interested in the relationship between formal education and other social processes, rather than with either the history of educational institutions as such, or with the history of changes in the curriculum and scholarship as such. Their concern is therefore with what is at present a highly unsatisfactory body of theory and knowledge, namely the sociology of education.

Every institution partly reflects the social, economic, and political system, but partly also it lives a life of its own, independent of the interests and beliefs of the community. The university, like the family and the church, is one of the most poorly integrated of institutions, and again and again it has been obstinately resistant to changes which were clearly demanded by changing conditions around it. And yet, in the long run, no institution can survive indefinitely in glorious isolation, and the interaction between the university's own built-in conservatism and the pressures upon it to adapt to new external conditions is one of the most potentially illuminating, but most practically obscure, aspects of the process of historical change.

What is abundantly clear is that the response of the university to external change has been neither simple nor immediate. There were no uniform series of changes in the universities of Europe in conformity with such major upheavals as the Renaissance, the Reformation, secularism and the Enlightenment, the rise of the bureaucratic nation-state, the rise of the bourgeoisie, or the Industrial Revolution, and any attempt to force the history of higher education into any such Procrustean mold is bound to fail. Nor does the history of the university lend any support to theories about its simple function to inculcate established values and transmit established cultural norms. It has certainly performed such functions in all countries and at all times, but its obstinate resistance to the values of an industrialized society in the 19th century, for example, or its encouragement of subversive and even revolutionary ideas such as 14th century Lollardy or 20th century Marxism, hardly lends support to any notion of its role as no more than an agency of socialization. The university has not been a Parsonian functionalist institution responding slavishly to social needs. Nor has it been a Marxist superstructure, automatically providing the ideological props for the group which currently controls the means of production. Nor is it helpful to apply Max Weber's division of functions between the training of a cultivated gentleman and the training of a specialized expert, since most universities have always tried to do both at the same time.

The contributors to this volume attempt to throw light on the relationship of the university to society by adopting a series of tactical approaches to specific problems, rather than by evolving grand strategic theory and then trying it out on the empirical data. They ask such questions as: Who were the students? How many were there? How did they get to the university? Why did they come? How did they spend their time? What did they learn? What jobs did they fill afterward? How did they get them? And how, if at all, did what they learn help them or change them? They also ask such questions as: Who were the faculty? What careers did they aspire to? How did they relate to the patronage system of the society? And how did they view their role and obligations? It is by asking these kinds of questions, rather than by thinking up macrocosmic theory or by studying the internal administrative history of the individual institutions, that new understanding of the shifting relationship of the university to society is most likely to emerge.

One group of essays asks questions about the relationship of students and faculty to that peculiarly Oxbridge institution, the college. Professors Lytle and McConica show that the colleges were as much concerned to exploit and reflect the two principles of patronage and privilege as any other institution in the society. To look at students from the point of view of patronage and promotion sheds quite new light on the nature and function of the colleges and the university. Mr.

Morgan carries this interpretation a stage further, by showing the intimate two-way relationship between the colleges and the "country" society from which the alumni were drawn and to which they returned.

It is a fond belief of academics that what really matters is what goes on in the classroom and in the library, but some of the contributors call this belief seriously into question. Dr. McLachlan and Professor Rothblatt show that much of the social and intellectual life of the students was organized by the private initiative of the students themselves. At some periods the statutory curriculum played only a modest role in determining what actually went on at Oxford or Cambridge, or indeed at Princeton.

One common methodological characteristic of most of the contributors is their attempt to replace ignorance or wild guesses by solid quantifiable evidence, wherever it is both available and appropriate. One discovery, stressed by Professor Kagan and myself, is the importance of the rise and fall of student numbers in affecting the quality of life at the universities. We can now dimly see the shape of a vast seismic shift in west European cultural arrangements over the last four centuries. First there came a period of astonishing growth after the middle of the 16th century, so that by 1640 in England, Germany, and Spain (and also, as Professor Kagan is now discovering, in France and Italy) a staggering number of students were pouring into the universities. This boom was followed everywhere by a long period of decline and low enrollment which lasted from about the middle of the 17th century until the first decade of the 19th. Then came another period of huge expansion, first immediately after the Napoleonic Wars and then again after 1860. So widespread were these movements, and so dramatic in their impact on the universities, that in the future much of the history of higher education is clearly going to have to be articulated around them. Accounting for such changes, however, and analyzing their results, is not going to be an easy task.

Other contributors are concerned with the two-way relationship between what went on in the university and the values and culture of the wider society. Dr. Phillipson describes how, in the 18th century, the provincial elite of Edinburgh encouraged the university, and was in turn stimulated by it, to help create an Enlightenment society led by literati. Professor McLachlan shows how, when that Enlightenment culture was threatened at Princeton in the early 19th century by a reinforcement of the official curriculum in the classics, moral philosophy, and piety, the students set up a fully institutionalized educational system of their own, which managed to preserve the more secular and vernacular culture of the 18th century. Professor Rothblatt has found a similar development of student culture at Oxbridge, but a much more hostile official reaction to it. Professor McPherson describes the imposition of an alien Puritan ideology upon black freedmen by white New England educators after the American Civil War. Professor Jarausch traces the relationship between radical ideas current in society at large and the rise of student unrest in early 19th century Germany.

Another group of contributors is concerned with the emergence of the academic profession as we know it today. Professor Turner explains how late 18th century German professors viewed the relative importance of teaching and scholarship before the impact of the well-known Humboltian reforms. Mr. Engel shows how the Oxford dons struggled to obtain the necessary requirements for a professional career, namely a well-defined ladder of advancement and freedom from religious ties and celibacy restrictions. Professor Church traces the evolution of the social scientists as professional men in late 19th century America, as they balanced uneasily between pure scholarship and the provision of expert guidance for politicians and men of action.

It is hoped that these essays will play some role in the rapidly developing historiography of the subject, by drawing the attention of scholars to certain questions, methods, and findings which need to be more fully explored. Few fields are today more ripe for the application of modern research strategies and tactics, and few offer greater promise of rich intellectual rewards, than the history of education.

Lawrence Stone

Princeton, New Jersey
December 1972

Contents

THE UNIVERSITY IN SOCIETY

7

Universities in Castile
1500-1810

by Richard L. Kagan

The history of the Castilian university during the Golden Age fits well with the general historical pattern of Habsburg Spain: a century or more of almost uninterrupted expansion in numbers and size ending in 1600 or, in some cases, 1620; a period of stagnation from the 1620s to approximately 1640; and after that date, steady decline lasting well into the 18th century. The reasons for this are many: population trends, economic and political developments, job opportunities, the educational and career interests of diverse social groups, particularly those of the rich and powerful, religious attitudes, and intellectual currents all contributed to the university's ups and downs. But so little is known about how this institution reacted to changes in the society which it served that the purpose of this article is only exploratory, a tentative outline of some of the complexities behind the growth of higher education and the development of the university in early modern Spain.

The evidence for such an exploration is sketchy, often unreliable. Matriculation records, perhaps the single most valuable source for uni-

* An earlier draft of this article appeared in *Past and Present* 49 (November 1970). In the present version some statistical material has been revised, the text has been emended and expanded to carry the story down to 1810. Maps, graphs, and tables have been added.

The following abbreviations have been adopted in the footnotes:

I. Archives
AGS Archivo General de Simancas, Valladolid
AHN Archivo Histórico Nacional, Madrid
AUG Archivo de la Universidad de Granada
AUS Archivo de la Universidad de Salamanca
AUSA Archivo de la Universidad de Sevilla
AUSC Archivo de la Universidad de Santiago de Compostela
AUV Archivo de la Universidad de Valladolid
BNM Biblioteca Nacional, Madrid
BSC Biblioteca Santa Cruz, Valladolid

II. Other abbreviations
Cons. Sección de Consejos Suprimidos
leg. legajo
Univ. Sección de Universidades

veristy enrollments, are not always available and then usually in broken series. Also, their accuracy is questionable. Spanish scribes of the 16th and 17th centuries are not to be trusted, their mathematical ability is poor, and there is no indication that the annual lists of students they produced are complete. On the other hand, these lists may be inflated; instructors at many universities were elected by student vote and for a clandestine fee may have persuaded university scribes to enroll local street urchins as students for the sole purpose of creating a claque. However, since there is no way to test the precision of these lists, they must be taken at face value, albeit of course with caution.

Unlike student registers at the University of Cambridge after the reform of 1544, Spanish matriculation books, like those of most continental universities, provide little or no biographical information about students. Titled noblemen, church canons, paupers, and the like are usually recorded as such, but family backgrounds, father's occupation, and clerical status go unrecorded, making any general statement about the social origins of the student body difficult. The problem of determining what students did after graduation is more troublesome; except for a few small colleges, no such records exist. This problem could be partially remedied by detailed family biographies and studies of men other than kings, grandees, prime ministers, and bishops, but these too are scarce, often limited in scope, and generalizations about the educational habits and career patterns of particular social groups remain guesswork at best.[1] The same applies to ecclesiastical, royal, and municipal officials, the learned professions, army officers, etc.; none have been examined in any systematic way. Unfortunately, even the religious orders, so important for the educational development of Spain, have attracted few modern historians, and the records of student enrollments at the Jesuit colleges have apparently disappeared.[2] Spanish archives remain largely unknown but despite the flimsy evidence at least some suggestions about the place of the university in 16-17th century Castile can be made.

I

Universities in Castile, as in other European states, grew rapidly both in number and size during the 16th century, responding to quick dem-

[1] The careers of one 16th century family are outlined in Guillermo Lohmann Villena, *Les Espinosa, une famille d'hommes d'affaires en Espagne et aux Indies à l'époque de la colonisation* (Paris 1968).

[2] For the Jesuits, see A. Astraín, *Historia de la Compañía de Jesús*, 7 vols. (Madrid 1912-25). The Jesuit papers assembled in the AHN, Sección de Clero: Jesuitas, contain enrollments only for the college in Pamplona (libro 192J).

ographic and economic growth and the needs of a militant church, a newly reorganized and expanding royal administration, and the cultural and professional interests of an increasingly sophisticated nobility. Beginning in the late 15th century prelates and churchmen, apparently eager to educate the laity in sound Christian doctrine, to bolster the ranks of both church and state with "educated" men, and to flatter local and family pride, contributed heavily to higher education.[3] Although the crown participated indirectly in all new educational foundations with special privileges and tax exemptions, direct royal sponsorship was infrequent; only Granada and Philip II's university at El Escorial were purely royal foundations. The titled nobility of Spain managed to establish only two additional universities, that at Osuna in Andalucia and Gandía on the Mediterranean littoral near Valencia. But together, sufficient benefices, rents, and taxes were set aside between 1474 and 1620 to establish no fewer than seventeen new universities in the Crown of Castile alone and within them, a host of small colleges providing support to a limited number of supposedly impoverished scholars who could not otherwise pay the costs of higher education.[4] Thus by the early 17th century, Castile, having inherited two institutions of higher learning from the Middle Ages, supported a total of nineteen universities; and if the kingdom of Aragon is included, Spain boasted a grand total of thirty-three.[5] (See Map 1.)

Aided by rapid economic growth, most of Castile's new foundations prospered, notably Alcalá de Henares, Baeza, Granada, Santiago de Compostela, and Seville, while the older, medieval universities at Salamanca and Valladolid continued to grow. Youths, generally ranging in age from the 15- to 16-year-olds in the lower faculty of grammar—actually a secondary school under university auspices—to those between 20 and 25 in the higher faculties, flocked to the universities to pursue studies in the new liberal arts as well as the traditional professions of law, medicine, and theology. Enrollments grew steadily, reaching a peak only in the closing decades of the 16th century. By then, the average yearly enrollment at Salamanca ranged between 5000 and 7000

[3] The best general account of Spanish universities is G. Ajo y Sainz de Zúñiga, *Historia de las Universidades Hispánicas*, 8 vols. (Ávila and Madrid 1957-68). Still useful is Vicente de la Fuente, *Historia de las Universidades*, 4 vols. (Madrid 1884-89).

[4] Collegiate foundations were numerous. For example, the University of Salamanca during the 16th century acquired twenty-eight new colleges, excluding those of the religious orders. The best guide to Salamanca's colleges is L. Sala Balust, *Constituciones, Estatutos y Ceremonias de los Antiguos Colegios Seculares de la Universidad de Salamanca*, 4 vols. (Madrid 1962-66).

[5] In addition, Castile established five universities in the New World before 1600 with a few others following in the 17th century.

Map 1

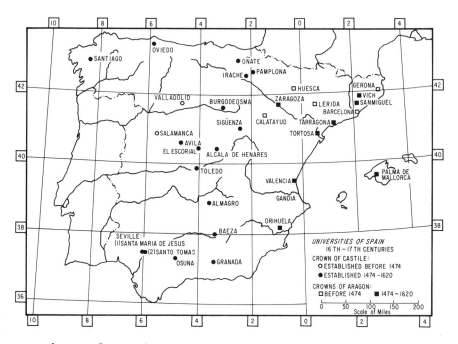

students, a figure which made this university easily the largest on the peninsula (Graph 1; see also Tables 1-7 at the end of this essay).[6] The new university of Alcalá de Henares which normally registered between 3000 and 4000 students was in second place and another new university, Santiago de Compostela, whose enrollments topped the 3000 level in various years was close behind (Graph 1).[7] Almost at a par with Santiago was the older and more famous university at Valladolid. Its matriculation books for the 16th century are fragmentary but in some years Valladolid appears to have registered 2000 students or more (Graph 1).[8] Lower still was Baeza, located in the olive-rich province of Jaen, supporting a maximum of approximately 600 students. Baeza's enrollments were matched and possibly exceeded by other Andalucian universities at Granada, Osuna, and Seville, but incomplete records for these institutions during this period do not allow for an exact estimate

[6] AUS, Libros 268-405.

[7] For Alcalá, see AHN, Univ., libros 431F-459F. For Santiago de Compostela, see AUSC, leg. 65; libros 227-31.

[8] For Valladolid, see AUV, libros 32-64. The Cámara de Castilla noted that Valladolid's enrollment in 1584-85 was approximately 2400 students; see Bartolomé Bennassar, *Valladolid Au Siècle D'Or* (Paris 1967), 358.

Graph 1

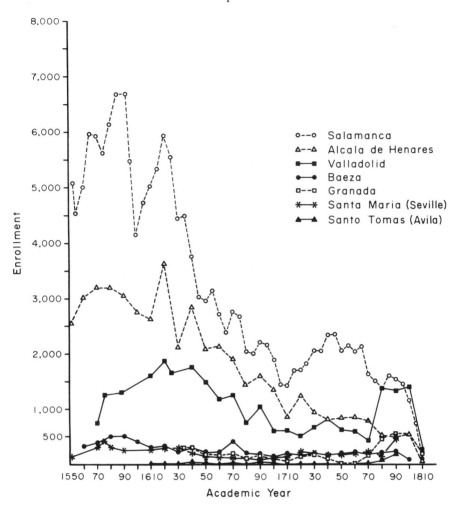

Universities of Castile: Total Matriculations by Faculty

of their size (Graph 1).[9] At bottom were small universities such as Sigüenza, which suffered from the competition of nearby Alcalá de Henares, with never more than a mere 60 or 70 students and a Domini-

[9] For Baeza, see the Archivo del Instituto de Enseñanza Secondaria, Baeza, Libros de Matrículas. For Granada, see AUG, libro 1440. For Osuna, see the Libros de Matrículas in the archive of the former university which is now a secondary school. For Seville, see AUSA, libros 478-84.

can-run institution in Ávila, with even fewer (Graph 1).[10] The severe plague of 1596-1602 which cost cities like Valladolid nearly 20 percent of their total population kept many students away from university towns for several years and the upward swing in enrollments was temporarily halted.[11] But most universities recovered quickly and by 1620 student populations neared their previous record levels.

Much of the resiliency of university enrollments in the years following the plague can perhaps be attributed to the relatively high social rank of the average student. It can probably be assumed that most students came from Castile's wealthier families, groups normally removed from the worst ravages of famine and disease. For this same reason, it would be unwise to attribute enrollments to total population trends alone; in many cases, the two curves bear little or no relation to each other.

Faulty records at many universities, the absence of figures on the size of incoming classes, and inadequate population statistics make difficult an accurate assessment of the proportion of Castile's youth attending university. However, with some statistical reservations, one can estimate that during the last quarter of the 16th century, Castile out of a population of roughly 6.9 million supported nearly 20,000 university students annually, a figure roughly equal to 3.2 percent of the male, adolescent age group (15-24 years).[12] (See Graph 2.) But if

[10] For Sigüenza, see AHN, Univ., libros 1283F-1287F. For Ávila, see the Archivo del Real Convento de Santo Tomás, Ávila, Libros de Matrículas.

[11] Bennassar, *Valladolid*, 205 gives estimates of losses caused by the plague.

[12] I have put the population of Castile, Navarre, and the Basque Provinces at about 6.9 million, the figure offered recently by Antonio Domínguez Ortiz, *The Golden Age of Spain 1516-1659* (New York 1971), 174. Males, ages 15-24, represented about 9% of the total population, or about 621,000 persons. On the basis of these figures, I calculated the percentage of youths attending university. One must understand that the 9% figure is not intended to be exact but only a rough guess; lack of accurate demographic statistics for the 16th century prevents anything more. I arrived at this estimate by applying the birth and death rates in the province of Valladolid published in Bennassar, *Valladolid*, 171-90 to age distribution tables in Ansley J. Coale and Paul Demeny, *Regional Model Life Tables and Stable Populations* (Princeton 1965). The stable population: Model South, Mortality Level 4 with a growth rate standing between 0/1000 and 5/1000 (Coale, 782) may apply to 16th century Valladolid and, by extension, all of Castile. However, T. H. Hollingsworth, *Historical Demography* (Ithaca 1969), 344, on the basis of his studies on the British peerage, has recently called into question the validity of applying life tables of stable populations to early modern societies. Whether his criticism, which is apparently based on a rather narrow sector of society, is correct, one does not know. On the other hand, conversations with Professor Pierre Goubert of the Sorbonne have assured me that the 9% figure corresponds to what he believes to be the case in populations of northern France

one also takes into account the several thousands of students being educated by the Jesuits in arts and grammar, that is, at the university level, then this percentage should be slightly raised.[13] It is also important to note that since students stemmed largely from the nobility, particularly the numerous *hidalgo* class which may have constituted up to one-tenth of Castile's total population, perhaps as many as one-fourth to one-third of Castile's young noblemen may have received some form of university or university-level education.[14] Such estimates

Graph 2

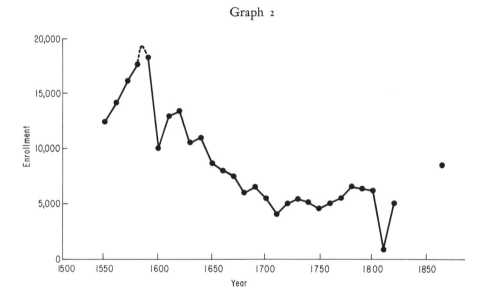

suggest that Castile ranked among Europe's most highly educated nations, a position which in part accounted for her cultural fluorescence during the Golden Age as well as her ability to create and sustain a worldwide bureaucratic empire.

Lawrence Stone has estimated that in 17th century England approximately 2.5 percent of 17-year-olds entered university each year.[15] To

at the same time period. Until more evidence is amassed, this estimate should serve only as a guide, not as an infallible answer.

[13] No complete figures for Jesuit enrollments are available. For some isolated estimates, see Astraín, *Compañía de Jesús*, I, 588-89; IV, 174.

[14] On the proportion of *hidalgos* in Castile, see J. Gentil da Silva, *En Espagne, Developpement Economique Subsistance Déclin* (Paris 1965), 110, and A. Domínguez Ortiz, *La Sociedad Española en El Siglo XVII*, I (Madrid 1963), 167-69.

[15] Lawrence Stone, "The Educational Revolution in England, 1560-1640," *Past and Present* 28 (1964), 57.

compare this figure with Castile is troublesome. Spanish matriculation books are usually arranged so that it is difficult to know what proportion of each year's enrollment constituted new, first-year boys. Moreover, the entrance age of Castilian students varied widely from faculty to faculty although the average age of first-year students in the late 16th century was in the neighborhood of 17 or 18. If we allow for these differences and remove the students of grammar from Castilian university enrollments in order to improve the bases for comparison with England, Castile in the last decades of the 16th century is left with a university population of around 15,000. Of these approximately one-fourth were newcomers, and such a figure would allow us to estimate that at least 5.43 percent of 18-year-olds entered university each year.[16] If this is correct, then Castile was far ahead of England in terms of access to university education and although similar estimates do not yet exist for other nations, Castile was possibly the most educated society in western Europe at that time.

Possible flaws in this estimate are several. The matriculation books may be either wildly exaggerated or our estimates of what proportion of the population represented males, aged 17 or 18, may be far off, but neither of these two possibilities is very likely. Alternately, the replacement rate at the universities, that is, the figure which represents the length of time the average student remained in residence and allows us to calculate what percentage of the students were new each year, may be incorrect. "Dropouts" were common to Castilian universities of the Habsburg era. In the arts faculty at Alcalá, for example, approximately one-third of all new students during the 16th century never went beyond the first year and only about one-third to one-half of those who matriculated initially took degrees.[17] Other faculties and universities differed little. These high attrition rates may complicate estimates of the number of first-year students at the universities since one does not know whether dropouts really dropped out or if they returned the following year, transferred to another faculty, or even to another university. In any event, it would seem likely that the average

[16] I reached this estimate on the basis that male 18-year-olds constituted about 1% of the total population of Castile or about 69,000 persons. One-fourth of the university population of 15,000 was approximately 3750 students: $\frac{3750}{69,000} = 5.43\%$. Once again, I would like to offer this figure only as a rough guide, not the gospel truth. My thanks go to Lawrence Stone for advice on these calculations.

[17] I have calculated these figures by comparing enrollments in the four years of the arts course at Alcalá over a number of consecutive years with graduation records. For the latter, see AHN, Univ., libros 400F-413F, and Juan Urriza, *La Preclara Facultad de Artes y Filosofia de la Universidad de Alcalá de Henares en el Siglo de Oro, 1509-1621* (Madrid 1942).

stay of most students approached four years even though the four years may not have been consecutive or at the same institution. Consequently, it is probably safe to assume that the above-presented proportion of Castile's youth attending university is a fairly reliable estimate, if not absolutely correct.

But if students were many, graduates were relatively few. In the late 16th century fewer than one-third of the students who began their course took a degree, and in succeeding decades the proportion fell off[18] so that even at their peak Castile's universities never awarded more than 1200 baccalaureates a year.[19] Assuming that the average age of these graduates was about 22, this meant that less than 1.73 percent of male youths at this age had earned a university degree.[20] Of these, only a handful managed to obtain one of the advanced degrees of master, licentiate, and doctor. The University of Salamanca, for example, graduated close to 400 *bachilleres* in law each year, but in the same period of time fewer than twenty advanced degrees in this subject would be conferred.[21] In total, Castile's universities could not have turned out more than 150-75 licentiates and perhaps 50-60 doctors annually,[22] the majority of whom were in the arts faculty where these honors were both cheaper and easier to obtain than in medicine, law, or theology.[23] Thus, from a university population which numbered in the thousands, only a handful of students ever became fully licensed professionals. Yet it was this same small group that staffed Castile's cathedrals, law courts, and councils and directed much of the administrative and religious policy of the empire while shaping the education of the nation's young.

Total enrollment and graduation figures, however, tell very little

[18] By the mid-17th century only one in four first-year students managed to earn degrees, and in the following century the ratio was only one in five.

[19] About 70 to 80 of these degrees were in medicine while 100 were in theology. The remainder were divided more or less evenly between arts and the laws. Together the universities of Alcalá de Henares, Salamanca, and Valladolid awarded close to 80% of the baccalaureates in Castile.

[20] Males, aged twenty-two, like those at seventeen or eighteen, presumably accounted for about 1% of the total population. The arithmetic used in this estimate is the same as that employed in footnote 16.

[21] See AUS, Libros de Grados.

[22] As in the case of the baccalaureates, most of these degrees came from Alcalá, Salamanca, and Valladolid.

[23] At the University of Santiago de Compostela a Master of Arts degree, the equivalent of a doctorate in this faculty, cost 150 *reales* in 1610. In law a doctorate required a minimum expenditure of 300 *reales*. See S. Cabeza de Leon, *Historia de la Universidad de Santiago de Compostela* (Santiago 1945), I, 246-47. The differences in the relative costs of an arts degree and that in one of the professional faculties at one of the major universities was significantly wider.

Richard L. Kagan

about the university itself. Matriculation Registers, while omitting family backgrounds, generally list the geographical origins of students, usually by town and diocese. The main shortcoming of such information is that it is difficult to determine whether the town listed represents the student's actual place of origin or merely his current residence, and many students apparently gave the university town in which they were then residing as their place of origin. With these reservations, some generalizations about the geographical origin of students are possible.

In the first place it appears that a majority of students were town-dwellers, not residents of the rural countryside. At Seville in 1570, for example, six Andalucian towns, including Seville itself, provided a little over half the university's total enrollment, with the remainder of students coming from a large number of towns and a few villages.[24] The same basic pattern applies to other small and medium-sized universities like Ávila or Baeza: a majority of the students came from the university town itself and one or two other nearby towns, with a lesser number coming from small towns and villages in the same region.[25] Other universities displayed similar patterns of distribution, and the reason for this is not very complex. The towns harbored most of the nation's wealth, they provided organized elementary and Latin instruction for local youths, and they contained a majority of Castile's *hidalgos*, merchants, office-holders, and professionals, the social groups most likely to educate their sons at university for purposes of career and status. The countryside—poor, illiterate, backward, and immobile—could provide few university students and even these were possible mainly because of clerical sponsorship or a college scholarship.

Secondly, most students tended to come from the north and center of the peninsula: the Basque regions, Asturias, León, Old Castile, and the northeastern part of New Castile around Cuenca. This too is not surprising: these regions were the most wealthy and populous parts of the Crown of Castile, and they contained a relatively high concentration of *hidalgo* families in comparison with the south and west.[26] It thus follows that thirteen of Castile's nineteen universities were found north of the Rio Tajo which cuts across the center of the peninsula separating New Castile, Andalucia, and Extremadura from the rest of the

[24] AUSA, libro 480. Xerez de la Frontera, Utrera, Arascena, Carmona, and La Palma del Condado were the other leading contributors.

[25] See the Libros de Matrículas for these universities, cited previously above in nn. 9, 10.

[26] See Domínguez Ortiz, *Sociedad Española*, I, 169; A. de Castillo, " 'Population et richesse' en Castille," *Annales E.S.C.*, vol. 20, 1965, pp. 716ff.

nation. Moreover, the largest universities—Alcalá, Salamanca, Santiago, Valladolid—were located in these same regions while the *hidalgo*-poor lands to the south supported relatively few universities, none of which attained a size comparable to their northern counterparts. One is again tempted to draw the conclusion that universities followed in the wake of wealth and privilege.

And finally, the Matriculation Registers reveal that except for Alcalá, Salamanca, and Valladolid, all of which enrolled students from across the peninsula and even abroad, Castile's universities drew the vast majority of their students from the diocese or province in which they were located.[27] For example, Santiago de Compostela, situated in the extreme northwest of the peninsula, drew almost exclusively from the surrounding provinces of Asturias and Galicia, particularly the latter in which the university was centrally located.[28] In the south the universities at Granada and Seville tapped Andalucia although Granada's students came predominantly from the east of that region; Seville's, from the west.[29] However, the busy port and commercial city of Seville also attracted a number of students from the center of Castile as well as the Canary Islands. Other universities, like Ávila and Baeza, as we have already seen, had even more limited areas of attraction, generally limited to the university town itself and the nearby countryside.

This pattern suggests that economic considerations in large part determined where parents chose to send their sons to university; one presumes that students, many of whom must have lived on meager allowances, attended a local university where the costs of travel and maintenance were ostensibly lower than at a more distant university.[30] Moreover, parents may have preferred local institutions if only because they were in a better position to watch over their young son's discipline and behavior. If this was the case, then the proliferation of small universities across the peninsula in the 16th century can be more readily understood; individual regions for reasons of economy as well

[27] The foreigners who appeared most frequently at these universities were the Portuguese. English and Irish students were also in evidence after colleges were established for Catholic emigrés of these nations in the second half of the 16th century. Before the late 17th century, students from the New World appeared sporadically.

[28] AUSC, libros A227-A330; leg. 65.

[29] AUG, libro 1440; AUSA, libros 478-84.

[30] The picaresque novels paint an excellent picture of student life. See especially Mateo Aleman, *Guzman de Alfarache* (1599) and the *Novelas Exemplares* of Cervantes, particularly "El Licenciado Vidriera" and the "Colloquio de los Perros." Also interesting is J. García Mercadel, *Estudiantes, Sopistas, y Pícaros* (Madrid 1934).

as prestige obviously desired universities of their own. And it follows that bishops and churchmen, in relatively close touch with the local populace, were in a better position to respond to local educational needs and to take the initiative in the establishment of new institutions than a recently hispanicized, peripatetic, and then stationary but distant and isolated crown.

But this localized educational pattern does not fully explain why Alcalá, Salamanca, and Valladolid, notwithstanding their location in the central provinces of Castile, proved so universally popular. At Alcalá, for instance, most faculties drew fewer than half their students from the large, populous Archdiocese of Toledo in which the university was situated.[31] The remainder came mainly from the neighboring Dioceses of Cuenca and Sigüenza and the more northerly regions around Burgos, Calahorra, Palencia, and Pamplona, etc., most of which supported universities of their own. Alcalá also drew regularly from Aragon, Andalucia, and various coastal regions, all distant and whose students could have attended universities closer to home (Map 2). The University of Salamanca had a wider and more evenly balanced geographical representation. Its Faculty of Canon Law, the largest in the nation, enrolled students from every region of Spain on

Map 2

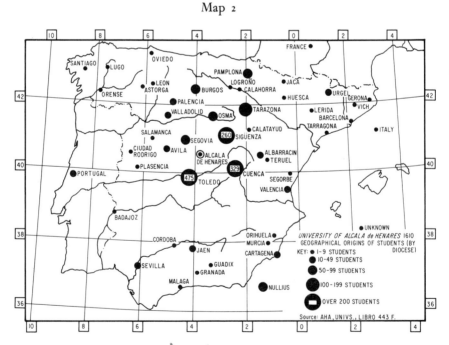

[31] See AHN, Univ., libros 431F-459F.

a regular basis in spite of Salamanca's location near the Portuguese border (Map 3). Valladolid, smaller than either Alcalá or Salamanca but noted for its legal faculties, also managed to draw upon the entire peninsula although the majority of its students came from Old Castile and the north. Naturally, Salamanca and Valladolid, famous since the Middle Ages, and Alcalá de Henares, the much heralded "Renaissance" university of Cardinal Cisneros, endowed with special royal privileges, large numbers of teaching chairs, and distinguished instructors, would attract students from an area far wider than their own im-

Map 3

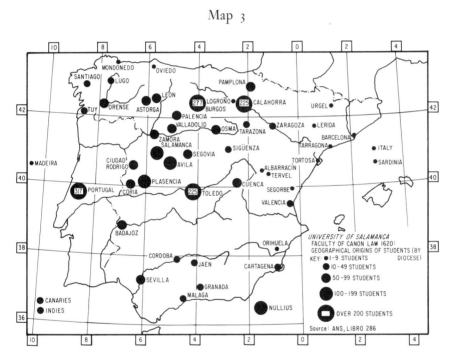

mediate environs. In many cases students from faraway regions studied grammar and arts at a small university close to home and transferred subsequently to a higher faculty at one of the larger universities, possibly hoping to take advantage of the variety of instruction they offered. But there are other and perhaps more impelling reasons which account for the large, diversified enrollments of these three universities.

Although information regarding students' postgraduate lives is available for only a few small colleges, university graduates in Castile generally entered a number of professional careers. The upper ranks of the clergy and important places in the royal administration, both associated with wealth and social prestige, were undoubtedly the students' preferred choice. A private professional career as a lawyer, especially if attached to a royal council, a provincial court, a cathedral, or municipal corporation, or even a wealthy nobleman's estates, probably ranked second, with careers in medicine and school-teaching tied for poor third. In the 16th century such "careerism," particularly among the *hidalgos*, may have been partially spurred by population growth combined with the simultaneous spread of the *mayorazgo* or entailed estate upon which the eldest son had first claim, two developments which may have left large numbers of landless younger sons in search of other livelihoods. Furthermore, the Habsburg monarchy offered growing numbers of offices specifically reserved for university graduates while the Spanish church had, since the days of Ferdinand and Isabella, put a high premium upon clerics with university degrees.[32] With these opportunities for advancement, many *hidalgos* in need of secure careers enrolled at the universities, apparently fulfilling the popular ethic, voiced first by the humanists, that the only true nobility was learning put to the service of one's prince. As most Spanish contemporaries suggest, it was precisely this hope of obtaining high office, the *premio* or reward as they put it, that brought young men to the university in the first place,[33] although high dropout figures after the first year suggest that youthful aspirations were frequently cut short by an empty purse or mistaken aptitude. If such an interpretation is correct, then the enrollments of a particular university may in part be linked to the success of its graduates in obtaining valued posts or, even more importantly, the reputation of such success.

An examination of top clerical and secular positions in Castile during the Habsburg period reveals that graduates of Alcalá, Salamanca, and Valladolid enjoyed a majority of places and in some agencies, such as the royal councils and the provincial courts of justice, the

---

[32] On the place of university graduates in Castilian government, see M. J. Gounon-Loubens, *Essais sur l'Administration de la Castille au XVIe Siècle* (Paris 1860); the Introduction by J. M. Batista i Roca in H. Koenigsberger, *The Government of Sicily under Philip II of Spain* (London 1948); and my unpublished dissertation, "Education and the State in Habsburg Spain" (Cambridge Univ., 1968), chs. I, II (hereafter cited as Kagan).

[33] Perhaps the best example of such thinking lies in the memorandum prepared by the *Junta de Educación* on 12 January 1636 (Biblioteca de la Universidad de Salamanca, MS 1925, fol. 8):

And because they [the students] direct their studies towards the rewards, both ecclesiastical and secular they hope to gain afterwards, the principle that must stimulate those within the university to work and to take advantage of their surroundings must be the just distribution of the rewards. . . .

For other examples, see Kagan, 141, 159-60.

audiencias, almost a complete monopoly.[34] Despite the establishment and growth of the new, "provincial" universities, graduates of the three major institutions received continued favor. So neglected were other students in appointments for important magistracies that Philip IV, acting on the advice of his favorite, the Count-Duke of Olivares, found it necessary to remind the royal councillors charged with the business of patronage that graduates of other institutions should be recommended for the posts in question.[35] What the neglected students did is unclear: there was always the military, lesser offices, and the New World; some may have added to the swell of petitioners at court while others, hoping for better success, may have left their small university for one of the larger institutions.

In light of the *hidalgo*'s quest for office, a desire termed by one historian as "empleomania,"[36] the large enrollments of Alcalá, Salamanca, and Valladolid can probably be attributed as much to the fame and prestige of their degrees in the competition for honors as to their proximity to wealthy, urbanized regions or the ability of their instructors to attract large student followings. Conversely, the newer and smaller universities may have suffered accordingly since they lacked the reputation which could earn their graduates important posts, a problem aggravated by the fact that the former students of the major universities who controlled the agencies in charge of appointments tended to make their decisions upon the twin bases of favoritism and precedent.[37] Such a situation may have encouraged students living outside the center of Castile to matriculate at one of the major universities while convincing those already living nearby to study close to home.

The result was a migration of manpower from the periphery and more remote areas of the peninsula toward the center, to those institutions offering the possibility of the choicest rewards. Whether this 16th century internal "brain drain" resulted in a permanent concentration of "educated" men in central Castile to the detriment of outlying provinces is not clear. It can be noted, however, that in 1588 Philip II instructed the members of the Royal Council of Castile who formed the new Council of the Cámara in charge of royal patronage to send the numerous office-seekers crowding about the court back to their homes.[38] And a half century later Philip IV issued a similar order prohibiting university graduates from traveling to Madrid without special license—a ban designed to keep petitioners away from court.[39]

[34] Kagan, ch. v.
[35] AHN, Cons., leg. 4422, *consulta* of 22 December 1622.
[36] K. W. Swart, *Sale of Offices in the 17th Century* (The Hague 1949), 32.
[37] Kagan, chs. IV, V.   [38] AHN, Cons., libro 666, fol. 3v.
[39] AUS, MS 939, fol. 135.

Provincials attending the central universities undoubtedly heightened competition within the Castilian job market, but it is also true that an indeterminate number of students left the major institutions to take their degrees at smaller universities where the graduation fees were usually much less. The University at Irache in Navarre seems to have made this practice into a regular business since the number of degrees it awarded annually was frequently three or four times greater than the total number of students enrolled.[40] The University of Oñate, also located in Navarre, was in the habit of incorporating a *bachiller* from one of the larger universities one day, examining and then graduating him licentiate the next, and then awarding him a doctorate a day or so later.[41] Oñate's professors received their fees, shared in the graduation feast, and the new doctor could go back to his old university and register his degrees at a bargain price. However, until more information is obtained about the careers of university graduates, the net result of this migration of "intellectuals" will remain unknown.

What is certain is that Alcalá, Salamanca, and Valladolid acted as a magnet, attracting men from diverse geographical regions and then training them for the highest posts in Spain and her empire. These served as the true "imperial" universities of the Habsburgs. The provincial universities, on the other hand, remained relatively small, local universities serving local, probably clerical, needs. In the long run, the biased system of royal patronage, locked in tradition, failed to include the provincial universities in the distribution of national and imperial office. This problem, on top of other difficulties with recruitment and finance, implied that these institutions had continually to contend with instructors and student followings that were irregular, disloyal, and transient, always eager to transfer to the larger universities, to leave for higher rewards. Thus Castile may have lost an opportunity during the 16th and 17th centuries to develop and maintain a broad-based, pluralistic university system which could offer possibilities for competition, variety, and innovation. Moreover, the "imperial" universities, so vital to the needs of the monarchy, gradually lost their autonomy to the crown, preventing Castile from developing a strong tradition of university learning independent of royal interest and control.

The influx of students interested primarily in jobs and professional training also had profound effects within the universities themselves. In every institution which offered instruction in all of the major facul-

[40] Archivo General del Reino de Navarra, MSS 539-42.

[41] One example, dating from the 18th century, is Joseph Curaldo de Yvicta, a *bachiller* in canon law from Valladolid who enrolled at Oñate on 13 October 1761. Two days later he graduated licentiate and doctor in the same faculty. See AUV, libro 344.

ties—arts, law, medicine, and theology—there was a steady shift, beginning in the middle years of the 16th century, away from the study of arts and theology to the study of law, particularly canon law, gateway to both clerical and secular careers (Graphs 3-5, and Tables 1, 4, 6, 7 at end of this essay).[42] At the University of Alcalá de Henares, originally dedicated to the study of the liberal arts and theology with

Graph 3

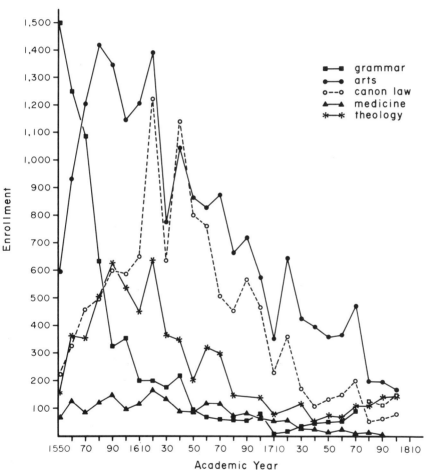

University of Alcala de Henares: Matriculations by Faculty

[42] See in particular the matriculation books of Alcalá, Salamanca, Santiago, and Valladolid, and Kagan, Graphs 2, 3, 4.

a curriculum limiting students to one course in canon law, the number of law students equaled that of theology by 1550, and by the opening of the 17th century, jurists outnumbered theologians almost two to one, a ratio which doubled before the century was out.[43] And under pressure from the Castilian Cortes, a body representative of the inter-

Graph 4

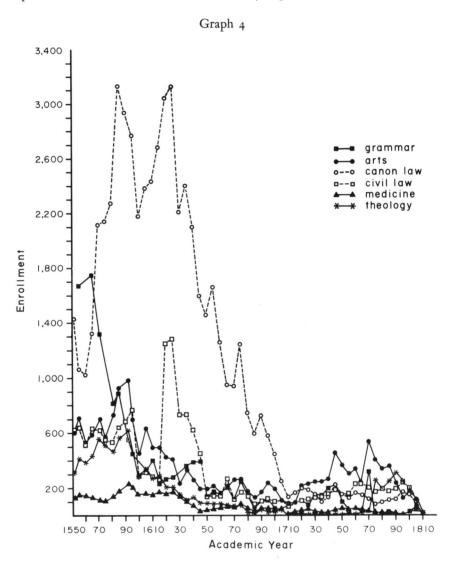

University of Salamanca: Matriculations by Faculty

[43] AHN, Univ., libros 431F-459F; Kagan, 220.

[372]

ests of the well-educated, office-holding *hidalgos* living in the major cities, Alcalá, in violation of her original statutes, began instruction in civil law.[44] At Salamanca and Valladolid which had no curricular restrictions, the theology faculty fared even worse; by the late 17th century, law students outnumbered theologians by twenty to one.[45] This sustained emphasis on juridical studies may have also prejudiced enrollments at the provincial universities, many of which lacked facul-

Graph 5

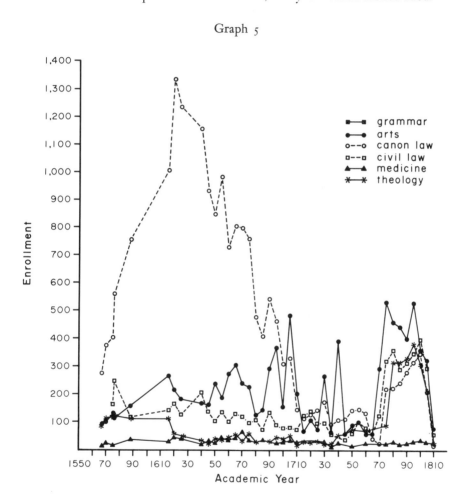

University of Valladolid: **Matriculations** by Faculty

[44] Cortes de Madrid, 1563, petition cxix in *Cortes de los Antiguos Reinos de León y Castilla*, v, 407; AHN, Univ., libro 1222F, fol. 234.
[45] AUS, libros 268-405; AUV, libros 32-64; Kagan, 220-21.

ties of law, thus contributing to the influx of students at Alcalá, Salamanca, and Valladolid.

According to the Matriculation Registers, students at Castile's leading universities eschewed studies in the liberal arts and theology for those in canon and civil law, either to prepare for a professional legal or office-holding career or to acquire a brief introduction to this subject for utilitarian reasons. Most of these dropped out, turning alternatively to the army, the church, offices not requiring university training or degrees, or independent lives as financiers, merchants, or *rentiers*; but those who did graduate, perhaps as few as one-third or less of those who matriculated initially, competed for scarce professorships and jobs. In this light the old, popular assertion that a one-sided, conservative preoccupation with theology thwarted educational and scientific progress in Spain and her universities is not borne out by the matriculation lists; the almost exclusive pursuit of law and office-holding careers would be a more credible answer. Experimental science, modern languages and history, studies in political economy had little place in an institution which was, and which regarded itself as, a professional training school for lawyers and legally trained clerics and noblemen. Law degrees, crown offices, and the prestige these conferred were the ultimate goals of the Castilian university, not the advancement of medicine nor scientific understanding of the world. And it is perhaps not surprising that the first sharp break from this legalistic university tradition in 18th century Spain came not from Castile but Valencia, whose university led the way toward a modern medical curriculum.[46]

Of course, the relative decline in the study of arts and theology as well as that in Latin grammar may have been compensated for by the growth of municipal secondary schools along with Jesuit and other religious colleges offering instruction in these disciplines to secular students. The sharp decline in the number of students studying grammar at the universities, the proliferation of local Latin schools and masters, and the rapid rise in enrollments at the Jesuit colleges in the late 16th century was no coincidence.[47] And by the middle of the 17th century the Society of Jesus was probably responsible for nearly half of all or-

[46] Richard Herr, *The Eighteenth Century Revolution in Spain* (Princeton 1958), 166.

[47] For example, enrollments at the Jesuit college in Seville rose from about 500 in 1563 to about 1000 in 1590. At their college in Córdoba, the growth rate was much the same: about 600 in 1573, about 1000 in 1588. See Astraín, *Compañía de Jesús*, I, 589; IV, 174. At the same time enrollments in grammar at the University of Salamanca fell from 1755 in 1565 to 331 in 1605. At Alcalá they dropped from 1493 in 1550 to 199 in 1610.

ganized instruction in the kingdom, the rest being supplied by private tutors, itinerant *pedantes* or preceptors, the odd convent of some other religious order, and colleges and masters supported by individual towns, private bequests, and student fees. Parents, perhaps in the hope of a less expensive or more rigorously disciplined education for their young sons, seem to have preferred a local Jesuit or municipal college to the increasingly turbulent universities where huge student bodies, the vast majority of whom lived outside protective college walls, hindered all attempts at proctorial control. Student riots, student gangs, armed clashes in the streets, and what may have been a rise in student gambling and vice undoubtedly created a climate which made many a pious Castilian father think twice before sending his young son off to university, even if he were accompanied by a responsible tutor.[48] Secondly, the costs of university attendance were undoubtedly far greater than at a local religious college where tuition was free. In many cases the student could save considerably by living at home or, if his family lived nearby, at least receive his basic provisions from his parents on market days.[49]

At any rate, the proliferation of Jesuit colleges in the late 16th and early 17th centuries and their rapidly growing enrollments suggest that the Society of Jesus responded to a popular demand for extra-university instruction in grammar, arts, and theology while they simultaneously provided a permanent home for these neglected subjects. Moreover, graduates of the Jesuit colleges, well-schooled in grammar, arts, mathematics, and other subjects, were ready to enter the world in their own right or to matriculate at a university for degrees or further higher education; thus, these colleges served not only as alternatives to the universities but also as complementary institutions, helping to educate thousands of youths for whom the universities could not adequately provide.

But although there may have been increasing reasons for not sending

[48] For some aspects of these problems, see García Mercadel, *Estudiantes, Sopistas y Pícaros*; A. García Boiza, *Intervención de los Estudiantes en la Universidad de Salamanca en el Siglo XVI* (Madrid 1933); U. González de la Calle, *Oposiciones a Catédras en la Universidad de Salamanca, 1550-60* (Madrid 1933); E. Esperabé Artega, *Historia de la Universidad de Salamanca*, 1 (Salamanca 1914); and AHN, Cons., leg. 7138.

[49] Room and board in university towns was expensive. At Alcalá, for example, boarding houses in the 1560s charged students between 40 and 60 ducats a year, while degree costs, incidental fees, etc. would push student expenditures even higher. At that time a judge in a royal court earned approximately 530 ducats a year, a master artisan about 70, a gardener only 7. It is obvious that the universities were largely the preserves of the rich with the exception of scholarship students and the clergy.

a 14- or 15-year-old to university for instruction in the arts and grammar, evidence also suggests that the major universities, geared primarily toward professional training, lost interest in these lower disciplines and allowed these faculties to fall into decay, thus helping to precipitate the rise of the Jesuit colleges. Shortages of qualified teachers in these faculties began in the middle of the 16th century and continued unchecked into the next.[50] At least one critic who noted these difficulties as early as the 1570s was prompted to write that since the universities lacked good Latin masters, they should hand instruction in this subject over to the Jesuits.[51] This dearth of teachers can be partially explained by the fact that the salaries of chairs in the lower faculties were among the lowest at the universities, but the failure of the universities to rectify this problem may be perhaps one indication of their relative unconcern. Nevertheless, even the well-endowed Trilingual Colleges of Alcalá and Salamanca which offered scholarship places in the classical languages suffered from a lack of student interest, and in 1597 Salamanca's college, without students, disappeared from the matriculation books for over fifty years.[52] Thus, with trained teachers in short supply, dwindling enrollments, and an apparent shortage of funds to raise salaries, some universities, including Valladolid and Santiago de Compostela, heeded their critics' advice and allowed the Jesuits and other orders to come in and take over.[53] The Jesuits, therefore, may have only filled an educational vacuum left behind by the professionally oriented universities.

If this vacuum existed, its origins lay deep in Spanish society. During the Middle Ages the jurist or *letrado* and not the theologian occupied the leading place in Spanish universities. The University of Salamanca, established early in the 13th century, did not acquire a Faculty of Theology until late in the 14th, and then by the beneficence of the papacy, not the crown.[54] At Lérida in Aragon and Valladolid in Old

[50] Commenting on this problem, the Royal Council, in reference to the University of Valladolid, complained of the "great shortage and necessity for Latin preceptors" (AUV, libro D-1, fol. 51, letter of 5 July 1581). See also M. Alcocer Martínez, *Historia de la Universidad de Valladolid* (Valladolid 1918-31), III, 315, 319; Esperabé Artega, *Universidad de Salamanca*, I, 568. Chairs in arts and grammar at Salamanca frequently received less than one half the salary of those in law; see AUS, libros 1027-28.

[51] AGS, Diversos de Castilla, leg. 5-106.

[52] By the mid-17th century one reformer urged the abolition of this college since its rents "served no purpose"; see AHN, Cons., leg. 7138, *memorial* of 22 July 1648. On this problem, also see Sala Balust, *Constituciones*, I, 21.

[53] AUV, libro 517, fols. 2-14; AUSC, libro 214; Alcocer Martínez, *Universidad de Valladolid*, III, 315, 319.

[54] La Fuente, *Universidades*, I, 208.

Castile, the two other leading universities in medieval Spain, the situation was much the same: the laws, civil and canon, were the honored faculties.[55] Moreover, doctors of law from Salamanca were granted certain of the fiscal and ceremonial privileges of nobility while some of their number regularly became advisers at the royal court, undoubtedly giving the profession at least a modicum of social prestige.[56]

During the 15th century, Spain's blossoming interest in Italian humanism and classical studies, while adding a new historical and philological dimension to law, nevertheless favored the study of liberal arts and theology. The first universities of this era, Sigüenza, Alcalá, and Santiago, reflected this trend and awarded the liberal arts and theology the leading place in their curriculum while the new interest in literary philology and classical antiquity gave these same faculties a boost at the older institutions. Lectures by noted humanist scholars such as Peter Martyr d'Anghera drew large crowds at Salamanca and this university, in imitation of Alcalá, added its own Trilingual College (Colegio Trilingüe) to pursue studies in Greek, Hebrew, and Chaldean.[57] Under the patronage of Isabella the Catholic, instruction in the liberal arts even entered into the world of the courtiers when Martyr and another Italian humanist, Lucio Marineo Siculo, opened a palace school for the benefit of young noblemen.[58] Moreover, Spanish prelates like Cisneros, conscious of the need to improve the intellectual standards of the clergy within Spain while extending the Catholic missionary spirit abroad, led the drive to establish new centers of learning and to make theology truly the queen of sciences and the liberal arts her leading handmaiden. At Alcalá, his own university, he may have hoped to guarantee their success by limiting studies in the law. Although records are scarce, it appears that these two disciplines won new popularity in the late 15th and early 16th centuries, with the need for trained clerics to "convert the heathen" in Granada, North Africa, and the New World sustaining this interest well into the Habsburg era.

But the challenge of the Renaissance did not last long. Although the study of classical languages and humanist theology remained popular among the convents of the religious orders and within the literary cir-

55 Ibid., 111.

56 See Conde de Torrenaz, *Los Consejos del Rey durante la Edad Media* (Madrid 1884), esp. 124, 150-51, 167.

57 Read Martyr's account of his reception at Salamanca in 1488 in *Opus Epistolorum Petri Martyris Anglerii Mediolanensis* (Paris 1670), I 57.

58 On this school and its pupils, see Caro Lynn, *A College Professor of the Renaissance* (Chicago 1937) and J. H. Mariejol, *Pierre Martyr d'Anghera: Sa Vie et Ses Oeuvres* (Paris 1887).

cles of the rich, the medieval legacy of the law proved triumphant within the lecture halls. The decade of the 1550s, heralded by the great debates between Las Casas and Sepúlveda over the issue of slavery and capped by the end of Erasmian influence in Spain at the famous auto-da-fé at Valladolid in 1559, was perhaps the symbolic era of change. After that decade, while arts and theology languished, students increasingly favored studies in law. But however professional their interests, these students still received preliminary training in the arts before studying a jurisprudence imbued with the critical, historical elements which the jurists of the Renaissance had bestowed upon it.[59]

Meanwhile, the arbiters of patronage in Castile, the presidents and members of the royal councils who were themselves normally graduates in law, continued to favor the *letrado* for royal and ecclesiastical office. Wherever a university education was a necessary or at least customary prerequisite for office, that is, at the upper echelons of the councils, in the royal and inquisitorial courts, bishoprics, cathedral chapters, and other church dignities, the jurist frequently merited the best chances for success.[60] Law graduates could also serve as crown officers in the towns (*corregidores*), royal inspectors, and municipal magistrates (*alcaldes*). In a private legal career, *letrados* could often earn substantial incomes and public notoriety and then hope eventually to win some form of public office. Castile's administrative and commercial cities supported considerable numbers of such men. According to tax rolls in the reign of Philip II, smaller provincial capitals like Cuenca, Murcia, and Plasencia normally listed from ten to fifteen *letrados* among their residents while larger capitals such as Seville or Toledo contained five or ten times as many.[61] And a metropolis like Madrid could list in 1597 234 *letrados*, many of whom possessed offices at the royal court.[62]

With wide opportunities for various office-holding careers, little wonder that the old doctor in Christóbal Suárez de Figueroa's famous work, *El Passagero* (1617), advised his son to study "laws and canons" which he termed a "noble and illustrious profession, the heart and soul of the cities" and to follow a legal career because of its "security of promotions."[63] It is only fair to mention that in this case, the son, a

[59] See Domenico Maffei, *Gli inizi dell' Umanesimo Giuridico* (Milan 1956).

[60] Kagan, chs. II, IV. Also useful is Gounon-Loubens, *Essais*.

[61] These figures are from the famous *vecindarios* of the 16th century; AGS, Expedientes de Hacienda, legs. 87, 89, 132, 143, 170, 183.

[62] AGS, Expedientes de Hacienda, leg. 121-22.

[63] Christóbal Suárez de Figueroa, *El Passagero* (Madrid 1617), ed. Sociedad de Bibliofilos Españoles (Madrid 1914), 171-73.

rather independent fellow, neglected his father's advice and decided to study theology, which he believed would lead to a secure clerical career. But for thousands of other students less willing to take vows of chastity and poverty, law was the chosen subject of study.

Other subjects may have had their liabilities. To matriculate in theology involved a long and difficult university career which led almost automatically into the church or religious orders; consequently, this faculty in the course of the 17th century became the preserve of the monks as secular students turned to other courses of study. Moreover, the Inquisition's activity against prominent theologians accused of emending or tampering with scriptural texts may have frightened some students off, but it is difficult, if not impossible, to say how many. Another choice was medicine: profitable, able to bring its successful practitioners to permanent positions in the king's household, but shunned by most students, perhaps because of a long-standing association of this profession with the stigma of *converso* blood. Finally, to remain in arts meant either school teaching or the church or heavy reliance upon the influence of family and friends to help secure an important secular or military charge.

Considering the limitations of other faculties and the doors to which legal training could lead, the average Castilian student matriculated in one of the laws. Furthermore, with court *letrados* achieving positions of influence and power, habits and lands in the aristocratic Military Orders, and even titles of noble rank, legal study seems to have shed whatever remained of its grim, "clerkly" reputation for that of the socially acceptable; therefore, it may have attracted young men in search of wealth, power, and rank.[64]

Moreover, in a society in which wealth was largely measured in land and in which nearly 90 percent or more of the total population lived, directly or indirectly, off the land, litigation was a regular feature of daily life. Suits involving boundaries, *mayorazgos*, taxes, seigneurial rights, rents, and the like involved representatives from every social class and group, and the volume of such business was probably enormous. Petitions on the need for more judges and more courts to help speed the time required to settle judicial disputes occurred repeatedly at meetings of the Cortes.[65] And although the character of

[64] On the wealth and position of letrados, see Bennassar, *Valladolid*, 122-24, 134-35, 235-72, 365-72.

[65] *Cortes de León y Castilla*, IV, V: Cortes de Santiago y La Coruña, 1520, pet. 56; Cortes de Valladolid, 1523, pet. 35; Cortes de Madrid, 1528, pet. 62; Cortes de Segovia, 1532, pets. 3, 4; Cortes de Madrid, 1534, pet. 128; Cortes de Toledo, 1538, pet. 110; Cortes de Valladolid, 1542, pets. 17, 24, 25; Cortes de Madrid, 1551, pets. 1, 9; Cortes de Valladolid, 1555, pets. 16, 122; Cortes de Madrid, 1576, pet. 3.

Castilian litigation has not yet received systematic attention, it is al-most certain that cases involving the land accounted for the bulk of Castile's court business. Thus a knowledge of the law was essential not only for those seeking *letrado* careers but also for noblemen, ecclesiastics, merchants, officials, anyone for that matter connected to the land in some manner. Castile's town-dwellers, the group best represented at the universities, would have directly benefited from juridical studies since much of the countryside was in their hands. And landless residents of the towns, hoping eventually to purchase rural estates and achieve the status and prestige of a landowner, may have optimistically directed their offspring into law in preparation for the future. The popularity of this subject among students was perhaps only one indication of the overwhelming importance of land ownership in 16th and 17th century Castile. It is not surprising that even sons of the titled nobility who occasionally attended university matriculated in law; the young Gaspar de Guzmán, future Count of Olivares, who enrolled as a student in canon law at Salamanca in 1600, is a case in point.[66]

Under these circumstances, the universities, filled with youths eager for honors, offices, and prestige as well as legal expertise, discarded their Renaissance mold for studies of a more professional, materialistic, and practical bent. The *studium generale* of the Middle Ages had also concentrated on the study of law but with an eye toward ecclesiastical careers; the university of Habsburg Spain made the production of lawyers and legally trained amateurs its primary goal, and thus dedicated to the study of jurisprudence, it neglected those subjects which did not directly serve that end.

II

Up to now this essay has considered the expansion of higher education in 16th and early 17th century Castile and the changes within the universities this prosperity brought. After 1620, however, the heyday of the universities came quickly to an end. The following section will suggest possible reasons for this reversal.

III

The emphasis of the 16th and 17th century university on the training of lawyers, many of whom were destined for the service of the crown, led to a situation in which the university practically invited royal intervention into its affairs. Absolute monarchy in Castile treated the university like any other institution which had to be brought under royal

---

[66] See U. González de la Calle, *Relaciones del Conde-Duque de Olivares con la Universidad de Salamanca* (Madrid 1931).

control in order to ensure maximum benefits for the crown. Precedents set by the Catholic kings and the decline of papal influence in Spain made the Royal Council of Castile into a primitive ministry of education, allowing it to act as the highest court of appeals for university disputes, guardian of collegiate and university statutes, and mediator of institutional, curricular, and fiscal reforms within the institutions of higher learning.[67] The growing volume of correspondence between the council and the University of Salamanca in the course of the Habsburg period testifies to the crown's strong interest in the internal affairs of its leading university: salary rises, new appointments, pensions to the widows of professors, student behavior all fell subject to the council's commands.[68]

One of the Royal Council's main interests was to secure the best of the growing crowd of *letrados* for important posts in the church and the royal administration. In a pattern which can be discerned as early as the reign of the Catholic kings, the "best" signified the professors and other instructors of law, and by the 17th century their appointments had become routine.[69] At this time the law instructor who did not leave his university post for clerical or secular office was rare indeed, and so rapid was this recruitment that many teaching positions regularly changed hands once or twice a year.[70] Complaints that this practice left the university without an experienced teaching staff usually went ignored, yet the Royal Council may not have been wholly at fault.[71] While it did little to ameliorate the university's loss of teachers, this exodus may have been spurred by falling professorial incomes as a result of declining university rents and a drop in student enrollments which implied fewer graduation ceremonies, fewer fees.[72] Certainly,

[67] The diminishing role of the papacy in 16th century Spanish universities is discussed in V. Beltrán de Heredia, *Bulario de la Universidad de Salamanca, 1219-1549*, 3 vols. (Salamanca 1966-67). On royal intervention, see Esperabé Artega, *Universidad de Salamanca*, vol. I.

[68] These are best followed in ibid.   [69] Kagan, chs. I, V, VII.

[70] See Esperabé Artega, *Universidad de Salamanca*, vol. II; Alcocer Martínez, *Universidad de Valladolid*, vol. III.

[71] The Royal Council questioned its policy only on one occasion; see AHN, Cons., leg. 13494, *consulta* of 7 November 1647. Twenty years earlier, the king had questioned this policy as well; see the *consulta* of 4 February 1627 in this same *legajo*.

[72] In the large faculty of canon law at Salamanca, for example, the number of licentiate's degrees awarded annually fell from over fifteen in the mid-16th century to only one, perhaps two, one hundred years later. Furthermore, the diocese of Salamanca, one-third of whose revenues supported the university, lost over 40% of its recorded number of laborers in the first two decades of the 17th century; the result may have been a sharp drop in professorial incomes, but records for the period do not exist. See Domínguez Ortiz, *Sociedad Española*, I, 119.

the rate of departure was highest in the short-term, lower Chairs of Law whose occupants were rather poorly paid in comparison with those enjoying the tenured positions.[73]

At the same time, complaints in the Cortes and elsewhere about the wildly corrupt and often violent student elections of professors at Salamanca and Valladolid led the young Philip IV in 1623, acting no doubt on the advice of his favorite, Olivares, to order the Royal Council to take charge of the selection of university instructors.[74] Supposedly designed to maintain university standards and to assure the students of qualified professors, this changeover, which became permanent after 1641, brought questionable results. In practice the council abused its new powers by extending its already biased and nepotic methods of patronage to the university chairs.[75] In the course of the century, all the council really achieved was to undermine the old tradition of the professional university scholar. Teachers, now appointed from Madrid for reasons often unrelated to their teaching ability and virtually guaranteed regular ascent to the highest chairs as a result of bureaucratic practices of advancement by seniority, neglected their lecture hall duties to petition the crown for further appointments.[76] Many frequently deserted the university for months, sometimes years at a time in search of higher office or to occupy ones they had already obtained, and university complaints about faculty neglect often went unresolved.[77] Thus chairs were left vacant, continuity of instruction in the major faculties disappeared, standards fell, and students were forced to learn from inexperienced substitutes who replaced the job-hunting professors. Such irregular instruction may have contributed toward student disenchantment with university life, perhaps encouraging extracurricular instruction by the colleges and religious orders. Leisure activities may have increased as well, but the overall consequence of

[73] For example, in 1633 the tenured chairs of Prima and Víspera in canon and civil law earned 200,000 to 300,000 *maravedís* each. The three-year *regencias* in these same faculties earned less than 60,000 *maravedís* apiece. See AUS, libro 1027. Esperabé Artega, *Universidad de Salamanca*, vol. II, and Alcocer Martínez, *Universidad de Valladolid*, vol. III, list appointments to chairs at these two universities. See also Kagan, ch. VII, Table 26.

[74] *Cortes de León y Castilla*, vol. XXV; Cortes de Madrid, 1617-20, petition of D. Pedro Mexia, 18 January 1619. An earlier complaint against student-run elections had been raised in 1608 by Doctor don Antonio Pichardo Vinuesa, Vísperas professor of law at Salamanca; see AUS, leg. 2109, fol. 8. For royal policy on the appointment of professors, see AHN, Cons., leg. 7138.

[75] See Kagan, chs. IV, V.

[76] The gravity of this problem can be readily seen in the fines levied upon professors for unauthorized absences; see AHN, libro 417F; AUSC, leg. 383.

[77] For example, see AHN, Cons. leg. 7138, "Pleitos de la Universidad de Salamanca sobre la renta de son Ambrosio Bernal."

this situation upon the quality of university education and thus upon the training and ability of *letrados*, clerics, and crown officials remains unknown.

The task of selecting only the most outstanding of university *letrados* for crown appointments combined with the corruption of the Royal Council also helped to disturb university life in other ways. Within Alcalá, Salamanca, and Valladolid were the six Colegios Mayores, all dating from the late 15th and early 16th centuries with the exception of San Bartolomé at Salamanca, established in 1401.[78] Founded by prelates to aid "poor" but otherwise qualified scholars, these criteria in practice meant that only *hidalgos* with moderate incomes who were already in possession of a bachelor's degree gained admission.[79] Supposedly elected on the basis of their ability and their freedom from Moorish and Jewish ancestry, members of the colleges were provided with room, board, dress, and expenses as they worked toward the higher degrees of licentiate and doctor. Able to devote their time wholly to study and benefited by special graduation privileges, these students rapidly earned the colleges a reputation for academic excellence as they frequently achieved the highest university honors and won professorships in the open, student-controlled elections. By the 17th century, candidates from the four Colegios Mayores at Salamanca and the two at Alcalá and Valladolid, successfully mixing scholarly prestige with a measure of bribery, intimidation, and violence, triumphed in enough of these competitions to dominate teaching positions at their respective universities.[80]

Through their outstanding university record, graduates of the colleges quickly won favor with the crown for its important posts, although much of this success rested upon the aid and influence of older graduates who, having reached high office, actively intervened on behalf of their old colleges in the distribution of royal and clerical office.[81] Consequently, the Colegios Mayores gradually became known as the ideal place from which one could begin a *letrado* career, a reputation which earned them both the respect and interest of many of Castile's most powerful office-holding families.

[78] The other colleges were Cuenca, San Salvador or Oviedo, Santiago el Cebedeo or Arzobispo, all at Salamanca; Santa Cruz in Valladolid; and San Ildefonso in Alcalá de Henares.

[79] The constitutions and statutes of the colleges at Salamanca are published in Sala Balust, *Constituciones*. Those for Santa Cruz are in the BSC, and the AHN, Univ. leg. 674F contains those for San Ildefonso.

[80] Esperabé Artega, *Universidad de Salamanca*, vol. II, lists college students holding chairs at Salamanca. See also Kagan, ch. VI, Table 26.

[81] The *consultas* for appointments to the *audiencias* demonstrate this situation; see AHN, Cons., legs. 13494, 13500-01, 13515-17, 13529. See also Kagan, chs. IV, V.

The colleges were not slow to exploit their favored role. With the autonomy granted them by their founders, college statutes were emended in order to accommodate the sons of wealthy and aristocratic families. And after the late 16th century the colleges tended increasingly to admit only those students related to former members, those who belonged to important noble houses, or those who enjoyed influential family connections at court.[82] High government officials, royal councillors, bishops, men who were often college graduates in their own right, often acted as court agents for one or more of the Colegios Mayores, helping them secure appointments for their members. Such cooperation usually brought the official a place in one of the colleges for a son or relative, a prize sure to further the young man's later career. The growing number of sons and nephews of royal councillors listed in the college records testifies to these ties which, after 1623, were considerably strengthened when the Council of Castile, except for a brief period in the 1630s, gained control of the elections to university professorships and added a new source of patronage to its already important place in the distribution of ecclesiastical and secular office. This council, like those of the Indies, Military Orders, and Supreme Inquisition, which were also important sources of patronage, was dominated by graduates of the colleges and their friends, forming what might be called a "Colegio Mayor" faction that openly favored younger college students for teaching posts and jobs.[83] In turn, the colleges, seeking to further their position at court, accepted the sons and clients of ministers into their ranks.[84] Continuing mutual interest brought the councils and the colleges ever closer together, and a student lacking family ties with either college graduates, court dignitaries, or influential noblemen normally found himself excluded from the Colegios Mayores, professorships, and, consequently, *letrado* offices. In this manner the family dynasties which dominated both the councils and the colleges kept other *letrados* out, and this develop-

[82] For biographical information concerning Colegio Mayor students, see J. Roxas y Contreras, *Historia del Colegio Viejo de San Bartolomé*, 3 vols. (Madrid 1766); L. Ferrer Ezquerra y H. Misol García, *Catálogo de Colegiales del Colegio Mayor de Santiago el Cebedeo, del Arzobispo, de Salamanca* (Salamanca 1956); for the College of Oviedo: BNM, MS 940; for Santa Cruz: BSC, libro 22; for Cuenca: BSC, MS 174; and for San Ildefonso: AHN, Univ., libro 1233F.

[83] Between 1566 and 1700, well over half of the members of the councils of Castile and the Indies were Colegio Mayor graduates. See Kagan, Tables 4, 5.

[84] Discussions of this situation can be found in Sala Balust, *Constituciones*, vol. 1, Introduction; and F. Pérez Bayer, "Por la Libertad de la Literatura Española" (unpublished MS), Biblioteca del Palacio Real, Madrid, MSS 277-78. See also BNM, MS 18.055, fols. 130-36r.

ment, by itself, may have been the most significant contribution towards the consolidation of a "robe nobility" in 17th century Spain.

The colleges, on the other hand, once the academic elite of the university now housed its social elite since they had become the almost exclusive preserve of the sons of a closed circle of powerful court families. They prospered, adding new scholarships, admitting fee-paying pensioners and acquiring luxurious new buildings while their members dedicated themselves more to leisure and the gentlemanly arts of dance, fencing, and horsemanship than to serious academic study.[85]

But to maintain that the Colegios Mayores, acting alone, caused university decline in 17th century Castile would be untrue. College students were relatively few in number, never amounting to more than 170 in any one year or never more than 3 percent of their universities' enrollments, and the posts they monopolized represented only a small fraction of the total places usually reserved for *letrados*.[86] However, their influence was greater than their numbers would indicate. The offices that they along with other university instructors who were not college graduates did control—presidencies of the councils and *audiencias*, councillorships and high magisterial positions, judgeships on the tribunals of the Inquisition, bishoprics, leading canonries, and royal chaplaincies, etc.—represented the important, prestige places.[87] And many students, frustrated by such overwhelming competition in a job market already overcrowded with *letrados*, apparently believed that promotion and advancement were almost impossible for those lacking the requisite family ties. Salamanca's three Colleges of the Military Orders, admittedly the outspoken enemies of the Colegios Mayores, may have summed up this problem in 1659 by recognizing that "for those who are not colegiales, the result is a dispair which urges them to abandon the university, as they see the door to offices is closed and that it will open only to a few accredited lawyers who are considered necessary in the tribunals. . . ."[88]

A shortage of contemporary diaries and letters makes any statement

[85] Records of the official "visits" to the colleges underscore this change. The best introduction to this subject is L. Sala Balust, *Colegio de Salamanca, 1623-1770* (Valladolid 1956). Also useful is AGS, Gracia y Justicia, leg. 959; AUV, libro D-6; BSC, Caja 31. The most grandiose of the new buildings erected by the Colegios Mayores is Salamanca's Palacio de Anaya, the 18th century home of the Colegio Mayor de San Bartolomé.

[86] The decade of the 1670s marked the apogee of the growth of the Colegio Mayores during the Habsburg era. See Kagan, Graph 1.

[87] See n. 73. Furthermore, nearly 40% of Castilian bishops during the 17th century were Colegio Mayor graduates. See Kagan, ch. v; Tables 4-7, 10.

[88] AHN, Cons., leg. 7138, Memorial de los Tres Colegios Militares, 1659.

about possible student "frustration" mere supposition, but in any case, student hopes may have been shattered by a probable diminution in the number of *letrado* places available which in turn tended to sharpen competition for scarce jobs and offices. With professors and college graduates in control of top positions, the average student who lacked strong family connections looked elsewhere for employment. Although evidence is often lacking, population loss, economic decline, mounting taxation, fiscal chaos, and the atrophy of Castile's industrial and mercantile cities may have combined to reduce the number of local *letrado* offices and to displace many lawyers from their careers; certainly, at the *Chancillería* in Valladolid, the number of registered attorneys fell sharply during the 17th century from a peak of around fifty in the 1590s to an average of approximately fifteen after 1640.[89] It is also possible that the economic squeeze produced a change in litigation habits during the 17th century which resulted in more cases being settled privately out of court or at a local level, circumstances which may have thrown the lawyers at the *Chancillería* out of work or encouraged them to work elsewhere. But until the manner in which families made use of the royal courts and the overall nature of Castilian litigation receive more serious attention, little can be known about such questions. *Letrados* may have also been shut out of local magistracies since many of these positions, particularly those in the larger towns, probably came under the control of one or two powerful families and were subsequently removed from the open, competitive market. Even school teaching as a career may have suffered; many towns, caught in a financial pinch, balked at payments to *maestros de niños* and Latin instructors while others in similar straits turned their schools over to the Jesuits or some other religious order, leaving the old, secular teachers without jobs. Guadalajara, La Coruña, and Logroño, and Pontevedra, where both of these occurrences took place, may be only a few examples among many.[90] Furthermore, Castile's economic troubles may have reduced either the number or value, perhaps both, of nonresident clerical benefices, a device through which the church had sent many students to a university.

[89] Archivo de la Chancillería de Valladolid, Libros de Acuerdos. The drop in the number of attorneys was apparently precipitated by an order of Philip III which set a ceiling of thirty *abogados* for this tribunal; see BNM, MS 12179, fols. 76-79.

[90] See Francisco Layna Serrano, *Historia de Guadalajara y Sus Mendozas en los Siglos XV y XVI*, 4 vols. (Madrid 1942), esp. IV, 21-24. For La Coruña, see AHN, Cons., leg. 13183, report on Galicia, 1772. Fernando Bujanda, *Historia del Viejo Seminario de Logroño* (Logroño 1948), deals with the history of the Jesuits in this town; see esp. 16-19. Pontevedra's educational problems are outlined in Enrique Fernandez Villamil, "La Preceptoria y Estudios de Pontevedra a tráves de Cuatro Siglos," *Cuadernos de Estudios Gallegos*, 1 (1944), 73ff.

All such estimates require statistical proof, but there seems to be sufficient evidence to indicate that the *letrado*'s world was shrinking at a time when the costs of university attendance were rising and the important posts remaining open to him were blocked by a favored minority. This contraction of the market served only to exacerbate Castile's long-standing problem of too many graduates competing for jobs which were always in short supply. Degree-holders, though never numerous in absolute terms, constituted a group too large for Castile's small, professional-job market to absorb. For these students preferment was not absolutely impossible, but the promise of promotion and advancement undoubtedly waned during a period when the investment demanded by a long *letrado* education no longer brought a sound return. Indeed, during the 17th century the costs of the higher degrees required by the important offices of the church, the royal administration, and the lawyer's profession spiralled out of control, dampening student motivation yet further or at least forcing many to take their degrees at the less renowned "provincial" universities.[91] Combined with the poor and irregular instruction in the lecture halls, such conditions allowed the pampered Colegios Mayores, whose members could graduate at reduced cost, to flourish while university enrollments steadily declined.

The Colegios Mayores, however, were not the only successful colleges in 17th century Castile. The communities of the religious orders, particularly the Jesuits, offered an alternative to university education. And since the late 16th century Jesuit colleges had accepted growing numbers of lay students, many of whom were possibly disillusioned with *letrado* universities which no longer catered for their tastes and with *letrado* careers which no longer offered secure rewards. Faced by a world of war, disease, famine, and uncertain employment, for many of these students the instruction offered by the friars, deeply engrained with lessons of Christian doctrine and example, may have offered not only an alternative to *letrado* education but also a new ideal and way of life. Given the special economic and social conditions of the time, the expansion of the regular clergy in 17th century Castile possibly represented one facet of a general reaction against university education and the competitive, office-holding world. Thus the church, acting as a sponge for frustrated students, may have channeled the

---

[91] According to one petition in 1703, the combined cost of a license and doctorate at Salamanca could amount to an incredible 20,000 *reales*, a sum which included gifts in money and kind, an elaborate feast, and, on occasion, bullfights, parades, and other performances which the degree candidate was obliged to provide. See Esperabé Artega, *Universidad de Salamanca*, I, 825.

energies of these possible discontents in a way 17th century England failed to do.

But falling university attendance may have also reflected a general increase in the number of salable financial and municipal offices open to those with sufficient cash.[92] Sons of the rich, rather than endure a long and sometimes arduous university career, could readily obtain brief training at home with a private tutor or in a local religious college, forgo a degree in law, and then purchase a lucrative, fee-paying office. It is tempting to compare the first signs of stagnation in university enrollments with the increases in the sale of office by the crown beginning in the reigns of Philip III and Philip IV. But until more information is gathered about the office buyers and the volume of total offices sold, this hypothesis must remain untested.

On another plane, the great international conflicts of the 1630s and 1640s and the coming of war to the Iberian peninsula itself after the Catalan Revolt of 1640, joined with the efforts of Olivares to revive a military spirit among Castile's courtly, office-holding aristocracy, may have encouraged the sons of *hidalgos* to discard their student robes for the sword and stirrup. Thus, the relative lack of interest in the universities after the 1630s may have only marked the triumph of old aristocratic ideas and values which in the course of the century turned the sons of the wealthy, including those of *letrado* officials, away from the professional universities and juridical study toward a more chivalric education and style of life. Only a careful, systematic study of career patterns among *hidalgo* and office-holding families can provide the answer; nevertheless, there is some evidence that graduates of the Colegios Mayores, traditionally oriented toward *letrado* careers, displayed a slight tendency in the later 17th century to become military officers, dignitaries in the royal household, and *rentiers* living off their own estates.[93] Indeed, it is not unlikely that the new robe nobility, eager for titles and the social status of the old landed aristocracy, attempted to live "nobly," and that this practice, perhaps akin to the well-noted *trahison de la bourgeoisie*, hindered university as well as economic development in 17th century Castile.

Whatever the exact cause, the outcome was the general decline of the university (Graph 2). After more than a century of new foundations, Castile after 1620 would not receive another new university until the 1830s when the practically defunct university of Alcalá was re-

[92] Little is known about the extent of the sale of offices in Castile. See Swart, *Sale of Offices*; E. Schäefer, *El Consejo Real y Supremo de las Indias*, vol. 1 (Sevilla 1935); AGS, Cámara de Castilla: Serie XII; AGS, Dirección General de Tesoro; Contaduría General de Valores, legs. 280-335.

[93] See n. 76; Kagan, Tables 19-22.

organized into the Central University of Madrid. Moreover, by 1660, Alcalá, Salamanca, and Valladolid attracted fewer than half the students they had had a century before, and this downward trend continued unabated into the 18th century (Graphs 1, 2). The small liberal arts colleges within these institutions, suffering from lack of interest, Jesuit competition, and adverse economic conditions, either disappeared completely or amalgamated, pooling students and rents. At the provincial level where universities had begun to languish even before the major institutions, enrollments at Santiago and Seville dipped to under 300 per year; Granada and Baeza barely managed the same; and poor Sigüenza after mid-century could never muster more than 30 students in any one year (Graph 1). By 1700 many of the smaller universities barely survived, while the major ones were rapidly losing both their influence and prestige.

The history of Castile's universities for the next seventy-five years simply confirmed those trends begun in the century before. Enrollments at the three major universities stagnated at relatively low levels: Salamanca attracted between 1500 and 2000 students a year; Alcalá rarely had more than 1000, Valladolid even fewer (Graph 1). At the provincial level the smaller universities continued to decay, while a few, notably Granada and Sigüenza, temporarily dropped out of sight. By mid-century the universities together could muster no more than 5000-6000 students, a figure less than one-third the total of two centuries before (Graph 2). In relative terms, these enrollments meant that Castile around 1750 sent only 2.2 percent of its 17-year-olds to university each year as compared to the 5.4 percent of the 18-year-olds who matriculated annually in the closing decades of the 16th century.[94] Since 1600 Castile had lost only a small fraction of her total population and by the middle of the 18th century demographic recovery was well under way, but during this same period her professionally trained, university-educated population had diminished by over one-half. Similarly, the number of students earning degrees—baccalaureates, licenses, and doctorates alike—had declined at a similar rate. Once the educational leader of Europe, Castile in the middle of the 18th century was well on the road that would turn her in the course of the next one hundred years into one of the Continent's educational backwaters.

Internally, the withered universities of the 18th century had little in common with their 16th century counterparts. Now that many of the law's attractions had slipped away, students were more or less evenly

[94] Castile's population at this time was about 6.3 million. For the mathematics involved in this estimate, see above, n. 16.

Richard L. Kagan

distributed about the various faculties, although arts was slowly becoming the universities' most popular discipline (Graphs 3-4). Students were also younger; the average age of first-year arts students at
the University of Alcalá de Henares had dropped by nearly two years,
from 18 in 1550 to 16 in 1771. Similar decreases were recorded in the
other faculties, partly because of improvements in primary and secondary education, but more importantly, because students were less
likely to defer university education until their late teens or early 20s.
In other words, by the mid-18th century education had become closely
associated with youth; children advanced through school and university classes as they advanced in age in a type of lockstep typical of
youngsters today.

Moreover, the majority of these younger students, rather than living
outside university auspices in private homes and lodging houses in the
fashion typical of the 16th century, resided in the universities' many colleges, religious and secular. Though the number of these "supported" or
scholarship students increased,[95] their growing strength within the
universities was primarily due to a decline in the number of those students who received no financial aid. As a result, 60 percent of the
students at Salamanca in the mid-18th century lived behind college
walls as compared to one-tenth of that figure two centuries before.
One consequence of this evolution is that, from outward appearances,
Salamanca and the other major universities were far more regimented,
far more peaceful, and less riotous institutions than they had been in
the past.

It would be a mistake, however, to attribute this new tranquility
solely to the cloistering of students at night; it had probably more to
do with the type of students who came to university in an age when
the professional job market remained relatively tight. These youths
were dedicated pre-professionals, and in general the universities
lacked students who enrolled merely for experience, an introduction
to the law, or for a lark, that is, those students who in the 16th century
had helped send enrollments to record heights. Eighteenth century
students for the most part appear to have been a dull and conservative
lot, interested less in curricular innovation and advance than in the
credentials which could help them toward a secure career. Instead of
pioneering ideas on the frontiers of science and philosophy, they
plowed through the rituals of learning required for a degree. Content
was less important than form so that when Norbert Caino visited
Sigüenza's medical faculty in the late 1750s, he reported that the question discussed in one public thesis was: "Of what utility or of prejudice

[95] College students at Salamanca before 1590 numbered fewer than 500. By the
1730s they had increased to over 1000.

would it be for men to have one finger more or less."[96] "If, in order to enjoy good health, it is necessary to begin with the right hand or the left" was supposedly another topic in dispute. Caino's reports, undoubtedly exaggerated, underscore the fact that ideas, however absurd, were subordinate to tradition, ceremony, and degrees in the universities of 18th century Castile.

One other reason for the peace, tranquility, and professional character of the universities in the 18th century was their decidedly monkish or religious character. In the 16th century less than 5 percent of the University of Salamanca's students belonged to the religious orders; the vast majority were either laymen or members of the secular clergy, and the same was true for the other important universities of Castile. In the following century the university colleges which housed the monks increased both in numbers and size while secular students increasingly stayed away.[97] By the 1750s almost half of Salamanca's students were religious, and the same was true at the Universities of Alcalá de Henares and Valladolid. In all of Castile a veritable "Christianization" of higher education had taken place. In the north of Europe just the opposite was true, and this difference no doubt helps to explain the continuing intellectual isolation and backwardness of Castile's universities. The new philosophical and scientific currents of the north were anathema to Castile's overwhelmingly orthodox regular clergy who, in control of the university Faculties of Arts and Theology, relied upon their brethren in the Inquisition to help keep Europe's intellectual "poison" out.[98]

In the 1770s the monks' presence at the universities was dramatically reduced. At Salamanca the total number of *religiosos* slipped from over 900 in the 1760s to one-third of that figure in the space of ten years, while in proportional terms, their share of the university's enrollments dropped from close to one-half to one-quarter. This about-face, common to other universities as well, can be partially explained by the expulsion of the Jesuits from Spain and its dominions in 1767, but at the same time university colleges belonging to the other religious orders, for reasons yet to be discovered, lost most of their students.[99] What is certain is that as the monks abandoned the univer-

[96] Cited in J. Garcia Mercadel, *Viajes de Extranjeros por España y Portugal* (Madrid 1962), III, 401.

[97] Between 1560 and 1760, religious at Salamanca increased from just over 200 to 900 and more.

[98] The University of Seville, for example, expressed its hostility to new Dutch and English ideas which were "perverting" Aristotle, Galen, and Hippocrates; see Ajo, *Historia de las Universidades*, V, 235.

[99] Salamanca's largest religious college, San Esteban, a Dominican house, had 175 members in 1765. Ten years later its membership had fallen to 36.

sities, secular students took their place. Students of arts and theology who would have been previously educated by the Jesuits returned to the universities, while the instruction offered by the other religious orders to secular students collapsed because of a royal decree in 1771 which ordered that such classes could no longer receive university credit.[100] Consequently, the universities recovered many of the students they had lost to the religious orders a century before, and their return helped to push enrollments at many universities to 18th century highs.

These increases were also linked to a series of university reforms introduced in the 1770s and 1780s by the "enlightened" ministers of Charles III.[101] Spearheaded by the Count of Campomanes, *fiscal* of the Royal Council of Castile, by Pablo de Olavide, a Castilian version of a French physiocrat, by Francisco Pérez Bayer, an outspoken enemy of the Colegios Mayores who was also a court tutor for the royal princesses, and later by Jovellanos, minister to Charles IV, these measures first humbled, and then in the 1790s, finally suppressed the Colegios Mayores, ending their 200-year domination of the universities and *letrado* posts. The costs of university degrees, prohibitively expensive at the major institutions, were also cut, enabling more students to obtain the valuable titles of licentiate and doctor.[102] Meanwhile, the university curriculum was modernized along European lines: medicine shed many of its classical vestiges for studies of a more empirical bent; Newton and Galileo, algebra and experimental physics were added to the liberal program, long dominated by the works of Aristotle; and in the laws, new emphasis was given to national as opposed to Roman and canon law.

Together these changes kindled new enthusiasm for university study, although it is important to note that students in the arts faculty showed little interest at first in "modern" subjects such as experimental physics. On the whole they preferred Aristotle; science in the late 18th century was still a pastime for gentlemen-dilettantes whereas the traditional course offered the meal-ticket the job-hungry students had in mind. Indeed, before attributing these late 18th century increases in

---

[100] See Ajo, *Historia de las Universidades*, v, 47-49.

[101] On these reforms see L. Sala Balust, *Visita y Reforma de los Colegios Mayores de Salamanca en el Reinado de Carlos III* (Valladolid 1958). Also useful is George M. Addy, *The Enlightenment in the University of Salamanca* (Durham 1966), and F. Aguilar Piñal, *Plan de Estudios para la Universidad de Sevilla por Pablo de Olavide. Estudio Preliminar* (Barcelona 1969).

[102] See above, n. 85. The high costs of advanced degrees were initially reduced in 1742, then again in 1772; see Esperabé Artega, *Universidad de Salamanca*, I, 919-20, 966. As a result, the number of licenses and doctorates awarded in the 1770s and 1780s was approximately three times that of preceding decades.

student enrollments to curricular changes alone, it is necessary to set them against the background of an expanding job market now freed from Colegio Mayor control and fueled by Castile's economic advance. Although much is yet to be known about the social, economic, and administrative history of this period, it seems likely that the last decades of the 18th century brought to graduates new opportunities in education, government, and law. These developments, together with curricular advance and the end of competition from the religious orders, fostered the recovery of the universities after 1770.

In some instances, this recovery was remarkable. Sigüenza, in and out of existence for much of the century, suddenly recorded enrollments of 100 students and more. Ávila, which had only 5 students in 1740, had close to 200 fifty years later; and the University of Osuna in 1790 managed to enroll close to 300 students, nearly six times as many as in the century's opening decades. Similar advances were recorded at Granada, Oviedo, Seville, Toledo, and Valladolid. The only major universities not to share in this general epoch of prosperity were Alcalá de Henares and Salamanca (Graph 1), but their failure to do so was significant. Though attendance at the smaller universities was up, losses at Alcalá and Salamanca made sure that total university attendance in Castile rose marginally if at all. And owing to the fact that population was rapidly on the rise, the overall position of the university at the opening of the 19th century continued to deteriorate (Graph 2).

What actually seems to have happened to enrollments was not an absolute rise but a shift away from the old university centers of Castile toward smaller institutions in the provinces. For Alcalá and Salamanca, years of Colegio Mayor domination, inordinately expensive degrees, and resistance to innovation and change had taken their toll. In fact, for much these same reasons, Alcalá and Salamanca after 1700 resembled the other universities of the kingdom in that they too had become "regional" institutions, drawing the majority of their students from the provinces in which they were located. In the 16th century these two universities along with Valladolid had helped to unite the kingdom, mixing together intellectuals and professionals from every province and region. But two centuries later, Alcalá and Salamanca, like the other universities, were catering mainly to a local clientele. This helped to keep the nation's educated populace apart, possibly reinforcing Spain's deep cultural and political divisions.[103]

When interest in university study revived during the reign of

---

[103] To some degree the advent of scholarly journals with a nationwide subscription had rendered this function of the university obsolete. On journals, see Herr, *Eighteenth Century Revolution*, ch. VI.

Charles III, would-be students, rather than trek to Alcalá or Salamanca, universities which could no longer guarantee either scholarly excellence or future jobs, attended the cheaper, sometimes more flexible and innovative institutions closer to home. Accordingly, Alcalá and Salamanca lost ground, but their inability to keep apace of the other institutions was coincident with the demise of Castile itself. The region's economic and demographic preponderance within the peninsula had long been eroded; its political leadership was under attack; and its empire in the Americas, increasingly independent of the mother country's control, was soon to fall apart. It was only fitting that in educational, perhaps even in intellectual terms, Castile's two universities, linked closely to the government in Madrid, would give way to other institutions located in the more prosperous and dynamic parts of the kingdom. Barcelona and Valencia, along with Oviedo, Seville, and the medical faculties of Cadiz, were to be the intellectual leaders of the nation for the next generation. And it was not until the establishment of the Central University of Madrid in 1836 that Castile and its monarchy attempted to reassert its educational mastery over the kingdom as a whole.

At the opening of the 19th century, the fortunes of higher education in Castile were relatively bleak. Though some gains had been made in the last twenty years, enrollments continued to languish, quality of instruction was poor, and most of the universities were nearly broke. To improve matters Charles IV in 1804 pushed through a new series of curricular reforms, and three years later he suppressed the multitude of Castile's universities, leaving only seven behind.[104] This measure, designed to concentrate the remaining financial and intellectual resources of the universities and to ensure graduates of a superior and more uniform caliber than before, initially lost its chance to succeed. The Napoleonic invasion of Spain in 1809 and the bitter civil war that ensued closed the universities which survived Charles IV's reforms, leaving Castile without university education for nearly a decade. The 1820s brought the beginnings of recovery, but it would take most of the 19th century before Castile's universities could rival the position and importance of their counterparts three centuries before.[105]

[104] See Ajo, *Historia de las Universidades*, v, 90. The survivors were Alcalá, Granada, Oviedo, Salamanca, Santiago, Sevilla, and Valladolid.

[105] Nineteenth century enrollments at Castile's universities are difficult to trace. For reasons I have yet to discover, most of the Matriculation Registers after the 1830s have been lost or misplaced or they are in such a state of disarray as to make them almost impossible to use. Madrid's few remaining registers, for instance, have suffered from a recent archival flood, and when I last saw them in the summer of 1970, they were damp, covered with mold, and soon to fall apart. Furthermore, no

IV

The dynamic shift in the importance of the university within Castilian life in the century between 1550 and 1650, the year which can be said to mark the beginning of a century of stagnation and decay, was perhaps more a readjustment than absolute decline. One could postulate that in the 16th century the university, despite its large enrollments, rested upon weak foundations. Primary and secondary education were limited to a small elite within the cities and towns while the urban and rural masses remained practically illiterate and undereducated. For the popular classes the university represented only a tax collector seeking his rents, an official in a scholar's gown claiming to buy wine and meat free of tax, or an imposing plateresque edifice inhabited by the sons of the rich. The university, dependent upon this wealthy, cultured elite, was sensitive to its educational interests and tastes. When, in the course of the 17th century, these apparently changed, the universities were stripped of their larger clientele and were left to the monks, scholarship students, and hard-core professionals. In other words, by the mid-17th century the university, after passing through a phase— we may call it the "Renaissance"—somewhat resembled its medieval counterpart: small, dominated by churchmen, highly vocational, and overwhelmingly legalistic. And enrollments, however diminished, may have reflected the nation's actual need for lawyers, theologians, and physicians rather than the social and cultural interests of the elite. Thus the university regained its predominantly professional spirit while its popular, pedagogical, Renaissance element passed into the hands of the regular clergy. Not until the late 19th century would the two be reunited under university auspices.

But ultimately, the reasons for the vulnerability of this institution to social change must be sought in the way the members of the university, both students and faculty, viewed themselves and their place in Castilian life. This community, under pressure from an expanding absolute monarchy in search of trained officials, neglected its lower faculties and developed its older, medieval character to become a professional school with an emphasis upon the study of law, leaving the religious orders behind to instruct the nation's youth in grammar, arts, and theology. The pursuit of abstract knowledge, the development of scientific learning, practical and pure, had little place in an institution aimed at the production of lawyers, or, at the very least, of gentlemen lightly schooled in the law for reasons of practicality and prestige. And

---

archive or library I visited in Spain had in its possession a complete set of the enrollment summaries that each university published annually.

having developed this particular role, the fate of the university rested largely with the market it served, the classes to whom it catered. Lacking the protective family ties of the Colegios Mayores, the spiritual bulwarks of the religious colleges, and controlled by a narrow-minded, selfish, and often short-sighted group of royal officials, the university fell apart as this market contracted and its following turned to other careers and alternate forms of education. Its revival would come only after Castile's own economic recovery, beginning in the late 18th century; after the introduction of modern medical and scientific studies, first underway at the turn of the 19th century, which would eventually give the university a new role in Castilian society; after a widening of its social bases, possible only after the establishment of popular elementary and secondary schooling in the course of the 19th century; after the gradual elimination of an aristocratic bias among the monied classes and the renewed interest of these classes in university careers, again a development which only began in the 19th century; and finally, after being granted a measure of independent, autonomous life, free of strict ministerial censorship and control, an emancipation still unrealized today.

APPENDIX

TABLE 1

University of Alcala de Henares: Enrollment by Academic Year, 1550-1830

	1550	1560	1570	1580	1590	1600	1610	1620	1630	1640	1650	1660	1670	1680	1690	1700
Grammar	1493	1250	1085	634	323	351	199	200	175	217	94	65	58	54	53	77
Arts	594	931	1202	1417	1346	1145	1206	1390	776	1032	862	828	874	662	714	571
Canon Law	221	325	457	497	599	587	650	1223	636	1140	799	760	505	452	565	465
Medicine	67	126	86	121	148	97	117	165	133	88	88	119	118	72	81	61
Theology	157	364	354	506	627	537	450	637	367	348	202	316	299	147	143	139
College	35	34	33	33	23	19	18	17	18	30	28	43	45	45	41	38
Totals	2567	3030	3217	3208	3066	2736	2640	3632	2125	2855	2083	2131	1899	1432	1597	1351

	1710	1720	1730	1740	1750	1760	1770	1780	1790	1800	1810	1820	1830
Grammar	7	12	33	44	48	50	88	–	–	–	–	20	–
Arts	353	641	425	392	358	364	470	197	195	169	–	183	105
Canon Law	228	359	170	106	132	148	198	51	61	77	–	12	19
Civil Law	–	–	–	–	–	–	–	125	110	149	–	198	251
Medicine	52	54	28	23	12	23	9	12	4	–	–	3	–
Theology	78	95	115	50	71	67	106	107	140	147	–	26	38
History	–	–	–	–	–	–	–	27	–	–	–	–	–
College	32	34	38	42	34	31	–	–	–	–	–	–	–
Other Colleges	121	61	156	196	236	214	–	–	–	–	–	–	–
Totals	864	1244	932	809	843	847	783	519	492	542	46	451a	413

Source: 1550-1831 AHN: Univ. Libros 431 F ff.

a Includes 34 students labeled "protestors."

TABLE 2

University of Baeza: Enrollment by Academic Year, 1560-1820

	1560	1565	1570	1575	1580	1585	1590	1595	1600	1605	1610	1615	1620	1625	1630	1635
Grammar	214	239	250	304	297	331	326	342	205	99	165	193	195	132	126	153
Arts	84	118	99	149	112	97	130	154	144	101	90	104	105	55	60	67
Theology	33	51	47	73	93	82	52	75	55	51	39	52	32	28	33	26
Totals	331	408	396	526	502	510	508	571	404	251	294	349	332	215	219	246

	1640	1645	1650	1655	1660	1665	1670	1675	1680	1685	1690	1695	1700	1705	1710	1715
Grammar	166	81	116	100	128	108	209	76	85	46	59	21	19	27	99	57
Arts	102	90	68	59	67	98	144	110	85	45	67	58	66	93	58	54
Theology	26	33	33	24	25	39	52	41	28	29	25	39	37	39	36	29
Canon Law	–	–	–	–	–	–	–	–	–	6	20	21	7	10	4	–
Totals	294	204	217	183	220	245	410	261	198	126	171	139	129	169	197	140

	1720	1725	1730	1735	1740	1745	1750	1755	1760	1765	1770	1775	1780	1785	1790	1795
Grammar	73	37	73	55	71	64	85	86	87	63	40	71	75	91	113	128
Arts	73	82	75	92	64	78	59	106	95	72	86	49	80	87	87	–
Theology	13	35	43	39	34	23	40	39	36	33	47	31	49	42	73	84
History	–	–	–	–	–	–	–	–	–	–	–	–	–	–	5	–
Totals	159	154	191	186	169	165	184	231	218	168	173	151	204	220	228	212

	1800	1805	1810	1816	1820
Grammar	90	72	–	112	102
Totals	90	72	–	112	102

Source: Archivo del Instituto de Enseñanza Secondaria, Baeza: Libros de Matrículas.

TABLE 3
University of Granada: Total Enrollment
(Quinquennial Averages)

Academic Years	Students	Academic Years	Students	Academic Years	Students
1635-40	222.6	1710-15	42.6	1785-90	555.6
1640-45	240.6	1715-20	66.6	1790-95	613.6
1645-50	238.8	1720-25	159.2	1795-1800	684.4
1650-55	175.8	1725-30	119.2	1800-05	703.6
1656-60	182.2	1730-35	89.0	1805-10	605.0
1660-65	168.4	1735-40	64.0	1810-15	220.6
1665-70	160.4	1740-45	118.0	1815-20	716.4
1670-75	160.8	1745-50	35.6	1820-25	947.8
1675-80	126.2	1750-55	1.0	1825-30	1157.0
1680-85	110.2	1755-60	6.4	1830-35	1408.0
1685-90	97.8	1760-65	34.8	1835-40	1478.0
1690-95	156.0	1765-70	37.4	1840-45	1032.0
1695-1700	128.4	1770-75	204.6	1845-50	777.0
1700-05	84.0	1775-80	373.8	1850-55	982.0
1705-10	65.4	1780-85	468.2		

Source: Francisco Montells y Nadal, *Historia del Origen y Fundación de la Universidad de Granada* (Granada 1870), 799-806.

TABLE 4
University of Salamanca: Total Enrollment
(Quinquennial Averages)

Academic Years	Students	Academic Years	Students	Academic Years	Students
1550-55	5982.0	1650-55	2949.4	1750-55	2054.8
1555-60	4511.6	1655-60	3133.4	1755-60	2139.0
1560-65	4998.8	1660-65	2709.6	1760-65	2035.4
1565-70	5958.3	1665-70	2383.4	1765-70	2112.0
1570-75	5917.6	1670-75	2747.4	1770-75	1609.2
1575-80	5607.0	1675-80	2659.8	1775-80	1499.4
1580-85	5976.5	1680-85	2029.0	1780-85	1385.2
1585-90	6633.3	1685-90	2001.2	1785-90	1599.4
1590-95	6359.0	1690-95	2201.0	1790-95	1533.0
1595-1600	4740.8	1695-1700	2150.4	1795-1800	1452.6
1600-05	5131.0	1700-05	1894.8	1800-05	1149.4
1605-10	4711.0	1705-10	1429.4	1805-10	717.6
1610-15	5006.0	1710-15	1420.6	1810-15	82.4
1615-20	5314.6	1715-20	1692.8	1815-20	420.8
1620-25	5918.6	1720-25	1698.4	1820-25	517.0
1625-30	5534.4	1725-30	1809.0	1825-30	611.2
1630-35	4428.0	1730-35	2041.6	1830-35	602.2
1635-40	4484.2	1735-40	2038.0	1835-40	654.2
1640-45	3748.4	1740.45	2336.0	1840-45	567.2
1645-50	3009.6	1745.50	2350.0		

Sources: AUS, Libros 268-359 and A. Vidal y Diaz, *Memoria Histórica de la Universidad de Salamanca* (Salamanca 1869), Appendix II.

TABLE 5

University of Salamanca: Enrollment by Faculty

	1551	1555	1560	1565	1571	1575	1581	1585	1592	1595	1599	1605	1610	1615	1620	1625
Grammar	—	1668	—	1755	1320	—	816	893	547	448	—	331	401	227	265	279
Arts	596	706	533	583	701	570	728	924	977	693	448	627	495	496	522	408
Canon Law	1436	1063	1026	1324	2118	2147	2277	3137	2939	2776	2178	2386	2437	2682	3043	3128
Civil Law	621	636	518	637	623	556	537	643	686	768	289	314	282	258	1244	1282
Medicine	129	157	148	138	115	110	144	194	234	208	161	164	155	178	163	177
Theology	318	420	391	440	565	519	470	571	626	—	294	343	278	293	210	211
Greek & Rhetoric	—	48	18	8	—	—	—	—	—	—	—	—	—	—	—	—
Hebrew	—	1	—	—	—	—	—	—	—	—	—	—	—	—	—	—
Surgery	—	—	—	—	—	—	—	—	—	—	—	—	—	9	10	20
Mathematics	—	—	—	—	—	—	—	—	—	—	8	7	—	22	3	—

	1630	1635	1640	1645	1650	1655	1660	1665	1670	1675	1680	1685	1690	1695	1700
Grammar	—	359	391	288	142	173	166	208	110	247	158	70	102	115	53
Arts	233	329	257	190	192	214	162	207	257	264	173	126	166	231	188
Canon Law	2209	2407	2099	1595	1459	1652	1259	952	940	1246	745	596	724	581	444
Civil Law	734	733	618	455	138	143	139	265	121	174	141	83	107	121	103
Medicine	143	108	75	38	42	49	61	70	60	88	59	39	57	52	50
Theology	156	107	137	95	89	84	89	70	66	80	34	32	45	32	27
Surgery	—	20	12	3	5	2	1	—	2	1	1	—	—	—	—

	1705	1710	1715	1720	1725	1730	1735	1740	1745	1750	1755	1760	1765	1770	1775	1780
Grammar	69	70	83	105	78	168	151	199	228	100	43	69	30	316	32	24
Arts	105	88	90	207	225	239	142	262	451	358	322	331	241	532	398	328
Canon Law	245	130	167	194	184	151	93	131	224	147	126	159	142	114	81	96
Civil Law	111	72	104	111	120	132	137	150	187	155	163	225	223	199	177	193
Medicine	52	12	33	42	49	33	24	23	46	57	46	54	46	31	15	24
Theology	36	8	16	17	11	7	18	15	19	9	14	12	22	27	255	196

(Table continues)

TABLE 5 (*cont'd.*) University of Salamanca: Enrollment by Faculty

	1705	1710	1715	1720	1725	1730	1735	1740	1745	1750	1755	1760	1765	1770	1775	1780
Greek & Rhetoric	1	—	—	—	1	1	1	—	—	—	—	—	—	—	16	41
Surgery	—	2	1	—	—	—	—	—	3	—	3	14	4	2	13	8
Mathematics	—	—	—	—	—	—	—	—	—	—	—	—	2	1	16	—
Music	—	—	2	2	2	4	4	4	4	8	21	15	10	7	14	4
Algebra	—	—	—	—	—	—	—	—	—	—	—	—	—	—	—	2
Experimental Physics	—	—	—	—	—	—	—	—	—	—	—	—	—	—	—	1

	1785	1790	1795	1800	1805	1810	1815	1820	1825	1830	1835	1840	1850	1855	1860
Grammar	23	7	8	30	58	—	18	—	—	—	—	—	—	193	—
Arts	351	230	125	163	115	9	55	23	59	180	275	111	—	72	—
Canon Law	110	116	169	149	95	1	13	34	35	33	9	12	—	—	—
Civil Law	175	188	238	196	126	5	16	146	138	158	247	197	136?	149	126
Medicine	13	19	12	—	46	29	14	17	36	24	32	157	—	32	—
Theology	246	307	237	172	128	3	8	22	44	34	105	53	—	—	33
Greek & Rhetoric	22	13	5	2	6	—	—	—	—	—	—	—	—	—	—
Hebrew	—	—	—	1	—	—	—	—	—	—	2	—	—	—	—
Surgery	10	8	—	—	—	—	—	—	—	—	—	8	—	11	—
Mathematics	1	2	71	4	1	1	—	300	—	—	21	—	—	—	—
Music	4	2	—	—	—	—	—	—	—	—	—	—	—	—	—
Algebra	6	6	9	14	4	—	—	—	—	—	—	—	—	—	—
Experimental Physics	12	6	14	6	15	—	—	—	—	—	—	—	—	—	—
Moral Philosophy	—	—	95	66	—	—	—	—	—	1	—	—	—	—	—
Political Economy	—	—	—	—	—	2	—	—	—	—	—	—	—	—	—

TABLE 5 (*cont'd.*) University of Salamanca: Enrollment by Faculty

	1785	1790	1795	1800	1805	1810	1815	1820	1825	1830	1835	1840	1850	1855	1860
Humanities	–	–	–	–	–	–	–	11	3	–	–	–	–	–	–
Greek	–	–	–	–	–	–	–	–	–	–	41	25	–	–	–
Astronomy	–	–	–	–	–	–	–	–	–	–	2	11	–	–	–
Botany	–	–	–	–	–	–	–	–	–	–	–	68	–	–	–

	1865	1870	1880	1885	1890	1900
Arts	–	134	186	149	156	68
Civil Law	133	672	216	164	617	129
Medicine	–	603	129	132	206	–
Theology	34	–	–	–	–	–
Sciences	–	82	118	138	82	–
Notary	–	30	–	3	3	–

Source: AUS, Libros 268-539. After 1840, matriculation books for Salamanca are difficult to find. Some are located in the archive of the university rector. Other information regarding 19th century enrollments can be found in the *Memoria histórica* published annually by the university, but no complete series of these booklets exists.

TABLE 6

University of Santa Maria de Jesús, Seville: Enrollment by Academic Year

	1546	1550	1566	1570	1575	1580	1590	1605	1610	1620	1630	1640	1650	1660	1670	1680
Arts	64	43	–	42	–	–	–	5	–	–	–	–	–	–	–	–
Canon Law	57	59	–	188	–	–	–	185	236	250	235	178	121	108	80	73
Civil Law	8	1	–	24	–	–	–	–	–	5	–	–	*	*	*	*
Theology	1	7	–	32	–	–	–	1	3	1	23	–	–	–	–	–
Medicine	2	5	–	16	–	–	–	24	33	24	34	26	17	19	34	35
Totals	132	127	321**	302	407**	303**	244**	215	262	280	292	204	138	127	114	108

	1690	1700	1710	1720	1730	1740	1750	1760	1770	1780	1790	1800	1810	1820	1830	1840
Arts	–	1	5	–	–	–	–	–	–	–	–	–	29	323	154**	254
Canon Law	163	88	73	201	133	–	122	122	140	47**	265	46	**	72	**	**
Civil Law	*	*	*	*	*	*	*	*	*	*	–	32	–	64	**	**
Theology	–	–	4	–	3	–	–	–	16	50	44	**	–	–	–	–
Medicine	19	26	38	22	58	35	47	64	74	41	67	**	22	57	92	279
Totals	72	115	120	223	194	**	169	186	230	138**	440	**	**	516	**	**

Source: AUS, Libros 478-502.

* Canon and Civil Law are combined.

**Total incomplete.

TABLE 7

University of Valladolid: Enrollment by Faculty

	1567	1570	1575	1576	1588	1616	1620	1625	1640	1645	1650	1655	1660	1665	1670	1675	1680
Grammar	231	138	–	220	130	61	55	34	7	18	8	11	–	73	–	–	–
Arts	91	98	129	111	158	264	215	181	167	160	236	184	269	302	237	225	122
Canon Law	273	373	403	558	755	1005	1335	1236	1157	930	847	981	725	801	796	758	474
Civil Law	–	–	161	245	113	140	164	126	204	137	101	135	100	129	118	95	105
Medicine	11	22	14	–	35	28	43	38	19	30	22	42	34	43	64	32	26
Theology	90	112	119	123	114	112	57	38	31	19	36	31	43	53	38	56	24
Colleges	–	–	–	–	–	–	–	–	172	232	242	225	–	241	–	–	–

	1685	1690	1695	1700	1705	1710	1715	1720	1725	1730	1735	1740	1745	1750	1755	1760	1765
Arts	141	290	366	152	481	202	64	105	71	262	60	392	56	87	99	55	55
Canon Law	405	540	462	307	328	142	110	123	140	171	91	106	109	140	145	131	38
Civil Law	71	133	87	76	78	70	120	136	93	95	55	–	35	56	98	76	60
Medicine	33	28	22	29	32	26	32	33	32	28	10	23	–	12	–	23	–
Theology	37	26	43	38	49	12	26	25	26	17	19	50	56	71	–	67	–
Colleges	254	–	264	–	–	153	–	95	–	194	162	238	–	251	289	245	–

	1770	1775	1780	1785	1790	1795	1800	1805	1810	1815	1820	1825	1835	1840	1845	1850	1855	1860
Arts	285	529	456	440	397	526	358	319	75	148	336	453	593	336	–	67	115	55
Canon Law	22	217	219	230	276	313	343	207	14	19	44	59	59	20	–	404	394	–
Civil Law	121	318	357	286	310	344	395	292	54	87	277	446	802	566	–	*	*	365
Medicine	–	20	28	19	23	29	33	26	22	10	8	42	96	165	–	–	–	155
Theology	–	86	312	312	326	378	301	206	19	24	30	43	223	56	–	88	–	–
Sciences	–	–	–	–	–	–	–	–	–	–	–	–	–	–	–	–	–	–
Notary	–	–	–	–	–	–	–	–	–	–	–	–	–	–	134	–	132	19
Medical Clinic	–	–	–	–	–	–	–	–	–	–	–	–	–	70	–	–	–	17

Source: AUV, Libros 32–86.

Notes:

Sixteenth century figures are apparently incomplete.

The fluctuations of the arts enrollment between 1715 and 1765 are partly the result of inconsistencies in the matriculation books.

Canon and Civil Law enrollments for 1850 and 1855 are combined.

8

Culture and Society in the 18th Century Province: The Case of Edinburgh and the Scottish Enlightenment

by N. T. Phillipson

Provincial culture is arguably the most neglected area in the study of the Enlightenment, yet it is surely one of its most characteristic manifestations.[1] Throughout the large provincial cities of continental Europe and the Anglo-Saxon world, in places such as Boston or Philadelphia, Dublin or Copenhagen, Bordeaux or Dijon, in countless German principalities or at Edinburgh, which is to be the subject of this essay, the same pattern is observable. We can see societies of men of letters, recruited from the local professions, closely linked with local mercantile or landed oligarchies, meeting in assembly rooms, university classrooms, Masonic lodges, coffee houses, salons, and taverns, founding and patronizing academies, debating societies, theaters, libraries, and publishing houses. In so doing we can see them seeking in some sense to improve themselves, and the wider society for which they felt responsible by acquiring a code of values that would be secular without necessarily being skeptical, that would encourage them to improve though not transform their world, that would provide them with a cultural style to identify them as a modern-minded elite, firmly established in the government of their province yet linked to a wider world by a shared, cosmopolitan scale of values. And while that style might be qualitatively different from that of the small, cosmopolitan, and terrifying secular elite of moralists, the philosophes, it had at least enough points of contact with the latter to give its adherents a sense of belonging to a wider, critically minded, progressive culture which could instruct and entertain provided that its self-evident follies were ignored.[2]

* I am very grateful to Messrs. S. H. Blumm, J. P. Cornford, R. L. Emerson, Jack P. Greene, and Carle E. Schorske for very valuable comments on this essay.

[1] One excepts from this generalization the work of D. Mornet and D. Roche. See D. Mornet, *Les Origines Intellectuelles de la Révolution Française* (Paris 1933), and D. Roche "Milieux académiques provinciaux et société des lumières," in *Livre et Société dans la France du XVIIIe Siècle* (Paris 1965), 93-184. See also D. Roche, "Encyclopédistes et académiciens. Essai sur la diffusion sociale des Lumières," in ibid., II (Paris 1970), 73-92.

[2] The term "Enlightenment" remains so controversial that clarity demands that one states one's allegiances. My own understanding of who the philosophes were

It would be interesting to know why so many like-minded elites emerged in so many different cities in the West at the same time. Presumably a necessary historical condition was the general relaxation in the centralizing pressures exerted on its provinces by the various metropolitan centers of power. This was a development which occurred at different periods and for different lengths of time between the 1660s and the 1760s and was particularly noticeable in France and in the Anglo-Saxon world. In these places, at least, it was a function of financial and military exhaustion, of the remoteness of the provinces from the metropolis and, above all, of the success of provincial oligarchies in vindicating their right to exercise fairly unfettered control over the government of their provinces. There was a tacit recognition that provincial oligarchies were, for better or for worse, *de facto* sources of effective government, and that their rule should be circumscribed by only the loosest financial and political controls from the metropolis. This development necessarily increased their status and a corresponding sense of their self-importance and so encouraged the search for institutions and ideologies to explain their role as a governing elite, to define their responsibilities and to relate them to that metropolitan world from which they had acquired an unwonted degree of autonomy. It is in this setting that provincial culture as a whole is perhaps best considered and it is thus that we shall consider it in its peculiarly Scottish setting.

Having said that, however, it is necessary to observe that Scotland, like the American colonies, provides a variation on the model just described. These were provinces whose ruling elites came to question, quite radically, the very foundations upon which their relations with the metropolis and their place in the world rested. In each of these areas, at different times, it is possible to see ruling elites growing increasingly and ever more fundamentally dissatisfied with their relations with metropolitan England, precipitating a crisis in these relations in the name of independence, seeing that crisis resolved more or less in their favor, and entering upon an entirely new pattern of relationships with the mother country. In Scotland, the period of dissatisfaction began in the 1670s, developed rapidly in the early 1700s, transforming a provincial legislative assembly, normally tightly controlled by the court in London, into an institution which could draw together a homogeneous, vociferous, and aggressively minded oligarchy, capable of seriously embarrassing the metropolitan court and

---

and of their rejection of philosophy for ideology is overwhelmingly that of Peter Gay, though I should want to state his argument in rather different terms. Some of my reservations to his thesis as a whole are implicit in this essay.

Parliament. The crisis was resolved by the Act of Union of 1707, which made possible the development of a new sort of relationship between province and metropolis in the ensuing century. In America the same sort of development took place in several of the colonial assemblies—notably those of Massachusetts, Pennsylvania, and Virginia—in the early 18th century, precipitating a prolonged crisis in Anglo-American relations that began with the Stamp Act and was finally resolved in 1782 by the Treaty of Paris. Where the provincial oligarchies differed was in their conception of the independence they believed to be threatened and which they sought to preserve. In the dissident American colonies, independence was defined in political terms and involved the creation of a sovereign assembly freed from the corrupting influences of metropolitan England. In Scotland, however, independence came to mean encouraging the economic growth upon which it was believed that political stability and national progress depended. The paradox was that this economic growth would be achieved, not by abandoning all existing political relations with England, but only by making them closer than they were at present, even though it was recognized and uneasily accepted that this would compromise the existing status of the Scots parliament and that it might even threaten the continued existence of the oligarchy that had brought it about. Thus, for the Scots, the period between 1707 and the American War was a post-revolutionary age in which a provincial oligarchy had to learn to live with a successful revolution. This necessitated a redefinition of their relationship with metropolitan England and of their role as a governing elite. For the American colonists, the period was a pre-revolutionary age in which provincial institutions were being subtly transformed by means of a growing sense of self-importance on the part of their elites and by a growing awareness of the inhibiting influences of the traditional structure of colonial government. And in the middle decades of the century the provincial oligarchies of Scotland and of the most dissident American colonies were to bring forth the most remarkable manifestations of the provincial culture of the Enlightenment, the Scottish Enlightenment and the American Revolution.[3]

[3] This comparison necessarily recalls the brilliant and influential comparison of Scotland and America as cultural provinces of England by John Clive and Bernard Bailyn in "England's Cultural Provinces: Scotland and America," *William and Mary Quart.*, 3d ser., 11 (1954), 200-213. John Clive has related the argument in this paper to the problem of the origins of the Scottish Enlightenment in "The Social Background of the Scottish Renaissance," in *Scotland in the Age of Improvement: Essays in Scottish History in the Eighteenth Century*, ed. N. T. Phillipson and Rosalind Mitchison (Edinburgh 1970), 225-44. In their essay and in this, the notion of the province and of the identity problems of provincial elites is of central importance. It will be found, however, that we use both of these terms

Nicholas Phillipson

It is with Edinburgh and the role of culture in that post-Revolutionary society that this essay is concerned. More particularly, it is an
attempt to construct a model to define the precise social role that the
literati of Edinburgh played in what will be shown to be a distinctively
motivated and energetic aristocratic society. The galaxy of philosophical, scientific, and literary talent that lived in the city or treated it as
the focal point of their cultural life does not need to be described here.
Nor is it necessary to review the history of Edinburgh University,
which during the 1760s and 1770s was rapidly developing as a center
of higher education of an importance comparable to that of Leiden a
century earlier. Edinburgh's literati and its university gave the city its
well-known and remarkable international reputation as a center of
learning from the 1760s onward and allowed Edinburgh to appear in
foreign eyes as the Athens of the North. Here, it is far more interesting
to notice that Edinburgh's society was structured so as to allow us to
think of its literati as forming its dominant elite about a decade before
international recognition came its way. Thus the first concern of this
paper is with the structure of the society that this literati came to lead,
for only then can we understand the sort of social leadership that the
literati offered and the reasons for which it was later accepted by a
highly aristocratic society. More specifically, it will be suggested that
this society is to be thought of as the rump of what will be called the
"old provincial oligarchy" which had brought about the union with
England in 1707 and which continued to make Edinburgh the focal
point of its collective life long after the union and the abolition of the
parliamentary and executive institutions which had provided the city
with its distinctive function. Disorganized and disorientated, too poor
to be able to transfer its social and political allegiances from provincial Edinburgh to metropolitan London, this society had to adjust itself
to the changed conditions of post-union Edinburgh and was to seek an
honorable collective role to play in a new and hopefully better world.
Technically, this essay will be concerned with the relationship between
the institutional and ideological forms which together provided that
group with its identity. An ideology provides members of a group with

---

differently. For Clive and Bailyn provincialism and the complex sense of inferiority
that a provincial experiences when confronted with metropolitan culture are para-
mount and made the key to their conception of provincial identity. In this essay,
however, the attempt of a provincial society to recast and to fulfill a long-standing,
honorable though rather curious role is to be the key to understanding their
pursuit of identity. In this respect my argument has some affinity to that of Jack
P. Greene, "Search for Identity: An Interpretation of the Meaning of Selected
Patterns of Social Response in Eighteenth Century America," *J. Social Hist.* 3.3
(1970) 190-220.

a sufficiently coherent and convincing pattern of legitimate forms of action to support the individual as well as the collective sense of identity of its members. But the possession of such an ideology necessarily predicates the institutional forms necessary to provide the group with the means of acting collectively. For in this sense, institutions and ideology have complementary functions. An institution without an ideology is a contradiction in terms; an ideology unsupported by an institution is simply a generalized expression of a desire to act on the part of an inchoate collection of individuals whose capacity to act collectively can only be realized once the institutional mechanisms which translate hopes into action have been devised or discovered.[4]

II

What defined the old provincial oligarchy that had brought about the union with England was its control of the membership of the Scots parliament, an institution which it was to transform and later abolish. What made it remarkable was the degree of ideological homogeneity which characterized its collective life. On the issue which was to become its major preoccupation, the question of economic growth, the various major groupings within the oligarchy, the greater and lesser nobility, the gentry and the merchants, came to share the same assumptions and to see the same sort of problems. For if the debate about the economy and about the relations between England and Scotland was sometimes conducted with great intensity and bitterness, it was nevertheless carried on within a single categorical framework. After 1707, however, things were rather different. The loss of Parliament and the Privy Council meant the departure of the great nobility to the new centers of power in London and the withdrawal of the merchants to their own cities, leaving Edinburgh as the resort of the minor nobility and gentry who were too poor to take the high road to London unless they were obliged to do so for parliamentary reasons which were normally underwritten by heavy subsidies from secret service funds. Without the means to assimilate themselves to the wider English-orientated society to which they had been joined, without the institutions to allow them to carry on their traditional role as a governing elite in the traditional way, without the support and sense of social cohesion the presence of the greater nobility and even the merchants

[4] In other words, "ideology" will be used in a sense recognizable to the psychologist and social psychologist rather than to the philosopher or student of mass politics. The sense in which I shall use the term derives from Erikson, though it is designed to centralize the role of ideology in legitimizing collective forms of action and to stress that it is action itself which is the mechanism by which a collective sense of identity is ultimately sustained.

could have provided, they were faced with the task of deciding whether they had any public, collective function to perform in the new Scotland and, if so, how it should be organized. And if they sought an identity as a governing elite, they had to face the problem of relating their present position and their new role to that of the former, homogeneous elite of which they formed the rump, and of discovering the institutional forms by which its ideology could be reanimated and used to give their society an identity in a changed world.

To what sort of oligarchy did the old Scottish parliament offer cohesion and how did that oligarchy construe its responsibilities? What was the nature of that revolutionary ideology that remained in existence long after the institutions which had enabled it to provoke collective action had been abolished?

Seventeenth century Scottish government is generally misunderstood.[5] Traditionally, it has been believed that Scotland was, in some sense, an independent country before 1707 with a "sovereign" parliament. In 1603, the Union of the Crowns gave Scotland and England the same king who governed, formally at any rate, two distinct societies through two completely different sets of legislative and executive institutions. Leaving aside the question of how far the word "sovereignty," in its modern sense, can be used in a 17th century context, it is clear that Scotland was governed from London in much the same way as the other provinces in Ireland and America; that is, through local men and local institutions which could somehow he controlled by the court in London. As far as the government of Scotland between the Restoration and 1707 is concerned, the most striking development was to be found in the development of the Scots parliament. Hitherto an almost entirely passive institution, it developed in independence throughout the latter decades of the century and became increasingly difficult for the crown to control. And when the Lords of the Articles, that essential mechanism through which royal control was exercised, were abolished in 1690, the crown was left with no formal means of controlling an increasingly intractable and troublesome provincial assembly.

To know exactly why this happened, it would be necessary to have the collective biography of members of the last Scottish parliament, which has not yet been written. However, it is clear that one of the

---

[5] There is very little to read on 17th century government in Scotland. But see R. S. Rait, *The Parliaments of Scotland* (Glasgow 1924); C. S. Terry, *The Scottish Parliament: Its Constitution and Procedure, 1603-1707* (Glasgow 1905); A. Dicey and R. S. Rait, *Thoughts on the Union* (London 1920); T. Pagan, *The Convention of Royal Burghs* (Glasgow 1926). See also G. Donaldson, *Scotland, James V-VII* (Edinburgh 1965) 276-91.

things that most worried their members was the existing pattern of relationships with England, which seemed quite unable to stimulate the sort of economic growth that was universally desired within parliamentary circles. It is true that the Scottish economy was underdeveloped and that her social and economic system remained largely feudal in structure. It is also true that throughout the century her merchants had found it difficult to develop profitable patterns of trade, partly because of a shortage of capital, and partly because English merchants were reluctant to allow the Scots to encroach on English or colonial markets. But it is a fallacy to assume that the governing classes of underdeveloped societies are necessarily bound to pursue a program of modernization, and it is necessary to ask why the Scottish governing classes became so preoccupied with the problem of economic growth in the later 17th century. To repeat, such a question can be answered only by a full collective biography. Such an analysis should show us what it meant for these classes to live in a small, underdeveloped country surrounded not only by large trading nations like England and France, but by small states like the Baltic countries and above all, Holland which could provide the Scots with relevant models to emulate. It would also help us to understand the importance of the physical contact the Scots had with these societies through the colonies of Scotsmen which could be found in so many European countries. Finally, it would help us to understand the extraordinary sense of community that the Scottish governing classes possessed from at least the late 1630s; the sense that the Scots were a distinct people with a unique history, with a political and religious tradition at least as old as that of any other nation and certainly as old as that of England and that they had a peculiar historical role to act out.[6] Indeed, when provoked by the inept efforts of Laud to impose the English prayer book on a largely Presbyterian society, the Scots could show a quite remarkable capacity to unite under an ideological banner which assured them that they were a chosen people, the guardians of the true values of a reformed church which was being betrayed everywhere in Europe (the parallels with the corresponding secular ideology of the American Revolution are striking). "Now, O Scotland, God be thanked thy name is in the Bible," exclaimed Samuel Rutherford in a memorable phrase which perfectly captures the Scots' slightly preposterous sense of their own consequence.[7]

[6] T. I. Rae touches on this problem in a different context in his essay "Historical Scepticism in Scotland before David Hume," in *Studies in the Eighteenth Century*, ed. R. F. Brissenden (Canberra 1973), 205-21.

[7] S. A. Burrell, "The Apocalyptic Vision of the Early Covenanters," *Scottish Hist. Rev.* 43 (1964), 16.

Contact with a wider, economically more progressive world, a sense of community, and historical purpose are all part of the ideological background of the political development of the Scottish parliamentary oligarchy in the later 17th century. Between the 1670s and the 1700s these pressures somehow came to be secularized and cast in economic terms to provide the foundations of a series of deeply seated assumptions about the duties of a governing class in a backward society in a situation in which it had become clear that they and they alone were responsible for the destinies of their country. What was remarkable about these assumptions was that they were so generally shared among the various sections of the governing class—the greater and lesser nobility, the gentry, and the merchants—and that they can be found at work not simply in a parliamentary context but in the Privy Council and in the Convention of Royal Burghs. And they were as much taken for granted in 1707 as they had been a generation earlier. They were never clearly or systematically articulated; indeed they can be excavated only in fragments from Acts of Parliament and Privy Council and from parliamentary petitions. But they are all the more significant for that; for it is out of them that the provincial oligarchy came to acquire its identity.

What were these assumptions? In the first place, as Professor T. C. Smout has noticed, it was assumed that Scotland was poor, that her economy was backward, and that the road to wealth lay in turning Scotland into a trading nation by following the example of more modern countries, Holland and England in particular. In the second place, it was assumed that the end toward which economic improvement should be directed was the creation of a self-sufficient economy in which Scottish producers and manufacturers would provide for all the needs of their countrymen (no doubt according to the most modern methods). In the third place, it was assumed that the responsibility for realizing these two objectives lay with the governing class, using all the encouragement that statutes, executive acts, and royal patronage could provide.[8] The values attached to these assumptions are of great interest. To assume that Scotland was poor was to admit that something had gone wrong. To assume that failure could be overcome by the proper use of state patronage meant that the governing elites placed upon themselves the responsibility for overcoming failure. The connection made between economic progress and the use of models derived from the examples of more modern countries directed them, in some

[8] Smout, *Scottish Trade on the Eve of the Union* (Edinburgh and London 1963), 20-23. W. R. Scott, "The Fiscal Policy of Scotland before the Union," *Scottish Hist. Rev.* 1 (1904), 173-90, gives a useful summary of state policy with respect to economic improvement.

sense, to associate economic growth with the assimilation of their economic life to that of a wider world by practices and values quite different from and, in some sense better than their own. It is interesting to see how strongly directed toward legitimizing such assimilation to the values of a modern world these assumptions were. As Professor Smout has noticed, the improvers' economic calculus exaggerated Scotland's poverty by ignoring entirely her real economic strengths, her capacity to feed her population in most years, her export of coal, black cattle, hides, etc.[9] Economic weakness was defined quite simply as the failure to produce those things currently imported from abroad.

What sort of action was necessary to bring about economic progress? Functionally, the answer was clear. If the Scots wished to pursue wealth by transforming themselves into a trading nation, they would have to manufacture those goods for which there was a foreign market; to put it another way, they would have to assimilate the pattern of their economic life to that of the wider trading world to which they sought entry. But the Scots seemed far less interested in penetrating foreign markets than in satisfying the domestic market by encouraging the manufacture of goods at present imported from abroad with the quite deliberate intention of creating a self-sufficient economy. There can be no doubt about the dedication of the whole governing class to this goal. From the 1660s to the 1700s a stream of acts of Parliament and Privy Council, Royal Charters, monopolies, and protective tariffs flowed to encourage sugar-refining, fishing, soap-boiling, the manufacture of textiles, glass, paper, hardware, pottery, rope, and gunpowder —all those goods at present being imported in quantity from abroad. But of all these exercises in public patronage, only that in sugar refining had any success at all and that because it had some natural economic basis. For the rest all this elaborate effort had little effect. As Professor Smout remarks, "The new concerns did not make Scotland self-sufficient in their various products as they were intended to . . . the fuss that went into their creation must not blind us to the small contribution they made to the economy." Yet, while the Scots periodically puzzled over their lack of success, they were not discouraged and simply redoubled their efforts.[10] What underlay this tension in the values of the governing class and in a sense resolved them was the belief that Scotland, like Holland, France, or England was a nation destined for greatness, able to fulfill her destiny as a great trading nation by creating a formidable manufacturing and trading economy capable of satisfying both domestic and foreign markets. The trouble was that this belief was totally unrealistic. The shortage of domestic capital and the

---

[9] Smout, *Scottish Trade*, 20.　　　　[10] Ibid., 22.

absence of an expanding domestic market meant that the capital resources necessary to bring about this desirable situation could be acquired only by opening up new markets abroad and by encouraging the manufacture of goods to sell in them. In other words, the Scots could acquire the wealth they so much desired only when they had come to accept that it was impossible for a small, underdeveloped country to pursue both these goals simultaneously and that the road to wealth and national greatness lay in the assimilation of their patterns of economic life to those provided by the trading world in which they were placed. A sense of national destiny had to be reconciled with the understanding that unlike England or France, Scotland was not a great state.

These lessons were learned in the 1690s, one of the grimmest decades in modern Scottish history. Already tenuous trading links with Europe were dislocated by incessant international war and by the Navigation Acts which prevented legal free trade with England and the American colonies. A series of bad harvests in the later years of the decade had resulted in widespread famine and in the death of perhaps one in five of the population.[11] The Darien Scheme—that misconceived, mismanaged, and unlucky attempt to establish a colony on the swamps of the Darien isthmus proved to be a costly fiasco for which the English were, hysterically and with only partial justice, held responsible.[12] Politically and ecclesiastically, it was a period of chronic instability in which no government seemed able to control either parliament or the kirk. In 1703 the Scots parliament precipitated a crisis in their relations with England by refusing to recognize the Hanoverian succession as a matter of course, thus opening the possibility of compounding the instability of the already far from stable politics of England. Most Scots would have liked to resolve this crisis by agreeing to recognize the Hanoverians in exchange for inclusion within the Navigation Acts and a federal relationship with England. But the Eng-

[11] Smout, *A History of the Scottish People, 1560-1830* (London 1969), 154-56.

[12] It seems likely that the failure of the Darien Scheme did more than anything else to break down the inhibitions that had stood in the way of economic progress. One of the Scottish Commissioners who negotiated the union, Sir John Clerk, an exceptionally well-informed and observant man, believed that people were perfectly prepared to put up with economic hardship throughout the 1690s. See "Sir John Clerk's Observations on the Present State of Scotland, 1730," in *Scottish History Society*, ed. T. C. Smout, 4th ser., vol. 2, Miscellany 10 (1965), 191. But a full-scale study is needed. See *Darien Papers (1695-1700)*, ed. J. H. Burton, Bannatyne Club; *Papers Relating to the Ships and Voyages of the Company of Scotland Trading to Africa and the Indies, 1696-1707*, ed. G. P. Insh, *Scottish Hist. Soc.*, 3d ser., vol. 6 (1924). There is useful information in G. P. Insh, *The Company of Scotland* (Edinburgh 1932).

lish would settle for free trade for the Scots only in exchange for the abolition of a troublesome and intractable parliament and the absorption of the Scots parliament and executive into that of England.[13] It was evidence of the cumulative effect of the failures of the 1690s and particularly of the failure of the Darien Scheme that while many—perhaps most—of the governing class were unhappy with the idea of an incorporating union and while intensive management was needed to pass it through the Scots parliament, few found it disagreeable enough to continue their opposition after 1707.[14] For between 1700 and 1707 the provincial oligarchy, as a whole, had come to accept that economic progress was impossible within the existing framework of Anglo-Scottish relations and through the sort of public patronage they had pursued in the last generation. Progress was possible only if their relations with England were transformed and if the role that they had chosen for themselves as agents of progress and guardians of their country's independence were redefined. Paradoxically, the Scottish provincial oligarchy was to reach its highest degree of integration and political vociferousness and was to bestow upon its parliamentary assembly its highest prestige at a period in which not only its interests but even its identity would have to be sacrificed in the cause of economic progress.

To say this is not to suggest that all the interests within the oligarchy were agreed upon the proper course of action to be pursued; indeed the violence, not to say virulence, that characterized the politics and the jockeying for position that took place in this period is one of its most striking features.[15] Nevertheless it is important to recognize that disagreement was contained by a wide range of agreement over fundamentals, which can only be explained as a function of a governing class that was ideologically, at least, highly integrated. Thus both the supporters and opponents of the proposed incorporating union agreed in their diagnosis of Scotland's present condition. Not only was the country seen to be poor, but her poverty was now seen to threaten her "independence." William Seton of Pitmedden, the union's chief spokesman, drawing on the writings of his leading opponent, Andrew Fletcher of Saltoun, remarked: "This nation is backward behind all other nations of Europe, for many years, with respect to the effects of an ex-

13 The most recent summary of the crisis is by W. Ferguson, *Scotland 1689 to the Present* (Edinburgh 1968), 36-69. See also T. C. Smout, "The Road to the Union," in G. Holmes, *Britain after the Glorious Revolution, 1689-1714* (London 1969), 176-96.

14 Smout, "Road to the Union," 191.

15 W. Ferguson, "The Making of the Treaty of Union of 1707," *Scottish Hist. Rev.* 43 (1964), 89-110. Ferguson's principal thesis is effectively refuted by Smout in "Road to the Union," cited above.

Nicholas Phillipson

tended trade." Unless something was done to stimulate economic growth, Scotland would become increasingly dependent upon the movements of the English economy and upon the whims of the English court: "Our sovereignty and independency will be eclipsed; the number of our nobility will increase; our commons will be oppressed; our Parliaments will be influenced by England; the execution of our laws will be neglected; our peace will be interrupted by factions for places and pensions; luxury, together with poverty (though strange) will invade us; numbers of Scots will withdraw themselves to foreign countries; and all the other effects of bad government must necessarily attend us."

One solution to this problem, Pitmedden observed, was to break all connections with England. But independence of this sort would altogether end any chance of achieving prosperity: "Hereby we may be in danger of returning to that Gothic constitution of government, wherein our forefathers were, which was frequently attended with feuds, murders, depredations and rebellions."[16] In other words, independence, either in the sense of continuing the *status quo* or of rejecting the existing connection with England altogether, was now seen as something which threatened the sort of integrity an earlier generation had thought would be compromised by becoming dependent upon foreign imports. Independence was now coming to be associated with the sort of prosperity that the Union of the Crowns had failed to bring with it, and with the sort of economic and political assimilation which would bring about the destruction of that formalized system of politics which gave parliament its life and the governing class its identity.

Significantly, the union's opponents agreed with this diagnosis and only doubted the capacity of the proposed union to secure this promised independence. Indeed, men like Fletcher believed it would only compromise it further. In the first place, as Fletcher had observed in 1703, it was by no means clear that the union could bring about economic growth. "Our trade, which is the bait that covers the hook, will be only an inconsiderable retail, in a poor, remote and barren country, where the richest of our nobility and gentry will no longer reside."[17] English textiles, he continued, would flood the markets; merchants in the Atlantic trade would be outclassed by the English; the poor, impoverished through lack of work, would multiply and migrate to Eng-

[16] D. Defoe, *The History of the Union between England and Scotland* (London 1786), 313-16.

[17] *The Political Works of Andrew Fletcher, Esq.* (London 1737), 396. Fletcher badly needs full-scale treatment. A brilliant start has been made by J.G.A. Pocock, "Machiavelli, Harrington, and English Political Ideologies in the Eighteenth Century," *William and Mary Quart.*, 3d ser., 22, no. 4 (1965).

land; political dependence upon the English court, already serious, would be intensified.[18] This sense that loss of identity and assimilation to England were connected is the theme of the most famous and most often reprinted of the speeches made during the union debates, Lord Belhaven's prophetic lament for a nation whose integrity and honor were threatened. The church, the nobility, the gentry, the merchants, the lawyers, the tradesmen, would all be impoverished, degraded, and dispersed by a union that would make the lives of every one of them dependent upon the whim of the English: "But above all, my Lord, I think I see our ancient mother, Caledonia, like Caesar, sitting in the midst of our senate, ruefully looking about her, covering herself with her royal garment, attending the fatal blow, and breathing out her last with a *et tu quoque mi fili.*"[19]

As we shall see, this fear that an incorporating union would result in the dispersal of a homogeneous governing class was to be justified by events and it is interesting to see that the union's protagonists ducked the issue simply by taking it for granted that prosperity would somehow guarantee national integrity and the integrity of the governing class. As Pitmedden remarked, "In general, I may assert, that by this Union *we* [my italics] will have access to all the advantages in commerce the English enjoy; we will be capable, by a good government, to improve our national product, for the benefit of the whole island; and we will have our liberty, property, and religion, secured under the protection of one Sovereign and one Parliament of Great Britain."[20]

What alternative remedies did the union's opponents propose to overcome the difficulties that stood in the way of an incorporating union? How did they believe the twin objectives of independence and economic progress could be secured? The answer, ironically, was by a closer union with England which would absorb Scottish life and government into a wider framework, dominated by England. But whereas an incorporating union meant absorption to England as it was, Fletcher wanted absorption to England as it ought to be, purged of corruption by the sort of reforms dear to the heart of country ideologists in England. London, Fletcher believed, was the seat of corruption and its power could be broken only when it had been redistributed among various seats of regional government. In a passage describing what is, in effect, an 18th century Anglo-Saxon provincial capital, he wrote:

[18] *The Political Works of Andrew Fletcher*, 396-402, 389.

[19] D. Defoe, *History of the Union*, 318.

[20] Ibid., 316. For a later instance in which the unconscious use of "we" had considerable ideological significance, see my essay "Public Opinion and the Union," in *Scotland in the Age of Improvement*, 125-47, esp. 132-34.

So many different seats of government will highly encourage virtue. For all the same offices that belong to a great kingdom, must be in each of them; with this difference, that the offices of such a kingdom being always burdened with more business that any one man can rightly execute, most things are abandoned to the rapacity of servants; and the extravagant profits of all great officers plunge them into all manner of luxury and debauch them from doing good: whereas the offices of these lesser governments extending only over a moderate number of people, will be duly executed, and many men have occasions put into their hands of doing good to their fellow citizens. So many different seats of government will highly tend to the improvement of all arts and sciences; and afford great variety of entertainment to all foreigners and others of a curious and inquisitive genius, as the ancient cities of Greece did.[21]

Thus, by 1707, no one doubted that a closer union with England was necessary to secure the sort of economic prosperity and independence they believed to be desirable. No one doubted that independence would somehow follow the acquisition of economic growth. The debate was about the means by which these objectives could be achieved. The willingness of the provincial oligarchy to countenance or tacitly to accept *ex post facto* a union which offered them no clear expectation of what would happen in the future, and no clear place in the new post-union world, which failed to provide them with institutions to organize their collective life thereafter, coupled with a fear, reaching back to the 1670s that economic progress might in some way involve the destruction of the oligarchy itself, suggests that these fears, deeply rooted though they might be, had lost their capacity to alarm the governing class seriously enough to drive them to defensive reaction. It was a state of mind that was well suited to encouraging the Scots to take things as they came and to improvise.

III

The first twenty years of the union was a period of economic depression and great political uncertainty. International war continued to dislocate trade; capital flowed south to be invested in more lucrative English ventures; the textile industry was severely dislocated by intensive English competition; in short, the economy as a whole remained as depressed immediately after the union as it had been before.[22] The unstable parliamentary politics of the pre-Walpolian era

[21] *The Political Works of Andrew Fletcher*, 445-46.

[22] Smout, *Scottish Trade*, 277-80. The manufacture of wool for the open market does not seem to have suffered as badly as other textile industries. C. Gulvin, "The Scottish Woollen Industry, 1707-60," *Scottish Hist. Rev.* 50 (1971), 121-37.

and incessant jockeying for position among the Scottish nobility created political conditions in which government had to be improvised.[23]

These unsettled conditions, so gloomily forecast by the union's opponents, extended to the governing class itself. As had been feared, the abolition of the Scots parliament and Privy Council and the removal of the center of power from Edinburgh to London resulted in the fragmentation of that once homogeneous governing class. For the merchants and the greater nobility, exploiting the possibilities opened up by the union meant the development of Atlantic trade routes and assimilating themselves to the political and social life of London; Edinburgh and the traditional life style of the old parliamentary class had little to offer them. The withdrawal of the greater nobility from Edinburgh was particularly striking; their great town houses in the Canongate were abandoned and allowed to degenerate into slums, a physical testimony to the city's loss of status on which many observers were to comment. As William Maitland exclaimed in 1753: "Having, before that Period, [the union] been the residence of the chief of the Scotish (sic) Nobility, it was then in a flourishing Condition; but being deserted by them, many of their houses are fallen down, and others in a ruinous Condition; it is a piteous case."[24]

The departure of the greater nobility from Edinburgh is normally taken to signify the destruction of Edinburgh as a center of aristocratic society.[25] But it is clear that this was not the case. No doubt the less prosperous members of the nobility and gentry would have liked to follow the greater nobility to London but in the early 18th century they were in no financial position to do so and those who had parliamentary duties to perform in London had to be heavily subsidized from secret service funds. Poverty forced them to confine their social horizons to Scotland and to continue to think of Edinburgh as the focal point of their social existence. At present it is impossible to be as precise as one would like about the structure and organization of Edin-

[23] P.W.J. Riley, *The English Ministers and Scotland, 1707-27* (London 1964), passim; J. M. Simpson, "Who Steered the Gravy Train, 1707-1766?" in *Scotland in the Age of Improvement*, 47-72.

[24] W. Maitland, *The History of Edinburgh from Its Foundation to the Present Time* (Edinburgh 1753), 151.

[25] On the early social history of Edinburgh in the early 18th century there is no adequate study of any sort. However, valuable material is to be gathered from R. Chambers, *The Traditions of Edinburgh*, 1st ed. (Edinburgh 1825), id., *Minor Antiquities of Edinburgh* (Edinburgh 1833), id., *Domestic Annals of Scotland* (Edinburgh 1858); J. Grant, *Cassell's Old and New Edinburgh* (London 1880-83); H. G. Graham, *The Social Life of Scotland in the Eighteenth Century* (Edinburgh 1899), ch. 3. W. Scott's little essay in *Provincial Antiquities of Scotland* (London 1826) is virtually unknown but brilliant.

burgh's society in the decades immediately following the union. Nevertheless, it is clear from literary and antiquarian evidence and, more precisely, from the annual almanacks that began to appear in 1773, that between the union and the 1780s Edinburgh remained a highly aristocratic city whose social life was dominated by the minor nobility, the more substantial gentry, and their dependents. Some lived permanently in the city; some visited the city for the social season and lived in flats and houses they either owned or rented; others lived on estates which were in easy riding distance from the city. This aristocratic society provided the city with those social foundations which would shape its character and define its position in the Anglo-Saxon world throughout the 18th century. It dominated the professional life of the city, monopolizing the bench of the Court of Session,[26] providing the Faculty of Advocates (the Scottish bar) with 87 percent of its members between 1707 and 1811,[27] having in its gift church livings, schoolmasters' houses, and private tutorships, able to offer local doctors lucrative practice and university professors private pupils. But what this society lacked immediately after the union was any institution which would, of itself, provide the sort of cohesion and sense of identity that the Scots parliament had provided for the old provincial oligarchy. In this period it was, quite simply, the disorganized rump of a once homogeneous society, stranded in Edinburgh through no fault of its own. All it possessed was the memory of a conception of the traditional role of a provincial elite in Scotland, which derived from the ideological world of the Scots parliament in its last days.

For the first twenty years of the union this problem did not seem to worry the members of this new provincial oligarchy for it made little effort to organize itself formally. As far as we can see, its collective life remained aimless and inchoate. Some no doubt continued to visit the city out of habit and others, like the Jacobite gentry who had been ruined by the Darien Scheme, were permanent residents.[28] Some went to London for parliamentary duties and some withdrew to their estates. Certainly the quality of the city's social life seems to have declined and by 1718 the master of the high school could be heard complaining of "it being well known . . . that there is a great decay of the inhabitants of this city, there being now scarce any of the nobility and

[26] G. Brunton and D. Haig, *An Historical Account of the Senators of the College of Justice from its Institution in 1532* (Edinburgh 1832).

[27] N. T. Phillipson, "The Scottish Whigs and the Reform of the Court of Session, 1785-1830," Ph.D. diss., Camb. Univ. (1967), 349-58.

[28] J. Clive, "The Social Background of the Scottish Renaissance," in *Scotland in the Age of Improvement*, 235-36.

very few of the gentlemen of the country residing here."[29] In general, while there are contemporary references to the existence of assemblies and balls and salons, it is clear there were no institutions to take the place of the old Scots parliament. Daniel Defoe, one of the union's leading propagandists, returned to Edinburgh to try to arouse the public spirit of the landed classes to exploit the advantages he believed the union offered ("Wake, Scotland, from thy long lethargic dream!").[30] But his efforts met with no response.

Organization could have taken two forms. In the first place, either a new institution could have been devised in which the ideology of the old provincial elite could have been adapted and made the vehicle of the collective life of a different sort of elite in different circumstances. Or existing institutions, devised for other purposes, could have been adapted to serve these ends. Perhaps the latter development was the one most to have been expected. Edinburgh possessed two institutions —both of which survived the union—which seemed admirably suited to this purpose, the kirk and the legal system. Each was a traditionally Scottish institution different from its English counterpart and each had the sort of functional importance that naturally placed it at the center of Scottish politics and government. The kirk was governed by a General Assembly which had been in existence since the reformation. Moreover, the history of the National Covenant in 1637-38 had shown that religion was capable of providing an institutional and ideological framework to allow the governing classes to express for a short period a remarkably unanimous opposition to the attempts of Charles I and Laud to impose the prayer book on Scotland.[31] The legal system, for its part, while it had never played such an important role in the past, was to do so in the early 19th century, in the age of Francis Jeffrey and Walter Scott at a time when the city had lost its aristocratic society. Not only would observers see in the legal profession (and especially the bar) the city's dominant elite;[32] they would also think of it in some sense as a metropolitan class not unlike that of parliamentary society in London, "keeping alive the sorely threatened spirit of national independence in the thoughts and in the feelings of their fellow-country-

[29] Quoted in A. Law, *Education in Edinburgh in the Eighteenth Century* (London 1965), 11, 59.

[30] Quoted in D. D. McElroy, *Scotland's Age of Improvement* (Washington 1969), 5.

[31] S. A. Burrell, "Apocalyptic Vision." The voluminous and intricate literature on this subject and on the later history of the convenanting movement is reviewed by I. B. Cowan, "The Covenanters: A Revision Article," *Scottish Hist. Rev.* 47 (1968), 35-52.

[32] N. T. Phillipson, "Scottish Whigs," 76-85.

men," as J. G. Lockhart put it.[33] But in the early 18th century neither the kirk nor the legal system came to occupy this position. The reason for this is not altogether clear. The kirk was probably in no position to take on such a role. In the first place it was deeply and bitterly divided internally between its latitudinarian wings and its evangelical wings and was haunted by not unreasonable fears of the supposedly Erastian designs of a largely English parliament—fears which seemed all too well founded when Parliament restored lay patronage in 1712. Moreover, even had it been in a position to offer the sort of leadership it had provided in the days of the National Covenant, it was far from certain that it would have been accepted by the many Episcopalian landed gentlemen who had little reason to identify themselves with a Presbyterian Kirk that was not only different to their own but bitterly opposed to it. As far as the legal profession is concerned, its failure to develop in this way is partly due to the fact that it was serving as an appendage of an already disorientated oligarchy which, as we have already seen, provided the bench and the bar with the vast majority of its members.

In fact, the identity crisis came to be resolved in rather a curious way. First, a tiny, distinctive new elite of literati developed in this period of general social institutional and ideological disorientation quite independent of any existing social or professional groupings. Rather later, in the 1720s, the landed classes devised for themselves a new, original, and equally distinctive organization and ideology to give themselves the identity they had hitherto lacked and in the process began to assimilate members of this literati to the institution they had already created. In the 1750s, however, an astonishing qualitative change took place in the structure of that society, and the literati suddenly and without warning found themselves assimilating the landed classes to their own institutions, providing the institutions and the ideology in which a later generation of the new provincial oligarchy could find its sense of identity. Almost without warning, and in a very strict sense, the literati became leaders of the new aristocratic society in which they moved, filling a role which they and only they could

[33] J. G. Lockhart, *Peter's Letters to his Kinsfolk* (Edinburgh 1819), II, 6-7; cf. R. Mudie, *The Modern Athens: A Dissection and Demonstration of Men and Things in the Scotch Capital* (London 1825), 163, 192-99. Thus Robert Chambers could write in 1825, "The members of the College of Justice may, in general, be described as the present aristocracy or predominant class in the population of Edinburgh; and that the cessation of their labours naturally produces a depression in the lower grades of society, similar perhaps to that which is occasioned in London by the rising of Parliament," in *Walks in Edinburgh* (Edinburgh 1825), 93.

have filled. In that sense at least, the Athens of the North was a real re-public of letters. Let us see how these developments took place.

It would be convenient to be able to think of the literati which de-veloped in early 18th century Edinburgh as an elite recruited from a single class, institution, or political or religious grouping, educated distinctively and single-mindedly in a particular framework of values. But it would not be true. For, while members of the literati were drawn from the legal profession, the kirk, and landed society, as an elite it was the protégé of no single institution, social group, or political grouping. It developed *de novo* from that rootless, heterogeneous, and largely youthful population which every administrative and social capital attracts, from the ranks of the students and ex-students from the university, young ministers, doctors, and lawyers from the ranks of the gentry, bourgeoisie, and poorer classes who were on the thresh-olds of careers in professions whose precise status had been rendered ambiguous by the union; from older ministers, both Episcopalian and Presbyterian, in search of livings or jobs as schoolmasters or tutors; from the ranks of law-clerks and law apprentices and young men of all sorts in search of a fortune or simply anxious to escape from home.[34] It is quite impossible to know how numerous they were, but in a city whose population was around 30,000 they must have run into the hundreds. Many of them were at that post-adolescent stage of life in which choices about their relation to the adult world had to be made; they were neither integrated into nor alienated from a social and pro-fessional universe which was itself thrown adrift as a result of the union. It was from this world that an elite emerged who were preoccu-pied with polite learning, anxious to absorb and to transmit to a wider society the values contained in the ideology of the old provincial oligarchy which they now expressed in cultural terms.

It is at this point that we confront the difficult problem of estimating the part played by the University of Edinburgh in equipping this elite to fill this role; needless to say, many members of the society from which this elite was drawn had spent some time there.[35] Highly organ-

[34] See, for example, H. G. Graham, *Scottish Men of Letters in the Eighteenth Century* (London 1901), 1-11; *Writings of Alexander Pennicuick, M.D. and Alex-ander Pennicuick, Merchant*, ed. W. Brown (London 1906); N. S. Bushnell, *Wil-liam Hamilton of Bangour* (Aberdeen 1957); J. Ramsay of Ochtertyre, *Scotland and Scotsmen in the Eighteenth Century. From the MSS of John Ramsay of Ochtertyre*, ed. A. Allardyce (Edinburgh 1888), I, ch. 1.

[35] No modern history of Edinburgh University exists. One makes do with A. Bower, *History of the University of Edinburgh* (Edinburgh 1830); A. Grant, *Story of the University of Edinburgh* (London 1884); D. B. Horn, *A Short History of the University of Edinburgh* (Edinburgh 1967). On the history of the university between 1660 and 1715, see I. Kenrick, "The University of Edinburgh, 1660-1715:

ized, distinctively motivated educational institutions, staffed by able and charismatic teachers, can provide students with a clearly defined cultural and ideological universe to which they can respond. Edinburgh had certainly provided such a universe when it was first founded at the Reformation and it was to do so again in the 1770s and 1780s. In the first period it was a Presbyterian seminary, with the very distinctive style Andrew Melville and its first Principal, Robert Rollock, imposed upon it. Its function was to provide the church with a ministry and a godly laity instructed in the cautious, Calvinist humanism of Geneva. Similarly in the late 18th century, when the college had an enviable international reputation, it again sought to produce a ministry and a godly laity, this time instructed in the canons of polite learning and in the new natural theology inspired by Thomas Reid and the common sense philosophers.

But between the 1690s and the 1720s the college was in a state of disorientation. Throughout the 1690s it was desperately poor and unable to retain a competent faculty. Worse, like the other Scottish universities its activities were continually bedeviled by the activities of a parliamentary visitation, dominated by the Presbyterian Principal of Edinburgh, Gilbert Rule. The visitors had begun their work with the simple intention of removing the Jacobites and Episcopalians from the faculties of the various colleges.[36] Before long, however, they became deeply involved in the problem of devising courses of philosophy and science that would not be inconsistent with a conservative, scholastic, Presbyterianism. The only way this could be brought about, they believed, was to enforce the use of a single textbook in all the colleges of Scotland by Act of Parliament. Yet try as they would, they could neither find a suitable model among the existing textbooks in use on the continent nor in England. As the commissioners sent to visit the four colleges reported to the visitors in 1695, "Wee can not find any one intire pairt of Philosophy which wee can recommend as sufficient to be taught for many of them ar wryte by popish professors and yrin they Cunningly insinuate ye hereticall tenets mixing them with their philosophy which ar not so easyly discerneable by the Youth." One after another, the existing textbooks were rejected as impious; as for "Cartesius, Rohault and others of his gang beside what may be said

A Study in the Transformation of Teaching Methods and Curriculum," Ph.D. diss. (1956), Bryn Mawr Coll.; good on the Episcopalian era, 1660-90, less so on the later period.

[36] This aspect of the visitors' work, described by them and by the Episcopalians as the work of a Presbyterian Inquisition, is reviewed by R. K. Hannay, "The Visitation of the College of Edinburgh, 1690," in *Book of the Old Edinburgh Club*, VIII (Edinburgh 1916), 79-100.

agt. their doctrine they all labour under this inconveniency that they give not any sufficient account of the other hypothesis and of the old philosophy which must not be rejected and were never designed to be taught to students."[37] And, after a further five or six years of fruitless endeavor they, too, had to report themselves unable to compile a satisfactory alternative.

Tension between scholastic and modern philosophy was one of the most distinctive aspects of the intellectual life of the Dutch universities. In a large and prosperous university like that of Leiden, students were exposed to a debate of great vigor and sophistication between men of considerable ability. In Scotland, however, the same tension simply resulted in confusion. Impoverished, continually exposed to external political and ecclesiastical pressures, Edinburgh University had no means of attracting or holding onto teachers of intellectual capacity and sophistication. The investigations of the visitors show that students were confronted, not with the rival claims of the old and new vigorously and intelligently presented, but with an inconsequential mishmash of both lacking sophistication, coherence, and vigor, expounded by timid men of negligible capacity. The college could not offer a coherent ideological universe to be accepted or rejected; still less could it offer its students a secure world as a shelter from the uncertainties of the society in which they found themselves; indeed it could only compound them. It was a situation well suited to force the attention of the intelligent student upon the complex relations between culture and society and to encourage him to think of the one as a means of giving structure and coherence to the other. Moreover, it was a situation equally well suited to encourage those deeply preoccupied with learning and letters to create their own institutions and to fashion their own ideology in an attempt to provide themselves with a shelter from the moral uncertainty of the world around them and with a role to play in fashioning an alternative to it. Under these circumstances, whatever learning they pursued would clearly acquire a profound ideological importance.

It is important to notice that this intellectual and ideological uncertainty persisted into the 1720s, although it took a different form in the two latter decades. In 1703 William Carstares, one of the most influential ecclesiastical and secular statesmen in Scotland retired from politi-

---

[37] "Answers by the Commissioners of the Four Universities to ye Queries proposed by ye Commissioners of the Visitatione of Colleges, 31 July 1695." Proceedings of the Scottish Universities Visitation, Scottish Record Office (1695) repr. in a slightly amended form in *Munimenta Alme Universitatis Glasguensis*, Maitland Club (Glasgow 1854), II, 530-32. Some material relating to the attempts to compile a uniform course of philosophy is reprinted in the same volume.

cal life to become the principal of the college after the death of Gilbert
Rule.[38] His appointment could not have happened at a better time for
it coincided with the rise to local prominence of George Drummond
who, until his death in 1766, was to provide the tight little oligarchy
that constituted the Edinburgh Town Council with its most energetic
and influential citizen.[39] By himself, there was little that Carstares
could have done to reorganize the college for the Town Council was
the patron of the college and its approval was needed for every major
change. But Carstares and Drummond saw eye to eye on the business
of university reform. Each was a reformer, totally dedicated to the sort
of "modernization" for which the proponents of the union stood—indeed, Drummond had been one of the Union Commissioners and Carstares had played a crucial role in securing the approval of the kirk for
the union. Together, these two remarkable men brought about a root
and branch reorganization of the college that was to make possible its
emergence as the most influential single institution in the higher education of the western world in the later 18th century. The details of
these reforms are well known and need not be labored here.[40] The
model Carstares and Drummond used was that of the Dutch universities so well known to prosperous and aristocratic Scots who had re-
sorted to them in increasing numbers throughout the preceding century. It is clear that one of Carstares' aims was to provide Edinburgh
with a college which could offer the landed classes at home what they
had hitherto got abroad at great expense, and an institution which
would also attract the prosperous foreign student, with all the capital
he could bring with him to Edinburgh. Thus when the Town Council
established the Chair of Civil Law in 1710, it explained its action by
the fact that "through want of Professors of Civil Law in this kingdom,
the youth who have applied themselves to that studie have been necces-
sitate to travell and remain abroad a considerable time for their education, to the prejudice of the Nation by the neccessaie charges occasioned therebye."[41]

The reorganization which took place was as radical in its way as the

[38] Carstares badly needs a good modern biography. But see R. H. Story, *William Carstares: a Character and Career of the Revolutionary Epoch* (Edinburgh 1874). On his activities as Principal of Edinburgh see n. 36 above.

[39] Drummond is even less well served than Carstares. But see W. Baird, "George Drummond, an Edinburgh Lord Provost of the Eighteenth Century," *Book of the Old Edinburgh Club*, IV (Edinburgh 1912).

[40] See n. 35 above.

[41] *Extracts from the Records of the Burgh of Edinburgh, 1701-1718*, ed. H. Armet (Edinburgh 1967) 201-2. Cf. the minutes establishing the Chairs of Civil History, Anatomy, and Medicine; Alexander Bower, *History of the University of Edinburgh*, II, 141, 181, 199.

Act of Union. In twenty years the college which had been little more than a Presbyterian seminary, was transformed into a self-consciously modern academy with faculties of law and medicine as well as of philosophy and theology, offering, *inter alia* courses in the polite arts of history and criticism, in Scots law, and clinical medicine. But it took time for a new cultural style to emerge to fill out this modern structure. Property rights had to be respected and many of the first generation of professors in this new and hopefully enlightened academy were simply the timid mediocrities carried over from the old regime. Between the 1700s and the 1720s its role in shaping a literati was simply to compound the uncertainty of an already uncertain moral environment.

Our first evidence that the crisis precipitated by the union might have its cultural consequences comes from the literary life of the city which was remarkable for its range and variety rather than its quality. Books like Anderson's *Historical Essay Showing that the Crown and Kingdom of Scotland Is Imperial and Independent* (1705), Abercrombie's *Martial Achievements of the Scots Nation, etc.* (1711, 1715), endless volumes of antiquities, the spate of shabby, badly written histories of Scotland, James Watson's popular and important edition of the forgotten poets of the Scottish renaissance, the new editions of those heroes of Scottish humanism, George Buchanan and Gavin Douglas, are all comprehensible products of a society anxious to reaffirm its consciousness of its historical identity at a time when it was widely believed that it was threatened.[42] The intense and continuing preoccupation of students with rationalist and empiricist metaphysics and with the foundations of knowledge was expressive of a society anxious to acquire through philosophy the certainty and stability that seemed to be absent from the wider world in which they moved. The equally intense and continuing concern with popular ethics and particularly with those of the *Tatler* and *Spectator* which appeared in Edinburgh in cheap reprinted editions and in imitation as soon as they were published in London[43] is also comprehensible in a society anxious

[42] D. Duncan, *Thomas Ruddiman: A Study in Scottish Scholarship of the Early Eighteenth Century* (Edinburgh 1965), esp. 41-71. An important and neglected book. On Watson, see J. S. Gibb, "James Watson, Printer: Notes on His Life and Work with a Hand-List of Books and Pamphlets Printed by Him, 1697-1722," in *Papers of the Edinburgh Bibliographic Society*, 1 (1890-95), 1-8.

[43] W. J. Couper, *The Edinburgh Periodical Press* (Stirling 1908), 1, 244, believes that James Watson, who republished the *Tatler* had some special arrangement with Steele for the production of a local edition of the paper in Edinburgh. Three principal imitations are recorded—*The Examiner* (1710), *The North Tatler* (1710), and *The Tatler by Donald McStaff* (1710-11). The latter, published by Watson, is a particularly intelligent, lively, and well-written periodical, well worth study. It

to discover a system of ethics that was both modern and associated with the values of an English-orientated world. The host of "needy and thirsty men" as Henry Grey Graham has called them, "the broken school-masters, law clerks and students who had failed of a profession" who dashed off elegiac doggerel, composed in Latin, English, or Scots, to sell to bereaved local notables, simply illustrated the cultural ambivalence of a society that did not know whether to express publicly and formally its gravest emotions in the aristocratic Latin of a decaying humanist tradition, the English of the modern world to which they sought entry, or the Scots vernacular which, though it might be the language of everyday life, was not that of polite sentiments.[44]

This sort of activity was not evidence that Edinburgh possessed an intelligentsia or that she would ever do so. For in the 1690s and 1700s Edinburgh's cultural life lacked the dominant style that humanist culture had provided in the 1670s and 1680s and which polite culture would provide in later decades. More important, it lacked the institutional and ideological structures which would give it a clearly defined place in a wider society. The cultural life of this period shows, quite simply, that the tensions experienced within the old parliamentary oligarchy had extended outward to a wider society characteristic of any provincial capital and had been translated into generalized cultural terms. Not until the late 1710s and 1720s would a literati develop, organized institutionally and ideologically to provide Edinburgh's cultural life with a dominant style which would shortly prove to be particularly attractive to the disorganized society of post-union Edinburgh.

For a time it looked as though intellectuals would take up a nonconformist role in opposition to, or at least in tension with the values of the union. Socially and intellectually, Edinburgh was strongly

---

was the work of Robert Hepburn of Bearford, a young man destined for the Bar who had just returned from studying law in Holland. He was described by Lord Hailes as "ingenii praecosis et praefervidi." As Hepburn admitted, his journal began life as a simple imitation of the *Tatler* but later took on a more distinctive life of its own. Not only did Hepburn express his admiration of Epicurus but he resolved to set up a Court of Wit "Whose *Judges* shall impartially punish all those who do not become their Condition or Circumstances in human Life, by altering their Station, and obliging 'em to act that part for which nature seems to have design'd them." Such censoriousness probably lost him readers and probably accounts for the early demise of the paper (Couper, 254-56). On Hepburn see A. F. Tytler, *Memoirs of the Life and Words of Lord Kames* (2d edn., Edinburgh 1814), I, 228-29n.

[44] H. G. Graham, *Scottish Men of Letters in the Eighteenth Century* (London 1901), 5-6.

connected with Jacobitism in these early years of the union.[45] As we have seen, many Jacobite and Episcopalian gentlemen, ruined by the collapse of the Darien Scheme, lived in the city; indeed at one time there were more Episcopalian meeting houses than Presbyterian churches in the city.[46] As far as the philosophically minded were concerned, the union was connected with the Presbyterian Kirk which seemed the incarnation of anti-intellectualism and bigotry. It had been the kirk which was responsible in 1696 for the execution of a deist student, Thomas Aikenhead, for blasphemy.[47] And if the poetry of the Scottish renaissance had been forgotten and stood in need of rediscovery, that was owing simply to the continuing and intense hostility of the kirk to secular literature.[48] The connection between Jacobitism and learning in the early 18th century is close and striking. The publisher James Watson and minor poets like Hamilton of Bangour and Alexander Penicuik were all Jacobites by instinct. So too were men like Alexander Pitcairne and Thomas Ruddiman, raised in what may be called a latter-day humanist tradition, stemming from the humanism of the Scottish renaissance, revivified in the 1670s and 1680s during the Episcopalian and royalist era, placed on the defensive by the Whig Presbyterian *revanche* of 1690, finally to be overcome by the moderate polite unionist world of the early 18th century.[49] But few of these Jacobites were men of action who joined the Pretender's army. Indeed, the only intellectual of importance to have done so, who went out in the Forty-Five, was the interesting, neglected economist Sir James Steuart.[50] It is never surprising to find intellectuals occupying a non-

[45] H. R. Trevor Roper, "The Scottish Enlightenment," *Studies in Voltaire and the Eighteenth Century* 58 (1967), 1635-58, says much that is of interest about the cultural significance of Jacobitism, but exaggerates their importance. See also D. Duncan, *Thomas Ruddiman*, esp. chs. 4 and 8.

[46] J. Macky, *A Journey through Scotland*, 2d ed. (London 1729), 220.

[47] Macaulay, who is good on Scotland in the Revolutionary period, should be read on Aikenhead's trial. So should the sources which are an invaluable document on the early history of metaphysics in the 1690s. See *Cobbett's Collection of State Trials*, compiled by J. B. Howell (London 1811-17), xiii. See also J. Gordon, *Thomas Aikenhead: A Historical Review to Mr. Macaulay and "The Witness,"* 3d ed. (London 1856).

[48] D. Daiches, *Robert Burns* (London 1952), ch. 1.

[49] On those I have called "latter-day humanists" see D. Duncan, *Thomas Ruddiman*, passim. The myth that members of this group are to be seen as the ancestors of the Scottish Enlightenment was stated by H. W. Meikle, in "Some Aspects of late 17th Century Scotland," in *14th David Murray Lecture* (Glasgow 1947).

[50] There is valuable biographical information on Steuart in Sir James Steuart, *An Inquiry into the Principles of Political Economy*, ed. with an Introduction by A. S. Skinner, Scottish Economic Soc. (1966).

conformist position in relation to their society. What has to be explained is the failure of Jacobitism and Episcopalianism to provide a more satisfying haven for them than it was evidently able to do; for by the 1720s intellectual life had begun to flow in much more establishment-oriented channels. The reason, it may be suggested, lies in the disorientation of Edinburgh life in the period of the union. For the union, as we have seen, did not provide Scotsmen with a clearly definable set of values against which actively minded men could react. In an important sense it was something that everyone wanted, although no one quite knew what it involved. It was difficult to oppose after 1707 because no one knew quite what they were opposing, or whether enough time had been allowed to assess whether the union was capable of bringing about the benefits that had been promised. This meant that Jacobitism signified unease and irritation rather than dissatisfaction. This can certainly be seen in its ideology. As Andrew Fletcher pointed out, in practical terms Jacobitism could offer its supporters only an autocratic monarchy, a Catholic Church, inevitable civil war, and the danger of conquest and occupation by England.[51] In an important sense, Jacobitism was just as much of a threat to Scottish "independence" as the union. It could offer an ideology capable of inciting rebellion only to those who were politically acutely disappointed, the disturbed, or those far removed from the realities of life.

When an institutionalized and ideologically motivated literati did emerge, it set out not so much to legitimize the values of the union, as to try to define them and to do this by capturing the spirit of those who had been responsible for bringing it about. Intellectually, its preoccupations were with metaphysics, Augustan ethics, and neoclassical literature. Technically, these pursuits centralized problems relating to consciousness, personal identity, and the foundations of knowledge; they saw the individual as a more or less passive creature, dependent upon a changing external world for his knowledge, his values, and his identity; they validated a cheerful assimilation to the values of that changing world and stressed the connection between them and social progress. It was a program of philosophical and critical inquiry, selected from the technical problems that already preoccupied the world of professional philosophy, that was peculiarly appropriate to the condition of early 18th century Edinburgh. But for the literati the pursuit of this sort of philosophy went hand in hand with the development of institutions and an ideology which would give them an identity not simply as men of letters but as an elite charged with the task of defining the values of the union and encouraging their society to pursue

[51] Smout, "Road to the Union," 185.

them. Organized in literary clubs, they adopted an ideology which was a version of the ideology of the old provincial oligarchy. The first of these intellectual clubs came into existence in the 1710s. We do not know how many there were—certainly not many. But there were two of the greatest importance, the Easy Club (1712-15) and the Rankenian Club (1716-64).[52] The first was one of the main sources of polite literature of the Enlightenment, the second of its metaphysics. Both were very small; the first had a membership of around twelve young men all of whom were drawn from that amorphous society we have just considered. The second, which had a memberhip of nineteen by the mid 1720s drew largely on young professional men; by then it had six university professors, five advocates, two doctors, and four from other professions (three of the professors belonged to more than one professional body).

Interestingly and irritatingly, the records of these societies and contemporary accounts of their activities tell us very little of what went on in them; when contemporaries described them they did so in terms of their organization and ideology which gave them their identity. Thus they listed their rules and procedures governing admission of members, conduct of debates and preparations of papers and they stressed the importance of their activities in bringing about the improvement of the manners of their members and those of society at large. Thus the Rankenian's first historian, George Wallace, described the function of his club as "mutual improvement by liberal conversation and rational inquiry" and spoke of its value to Scottish society in "Disseminating freedom of thought, boldness of disquisition, liberality of spirit, accuracy of reasoning, correctness of taste and attention to composition."[53] Rather later, a far less august society of students was described in a report in an English augustan periodical in terms which show how quickly this style caught on. It was "A Society of Young Gentlemen, most, if not all of them, Students in the University of *Edinburgh*, who from a Sympathy of Affections, founded on a Similitude of *Parts*, and *Genius*, have united themselves into a Body, under the Title of THE GROTESQUE CLUB; . . . Their Business, to express it in the Words of one of their own Members, is *A Friendship that knows no*

[52] D. D. McElroy, *The Literary Clubs and Societies of Eighteenth Century Scotland*, Ph.D. diss., Edinburgh Univ. (1952). More accessible though less useful is his *Scotland's Age of Improvement* (Washington 1969).

[53] *Scots Mag.* 33 (1771), 340-44. For a short but important discussion of the intellectual importance of the Rankenian Club, see G. E. Davie, "Hume in his Contemporary Setting," in *David Hume: University of Edinburgh 250th Anniversary of the Birth of David Hume 1711-1961. A Record of the Commemoration Published as a Supplement to the University Gazette* (Edinburgh 1961), 11-15.

Strife, but that of a generous Emulation to excell, in Virtue, Learning, and Politeness."[54]

Perhaps the best-documented and most instructive account of the connection which this developing literati made between the pursuit of literature, social improvement and their own role as leaders of a progressive society, is to be found in the case of the Easy Club.[55] It was founded in 1712 by a group of young men, led by the poet Allan Ramsay. They announced "The gentlemen who compose this Society Considering how much ye immaturity of years want of knowing ye world and Experience of living therein Exposes them to ye Danger of Being Drawn away by unprofitable Company to the waste of the most valuable part of their time have resolved at sometimes to retire from all other Business and Company and meete in a Society by themselves in order that by a Mutual improvement in Conversation they may become more adapted for fellowship with the politer part of mankind and Learn also from one anothers happy observations. . . ."[56] This act of withdrawal from a society from whose values they wished to dissociate themselves in order to turn themselves into an elite defined in terms of the values of the polite world was reinforced by an even more striking act of identification with it. For the members of the club resolved to adopt pseudonyms drawn from the ranks of the heroes of the ideological world of augustan ethics and in this guise, to discuss the *Tatler* and *Spectator* essays at every meeting along with their own literary work. Interestingly too, they resolved not to discuss politics. This was natural enough. The union had spelled the end of formal politics as a legitimate means of pursuing wealth and national independence and as a legitimate form in which a post-union elite could acquire an identity. But the union was so recent that it was too much to expect a new elite to forget all associations between politics and identity overnight. Thus it is significant to find that under the pressure of a major crisis in Anglo-Scottish relations in 1713 members of the Easy Club abandoned their former resolution to eschew politics and resolved instead to petition the king to dissolve the union, "The first cause and fountain of all the greatest ills Scotland suffers or fears." Indeed, such was their indignation that they discarded their English pseudonyms for ones drawn from the political and cultural heroes of Scotland (Sir

[54] *The Plain Dealer*, no. 46 (1724) 393-94. I do not rule out the possibility that the interesting reports of the activities of polite society in Edinburgh in 1724, signed Fergus Bruce, are by Allan Ramsay.

[55] D. D. McElroy, *Scotland's Age of Improvement*, 14-19.

[56] Quoted in *The Works of Allan Ramsay*, ed. A. M. Kinghorn and A. Law, Scottish Text Society (Edinburgh 1970), IV, 11.

William Wallace, Lord Belhaven, Gavin Douglas, George Buchanan, et al.). But that did not lead them to abandon their cultural program and they still continued to debate augustan ethics behind these new masks. Only in this way would they sustain their love to their native country, "which we see dayle decaying and animate us to new projects for her interest." As with the old provincial oligarchy, they had learned to subordinate their defensive sense of independence to their belief in the need to assimilate themselves to a wider scale of progressive values represented by the culture of England.

IV

By the 1720s Edinburgh had acquired a structured literati, which associated its preoccupation with some of the most difficult and central problems of contemporary philosophy and literature with the improvement of a backward society. Indeed, this literati was developing as a modern-minded elite, anxious to provide a disorientated, leaderless society with a new identity. Given the condition of early 18th century Edinburgh it was perhaps understandable that various elites should have come forward to offer a disorientated society the leadership it lacked. But that does not explain why this leadership should have been accepted by the dominant social group in the city. Indeed, between the 1720s and 1740s it looked as though that aristocratic society would begin to provide *itself* with the institutions and ideology necessary to acquire an identity and in the process, to assimilate the literati to those dominant forms. In so doing, it looked as though the cultural life of 18th century Edinburgh was conforming to the conventional pattern observable in many provincial capitals in the West.

The 1720s to 1740s form a period in which post-union depression and political uncertainty eased. Politically the rise of Walpole marked the beginning of a period of political stability that would continue unbroken until the 1760s. The spasmodic and ill-advised meddling of Parliament and English ministers in Scottish business that had characterized the early years of the union, gave place to a more relaxed relationship between the two countries in which, for the rest of the century Parliament was to show little interest in Scottish affairs; what legislation appears in the statute book was, for the most part initiated and drafted in Scotland and simply forwarded to London for more or less formal parliamentary approval.[57] The Secretaries of State, too, for the most part were content to allow magnates like the 3d Duke of Argyll and later Henry Dundas, to manage the ordinary business of politics

[57] N. T. Phillipson, "Scottish Whigs," 4-7.

and government with only the most minimal interference from London.[58] In purely functional terms, while there might be no formally constituted Scottish Assembly or Governor's Court in Edinburgh, the city was as much a provincial capital as Boston or Dublin. The only difference was that Edinburgh functioned as a provincial capital on an informal and not a constitutional basis. In the last resort, its status rested on the fact that many of the Scottish landed classes were too poor to be able to do their ordinary political, administrative, and social business in London; it was a case of bringing institutions to the people. The growth of stability, and the consequent easing of the uncertainty and unpredictability of Scottish government in the preceding decades made it possible for a new provincial oligarchy in Edinburgh to take stock of its position and to seek an identity that would relate their collective interests to their sense of the traditional responsibilities of a governing class and to encapsulate the whole in an institutional and ideological framework that would recognize its honorable and preeminent role in Scottish society.

Just as the identity of the old provincial oligarchy had been formed by its preoccupation with economic improvement, so was that of its successor. This time, however, it took the form of a concern with agricultural improvement rather than with trade and manufactures. Previously, agricultural improvement had been a case of individual rather than collective effort. In 1723 it became a subject of collective interest with the foundation of the Honourable the Society for Improvement in the Knowledge of Agriculture, the first such society to be established in Britain and the model upon which those which followed were based.[59] Its three hundred members were drawn almost exclusively from the landed classes and included a majority of the peerage and substantial gentry. It was an Edinburgh-based organization managed by a committee of twenty-five, thirteen of whom were required constitutionally to be drawn from the Lothians, the agricultural counties which surrounded Edinburgh; its secretary and guiding spirit was Robert Maxwell of Arkland, an improver who ended up bankrupt.

To begin with, the society's efforts were confined to agriculture. Their committee was to offer general instruction in the principles of scientific agriculture and particular advice upon any specific problems that its members might have. But soon their horizons widened. They resolved to turn to educate their tenants "who work more like Tools or Machines, than men of Reason, going on blindly as led by custom in

[58] Ibid., 25-32; J. M. Simpson, "Who Steered the Gravy Train?" 47-72.

[59] The following material is drawn from *Select Transactions of the Honourable the Society for Improvement in the Knowledge of Agriculture in Scotland*, ed. R. Maxwell (Edinburgh 1743).

the often unaccountable ways of their fathers . . . their progress upon no Principles or if upon any, upon the wrong ones, makes it necessary that Agriculture should be taught in a college way as other sciences." Later they widened their interest to other forms of economic activity. Prizes were offered to fishermen to encourage them to take up deep-sea fishing; efforts were made to stimulate the linen industry by searching for Frenchmen who would teach the Scots the most modern methods of weaving and by imposing upon themselves a self-denying ordinance against buying or wearing foreign linen. In general, if we may judge from Maxwell's interesting preface to the Society's Select Transactions, they saw themselves as agents of economic progress, spurred on by the knowledge that such progress had, after all been attainable in England: "If the Agriculture and Manufactures were improved and carried on to the height they could bear, we might be near as easy and convenient in our circumstances as our sister kingdom of *England* seeing neither our soil nor our Climate is unfriendly, and, since we enjoy the same Priviledges of Trade with them. If we are far behind, we ought to follow the faster."

The society is of great significance. Although the union had brought about the fragmentation of a once homogeneous provincial oligarchy, the activities of the rump that remained orientated toward Edinburgh showed that by the 1720s they had devised the institutional means of identifying themselves as the heirs to that former governing class. They sought to encourage economic growth by assimilating their country's economy to the more modern patterns to be found in England. They sought to improve themselves and a wider community, and in so doing, began to see themselves, as did the literati, as a modern-minded elite whose duty it was to regenerate a backward society.

Under these circumstances it was not at all surprising that the literati and the aristocratic society of Edinburgh should have developed close links. The literati developed in strength and in social prestige and moved into a closer relationship with the new provincial oligarchy. Members of the Rankenian Club grew older and better established in their professions: by 1730 their average age was 31, by 1740, 38 and they could number among their members fashionable Edinburgh ministers like Robert Wallace and George Wishart, well-known professors like Colin McLaurin, John Stevenson, and Charles Macky, advocates at the head of the bar and heading for places on the bench like Alexander Boswell (James's father) and Alexander Murray, Sir Andrew Mitchell (an ambassador), and Charles Maitland, an M.P. The Rankenians, in short were becoming closely bound into the institutional fabric of Edinburgh society.

Perhaps the most striking development of this period was the emergence of the college as a university of reputation, closely identified with the polite learning associated with the literati.[60] By the 1720s its faculty had lost most of the cautious, elderly nonentities it had inherited from its earlier existence as a scholastically orientated seminary and had begun to acquire influential teachers of vigor, sophistication and merit who belonged to quite a different world. Charles Macky and John Stevenson, Professors of Civil History and Logic from 1719 and 1730, may not have published, but they were important teachers who introduced the teaching of Locke and the history of manners into the curriculum. Significantly, too, they both taught belles lettres—that quintessentially polite discipline—Macky by teaching the lives of the learned and Stevenson by teaching criticism. It was through their agency as teachers and as prominent members of Edinburgh's polite society that young men like David Hume, Adam Ferguson, and William Robertson were introduced to that most characteristic preoccupation of the Scottish Enlightenment.[61] At the same time the university acquired its medical school, the result of pressure put upon it by a small group of ambitious Edinburgh doctors who had studied medicine at Leiden, who used that celebrated medical school as a model upon which to found a rival establishment that would soon surpass its original as a center of medical learning and scholarship.[62]

Appropriately enough, it was at this time that the literati began to produce the first of those leaders who were quite deliberately to offer the landowning society of Edinburgh their services as purveyors of those polite values which they believed to be of some social consequence to them. The first two leaders were the poet Allan Ramsay and the mathematician Colin McLaurin.

In some respects, Allan Ramsay's career is a commentary on the cultural history of early 18th century Edinburgh.[63] Born in 1684 or 1685,

[60] This is illustrated in the prospectus issued by the college in 1741. While it is unreliable in some respects as a description of what was actually taught, it is a striking testimony to the college's intentions. *Scots Magazine* 3 (1741), 371-74.

[61] For Macky, see L. W. Sharp, "Charles Mackie, the First Professor of History at Edinburgh University," *Scottish Hist. Rev.* 41 (1962). Not much is known about Stevenson, but see *The Autobiography of Dr Alexander Carlyle of Inveresk, 1722-1805*, ed. J. H. Burton (London 1910), 47-49; T. Somerville, *My Own Life and Times, 1741-1814* (Edinburgh 1861), 12-14.

[62] D. Guthrie, *The Medical School of Edinburgh* (Edinburgh 1959).

[63] Ramsay deserves fuller treatment than he has so far received. At present see *The Works of Allan Ramsay*, ed. A. M. Kinghorn and A. Law, vol. IV: *A Biographical and Critical Introduction to the Works of Allan Ramsay . . .* ; B. Martin, *Allan Ramsay, A Study of His Life and Works* (Cambridge, Mass. 1931); A. Gibson, *New Light on Allan Ramsay* (Edinburgh 1927). For Ramsay's literary significance, see D. Craig, *Scottish Literature and the Scottish People* (London 1961) and A. H. Maclaine, "The Christis Kirk Tradition: Its Evolution in Scots Poetry to

the son of the Earl of Hopetoun's factor, he had moved to Edinburgh around 1700 to join its heterogeneous, youthful population. He became a wig-maker and soon moved into bookselling and poetry. He was one of the original members of the Easy Club which discussed and apparently even published some of his poetry. By 1719 he had begun to acquire something of a reputation in England as well as in Scotland for verse which reflected many of the cultural and ideological aims of polite culture in Scotland. He set out, quite deliberately, to stimulate a sense of national identity by awakening the cultural pride of his fellows, encouraging the republication of Scottish verse ancient and modern, stressing continually that there was nothing in it which was incompatible with modern taste. At the same time he set out to show that the forms, language, and idioms of that tradition, even though it had decayed through neglect since the renaissance, were things that could be revived and given cultural life in the modern world by being assimilated to the aesthetic framework provided by the existing cosmopolitan, neoclassical world.

It is clear that Ramsay wanted to do more than regenerate Scottish poetry ("I being a poet sprung from a Douglas' loin"—i.e., Gavin Douglas). He saw himself as the agent of a wider program of social and cultural improvement. Between 1720 and 1740 he was to open a bookshop, a lending library (the first in Britain), an academy of painting, and, to the horror of the evangelically minded, a theater. At the same time a stream of exhortatory verse began to appear. The Town Council was urged to improve the amenities of the city, the Convention of Royal Burghs was told to do something about the fisheries. The efforts of the Society for Improvement in the Knowledge of Agriculture received Ramsay's particular attention. Their ladies were commended for appearing at a public assembly wearing dresses made of native cotton. And the society thanked Ramsay for an ode written to encourage their improving labors:

> *Continou Best of Clubs Long to Improve*
> *Your native Plains and gain your nation's Love*
> *Rowze every Lazy Laird of each wide feild*
> *That unmanur'd not half their Product yield.*

It is for others to judge Ramsay's quality as a poet; the historian can notice only that his reputation and success were unparalleled in Edinburgh's literary history. The nobility and gentry took him into their circle and made his shop one of their favorite meeting places. During

Burns," *Studies in Scottish Literature*, II (1964-65), 3-8, 111-24, 163-82, 234-50, esp. 163-71.

the 1720s his three principal works, the *Poems* (1720), the *Tea-Table Miscellany* (1725), and the *Gentle Shepherd* (1725), soon to be known as the National Pastoral, collectively went through nineteen editions.[64] The 1728 edition of the *Poems* was sponsored by a list of 416 subscribers including most of the nobility and gentry. As Ramsay rightly observed, noble patronage had "raised the Stock of Fame amongst the Rank of native poets."[65] He might have added that it was also evidence of the rapidly growing respect of a largely landed society for the purveyors of polite culture.

Colin McLaurin's success was of rather a different sort, though in its way it was every bit as remarkable as that of Ramsay.[66] His appointment to the Chair of Mathematics at Edinburgh was an event of some significance for it was the first time the reorganized university had appointed a professor of established international reputation to its faculty. McLaurin was one of Newton's favorite pupils and he had been professor at Marischal College, Aberdeen, before being lured to Edinburgh for what was said to have been an exceptionally large salary. As the Town Council, with whom the patronage of the chair lay, minuted, "It was impossible for us to hope for any opportunity of doing a thing more honourable and advantageous for the city, that could contribute more to the reputation of the university, and advance the interest of learning in this country, than the giving Mr. McLaurin suitable encouragement to settle among us."[67]

McLaurin quickly emerged as the second of the two undisputed leaders of that early generation of literati. He was an influential and fashionable teacher who opened his classes to the polite society of the city as well as to the students of the university, giving a polished and highly intelligent series of lectures on Newtonian astronomy and methodology. Earnest and elegant, they provide a statement of the aims of science stressing the need for cautious induction rather than speculation and the value of science as an agent of social progress and true religion. It is a statement that embodies many of the methodological and ideological assumptions of the Scottish Enlightenment. McLaurin's stress on the social role of science and the scientist was not simple theorizing. It was typical of him that he should have been a

[64] B. Martin, *Bibliography of Allan Ramsay* (Glasgow 1931). *The Gentle Shepherd* is an important poem, and a careful reading of it provides a fascinating insight into the ideological world of Edinburgh society in the 18th century.

[65] *The Works of Allan Ramsay*, ed. B. Martin and J. W. Oliver, Scottish Text Society (1953), II, xxi.

[66] C. McLaurin, *An Account of Sir Isaac Newton's Philosophical Discoveries*, ed. with a biographical introduction by P. Murdoch (London 1750).

[67] A. Bower, *The History of the University of Edinburgh*, II, 222-23.

member of the Society for Improvement in the Knowledge of Agriculture. It was equally typical that in 1737 he should have encouraged (perhaps even initiated) a move to persuade the professors of the new medical school, who had set up a little society to encourage medical research, to widen their horizons. He urged them to range over the sciences in general, and to include the antiquities of Scotland, and at the same time to attract the nobility not only to become members but to become actively involved in its organization.[68] His teaching (he is said to have taught four to five hours per day) and his improving zeal exhausted him. As his biographer remarks, "His acquaintance and friendship was . . . courted by the ingenious of all ranks; who, by their fondness for his company, took up a great deal of his time and left him not master of it, even in his country retirement."[69] He died of overwork in 1746 at the age of 48, characteristically trying to organize the defense of the city against the Jacobite army.

Thus, by 1745 it seemed that Edinburgh society resembled that of many other provincial cities in the western world. The city was a provincial capital and, rather curiously, the political, administrative, and social center of Scottish government. In this setting a new provincial oligarchy developed, as many similar oligarchies were developing throughout the West, as a modern-minded elite concerned with the economic, social, and cultural improvement of themselves and a wider society. The primary organization through which this collective role was acted out was the Society for the Improvement in the Knowledge of Agriculture. Having been set up simply to further the economic interests of their own class, it had begun to engross a widening social and cultural program, and had assimilated to it a few, highly respected intellectuals. But what set the society apart from similar organizations elsewhere was the fact that the elite it served was the rump of a once homogeneous and politically active oligarchy which had precipitated and successfully concluded a revolution in their relations with metropolitan England. The society provided its members not simply with a means of asserting their identity as a provincial oligarchy, but with a means of compensating for the fragmentation and loss of status that it had suffered at the time of the union. Thus the ideology which defined the collective role of this provincial society not only defined their relations with metropolitan England but harked back to the pre-union days and to the ideology of that once homogeneous old provincial

[68] See, in addition to Murdoch's biography, W. Maitland, *A History of Edinburgh*, 355; D. D. McElroy, *Scotland's Age of Improvement*, 27-30, and *Literary Clubs*, 82-95. "Alexander Munro, *primus*," ed. H. D. Erlam, *Univ. of Edinburgh J.* (1954), 87-88.
[69] McLaurin, VII.

oligarchy that had brought the union about. Again, in assimilating a few, but highly respected members of the literati to their membership and, more generally, to their social world, the society seemed to be developing a relationship with the local intelligentsia that is very much what one would expect and is characteristic of society in the West as a whole. However, in the following generation this relationship underwent a remarkable transformation. From occupying an honorable, but dependent position in relation to the oligarchic society of Edinburgh, the literati suddenly and without warning found themselves in a position to offer the aristocratic society of Edinburgh both the institutional and ideological forms which could provide a later generation with its identity. They became, in a very strict sense, the leaders of the provincial society of Edinburgh, the custodians of the values of a pre-union oligarchy, providing their successors with the means of acquiring an identity that they were unable to provide for themselves. This development took place in the 1750s and we must now see how it happened.

V

The 1750s mark the beginning of an important period in Scottish history. It was one in which it seemed that the elusive goal of rapid economic progress, so crucial to the ideology of both the provincial oligarchy, and the literati, lay at last within reach. Rents, which had apparently begun to increase slowly in the later 1730s now began to increase more rapidly; the linen and iron industries, the cattle trade and above all the tobacco trade with America had begun to expand rapidly. More dramatically, the recent failure of the Jacobite rebellion of 1745 had shown, paradoxically, how stable Scotland had become; outside the highlands, few members of the landed and merchant classes had been prepared to disrupt the existing structure of the union, however imperfect it might be. Generationally, it was a period in which a new and younger society of literati, which had passed through adolescence and early manhood in the 1720s-1740s, reached maturity. Aristocrats and literati alike, and men of the greatest importance to the future history of Scottish culture, like David Hume, Adam Smith, Adam Ferguson, William Robertson, and Joseph Black had been through college, had studied or come into contact with that first generation of polite professors, Macky, Stevenson, and McLaurin and had perhaps visited Francis Hutcheson at Glasgow. They had all made their way through that nexus of polite student societies, had moved in Rankenian circles, had been exposed to the gradually cohering social and ideological world that was beginning to provide the city and its new provincial oligarchy with an identity. By the 1750s many of these men were in their late twenties and early thirties. They were becoming established in careers and were acquiring an adult life-style in a world that seemed at last to offer the fulfillment of those aspirations with which earlier generations had been so closely identified. Growing wealthier, with less cause than their fathers to confine their ambitions to Scotland and to Edinburgh, they could now begin to cast their eyes southward as the great nobility had done in 1707. Throughout the 1750s and 1760s, the drift away from Edinburgh to London became increasingly noticeable. At first it meant the sort of short visit to London James Boswell and his friends liked to make. By the 1770s and 1780s it meant giving up the social life of Edinburgh altogether. Indeed it is a striking paradox, spelled out in the almanacks that began to appear from 1773 onward, that the Georgian New Town of Edinburgh was planned and founded in the 1750s, to house the functions and society of a provincial capital, and that this new town began to take shape just at the time when the society it was designed to serve was planning its withdrawal from the city.[70]

In other words, the 1750s saw the beginning of that political stability and prosperity which was so deeply important to the identity of the new provincial oligarchy and to the literati. But it also saw the simultaneous and necessary loosening of the links which bound the new provincial oligarchy to Edinburgh; soon, like the great nobility in 1707, they would be able to take the high road to England and assimilate themselves to a wider, more modern society. As Alexander Wedderburn, a young advocate, literatus, and future Lord Chancellor, wrote in the preface to the first *Edinburgh Review* of 1755-56,

> The memory of our ancient state is not so much obliterated but that, by comparing the past with the present, we may see the superior advantages we now enjoy, and readily discover from what sources they flow. . . .
>
> If countries have their ages with respect to improvement *North Britain* may be considered as in a state of early youth, guided and supported by the more mature strength of her kindred country.[71]

In the 1750s, then, when their economic fortunes were at last beginning to turn upward, this new generation of a new provincial oligarchy required an identity that would define an honorable, traditional role for them in the setting of mid 18th century Edinburgh, but not one

[70] On the planning of the New Town, see A. J. Youngson, *The Making of Classical Edinburgh 1750-1840* (Edinburgh 1966).

[71] *The Edinburgh Rev.* 2 (Edinburgh 1755-56). This was by no means a unique sentiment. See the ironical broadsheet composed by the Moderate Clergy of Edinburgh, quoted by E. C. Mossner, *The Life of David Hume* (London 1954), 369. See also *Scots Mag.* 15 (1752), 370-80.

which would commit them too deeply to the city. And, instead of resurrecting the institution of their fathers, the Society for the Improvement in the Knowledge of Agriculture which had become defunct at the time of the Jacobite rebellion, they became parasite on an institution for which they held no responsibility, a society of intellectuals, the Select Society of Edinburgh.[72]

The Select Society was founded on 22 May 1754 by a little group of the younger literati led by David Hume, Adam Smith, and the younger Allan Ramsay, who clearly hoped to establish a society that would serve them as the Rankenian Society had served their elders. Intellectually, if we may judge from the subjects of their early debates, they set out to discuss the sort of questions about social structure, social progress and criticism about which Hume had recently written and on which Kames and Smith were soon to publish, not the metaphysical subjects which had interested the Rankenians. More formally, they proposed "by practice to improve themselves in reasoning and eloquence, and by the freedom of debate, to discover the most effectual methods of promoting the good of the country."[73] But the idea of a small society of literati had soon to be abandoned. From the very outset the society was bombarded with applications for membership. In the spring of 1755 Hume could write to Ramsay who was at that time in Rome: "It had grown to be a national concern. Young and old, noble and ignoble, witty and dull, laity and clergy, all the world are ambitious of a place amongst us, and on each occasion we are as much solicited by candidates as if we were to choose a Member of Parliament."[74]

By 1759 there were 135 members and there could have been many more, and they included, as Alexander Carlyle reported, "All the literati of Edinburgh and its neighbourhood, and many of the nobility and gentry who, though few of them took any share in the debates, thought themselves so well entertained and instructed that they gave punctual attendance."[75] No society could have had a more homogeneous membership. Not only did its members belong to the same age group—around 32 in 1754—but 51 of the total membership of 162 were closely related to at least one other member and many more be-

[72] D. D. McElroy, *Literary Clubs*, 138-98 and App. See also R. L. Emerson, "The Social Composition of Enlightened Scotland . . . ," in *Studies on Voltaire and the Eighteenth Century*, cxiv (1973) 291-329.

[73] *Scots Mag.* 17 (1755), 126.

[74] D. Hume to Allan Ramsay, April-May 1755, in *Letters of David Hume*, ed. J.Y.T. Greig (Oxford 1932), I, 219-21.

[75] Quoted D. Stewart, *Account of the Life and Writings of William Robertson* (London 1801), 212.

longed to a more distant network of cousinage. A majority were heirs apparent and most "could expect to be land-owners in an agrarian society rapidly increasing its productivity." Well over three-quarters were to fill significant and efficient places in government, in the military and ecclesiastical establishments, and in the universities. As Mr. R. L. Emerson remarks, "Their roles were conditioned by the expectation of inherited titles, places, responsibilities, wealth and power—the very stuff that human confidence is made of."[76] There, under the aegis of the literati, the Select Society debated what can only be described as the theme of modernization. They discussed the economy, the institutions, the manners, and the culture proper to a progressive society, the relations between different states of society and the mechanisms by which they progress from one state to another. Nor were the problems of the effects of progress upon the identity of a community forgotten, for this, in the guise of subjects relating to Virtù was frequently discussed: "Whether a nation may subsist without public spirit"; "Whether commercial and military spirit can subsist in the same nation"; "Can a body politick be virtuous," etc.

But the Select Society was more than an academic debating society. From the general they moved to the particular to debate more specific problems relating to current progress of Scotland, problems of agricultural and economic improvement, legal and political reform, the treatment of servants, etc. And from the particular they moved to the practical. Within a year the society had become the patron of what was nothing short of a campaign for the general improvement of Scottish society at large. On 7 April, they set up the first of what was to be a constellation of subsidiary societies, called the Edinburgh Society for the Encouragement of Arts, Sciences, Manufactures and Agriculture. Proposed by Colonel Oughton, and modeled on a similar Dublin establishment,[77] its purpose was "To encourage genius, to reward industry, to cultivate the arts of peace (for these) are objects deserving the attention of public spirited persons." For, it was observed that "the inhabitants of Scotland may become diligent in labour and excellent in arts in the concern of all who indeed love their country."[78]

Soon, under the directorship of the Duke of Hamilton and Lord Kames, an elaborate system of committees, prizes, and medals had been established to encourage an astonishing number and variety of projects (92 in 1756; 142 in 1759). The first committee was to encourage "National History and Chemistry"; another, "pure and mixt Mathematics"; a third, "Belles Lettres and Criticism"; and a fourth, "History

[76] R. L. Emerson, *op.cit.*   [77] "Alexander Munro, *primus*," 89-90.
[78] *Scots Magazine*, 17 (1755), 127-29, 407.

and Politics."[79] Next came a short-lived journal, the first *Edinburgh Review* (1755-56) intended to transmit the didactic, critical style of the Select Society to a wider public, and to bring before it the most noteworthy polite literature produced in England and abroad. Finally, the society launched its best-known project, the Select Society for Promoting the Reading and Speaking of the English Language in Scotland. Once again a constitution was drawn up and an elaborate organization established and the actor Thomas Sheridan was engaged to deliver a course of lectures. Given in June 1761, in a rich Irish brogue to an audience of 300 ("The most eminent in this country for their rank and abilities" as the *Scots Magazine* reported),[80] the lectures were the greatest success, were soon repeated, and later published.[81]

VI

The achievement of this remarkable society which provided Edinburgh's society with its institutional and ideological framework from 1754 until its gradual demise in the early 1760s cannot be thought of in narrowly functional terms. Indeed, apart from the few gentlemen who learned how to pronounce English tolerably, it is hard to believe that all the premiums, prizes, and organization had much effect in stimulating social or cultural progress. Its importance lay in providing an identity to an aristocratic society that was sensitive to the fact of its fragmentation and possessed traditional and deeply held convictions about its role as a governing elite. To do this, a small, private society of intellectuals had been transformed and had taken over the patronage of that distinctive and traditional program of improvement so necessary to the Scottish provincial oligarchy's identity. To be sure, the literati was well equipped for this task. As we have seen, in the early, confused days of the union they had come to see themselves as in some sense the heirs to a now apparently defunct provincial oligarchy. But simply to take up that role in a highly aristocratic city like Edinburgh did not mean that the leadership they offered would necessarily or even probably be followed by the dominant, aristocratic society in which they moved. Indeed, it is arguable that all the probabilities were against such a development. What made it possible was the changing circumstances of mid 18th century economic and political life which unsettled the younger members of the new provincial oligarchy, forcing them to look for institutional and ideological means of making their orientation to Edinburgh less positive than it had been in the days of

[79] Ibid.

[80] Ibid. 22 (1761), 390.

[81] T. Sheridan, *A Course of Lectures on Elocution: Together with Two Dissertations on Language* (London 1762).

their fathers. Hume and his friends had created an institution upon which they could become parasite, and as the Select Society was to hand, it was that institution that was taken over and transformed. And so the literati found themselves in the astonishing position of offering identity to a complex aristocratic society, in an important provincial capital. And while such a development could not, by itself, make them or anyone else better philosophers, it did ensure that polite letters had social importance and that their authors could enjoy quite remarkable social status, thus making the life of the literatus not only socially acceptable but an object of ambition to the motivated. It was a development well suited to channeling intellectual talent into the paths of polite culture.

The literati and the provincial oligarchy of enlightened Edinburgh thus formed a single extraordinarily complex social unit. Its identity rested upon institutional and ideological foundations which were the product of a tension within the traditional governing elite which desired simultaneously to identify with and to alienate itself from a society already crumbling as the result of long-hoped-for economic growth. But the willingness to suffer alienation from a traditional environment and to countenance a still further fragmentation of a governing elite was stronger than the defensive desire to identify with it. Thus when enlightened Edinburgh looked back defensively to their country's Gothic past, they taught themselves to see only a feudal society in which they had shared the same sort of society and institutions as the English. When they reflected on the historical process which linked the past with the present, they saw only a series of accidents, misunderstandings, petty jealousies on the part of Englishmen as well as Scots, which had stood in the way of the predestined union of the two kingdoms "divided from the earliest accounts of time, but destined, by their situation, to form one great monarchy," as William Robertson put it.[82] And, as I have shown elsewhere, they soon learned to express those occasional moments of fear and frustration, which the fear of lost identity made natural, by directing their hostility toward issues of no possible importance, which could in no way threaten the structure of the union and the process of assimilation that was bound up with it.[83]

The literati could teach their aristocratic followers not to act but to understand. They taught them that in all societies man is determined by an external world operating according to discoverable, secular mechanisms, which provide him with his knowledge of the God he

[82] *The Works of William Robertson, D.D.* (Oxford 1825), II, 235.

[83] N. T. Phillipson, "Nationalism and Ideology," in *Government and Nationalism in Scotland*, ed. J. N. Wolfe (Edinburgh 1969), 167-88.

worships, the things he senses, the values which govern his conceptions of right and wrong, his sense of the sublime and the beautiful, the critical and scientific skills by which he determines the limits of human action. For this mid 18th century society, the collective will to understand was a substitute for the sort of political action from which an earlier generation had derived its identity. The literati and their institutions provided the same function for the governing class as the old Parliament and perhaps the great nobility had once provided their ancestors. That is why enlightened Edinburgh was, in a strict sense a Republic of Letters, and why it could justly adopt the title, The Athens of Britain.[84]

[84] A. Ramsay to Sir A. Dick, 31 January 1762 in *Curiosities of a Scots Charta Chest*, ed. Hon. Mrs. A. Forbes (Edinburgh 1897), 198. I explore the social significance of the deterministic philosophy of David Hume, Adam Smith, Lord Kames, John Home, and their friends in my essay, "Towards a Definition of the Scottish Enlightenment," in *City and Society in the 18th Century*, eds. P. Fritz and D. Williams (Toronto 1973), 125-147.

In this essay I also explore the catalytic effect of their determinism upon thinkers like Adam Ferguson, John Millar, and particularly Thomas Reid, James Beattie, and the philosophers of Common Sense.

9

The *Choice of Hercules*
American Student Societies in the Early 19th Century

by James McLachlan

It is more in accord with nature to emulate the great Hercules and undergo the greatest toil and trouble for the sake of aiding or saving the world, if possible, than to live in seclusion, not only free from all care, but revelling in pleasures and abounding in wealth, while excelling others also in beauty and strength. Thus Hercules denied himself and underwent toil and tribulation for the world, and, out of gratitude for his services, popular belief has given him a place in the council of the gods.

From Cicero, *De officiis* III.5.25[1]

Go hence, Herculean Youth,
Clad in the might of truth
And reason calm,
To turn with high disdain
From Vice to Virtue's train:—
Such manhood must he gain
Who wins our palm.
From "Ode for the Centennial Celebration of The American Whig Society, Nassau Hall," 1869[2]

In January 1819, members of the American Whig Society, a student organization at the College of New Jersey in Princeton, decided that they needed a new "device"—or symbolic representation—to imprint upon the diploma they awarded to members of their group. The device (it turned out to be an engraving made from a painting) secured by the students over the course of the year, barely known even today, is one of the most revealing monuments in the history of American culture. The story of its commissioning is best told in the words of the students themselves: "The committee appointed in the winter ses-

---

[1] *Cicero: De officiis*, trans. Walter Miller, LCL (1913).

[2] N.a., *Ode for the Centennial Celebration of The American Whig Society: Nassau Hall, June 29th, 1869* (n.p. 1869), stanza 5. Copy in the Princeton University Archives, Firestone Library. The Archives are cited hereafter as PUA.

sion having during the vacation visited Philadelphia, there entered into engagements with an artist of eminence ([Thomas] Sully) to complete a device for a new diploma. This the Artist executed with much taste, the Subject being 'the choice of Hercules.' "[3]

The *Choice of Hercules* would adorn the diplomas of the Whigs for the next century. The painting (Fig. 3) depicts the youthful, beardless Hercules, clad in a toga-like garment, frowning in indecision as he stands, leaning on his club, in the middle of the scene. On his right the seductive figure of Pleasure, or Vice, one breast bared, hair swirling and clad in flowing garments, gestures toward the delights she offers Hercules—a low grove shading a scene where scantily clad nymphs and satyrs dance and play upon pipes and cymbals. On Hercules' left and slightly before him stands the stern figure of Virtue, clad in a dark mantle and holding a book. She points to her right, where we can see, in a distant, mountainous landscape, a classical figure of a reclining youth with a book, a globe, and a group of earnest philosophers. In the right foreground is placed a pile of books, scrolls, a compass, and a plumbline—the traditional attributes of Virtue in Western art.

This subject was not chosen by the Princeton students on a mere whim.[4] It is extraordinarily revealing of their intellectual world, their aspirations, and the nature of the American college and American culture early in the 19th century.

[3] J. J. Middleton, "Annual History for 1819, 3rd part," in MS vol., "Historical Annals of the American Whig Society, 1802-1869," in PUA. See too MS Records/Minutes of the American Whig Society, IX, entries for meetings of 9 January, 1819; 8 February, 1819; and X, entries for meetings of 2 July, 1819 and 27 September, 1819. The Whig Records are unpaginated and were not kept in chronological order. They are cited hereafter as *Whig Records/Minutes*. Sully's painting is now in the Princeton University Art Museum. The PUA has many examples of J. Neagle's engraving of the painting. Sully was paid $100 for the painting. The costs involved in the engraving (the first engraver chosen defaulted) amounted to about $400—a very large amount for the time. The students planned on recouping the sum over a long period of time by charging graduates for copies of the diploma. There is a brief discussion of the Princeton *Choice of Hercules* in Frank Jewett Mather, Jr., "American Paintings at Princeton University," in *Record of the Museum of Historical Art of Princeton University*, II (Spring 1943), 5-6.

[4] My assertion that the subject was the choice of the students rather than the artist rests on two grounds: (1) Sully was primarily a portraitist; in his vast *oeuvre* the *Choice of Hercules* represents almost the sole excursion into mythology (see Edward Biddle and Mantle Fielding, *The Life and Works of Thomas Sully* [Charleston, S.C. 1969]); and (2) in 1811 the other Princeton student organization, the Cliosophic Society, proposed exactly the same subject for its own device. The device, however, was never adopted by the Clios, apparently because of the expense involved in its execution. See MS *Records/Minutes of the Cliosophic Society*, III (1811), PUA.

The myth of Hercules confronted by Virtue and Pleasure (or Vice) at the Parting of the Ways has echoed down the corridors of time, stirring the imagination of artists, writers, and thinkers ever since Athens in the 5th century B.C., when it first appeared as the tale of Prodicus of Ceos in one of Xenophon's accounts of the Socratic dialogues.[5] "When Heracles was passing from boyhood to youth's estate," Xenophon wrote, "wherein the young, now becoming their own masters, show whether they will approach life by the path of virtue or the path of vice, he went out into a quiet place, and sat pondering which road to take. And there appeared two women of great stature making towards him." One was Vice ("my friends call me Happiness"), the other Virtue ("I company with gods and good men, and no fair deed of god or man is done without my aid"). Vice sought to tempt Hercules along the easy way of indolence and pleasure. Virtue exhorted him to take the hard but ultimately more rewarding path of duty and honor. At the youthful crossroads of his life, Hercules chose Virtue.[6]

In the twenty-two hundred years before the Princeton students adopted the myth as their own exemplar it passed through many transformations and accumulated several levels of meaning. In his *Works and Days* Hesiod added a specific landscape to Prodicus' story—the identification of the Way of Vice with a low and easy path, and the Way of Virtue with a high and difficult one.[7] It was an image which would influence visual representations for centuries. The early Chris-

[5] The literature on the *Choice of Hercules* is extensive. For a useful listing of the subject in works of art (but not including the Princeton *Choice*), see Andor Pigler, *Barockthemen* (Budapest 1956), 117-18. I have relied heavily on the classic discussion of the subject, Erwin Panofsky's *Hercules am Scheidewege und andere antike Bildstoffe in den neueren Kunst* (Berlin and Leipzig 1930), which prints scores of versions. Panofsky's work should be supplemented by E. Tietze-Conrat, "Notes on 'Hercules at the Crossroads,' " *J. of the Warburg and Courtauld Institutes* 14 (1951), 305-9; Theodor E. Mommsen, "Petrarch and the Story of the Choice of Hercules," ibid., 16 (1953), 178-92; John Rupert Martin, *The Farnese Gallery* (Princeton 1965), 24-27; and Theodore Reff's "Cézanne and Hercules," *Art Bulletin* 48 (1966), 35-44, which is broader than its title indicates. Among the non-art historical studies of the subject Marc-René Jung's *Hercule dans la littérature Française du XVIe siècle: de l'Hercule Courtois a l'Hercule Baroque* (Geneva 1966), esp. 132-36, is particularly valuable, though Jung's final conclusion ("En France, la jeunesse d'Hercule, c'est la Renaissance.") seems somewhat overstated. The most extensive collection of graphic representations of the myth is the *Choice of Hercules* file in the photographic library of the Warburg Institute, London, England.

[6] The quotations are from *Xenophon: Memorabilia and Oeconomicus*, trans. E. C. Marchant, LCL (1923), "Memorabilia," I, 20-34.

[7] See *Works and Days* in *Hesiod: The Homeric Hymns and Homerica*, trans. H. G. Evelyn-White, LCL (1926), 25.

James McLachlan

tian fathers were suspicious of the myth, as they were of so many other aspects of late Graeco-Roman culture. For almost a millennium after the decline of Rome in the West the image of Hercules *in bivio* languished, until it was revived second hand from a passage in Cicero's *De officiis* by Petrarch in his *De vita solitaria*. In *De officiis*, Cicero had used the myth to illustrate his discussion of the choice of a career, "the most difficult problem in the world."

> It is in the years of early youth, when our judgement is most immature, that each of us decides that his calling in life shall be that to which he has taken a special liking. And thus he becomes engaged in some particular calling and career in life, before he is fit to decide intelligently what is best for him.

"We all cannot have the experience of Hercules" of a clear choice between vice and virtue, Cicero wrote, going on to illustrate his point by recounting the tale of Prodicus. Too often the most important decision in one's life was decided merely by accident.[8]

Over the centuries the myth of Hercules became intertwined with other elements, biblical and Christian, particularly the passage in the gospel of Matthew (7:13-14) which reads: "Enter ye in at the strait gate: for wide is the gate, and broad is the way, that leadeth to destruction, and many there be that go in thereat; because strait is the gate, and narrow is the way, which leadeth unto life, and few there be that find it."[9] In the Renaissance the myth proved to be particularly attractive to the early humanists; visual representations of it received wide circulation in works such as the illustration (Fig. 1) to a 1515 edition of Sebastian Brant's famous *Ship of Fools* (1494), in which a youthful, knightly Hercules dreams of a voluptuous but deadly Vice surrounded by roses at the end of the easy way, and a stern Virtue surrounded by thorns at the end of the narrow way.[10]

In the 1590s the subject received what Erwin Panofsky has called its "canonical formulation," which would fix the image for centuries, when it formed the centerpiece of an elaborate iconographic program painted by Annibale Carracci for the Camerino in the Palazzo Farnese in Rome (Fig. 4).[11] In his work on the Farnese Gallery, John Rupert Martin describes Carracci's painting thus:

[8] Mommsen, "Petrarch and Hercules," 188, n. 3; *De officiis*, I, 32, 118.
[9] Samuel C. Chew, *The Pilgrimage of Life* (New Haven 1962), 175-76.
[10] As reprinted in Bonnie Young, "Scenes in an Ivory Garden," *Metropolitan Museum of Art Bull.* 14 (June, 1956), 255. Reproduced here by permission of the Metropolitan Museum of Art.
[11] Panofsky, *Hercules am Scheidewege*, 124ff. Reproduced here by permission of Villani and Figli, Bologna.

The nude, beardless Hercules, frowning in his indecision and clasping a mighty club, sits on a rock in the middle of the scene. At his left the elegant figure of Voluptas, seductively clad in swirling and diaphanous garments of yellow hue, indicates the sweet but false delights that await him along the "primrose path of dalliance": a book of music, masks, musical instruments, and playing cards—and, deep within the grove, clusters of grapes. On the other hand stands the sterner figure of *Virtus*, holding a sword and pointing upward along the stony way that leads to the mountaintops, where the winged horse Pegasus can be seen amidst the trees. . . . Seated at her feet is a poet wreathed with laurel; holding an open book before

Figure 1: An Early Humanist *Choice of Hercules* (1515)

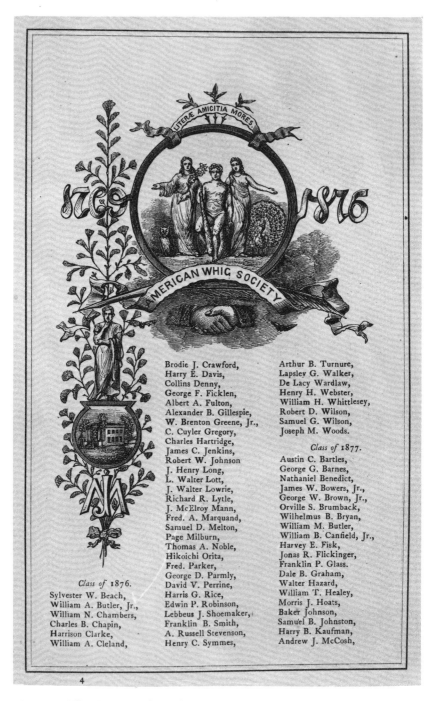

LITERÆ AMICITIA MORES.

1769   1876

AMERICAN WHIG SOCIETY

Brodie J. Crawford,
Harry E. Davis,
Collins Denny,
George F. Ficklen,
Albert A. Fulton,
Alexander B. Gillespie,
W. Brenton Greene, Jr.,
C. Cuyler Gregory,
Charles Hartridge,
James C. Jenkins,
Robert W. Johnson
J. Henry Long,
L. Walter Lott,
J. Walter Lowrie,
Richard R. Lytle,
J. McElroy Mann,
Fred. A. Marquand,
Samuel D. Melton,
Page Milburn,
Thomas A. Noble,
Hikoichi Orita,
Fred. Parker,
George D. Parmly,
David V. Perrine,
Harris G. Rice,
Edwin P. Robinson,
Lebbeus J. Shoemaker,
Franklin B. Smith,
A. Russell Stevenson,
Henry C. Symmes,

Arthur B. Turnure,
Lapsley G. Walker,
De Lacy Wardlaw,
Henry H. Webster,
William H. Whittlesey,
Robert D. Wilson,
Samuel G. Wilson,
Joseph M. Woods.

Class of 1877.
Austin C. Bartles,
George G. Barnes,
Nathaniel Benedict,
James W. Bowers, Jr.,
George W. Brown, Jr.,
Orville S. Brumback,
Wilhelmus B. Bryan,
William M. Butler,
William B. Canfield, Jr.,
Harvey E. Fisk,
Jonas R. Flickinger,
Franklin P. Glass.
Dale B. Graham,
Walter Hazard,
William T. Healey,
Morris J. Hoats,
Baker Johnson,
Samuel B. Johnston,
Harry B. Kaufman,
Andrew J. McCosh,

Class of 1876.
Sylvester W. Beach,
William A. Butler, Jr.,
William N. Chambers,
Charles B. Chapin,
Harrison Clarke,
William A. Cleland,

4

Figure 2: The Degeneration of a Symbol: the Princeton Whig *Choice of Hercules* of 1876

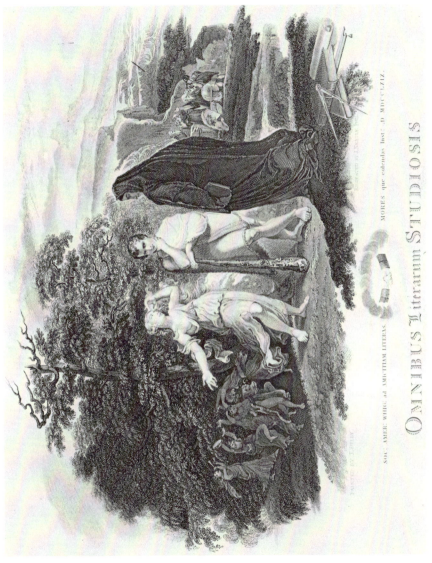

Figure 3: Thomas Sully's *Choice of Hercules* of 1819

[455]

Figure 4: The Canonical Formulation: Annibale Caracci's *Choice of Hercules* of the 1590s

Figure 5: The Progress of Reason: The Princeton Whig Device of 1799-1800

him, he seems to promise eternal fame for Hercules if he will choose the way of goodness. The outcome, to be sure, is obvious. Already the hero's eyes are turned towards Virtue, and the palm tree behind him is, as Bellori observes, a "presagio ben certo delle sue vittorie."[12]

The iconographic program was probably designed by an internationally famous humanist scholar, Fulvio Orsini. It was meant not only to celebrate the House of Farnese but to inspire and flatter the young Odoardo Cardinal Farnese to emulate his famous uncle, Alexander Cardinal Farnese. "The winged horse," Martin observes, "serves not only as a symbol of 'fame as the consequence of virtue,' but also as a reference to Alessandro himself, who bore an *impresa* [device] showing Pegasus on Mount Parnassus, to signify his patronage of *letterati*. The same two meanings—fame engendered by virtue, and the fostering of arts and letters—are combined in the figure of the poet who fixes his gaze on the young Hercules, and promises to sing his praises forever."[13] It was a meaning to which every struggling humanist man of letters could heartily subscribe.

Though the subject underwent many variations over the next two centuries, the ultimate, if not the immediate, iconographic origins of the Princeton *Choice of Hercules* in the Farnese *Choice* seem clear enough. However, the reasons why in 1819 the students at a tiny, provincial, Presbyterian college on the shores of North America should have adopted as their device a theme which had received its classic statement over two centuries earlier, on the ceiling of a palace of a humanist-influenced Roman Catholic prince of the Counter-Reformation, seem anything but clear. What in their experience led the Princeton students to make such an apparently arcane and unlikely selection? What did the *Choice of Hercules* mean to them? We can answer these questions only by reconstructing the world of American college students in general, and of Princeton students in particular, during the early 19th century.

To do so is no easy task. "Things go with so much sameness here," wrote James Garnett, a student at Princeton in January 1813, "that the occurrence[s] of a week seldom furnish sufficient matter for a letter; I can do little more, therefore, than to tell you how often I wish myself out of this western siberia."[14] For historical purposes Garnett and his

---

[12] Martin, *Farnese Gallery*, 24.

[13] Ibid., 28-38, 26. The *Choice of Hercules* now in the Camerino Farnese is a poor copy; the original is in the Galleria Nazionale in Naples.

[14] James M. Garnett, Jr., to Mary E. Garnett, 30 January 1813, Bound Collection of Typescript Copies, Rare Book and Manuscript Room, Firestone Library, Princeton University. Cited hereafter as Garnett Papers.

fellow students might almost as well have been in the eastern Siberia. His is a lonely voice speaking for what is surely the least-studied and most mysterious group in the history of American higher education— the students, who composed the largest single group on the rosters of colleges and universities, and who were, ostensibly, the primary objects of the institutions' concern.

Characteristically, students are conspicuous by their absence in the first volume of what promises to be the most authoritative history of American education in our time, Lawrence Cremin's fine *American Education: The Colonial Experience, 1607-1783* (1970). Cremin can hardly be faulted for his omission; the only effort yet made to write a comprehensive history of students was published as long ago as 1901. It is a book that Cremin—rather generously—has characterized as "primordial." Beyond the merely anecdotal, the history of the student before the 20th century would seem to belong to the history of the in-articulate—to the history of groups like the poor, youth, slaves, mobs, children, peasants; shadowy but important groups that leave little or no written record, that surge unexpectedly onto the historical stage, provide a colorful melee, wreck the scenery, and then retire to the wings, leaving the task of reconstructing the action to various well-documented elites.[15]

James Garnett arrived at Princeton in August 1812. It was a crucial moment of transition in the college's history. "I understand that Dr. Green has accepted his appointment as president," he wrote home a

[15] Despite its faults, Henry D. Sheldon's *Student Life and Customs* (New York 1901) must be consulted by anyone interested in the subject. Written as a Ph.D. dissertation under G. Stanley Hall at Clark University at the turn of the century, it contains much useful information. Only 80 of the book's 366 pages are devoted to European students.

Recent work in the history of European—particularly French—higher education, some of which concerns students, is surveyed in John Talbott, "The History of Education," *Daedalus* 100 (Winter 1971), 133-50. On British students, see Eric Ashby and Mary Anderson, *The Rise of the Student Estate in Britain* (London 1970), a good example of what I call, below, the "social institutional" approach to the history of students. Though brief and without references, a most suggestive introduction to the history of the American college student is Frederic Rudolph's "Neglect of Students as a Historical Tradition," in Lawrence E. Dennis and Joseph F. Kauffner, eds., *The College and the Student* (Washington 1966), pp. 47-58. Rudolph's *The American College and University, A History* (New York 1962) and Lawrence A. Veysey's *The Emergence of the American University* (Chicago 1965) contain much valuable material on the history of students. The most satisfactory single article on the history of the American college student is Edmund S. Morgan's "Ezra Stiles and Timothy Dwight," Mass. Hist. Soc. *Proceedings* 72 (1963), 101-17. Like all good historical essays, Morgan's raises more questions than it answers; it is both a model of historical inquiry and a warning against the pitfalls that lay in wait for the researcher on this subject.

few days after his arrival, "and I believe that the great desire he expressed to refuse it before he was actually elected, was nothing more than an electioneering trick."[16] It was a harsh judgment, but historians have been little kinder to Ashbel Green's presidency than were his contemporaries.[17] Although Princeton was only sixty-six years old in 1812, it seemed to many that the college's best days were behind it; on the face of it, nothing that occurred over the next few years would disprove such judgments.

Within a decade or two of its founding in 1746, Princeton and its alumni had come to exercise a major influence on cultural life in the American colonies. After the appointment of the Reverend John Witherspoon as president in 1768 the college's influence was intensified tenfold. Steeped in the brilliant intellectual world of the Scottish Enlightenment (albeit its more conservative wing), Witherspoon introduced hundreds of young Americans to the novel study of belles lettres, to natural philosophy, and to the newest in Scottish moral philosophy, a system of thought which would become for the next century the reigning academic philosophy in the United States. The only clergyman to sign the Declaration of Independence, by precept and example Witherspoon shaped a generation that would lead the colonies in revolt against the mother country in 1776.[18]

[16] James M. Garnett, Jr., to Mary E. Garnett, 5 September 1812, Garnett Papers.

[17] My general remarks on the history of the college are based mainly on five works: (1) John Maclean's *History of the College of New Jersey, from Its Origins in 1746 to the Commencement of 1854*, 2 vols. (Philadelphia 1877), a massive double-decker Victorian biography of an institution, which contains many primary documents and shrewd first-hand observations; (2) Varnum Lansing Collins' *Princeton* (New York 1914), a somewhat neglected work, very well written and based on much original research; (3) Thomas J. Wertenbaker's *Princeton, 1746-1896* (Princeton 1946), a fine and comprehensive internal history of an institution; (4) Douglas Milton Sloan's *The Scottish Enlightenment and the American College Ideal* (New York 1971), a series of often-acute intellectual biographies of the major figures connected with Princeton and other Presbyterian schools from the mid-18th to early-19th century; and (5) Guy Howard Miller's "A Contracting Community: American Presbyterians, Social Conflict and Higher Education, 1730-1820" (Ph.D. diss., Univ. of Michigan 1970). Miller's is the best work done on Princeton for this period. Viewing the college as the institutional embodiment of peculiarly Presbyterian ideas about man, society, and education, he firmly places Princeton—along with other Presbyterian academies and colleges—within the historical development of the denomination.

[18] For Witherspoon, see Lyman H. Butterfield, *John Witherspoon Comes to America* (Princeton 1953), and Varnum Lansing Collins, *President Witherspoon, A Biography*, 2 vols. (Princeton 1925). In the current long-overdue appreciation of the massive impact of the Scottish Enlightenment on American cultural and intellectual history it should not be forgotten that the Scottish Enlightenment was not a monolithic movement. There were two main trends to the Enlightenment

Long before Witherspoon's death in 1794 the effective direction of the college was taken over by one of his most promising disciples, his son-in-law, Samuel Stanhope Smith. Smith "was the well-bred, courteous gentleman, every where, at all times, in all companies, on all occasions," one of his students remembered.[19] He was, in fact, the perfect neoclassical divine, a balanced and somewhat chilly mixture of 18th century piety and rationalism.[20] But as the Enlightenment waned a second Great Awakening, a massive revival of the religious enthusiasm of the 1740s, began in America. From the mid-1790s on anything tinged with the "infidel philosophy of the French Revolution" (a brush that some used to tar most of Enlightenment thought) became suspect.[21] A new, more evangelical generation, viewed with distrust Smith's cool piety and willingness to explore in a disinterested manner some of the wilder shores of 18th century intellectual inquiry. While Smith in fact shared the general conservative abhorrence of "infidelity," neither his nor Princeton's reputation was enhanced by the recurrent student disturbances that began to break out at the turn of the century. Many thought that Princeton was not only failing to produce its proper quota of Presbyterian clergymen, but was becoming ideologically suspect as well. "Between 1808 and 1812," Princeton's most recent historian has concluded, the Presbyterians "essentially boycotted the school."[22]

In 1812 Samuel Stanhope Smith was retired as president. Waiting

within Scotland, a conservative—and ultimately dominant—one centered at the University of Aberdeen, and a more liberal one that radiated from the University of Edinburgh. Witherspoon was as much influenced by the former as the latter.

[19] Philip Lindsley, "Samuel Stanhope Smith," in William B. Sprague, *Annals of the American Pulpit*, 9 vols. (New York 1857-69), III, 343.

[20] For Smith, see Samuel H. Monk, "Samuel Stanhope Smith (1751-1819): Friend of Rational Liberty," in Willard Thorp, ed., *The Lives of Eighteen from Princeton* (Princeton 1946), 86-110, and William H. Hudnut III, "Samuel Stanhope Smith, Enlightened Conservative," *JHI* 17 (1956), 540-52. An incisive and judicious portrait of Smith as man and thinker is Winthrop D. Jordan's "Introduction" to his edition of Smith's 1787 classic, *An Essay on the Causes of the Variety of Complexion and Figure in the Human Species* (Cambridge 1965), vi-liii.

[21] On the question of "infidelity" see G. Adolf Koch, *Republican Religion* (New York 1933); Vernon L. Stauffer, *New England and the Bavarian Illuminati* (New York 1918); Herbert M. Morais, *Deism in Eighteenth Century America* (New York 1934); Charles D. Hazen, *Contemporary American Opinion of the French Revolution* (Baltimore 1897), and Charles E. Cuningham, *Timothy Dwight, 1752-1817: A Biography* (New York 1942). The idea of infidelity in America antedates, of course, the French Revolution. Until a careful and sophisticated study of this notion is made, much of late 18th and early 19th century American intellectual and educational history will remain obscure.

[22] Miller, "Convenanting Community," 443.

in the wings—rather impatiently, some thought—was Ashbel Green, a Princeton alumnus, trustee, and presently a Presbyterian clergyman in Philadelphia. If Smith had been a balanced compound of Enlightenment piety and rationalism, Green would prove to be an erratic mixture of 18th century piety and sentimentalism. A proto-Victorian, he was inducted as president of Princeton with an implied mandate to maintain strict order among the students and to restore ideological and religious orthodoxy.

Green's problems were those of many American college presidents of the time. From the 1790s on, American colleges experienced increasing unrest among their students, unrest that manifested itself in constant violence and riot. Part of this was due to tensions arising within student groups; as much, however, was due to a basic ambivalence among American educators and the American public as to the very nature of the college as an institution. Nowhere better was this ambivalence expressed than in a letter written by a contemporary of Green, Eliphalet Pearson, following student disturbances at Harvard in 1789. Pearson, a member of the Harvard faculty, raised questions about the nature of the college that would plague students, faculties, and administrators through the 19th century. Indeed, the issues he outlined are unresolved today. Since Pearson's letter is one of the half-dozen or so most significant documents in the history of American higher education, it demands quotation at considerable length:

> I take it to be a maxim in politics, that that system of jurisprudence will be most satisfactory, & most productive of good, which is best suited to the nature of the society, for whose benefit it is established. Writers on natural law usually, I believe, distinguish societies into two kinds, *domestic* & *civil*. The principal relations in the former are those of *husband* & *wife*, *parents* & *children*, *master* & *servants*. All which relations, as they usually coexist in the same family, which family is governed by the father, I shall consider together, & dominate the form of government *patriarchal*, *parental*, or *family*. The usual forms or species of *civil* government are well known to be *monarchy*, *aristocracy*, or *democracy*; or certain mixtures of these. Moreover, the respective rights & duties existing between magistrates & subjects, in all the numerous forms of *civil polity*, are, I believe, well stated & explained by writers on law. But I do not recollect a writer, who tells us what species of society a *university*, *college*, *academy*, or *school* is. It is true, they are called *literary* societies. But this points out the *object* of their institution, not the form. So that, perhaps, it may be a question, yet to be decided,

whether such societies ought to be denominated *domestic*, or *civil*, or *sui generis*, or *mixed*. If *domestic*, then it seems most proper that *parental* government should obtain in them; if *civil*, then such laws & such modes of executing them should be adopted, as would be most consonant to the particular form of civil polity established in them. But, if literary societies be societies *sui generis* their system of jurisprudence ought to be constructed accordingly; or, if they be of a mixed nature, so also should their laws & the administration of them be. These I conceive to be positions admissible by all.

I have been led into these speculations by the various & inconsistent remarks, I have often heard made by different persons, & sometimes by the same person, on the conduct of the officers of College. At one time they are censured for exercising *parental* authority, at another for conducting like *civil* officers. This difference of opinion probably arises from different views of the nature of such a society, & of the respective rights & duties of the governors & governed; or, possibly, from imperfect ideas of this subject. Those gentlemen, who consider college, as a *civil* society, naturally insist upon the right of the subject to a public trial, & to overt, confronted evidence; &, to effect this, would empower us to impose oaths. This open procedure, like that of a civil court, they say, is the sole method of preventing the charge of partiality. But, when you have given them a public hearing, why should they be denied the darling privilege of freemen, the right of trial by their peers, i.e., by a jury of classmates; & also the right of being heard by council? Nothing short of this would give them complete satisfaction.

On the other hand, those, who prefer *parental* government, are nevertheless unwilling to endow us with those discretionary powers, which are essential to *parental* authority. For I do conceive that *parental* authority is very nearly allied to unqualified *monarchy*, with respect to discretionary powers. The *civilian* says that the guilty party ought not to criminate himself, & that it is no immorality in him to deny facts, of which he is conscious. The advocate for *parental* government is equally hurt, when a scholar is censured, but upon the most direct evidence, notwithstanding the most plenary satisfaction on ye part of his judges. So that both the *civilian* & the *parent* are united in the exclamation of *tyranny*. While the students, as they mix with mankind, often hear such exclamations made, & some times by the most respectable characters, is it all surprising, that they are prejudiced against the officers & government of College? If they are taught from abroad . . . that they are entitled to all the civil rights of freemen; that, notwithstanding they are minors, they are still young

[463]

gentlemen *sui generis*; it is no wonder that they rebel against the constitution of College, which, at present, is not founded on such principles.

I do therefore most devoutly wish that this subject may be thoroughly explored; & that it may be determined, first of all, what *species* of society we are, whether *domestic* or *civil*. If the latter, whether *monarchical, aristocratical, democratical,* or *mixed.* So that it may be clearly understood, what the rights & duties of the governors & governed are; & that the laws & the mode of executing them may be made conformable to the nature of the society & of its constitution. For I conceive it to be an important truth, that that government will ever be the most happy, which is best suited to the nature of a particular society; & that those laws & statutes will ever give most satisfaction, which are founded in the *law of nature,* or on *rights* & *obligations* clearly defined & well understood.

What form of government will be best for College does not belong to me to determine; nor do I think myself capable of such a decision. I shall only observe that a *School* seems to be generally viewed in the light of a *family*; the masters of which appear to be clothed with *parental* authority, & vested with *discretionary* powers; the natural parents having, for a time, made an implied surrender of some of their rights, for the better government & education of their children. If College may be considered, as a School of a larger size, the same observations, in a degree at least, may be applied to us. And, perhaps, there would be as much safety in vesting 8 or 9 gentlemen, some of whom have *parental* feelings, with *parental* authority over 150 youths, as there is in committing 50 children to the discretion of one unexperienced youth, who has just left College, or who is still an undergraduate. However, I am very far from being an advocate for absolute discretionary powers. Nevertheless, I think it possible, that some extension of them may be found beneficial.[23]

Neither educators nor the public could decide whether college students were citizens, or children. They belonged to that unstable, unpredictable and ill-defined group called "youth." This basic uncertainty helps account for the seemingly capricious and arbitrary atti-

[23] Eliphalet Pearson to Edward Holyoke, 28 April 1789, Park Family Papers, Manuscript and Yale Memorabilia Room, Sterling Library, Yale University. Pearson (1752-1826) is best remembered as the first principal of the Phillips Academy at Andover, Massachusetts. He was later maneuvered out of the Harvard presidency when the established church in Massachusetts split into Orthodox Congregationalists and Unitarians. The Unitarians retained control of Harvard, and Pearson was instrumental in founding the Andover Theological Seminary in 1809 as a conservative redoubt against "infidel" Harvard.

tudes toward students that characterized the 19th century college. In fact, there were complex ideological reasons and objective circumstances that must be taken into account in any final explanation of their confusion. For the present we may simply note the confusion.

Toward the end of his letter Eliphalet Pearson seemed to embrace the "parental" or "familial" conception of the college. This would become the dominating, though hardly unchallenged, theme in the history of the 19th century American college. It would form, as well, Ashbel Green's conception of his role at Princeton. On taking up his duties Green made fifteen resolutions. They blend together to produce one dominating image: Ashbel Green was determined to be the archetypal *paterfamilias*:

> Resolved, 1st . . . I am to endeavour to be a father to the institution. I am to endeavour to the utmost to promote all its interests as a father does, in what relates to his children and property. 2d. To pray for the institution as I do for my family, . . . 9th. To endeavour that my own family be exemplary in all things. 10th. To view every officer of the College as a younger brother, and every student as a child. . . . 12th. To treat the students with tenderness and freedom, but yet as never to permit them to treat me with familiarity, or to lose their respect for me.[24]

In action, Green's resolves involved little more than a stilted attempt at intimacy by means of inviting eight students at a time to his home for dinner. Coupled with constant religious exhortation and his teaching, this described the parameters of Green's role as *paterfamilias*. Like that of most 19th century college presidents, his policy toward students was one of unsalutary neglect punctuated by capricious disciplinary raids in times of seemingly inexplicable crisis. Aside from the required attendance at classes and chapel, such discipline—or enforcement of consistent norms of conduct—as there was, was provided largely by student groups.

To say that patriarchy remained a nagging ideal rather than a reality is not to dismiss it as inconsequential. College faculties perceived students in terms of the patriarchical ideal and demanded that they behave like 19th century children. They did so, that is, when they were not perceiving students as citizens and threatening them with legal or police action. Students, on the other hand, saw themselves in terms of the civil ideal; college presidents were monarchs, students, responsible citizens. Like faculties, however, students were inconsistent. When it suited them they were often ready to play the role of the dependent

[24] Ashbel Green, *The Life of Ashbel Green, V.D.M.* (New York 1849), 343-44.

child. On the face of it, it would seem that all these conflicting roles could coalesce in only one place—the classroom.

The goal of late 18th and early 19th century American colleges was a "literary"—or intellectual—one. It is here, in the college curriculum, where the interests and activities of students and faculty intersected, that we might hope to discover something of the history of student thought. But such a supposition would be misplaced. By no educational criteria derived from any time, place, or philosophy, can the early 19th century American college curriculum as actually taught be made to look attractive. It consisted almost solely of a drill in Latin, Greek, and mathematics, with a cursory view of science and some moral philosophy and belles lettres as the capstone.[25]

The students disliked the curriculum and pursued their studies only grudgingly. "I have just begun to translate Greek today," James Garnett reported to his parents in 1812, "I find the study somewhat easier as I go on, but it affords very little entertainment; indeed geography is the only study of our class in which any one can take much pleasure." By the following year Garnett was even more despondent about the curriculum. "I lament very much that I did not attend to history more than I did before I came to college," he wrote, "for I shall have no time to read it here, and I often find myself much at a loss for historical information. As it is I shall be forced to neglect it until I graduate." By the end of the year Garnett's complaints had reached a peak:

> . . . I think the system of Natural Philosophy which they teach here, a very dry and unentertaining one. It is Enfield's. The chief fault that I find with it is, that every thing is put in the form of prop-

[25] The standard works on the history of the college curriculum are R. Freeman Butts, *The College Charts Its Course* (New York 1939), and Louis F. Snow, *The College Curriculum in the United States* (New York 1907). To a degree, for the colonial period both works are now superseded by Lawrence Cremin's *American Education: The Colonial Experience*, 459-68, 509-16. For a provocative discussion of the 19th century college curriculum, see Douglas Sloan, "Harmony, Chaos, and Consensus: The American College Curriculum," *Teachers College Record* (Fall 1971), 221-51. Sloan cites almost all secondary sources pertinent to a history of the 19th century curriculum.

The clearest place in which to trace the history and actual influence of the curriculum is in biographical accounts of the education of various individuals. See, in particular: Merrell R. Davis, "Emerson's 'Reason' and the Scottish Philosophers," *NEQ* 17 (January 1944), 209-28; Herbert D. Foster, "Webster and Choate in College: Dartmouth under the Curriculum of 1796-1819," *The Collected Papers of Herbert D. Foster* (n.p. 1929), 213-49; Jonathan C. Messerli, "Horace Mann at Brown," *Harvard Educational Rev.* 33 (Summer 1963), 285-311; and Joseph J. Kwiat, "Thoreau's Philosophical Apprenticeship," *NEQ* 18 (March 1945), 51-69.

ositions, and this too, when they are such facts as he can easily demonstrate, only by reasserting the proposition in different words, or
by directing an experiment to be made. In order to render the style
of a work on Philosophy as entertaining as possible, I think nothing
should assume the form of a proposition, except what is susceptible
of mathematical demonstration. But what I dislike most, is, that in
all probability, we shall be unable to finish our course of study; the
last Senior class only recited about sixteen pages of chemistry; and
we are now more behind-hand than they were at the same time; owing to our being obliged to study conic sections this winter, a study
which we ought to have finished in the junior year.[26]

Garnett was a haughty and somewhat priggish young Virginia aris-
tocrat; on the basis of his letters, he was also intelligent and a sharp
observer. And his complaints were not unique among students. A few
years later at Harvard young Ralph Waldo Emerson was making identical complaints about his studying his "accursed Enfield."[27]

No single reason why the formal curriculum could not have been
made interesting to students is immediately apparent. Moral philosophy was the intellectual ancestor of the 20th century social sciences—
sociology, economics, anthropology, and so forth—and could possess
the same attraction as its progeny.[28] The same was true of belles
lettres, from which much of the present humanities curriculum—
poetry, fiction, drama, criticism, history—derive.[29] The potential fas-
cination of the study of mathematics and the natural and physical sciences needs no special pleading, nor does the interest inherent in the
study of the whole sweep of Greek and Roman culture.

Educational reformers and contemporaries at other colleges often
argued that American colleges were reduced to teaching on the level
of the grammar school because of the wretched state of college prepa-

[26] James M. Garnett, Jr., to Mary E. Garnett, 18 July 1812; Garnett, Jr., to
James M. Garnett, Sr., 1 May 1813, and 18 December 1813, Garnett Papers.

[27] Davis, "Emerson's 'Reason,'" 215n. William Enfield (1741-97) was an
English Presbyterian clergyman, author, and rector (1770-83) of the influential
dissenting academy at Warrington, where Joseph Priestly also taught. The book
Garnett and Emerson were referring to was probably Enfield's *Institutes of
Natural Philosophy* (1785). On Enfield, see *DNB*, vi, 787-88.

[28] See Gladys Bryson, "The Emergence of the Social Sciences from Moral
Philosophy," *International J. of Ethics* 52 (1931-32), 304-23; Bryson, "The Com-
parable Interests of the Old Moral Philosophy and the Modern Social Sciences,"
Social Forces 11 (1932-33), 19-27; Bryson, "Sociology Considered as Moral
Philosophy," *Sociological Rev.* 24 (1932), 26-36; and George P. Schmidt, *The
Old Time College President* (New York 1930), 108-45.

[29] Wilbur Samuel Howell, *Eighteenth-Century British Logic and Rhetoric*
(Princeton 1971), 714.

ration in the United States. James Garnett could hardly expect to appreciate Xenophon without knowing Greek; Emerson must master Enfield before tackling Schleiermacher. No true universities could be established in the United States, the argument ran, until the quality of American secondary education was drastically improved. The very age of the majority of college students—mere boys of 15, 16, or 17—reformers claimed, mitigated against responsible intellectual achievement, let alone the maintenance of order. Moreover, a reckless proliferation of colleges (9 in 1776, 25 by 1800, about 516 chartered between the Revolution and the Civil War) was forcing all institutions to lower their standards in order to attract the students whose tuitions they needed in order to survive. The best the colleges could realistically hope to do, the more pessimistic claimed, was to try to inculcate the most basic elements of traditional high culture and hope for the best.[30] These arguments and observations contained a considerable amount of truth, but not all of the truth. And none explain what appears to have been a sudden deterioration in the standards of both the curriculum and teaching at Princeton under Ashbel Green.

The 18th century American college curriculum had been far more adventurous for its time than was the curriculum of the early 19th century college. Many colleges, including Princeton, had introduced the newest in scientific studies, had either dropped or tried to push the basic study of Latin and Greek into the secondary schools, and had introduced the study of modern languages. With Green's arrival in 1812, however, the tide of the Enlightenment was stemmed at Princeton. John Maclean, a brilliant chemist hired by his predecessor, was dismissed; Latin and Greek in the form of gerund-grinding returned in full force, and the curriculum was given a heavily religious cast. Moreover, the teaching suffered: the study of belles lettres apparently amounted to little more than basic English grammar, while moral philosophy consisted of dreary recitations. Green, essentially, tried to turn the college back thirty or forty years earlier, to his most basic memories of Princeton in his own student days. "The mold of Witherspoon," a recent exhaustive history of the Princeton curriculum has concluded, "was by 1812 too reactionary for the college . . . the curriculum was . . . an unrelated, undefined, and unsystematic collection of courses which were taught by whomever was momentarily qualified to teach them. All students had to take all the courses, regardless of taste or gifts, or future plans."[31]

[30] All of these subjects are dealt with in considerable detail in James McLachlan, *American Boarding Schools: A Historical Study* (New York 1970), 19-101.

[31] Darrell L. Guder, "The Story of Belles Lettres at Princeton: An Historical Investigation of the Expansion and Secularization of Curriculum at the College of

Green was not an unrepresentative college president of his time, the Second Great Awakening. Like Timothy Dwight at Yale in the 1790s he saw a French infidel lurking under every bed, a revolutionary conspiracy or attack on Christianity in every student disturbance. Like Dwight at Yale, Green would attempt to assert a conservative, Christian republicanism by bending his best efforts to inducing religious revivals among his students. A decade ago Edmund Morgan conclusively demonstrated that the source traditionally used to show "French infidelity" among students at Yale was completely unreliable, and that in fact students seem to have been just about as religiously inclined under Timothy Dwight as under his supposedly lax and "enlightened" predecessor, Ezra Stiles.[32] The same appears to have been true at Princeton under Ashbel Green: as we shall see, Princeton students were not noticeably "infidel," nor did Green's efforts at religious suasion meet with mass upsurges of religious feeling. Green, ironically, spent the best part of his time and energy trying to establish a Presbyterian theological school in Princeton—a course which, since it removed many of the religiously inclined from among their number, could only lessen religious interests among the mass of undergraduates. In the meantime, the curriculum and teaching in the college deteriorated.

If the formal curriculum acted more as a negative than a positive intellectual stimulus, within the college there remained at least one other obvious source of intellectual tools available to students of the late 18th and early 19th centuries—the college library. Indeed, the American college began with the gift of a library, in 1638, when the Reverend John Harvard left in his will to the infant Cambridge college about £780 and over three hundred books. These books, one of Harvard's early historians claimed, "rendered possible the immediate reorganization of the College on the footing of the ancient institutions of Europe."[33] During the 17th and 18th centuries American colleges tried assiduously to assemble collections of books, efforts often thwarted by expense, and worse, by the fires that periodically swept their collections. Their efforts were only modestly successful. At its peak in the 18th century Harvard's collections amounted to only 14,000 volumes. Yale managed to accumulate slightly fewer than 4000 by the time of the Revolution—only to see about 1600 of these de-

---

New Jersey with Special Reference to the Curriculum of English Language and Letters" (Ph.D. diss., Univ. of Hamburg 1964), 234, 235.

[32] Morgan, "Stiles and Dwight."

[33] Andrew M. Davis, *A Few Notes Concerning the Records of Harvard College* (Cambridge 1888), 6.

stroyed during the war. American college libraries were small libraries, but important: the introduction of a trunk of books from England at Yale in 1730 caused an intellectual revolution.[34]

Princeton's library in the beginning consisted, essentially, of the private libraries of the early presidents. The college did not have a real collection of its own until Governor Jonathan Belcher of New Jersey contributed his personal library of 475 volumes. The trustees early recognized the importance of books. In the first catalogue of the Princeton library, published in 1760, they complained of their "comparatively small assortment of modern authors," and their lack of "works on mathematics and the Newtonian philosophy, in which the students have but very imperfect helps, either from books or instruments. . . ."

A large and well-sorted collection of books is the most ornamental and useful furniture of a college, and the most valuable fund with which it can be endowed. It is one of the best helps to enrich the minds both of the officers and students with knowledge; to give them an extensive acquaintance with authors; and to lead them beyond the narrow limits of the books to which they are confined in their stated studies and recitations, that they may expatriate at large through the boundless and variegated fields of science. If they have books on hand to consult upon every subject that may occur to them, as demanding a more thorough discussion in their public disputes, in the course of their studies, in conversation, or their own fortuitous thoughts, it will enable them to investigate truth through its intricate recesses and to guard against the strategems and assaults of error.[35]

When the catalogue was published, in 1760, it listed 1281 volumes. Despite the trustees' (or, more properly, President Davies') faith in books, by 1802 the library's holdings had increased only to about 3000 volumes. In that year disaster struck: fire gutted Nassau Hall, destroying all but the 100 volumes President Smith had at his home.[36] Fortunately, the losses were made up fairly quickly. By 1804 the library had about 4000 volumes, and by 1816, 7000—the increase made up largely by the purchase for $1250 of President Smith's personal library. That

[34] Louis Shores, *Origins of the American College Library, 1638-1800* (Nashville, Tenn. 1934), 227, 226, and passim. Shores's is the standard work on the subject. For the 19th century, see Howard Clayton, "The American College Library: 1800-1860," *J. of Library Hist. Philosophy and Comparative Librarianship* 3 (1968), 120-37.

[35] *A Catalogue of Books in the Library of the College of New Jersey* (Woodbridge, N.J. 1760).

[36] Wertenbaker, *Princeton*, 106-7, 126.

was the last considerable increase in the size of the library until mid-century. By 1868, when James McCosh became president of Princeton, the library had increased only to 14,000 volumes. The library's acquisitions in the intervening period make a curious list: 1827—four books bought; 1828—no books bought; 1829—one book received as a gift. Eighteen-thirty was something of a banner year; the library purchased three books, one magazine, and a pamphlet. The only considerable gift (there were no significant appropriations) made to the library between 1812 and 1868 was the $1000 legacy it received in 1836 from an alumnus, President James Madison.[37]

Despite the trustees' 1760 encomium of books and reading, if a Princeton student wanted to use the library he had to be fast on his feet. In 1770 the library was open for only three one-hour periods a week, and students were limited to a single volume. By 1794 the library was opening only one hour on one day a week. Such policies were understandable in the late 18th and early 19th centuries, when books were still, to a degree, precious commodities, and when the librarian's position was apt to be occupied by a harassed junior member of a tiny faculty. But the Victorian period, when books were plentiful and cheap and faculties larger, saw only steady decline at Princeton, from five one-hour openings a week in 1831 to a single one-hour opening a week in the early 1860s. Books were carefully rationed, apparently by size rather than by content: "No student or other person, except members of the faculty," the 1813 library regulations read, "shall be allowed to take out of the library at one time, more than one folio, two quartos, or two octavos, or smaller volumes, which shall be returned before they shall have liberty to take out any other books."[38]

Princeton's niggardly circulation policies were not a Presbyterian eccentricity. Much the same rationing was followed by all other American college libraries through the 1860s. The attitude of John Langdon Sibley, a formidable scholar and mid-Victorian librarian at Harvard, was typical. Normally a rather forbidding individual, Sibley was seen in the Yard one day with a smile on his face. When asked why by a passerby, he replied, "All books but two are in, and I am on my way to get them."[39]

[37] [Ernest C. Richardson,] "The University Library," *Princeton Univ. Bull.* 9 (May 1898), 73-93. See too "A History of Princeton Libraries," *Princeton Alumni Weekly* 49 (April 1949), 5-9.

[38] *Laws of the College of New Jersey, Revised, Amended and Adopted by the Board of Trustees, September 30, 1813* (Trenton, N.J. 1813), 9; Richardson, "The Princeton Library," 84.

[39] Keyes D. Metcalf, "The Undergraduate and the Harvard Library, 1765-1877," *Harvard Libr. Bull.* 1 (1947), 47-48.

James McLachlan

What then was available to the student to stimulate the life of the mind? Quite simply, American students provided the tools themselves. In 1894 William Frederick Poole, a great bibliographer and mid-19th century graduate of Yale, remembered his undergraduate years thus:

> To those of us who graduated 30, 40, or more years ago, books, outside of the textbooks used, had no part in our education. They were never quoted, recommended, nor mentioned by the instructors in the class-room. As I remember it, Yale College Library might as well have been in Weathersfield or Bridgeport as in New Haven, so far as the students in those days were concerned. The College Societies, however, supported and managed wholly by the undergraduates, had good libraries, and here was where the students, and the professors besides, found their general reading.[40]

What was true of Yale seems to have been true of almost every other American college from, very roughly, the last third of the 18th century through the middle of the 19th. The student literary societies engrossed more of the interests and activities of the students than any other aspect of college life. Elaborately organized, self-governing youth groups, student literary societies were, in effect, colleges within colleges. They enrolled most of the students, constructed—and taught —their own curricula, granted their own diplomas, selected and bought their own books, operated their own libraries, developed and enforced elaborate codes of conduct among their members, and set the personal goals and ideological tone for a majority of the student body. When their operations faltered, the college collapsed. The meaning of the *Choice of Hercules*—and the history of the American college student—must be sought in the study of student societies.[41]

[40] William F. Poole, *The University Library and the University Curriculum* (Chicago 1894), 50.

[41] All histories of individual colleges and of American higher education have recognized the existence—and sometimes the importance—of student literary societies. However, they have never been systematically examined.

Aside from Sheldon's work cited above, the only general historical discussions of various aspects of student literary societies have been made by writers concerned mainly with the history of libraries or with speech education. See, in particular: David Potter, *Debating in the Colonial Chartered Colleges: An Historical Survey, 1642 to 1900* (New York 1944); Potter, "The Literary Society," in Karl R. Wallace, ed., *History of Speech Education in America: Background Studies* (New York 1954), 238-58; Thomas S. Harding, *College Literary Societies: Their Contributions to Higher Education in the United States, 1815-1876* (New York 1971); Roscoe Rowse, "The Libraries of Nineteenth-Century College Societies," in David Kaser, ed., *Books in America's Past: Essays Honoring Rudolph H. Gjelsness* (Charlottesville 1966), 25-42; and Catherine P. Storie, "The American College Society Library and the College Library," *Coll. and Research Libr.* 6 (June 1945), 240-48.

At Princeton early in the 19th century the two student literary societies, the American Whig Society and the Cliosophic Society, provided the main social and intellectual framework that gave meaning and interest to the lives of the students. Founded in 1765, by 1813 they were among the oldest student societies then in existence in America.[42] James Garnett's opinion of the college, we will remember, had not been high. But for the American Whig Society, of which he was a member, he had only praise. "I think," he informed his parents in July 1813, "as much improvement is to be derived from the Whig Society as from the College at present, for it is in a very flourishing state, and has forty-five members."[43] Since there were 110 students in the college at the time, the Whigs made up almost half the student body. Membership in the rival Cliosophic Society was probably about the same.[44]

[42] For histories of the societies, see Jacob N. Beam, *The American Whig Society of Princeton University* (Princeton 1933), and Charles Richard Williams, *The Cliosophic Society, Princeton University* (Princeton 1916).

[43] James E. Garnett, Jr., to Mary E. Garnett, 18 July 1813, Garnett Papers.

[44] The next few pages will concentrate on the years 1813-17 at Princeton. The following table gives an approximation of the numbers of students present at any one session. No catalogues for the College were published in these years. The figures in the table were pieced together from the following sources: (1) MS "Refectory Day-Book, 1803-1820," PUA; (2) MS "Minutes of the Faculty, College of New Jersey," 12 November 1812-25 August 1820, vol. II, PUA; (3) *Princeton University: General Catalogues, 1746-1906* (Princeton 1908); and the Alumni Biography Files in the PUA. These figures include all students present at a particular session, even if an individual spent only a few weeks in Princeton.

Students at Princeton August 1813 to September 1817

	Fresh.	Soph.	Jr.	Sr.	Grads.	Non-grads	Total
1) Aug.-Sept. 1813	11	33	32	34	85	25	110
2) Winter Session, Nov. 1813-May 1814	15	33	57	32	83	54	137
3) Summer Session, May 1814-Sept. 1814	13	31	48	31	90	34	124
4) Winter Session, Nov. 1814-May 1815	11	19	39	41	75	40	115
5) Summer Session, May 1815-Sept. 1815	17	40	40	42	90	54	144
6) Winter Session, Nov. 1815-May 1816	11	37	57	35	71	71	142
7) Summer Session, May 1816-Sept. 1816	24	41	40	36	80	60	140
8) Winter Session, Nov. 1816-May 1817	11	37	63	29	75	65	140
9) Summer Session, May 1817-Sept. 1817	19	42	44	21	85	41	126

All but a small minority of Princeton students, then, belonged to a literary society.

The records of both the American Whig and Cliosophic societies survive. Indeed, their manuscript records occupy almost 200 feet of shelf space in the Princeton University Archives. On the basis of these records it is possible to reconstruct the social and intellectual history of Princeton students for a period of almost a century. Since student literary societies existed in most other American colleges as well, if their records survive it should be possible to make a comprehensive study of the history of the American college student.

"The primary object of our convention here," the Whigs declared, "is mutual improvement by mutual attention and remarks."[45] In fact, their "mutual attention and remarks" added up to an extraordinarily intense and unremittent system of education by peers. Almost as soon as a student entered Princeton he would be solicited by one of the two rival societies. Once enlisted, he was sworn to absolute secrecy concerning the society's activities and ritual. Each society gained much of its internal cohesion from the simple existence of another, rival, society. Elaborate treaties were entered into between the two youth groups regarding their mutual relations, and ensuring their integrity against unwarranted incursions by the faculty. Members of a society were expected to conform to rigid forms of conduct, both during and outside of the society's meetings. The societies financed themselves through an elaborate system of self-imposed fines levied for breaches in the rules of conduct: twenty-five cents for laughing during a speech; fifteen cents for staying too long away from a meeting; ten cents for not returning a book, and so forth. A list of a society's fines reads like an applied neoclassical etiquette book for youth.[46] Serious breaches of decorum such as fighting in the college halls or failing to participate in an assigned society exercise were punishable not only by fines but by admonitions read to the offender during the society meeting by the censor, one of the elected officers. The length of time this public shaming among peers was to last was carefully stated in the official minutes of the society.

The early 19th century American college was characterized by constant and seemingly unmotivated student riot and violence, which historians have never explained convincingly, possibly because the main stabilizing organizations within the colleges, the student societies, have

[45] *Whig Records/Minutes*, vii, PUA, meeting of 13 January 1817.

[46] Some other fines were: talking, 10¢; out longer than one hour, 100¢; laughing, 20¢; impropriety, 20¢; putting in an improper Debate, 80¢; walking across the floor without permission, 6¢. See American Whig Society, MS *Small Fine Book, May 13, 1813-August 22, 1814,* PUA.

been so little investigated. Many disorders were, most probably, caused by disruptions in the internal dynamics of the student societies. It may well be that much of early 19th century student "unrest" was anything but haphazard and that a careful study of student records would reveal consistent patterns leading to student outbreaks hitherto seemingly unmotivated.[47]

While the social and intellectual histories of students are of equal importance and not completely separable, the meaning of the *Choice of Hercules* lies more in the intellectual than the social realm. The intellectual history of any age is difficult to reconstruct completely. In retrospect, a very few great books seem to dominate a particular era. We usually miss the multitude of forgotten books and pamphlets that together provided the common, day-to-day cultural context of thought and feeling through which the literate public actually perceived any particular work. We can reconstruct the contents of a few libraries, and often do the same with reading lists for individuals.[48] We know something of what books Americans have printed and purchased over the years.[49] But we have no information concerning the actual day-to-day reading habits of any group of people in American history, except for members of the American Whig Society.

Besides the college library, Princeton Whigs had their own collection of books, chosen by themselves. We can trace from week to week, from year to year, exactly which books the students purchased. For instance, at their meeting of 18 January 1813 the Whigs authorized the purchase of the following books:

 Beattie's works
 Burr's trial

[47] I hope to demonstrate this in a forthcoming essay on a major disturbance at Princeton which occurred in January 1817.

[48] For colonial libraries, see Cremin, *American Education*, 396-400, and his bibliography, 644-45; and also, Jesse H. Shera, *Foundations of the Public Library: The Origins of the Public Library Movement in New England, 1629-1855* (Chicago 1949). For a masterful account of the impact of reading on a particular school of thought, see Bernard Bailyn, *The Ideological Origins of the American Revolution* (Cambridge 1967), 1-54.

[49] See Charles A. Madison, *Book Publishing in America* (New York 1966); Hellmut Lehmann-Haupt et al., *The Book in America: A History of the Making, the Selling, and the Collecting of Books in the United States* (New York 1939); James D. Hart, *The Popular Book: A History of America's Literary Taste* (New York 1950); and Frank Luther Mott, *Golden Multitudes: The Story of Best Sellers in the United States* (New York 1947).

The only study I am aware of that bears any resemblance to the following pages is Albert Goodhue, Jr., "The Reading of Harvard Students, 1770-1781, as Shown by the Records of the Speaking Club," *Essex Institute Hist. Coll.* 73 (April 1937), 107-29.

Malthus on population
Rousseau social contract
Doddridge's rise & progress
Haller's Letters
Volney's Ruins
Humbolt's New Spain
Paine's Works, except the Age of Reason
Christian Panoply
Chase's trial
Austin's letters
Stuart's [*sic*] Metaphysical Essays[50]

A proper analysis of their choices can reveal much about the intellectual world of the turn of the century. Consider only Thomas Paine's *Age of Reason*. By 1813 the author of *Common Sense* was honored for his role in the American Revolution, but reviled for spreading his wicked "infidel philosophy," which could lead, President Dwight of Yale warned his students as early as 1797, only to "falshood [*sic*], perjury, fraud, theft, piracy, robbery, oppression, revenge, fornication, and adultry."[51] The *Age of Reason* apparently arrived with the rest of Paine's works; the Whigs promptly passed a resolution "that the censor be empowered to send that volume of Payne's [*sic*] works containing the age of reason to a bookbinder that that portion of it may be taken out."[52] Ashbel Green's admonitions against "infidelity" were, apparently, making themselves felt among the students. On the other hand, the works of Volney and Rousseau might be considered just as subversive as the *Age of Reason*, but they in turn were balanced by Philip Doddridge's *Rise and Progress of Religion in the Soul* (1753), one of the most influential works of dissenting piety published in the 18th century.

The possibilities for analysis presented by the records of books purchased by the Whigs are potentially of great importance for the social history of ideas. But lists of books bought tell only part of the story: infinitely more significant would be the determination of which books were actually read, and with what frequency. Biography aside, this question has long eluded historians. However, among the American Whig Society records are the yearly student librarians' records, which carefully note, day-by-day, every volume withdrawn by each member of the society. The earliest surviving library records date from 1813.

[50] *Whig Records/Minutes*, VII, PUA, meeting of 18 January 1813.
[51] Quoted in Kenneth Silverman, *Timothy Dwight* (New York 1969), 98.
[52] *Whig Records/Minutes*, VII, PUA, meeting of 15 February 1813.

In the four years between August 1813 and September 1817, undergraduate members of the American Whig Society made exactly 6481 withdrawals from their library. Student reading for this period can be broken down into the following categories:[53]

Volumes Withdrawn from the Library of the American Whig Society, Princeton, by Undergraduate Members
August 1813 to September 1817

Categories	Withdrawn	%
1) Current Periodicals	460	7.0
2) Greek & Roman History, Literature, etc.	425	6.5
3) Natural Philosophy, Science, Mathematics, Medicine	140	2.1
4) Moral Philosophy, Religion, Theology, Philosophy, Education, Religious Biography	230	3.5
5) Voyages and Travels	386	5.9
6) Political, Social & Economic Theory; Current & Recent Public Affairs	378	5.8
7) History, Historical Biography, Memoirs, Letters, etc.	942	14.5
8) Rhetoric & Logic; Speeches and Sermons	371	5.7
9) Literary Biography, Criticism, Letters, Memoirs, etc.	718	11.0
10) Poetry and Fiction	2108	32.5
11) Reference	325	5.0
12) Miscellaneous unidentified	46	0.7
Total for the period	6529	

[53] This table is based on a list of books drawn from the first four of the twenty-eight MS "Books Borrowed from the American Whig Society Library" ledgers in the PUA, as follows:

1) Books Borrowed, 1813-1815, volume 1
2) Books Borrowed, 1815-1816, volume 2
3) Books Borrowed, 1816-1817, volume 3
4) Books Borrowed, 1817, volume 5

Volume 4 of this series contains the librarians' accounts. The whole series of 28 volumes spans the years 1813 to 1880. The ledgers also record books borrowed by graduate members of the society and some faculty members. The table is based only on the books borrowed by undergraduates.

It must be remembered that many, if not most, works published in the late 18th and early 19th centuries were printed in multivolumed editions; the table is based upon withdrawals of single volumes, not of complete works. The master list (now deposited in the PUA) is at best an approximation of reality. The student librarians usually recorded only the title that appeared on the spine of a volume—for example, "Barrow, Travels, v. 1." Sir John Barrow—not to mention many other Barrows—wrote many books of travel. To take another instance: the ledgers record many withdrawals of "Knox on Education." Since Princeton was a Presbyterian college, the immediate assumption is that the students were still reading John Knox's 16th century writings on education. But, as it turns out, they also read many of the compilations of Vicesimus Knox (*Elegant Extracts in*

The table by no means represents all volumes read by the Whigs during the period. The college library, however briefly, was available to them; we know too that some students had their own collections of books.[54] But the list of books withdrawn by the Whigs from their library probably comes as close as is possible to marking with some precision the intellectual boundaries of the early United States. Only a brief indication of the variety of works read by the students will be given here.[55]

The volumes withdrawn by the Princeton students make up an intensely cosmopolitan and sophisticated list, drawing equally upon the classics of Greece, Rome and the Renaissance, the American, French, and Scottish Enlightenments, the by-then classic authors of Augustan England, the full range of late-18th century neoclassical literature as well as most of the important works of the early Romantic movement. Perhaps the most surprising thing about the list is the comparatively small number of American works on it. Such works were hardly ignored; the students read the memoirs of Richard Henry Lee, a Princeton alumnus, and accounts of the trial of Aaron Burr, another alumnus. Franklin's *Works* were read as well as Joel Barlow's *Columbiad* and the *Federalist Papers*. But American works form only a small proportion of the total. The list of student readings represents a provincial, but not a parochial, world-view.

The traditional classic authors, such as Cicero, were read in the formal curriculum of the college. But the Whigs extended the formal curriculum by reading Ovid, Tacitus, Terence, Virgil, Herodotus, Homer, Josephus, Juvenal, Pindar, Quintilian, Livy, and others on their own, most often in translation—Cowper's and Pope's *Homer*, for instance, or Dryden's *Virgil*. Their most frequently used guide to the ancient world was *The Ancient History of the Egyptians, Carthagenians . . .* (1740) by Charles Rollin, Rector of the University of Paris

---

Prose, Elegant Extracts in Verse, etc.), an English don who appears to have been a one-man anthology factory. It seems most likely, therefore, that the "Knox on Education" listed so often in the ledgers was not John's, but Vicesimus' *Liberal Education: or, a Practical Treatise on the Methods of Acquiring Useful and Polite Learning* (1782). In other words, the determination of the title of each volume represented an individual evaluation of likely candidates.

[54] For instance, on 5 January 1813 James Garnett reported to his parents: "Mr. Oliver from Baltimore . . . has brought with him a large collection of French authors, and he has been so good as to offer me the perusal of them" (Garnett Papers). Garnett's are the only extensive series of student letters to survive from this period.

[55] I hope to make an analysis of the works read by the Whigs the basis of a long work on colleges and the social history of ideas in the United States in the 19th century.

early in the 18th century and one of the most influential academic writers and scholars of his age.[56]

The category of "Natural Philosophy, Science, Mathematics, and Medicine" composes one of the smallest groups on the list. The students read classics such as Francis Bacon's *Essays* and Isaac Newton's *Works*. But the single most popular work in this category (and it is doubtful if it even belongs here) was a work by a fervent disciple of Rousseau, Bernardin de Saint-Pierre, best known as the author of *Paul et Virginie*. Saint-Pierre's *Studies of Nature* (1784) is a mixture of ardent nature-worship, exoticism, and pseudo-science. The second most popular book in this category was an even stranger—and perhaps most significant—work, Johann Kaspar Lavater's *Essays on Physiognomy* (1798), which eventually spawned the phrenology movement. A study of Lavater would lead naturally to the third most popular work, Benjamin Rush's *Medical Inquiries and Observations upon the Diseases of the Mind*. Somewhat sounder books in this category read by the students were the Marquis de Chaptal's *Elements of Chemistry* and the Comte de Buffon's *Works*. One hesitates on deciding in *which* category the poems of Erasmus Darwin—*The Loves of the Plants, The Botanic Garden*, or *The Temple of Nature*—should be placed. All of which suggests, perhaps, that to the average educated man of the early 19th century "science" still primarily connoted "natural philosophy."

The second largest segment of books on the list was made up of works of history and related subjects. The single most popular work here was David Hume's *History of England*. Oliver Goldsmith's *History of England* and his *History of Greece* were read, as were the historical works of three of the most popular historians of the 18th century, Gibbon, Voltaire (particularly his *Charles XII* and *Age of Lewis XIV*), and the Scotsman, William Robertson. American works were not slighted: John Marshall's *Washington* was read, as well as the histories of the Revolution by Mercy Otis Warren and David Ramsay.

Two categories together combine to make up almost half the volumes withdrawn by the Whigs from their library—poetry and fiction and the closely related topic of literary biography, criticism, etc. The classics of the Renaissance appear on the list: Tasso, Spenser, Burton, Milton, Cervantes, and, overwhelmingly, Shakespeare. As contemporary students in French colleges were probably doing, Princeton students read François de Fénelon's *Adventures of Telemachus* and the Abbé Barthelemy's *Travels of Anarcharsis*, two of the most widely circulated didactic novels of the 18th century, along with books now even more obscure, such as the works of Pietro Metastasio, mid-18th cen-

[56] Howell, *Eighteenth-century British Logic and Rhetoric*, 528.

tury court poet to the Austrian emperor, remembered today—if remembered at all—for his *Clemenza di Tito* (1734). The largest single segment in this category was made up of the English Augustan and neoclassical authors—Addison and Steele, Pope, Swift, Dr. Johnson, Goldsmith, Cowper, and others. The most popular novels were LeSage's *Gil Blas* and, above all others, Henry Fielding's *Tom Jones*. The most popular American novel was William Wirt's *Memoirs of the British Spy* (1803); the most widely read American man of letters, in one form or another, was Washington Irving.

Princeton students read the crucial texts of the early Romantic movement—Robert Bage's *Hermsprong*, a rhapsodic paen to natural man, Klopstock's interminable *Messiah*, Goethe's guidebook to adolescent revolt, *Goetz von Berlichingen*, and Wordsworth and Coleridge's *Lyrical Ballads*. They devoured Maria Edgeworth's genre studies of Irish country life (*The Absentee, Moral Tales, Scenes of Fashionable Life*, etc.), absorbing even today, and the works of her infinitely greater and more famous disciple, Sir Walter Scott. Each work of Lord Byron, from *English Bards and Scotch Reviewers* to *The Giaour*, was snapped up as soon as it appeared. One of the most influential books of the nineteenth century, Madame de Stäel's *Germany* (1813), was ordered when it was barely off the American presses. The students were as much at home with the two most influential journals in the English-speaking world, the Whiggish *Edinburgh Review* and the Tory *Quarterly Review*, as they were with the most prominent American journal of the time, Joseph Dennie's *Port Folio*.[57]

Students certainly read to escape the excruciating boredom created by Princeton winters and the limitations imposed by the "familial" college.[58] More important, they read in order to participate in the informal curriculum developed by themselves in the literary societies. The Whigs, for example, broke their membership down into an elaborate system of graded groups, each expected to pursue certain exer-

[57] For the British journals, see John Clive, *Scotch Reviewers: "The Edinburgh Review," 1802-1815* (Cambridge 1957). For the *Port-Folio*, see Frank Luther Mott, *A History of American Magazines, 1741-1850* (New York 1930), 218-52, and Harold M. Ellis, *Joseph Dennie and His Circle: A Study in American Literature from 1792 to 1812* (Austin, Tex. 1915).

[58] Cf. James Garnett to his mother, 13 February 1813: "It has not ceased to snow almost every day for a month, & if it continues any longer I shall be forced to run away; for I can not live without exercise, & Dr. Green has forbidden any noise or romping in the college—I was in hopes that we should have sufficient exercise in dancing and fencing; but I find with regard to that, that the students here have no more public spirit than you suppose they have at William & Mary." Garnett Papers.

cises during their stay in the society. If he successfully completed this course, the student would be awarded the society's diploma. The most frequent exercises were the compositions written by the individual students. James Garnett, for example, wrote essays on the following topics for the Whig Society in 1813 and 1814: Nature, The Improvement of the Mind, The Superiority of Beasts over Men, The Pleasures of Memory, Knowledge of Human Nature, The Farmer's Life, The Want of Independence, Party Spirit, and Genius.[59]

The composition topics were assigned by the more advanced members of the society, who also corrected them for grammar, spelling, punctuation, and to a lesser degree, content. (Student papers destined for a faculty member were supposed to be passed through this process before final submission.) We can reconstruct this informal curriculum for every member of the society. For example, in 1813-14 Charles Hodge, later a famous and influential Presbyterian theologian, wrote compositions on the following topics: The Education of Youth, Superstition, Envy, Friendship, On Reason and Revelation, Firmness, Happiness, Firmness and Decision of Character, and Love of Liberty.[60] One cannot escape the suspicion that the assignment of topics was deliberately tailored to a particular student's individual interests. Moreover, the composition topics appear often to have been assigned with a heuristic intent aimed at a particular student's faults. Did it seem to his peers that Charles Hodge lacked Firmness? Or, more likely had too much of it? Certainly this seems the most likely explanation for the constant assignment of the topic Drunkenness.

In the case of student compositions, art dictated experience. No matter what the immediate inspiration for assigning a particular topic, the subjects were usually couched in the idiom of the students' readings. They were framed, largely, in categories determined by the classics and by Augustan and neoclassical literature.[61] Consider the recurring

[59] From scattered entries in the *Whig Records/Minutes*, 1813-14.

[60] Ibid.

[61] The best general introduction to the intellectual world of this period is still John Theodore Merz's 1904-12 *A History of European Thought in the Nineteenth Century*, 4 vols. (New York 1965). For American literature and thought in this period, particularly valuable are the essays in Harry H. Clark, ed., *Transitions in American Literary History* (Durham, N.C. 1953), especially Leon Howard, "The Late Eighteenth Century: An Age of Contradictions," 49-90; M. F. Heiser, "The Decline of Neoclassicism, 1801-1848," 91-160, and G. Harrison Orians, "The Rise of Romanticism, 1805-1855," 161-244. The confusing and contradictory cultural trends of these years are best set forth in Robert Rosenblum, "Neoclassicism: Some Problems of Definition," in his *Transformations in Late Eighteenth Century Art* (Princeton 1967), 3-49.

composition topic of Luxury. In America luxury was condemned by Presbyterian and other Protestant ministers as early as the 1750s.[62] But clergymen had no monopoly on the topic. Abhorrence of luxury was a central concern and occasion for expression in 18th century British, American, and French thought and literature.[63] On opening the works of Oliver Goldsmith, one of the students' favorite poets, the Whig assigned the topic of Luxury could hardly have escaped these lines from Goldsmith's lament on the enclosure movement, *The Deserted Village* (1770):

> *O Luxury! thou curst by Heav'ns decree,*
> *How ill exchang'd are things like these for thee!*
> *How do thy potions, with insidious joy,*
> *Diffuse their pleasures only to destroy!*
> *Kingdoms by thee, to sickly greatness grown,*
> *Boast of a florid vigour not their own.*
> *At ev'ry draught more large and large they grow,*
> *A bloated mass of rank unwieldy woe;*
> *Till sapp'd their strength, and ev'ry part unsound,*
> *Down, down they sink, and spread a ruin around.*

The notion of luxury, in fact, is only one of many elements that go to make up a major theme in Western culture—the pastoral myth that so dominated the 18th century. Luxury led to dissipation, the destruction of empires, the depopulation of the countryside, the sucking of sturdy farmers—the backbone of the population—into cities. As Dr. Johnson, one of the students' favorite authors, put it in the greatest of Augustan odes, *London: A Poem* (1738):

> *London! the needy villain's gen'ral home,*
> *The common sewer of Paris, and of Rome;*
> *With eager thirst, by folly or by fate,*
> *Sucks in the dregs of each corrupted state.*
> *Forgive my transports on a theme like this,*
> *I cannot bear a French metropolis.*

Or New York, or Philadelphia, or Boston—and Thomas Jefferson would certainly have agreed. Perhaps it is unnecessary to continue:

[62] Miller, "Contracting Community," 101.

[63] There is no full-scale study of the idea of luxury in the 18th century. It has, of course, classical origins. For a study of pre-Revolutionary American uses of the concept, see Bailyn, *Ideological Origins*, 135-41. For a brilliant discussion of the place of the concept in Western thought from the Renaissance to the 18th century, see J.G.A. Pocock, "Virtue and Commerce in the Eighteenth Century," *J. Interdisciplinary Hist.* II (Summer 1972), 119-34.

most of the composition topics were directly inspired by the students' reading. The search for the self which the student necessarily conducted when he wrote was decisively shaped by the abstract, generalizing categories of the literature of Rome and Greece and of Augustan and neoclassical literature. By 1813 this style was thoroughly undermined by the Romantic movement, which developed a new sense of the self that could only have led to much student confusion and unrest. The 20th century has seen thousands of dim walking carbons of Jake Barnes, Holden Caufield, and Steppenwolf; the 18th and early 19th centuries had their mini-Addisons and would-be Byrons. Education both informs and forms; Tom Jones lives in all of us, Frodo never dies.

Today the student literary societies are remembered mainly for their debates. The debates, as we have seen, were only one part of a broader complex of activities. If the writing of compositions drew the student into the interior world of the *vita contemplativa*, the society's debates pushed him outward, upon the public stage of the *vita activa*. The student debates were in a way the capstone of the informal curriculum; they demanded much effort in preparation. For instance, on 20 December 1813 James Garnett and his friend Charles Oliver were assigned by their fellow Whigs to uphold the negative side in a New Year's Eve debate on the question, "Ought the right of suffrage to be extended to females." Garnett did not withdraw any work on women from the Whig Library. Instead, he renewed his loan of Lord Kames's *Elements of Criticism* (1762) which he had already had out of the library for three and a half weeks.[64] Kames's book was one of the most influential works on rhetoric written in the 18th century.[65] Garnett apparently studied Kames to good effect, for he and Oliver won the debate. In his somewhat stuffy way, Garnett was pleased. "Last night," he informed his parents on New Year's Day, "I performed the task of addressing a public audience, and you cannot imagine how much I felt relieved by its being over; I confess, however, that unlike other evils, it was much worse in anticipation than I found it to be in practice. It is certainly very unchristianlike to rejoice in the defeats of others; but I found great consolation in reflecting, that I should speak in company with one half of my class-mates, many of whom would succeed no better than myself."[66]

The debating topics had many origins: public affairs, personal concerns, long-standing philosophical, religious, and social questions. In 1812 the nation went into a hotly debated and widely opposed war.

[64] MS *Books Borrowed, American Whig Society*, I, 56, PUA.
[65] See Howell, *Eighteenth-Century British Logic and Rhetoric*, 377-78.
[66] *Whig Records/Minutes*, VII, PUA, meeting of 28 December 1813; Garnett to Mary E. Garnett, 1 January 1814, Garnett Papers.

For the next three years students discussed every aspect of public events, almost as they occurred. They discussed too the great domestic issues of the day, such as slavery. They debated on immediately personal questions, such as "Are early marriages conducive to happiness?" (5 August 1816). Some of the seemingly abstract propositions, such as the often-debated "Is a public or a private education more likely to produce intelligent and Virtuous citizens?" (31 May 1813), though traditional, probably began with a particular student. "Public education" then meant education in groups, while "private education" meant individual instruction by a tutor. It was a question that constantly agitated James Garnett. "Although I have made up my mind to remain here until I graduate," he told his mother, "rather than to quit this for the chance of finding a better college . . . nothing would give me greater pleasure than to pursue my studies at home, & should Uncle Hunter and my father procure a Private Tutor who could teach such branches of science as I would wish to study, I shall be willing at any time to leave this institution."[67]

Some propositions were drawn from the ancient stock of student debate questions. For instance, "Do Brutes possess reason?" (21 February 1815) derives from considerations of natural law. It was being debated by members of the Spy Club at Harvard as early as 1722, in the guise of "Whether the Souls of Brutes are Immortal."[68] Others, such as "Ought the Latin and Greek Languages to be made part of a liberal education?" (July 1815) were part of longstanding and also immediate educational concerns.[69] Samuel Smith would have preferred to limit them to the secondary level: Ashbel Green based Princeton's curriculum on them. Not only the composition topics but many of the debating topics as well derived from the students' reading. Thus, the question "Is there in human nature a principle of disinterested benevolence?" (12 April 1813), was possibly inspired by William Godwin's *An Enquiry Concerning Political Justice* (1793), for it perfectly expresses the main argument of the book. Through the public debate Godwin's ideas were spread among an audience many of whom probably never heard his name. The constant reappearance in one form or another of the question "Whether are the diversities of the human family, as of complexion and figure, referable to climate, or the original distinction" (13 January 1817) was in a way a tribute to Prince-

[67] 30 January 1813, Garnett Papers.
[68] William C. Lane, "The Telltale, 1721," *Publications of the Colonial Society of Massachusetts* 12 (January 1909), 220-31.
[69] Meyer Reinhold, "Opponents of Classical Learning during the Revolutionary Period," *Proceedings of the Am. Philosophical Soc.*, 112 (August 1968); McLachlan, *American Boarding Schools*, 40-41.

ton's former president, Samuel Stanhope Smith. It was precisely this question that Smith had addressed himself to in his classic *An Essay on the Causes of the Variety of Complexion and Figure in the Human Species* (1787), widely read among the Whigs.

The activities of the American Whig and other student societies outlined here suggest that the study of the formal curriculum of the early 19th century American college cannot be carried on in isolation from an equally intense study of the student extracurriculum. To do so produces a completely misleading—in fact, downright false—impression of the history of American higher education. That the early 19th century saw a retreat to basic drill within the formal curriculum seems unmistakable. But when we add the activities of the student literary societies to the formal curriculum we emerge with a completely different picture: a total educational process that was intellectually solid, rigorous, broad in scope, and surprisingly well tailored to the character and interests of the individual student. College faculties were perfectly well-aware of the value of the societies. At Princeton special rooms in college buildings were set aside solely for the use of the Whig and Cliosophic Societies. The surprising—and, at the moment, inexplicable—thing about the relation of the faculty to the student societies, however, is that it was almost nonexistent. At Princeton under Ashbel Green the faculty attitude toward the student societies seems to have been simply one of benign neglect.[70] We can conclude, however, that no history of American higher education is accurate without a full description of the student literary societies from their origins in the 1760s to their fading in the 1840s and 1850s, when they were gradually eclipsed by student fraternities. In the records of these scores of societies is preserved not only the basic social and intellectual history of the American college student but of the college itself.[71]

[70] The American Whig Society had both faculty and graduate members. Neither, however, appear to have taken part in any of the society's exercises. They merely availed themselves of their book-borrowing privileges. Ashbel Green's role in relation to Whig is particularly puzzling. In the years under study he made only one perfunctory appearance at a Society meeting. Yet he had helped reestablish Whig after the Revolution, when the college had been dispersed, and also went to the trouble of writing a history of the society. Whether or not the lack of relations between the literary societies and the faculty in these years was a peculiarity limited to Princeton or was generally true of other American colleges is uncertain. Jonathan Messerli's description of Horace Mann's education at Brown (where not even rooms were provided for the literary societies) in the same years suggests that the situation at Princeton was not unique. See Messerli, *Horace Mann, A Biography* (New York 1972), 47.

[71] The origins of permanent student organizations are at present unclear. Sheldon's *Student Life and Customs* is not helpful on this point. When John Witherspoon arrived at Princeton in 1768 he found two student societies (the Well-

Beyond the history of students, however, we must end with some broader questions: What was the aim of all the reading, the self-discipline, the writing of compositions and the endless debating? Why did boys want to go to Princeton or to other American colleges? Why did their parents send them? What was the goal the students were working towards so assiduously? What, finally, was the significance of the *Choice of Hercules*?

Curiously enough, historians have ignored the fact that in the late 18th and early 19th centuries the American college called itself and was called by others a *literary* institution. In the decades before and after 1800 the word "literature" had a far broader meaning than it carries at present. Today it has dwindled to "mere" literature—to fiction,

---

Meaning and the Plain-Dealing clubs, the precursors of Whig and Clio), which had been recently dissolved by the faculty. Witherspoon encouraged their re-formation in much the form that they are described above. It is possible that Witherspoon reshaped the societies in the image of the Scottish student societies of the mid-18th century (for the Scottish societies, see Howell, *Eighteenth-Century British Logic and Rhetoric*, 534), but this is unsure. The following list gives some indication of the extent of student societies in American colleges:

STUDENT SOCIETIES IN AMERICAN COLLEGES, 1750-1814

Year	Society	College
1750	Flat Hat Club	William and Mary
1750	Critonian	Yale
1753	Linonian	Yale
1765	American Whig	New Jersey
1765	Cliosophic	New Jersey
1768	Brothers in Unity	Yale
1770	Institute of 1770	Harvard
1771	Pronouncing	Brown
1776	Phi Beta Kappa	William and Mary
1776	Athenian	Queen's
1781	Phi Beta Kappa	Harvard
1783	Social Friends	Dartmouth
1786	United Fraternity	Dartmouth
1786	Belles Lettres	Dickinson
1787	Phi Beta Kappa	Dartmouth
1789	Union Philosophical	Dickinson
1791	Porcellian	Harvard
1791	Franklin	Jefferson
1794	Philermenian	Brown
1795	Dialectic	North Carolina
1795	Hasty-Pudding Club	Harvard
1795	Philanthropic	North Carolina
1795	Philologian	Williams
1795	Philotechnian	Williams
1795	Philomathean	Union

verse, and drama. In 1800 it meant, roughly, all knowledge; it conveyed much of the sense of the present German word *Wissenschaft*. Students went to college to become men of knowledge, men of literature, men of letters—to become *literati*.[72] Parents and guardians were clear about their motives in sending their sons to Princeton and to other colleges. "I have always considered you possessing Talents," a Princeton alumnus wrote to his student nephew in 1816, "which, if improved, might render you an ornament to Society, and a useful Character in the literary World. . . . While the multitude of mankind are grovelling in the Earth, convince them that you possess more escalted [*sic*] views . . . and that your wish is not to live for yourself alone, but for the benefit of Society, and for the glory of that divine being who hath created you, and endowed you with superior mental faculties, to the end that you might improve them for valuable and important purposes."[73] Students too agreed that becoming a member of the literary world was demanding but inspiring. "The manner in which I spend my time is attended with more labour than your present occupation," a Princeton student of 1812 wrote to his brother. "The satisfaction which is to be derived from the acquirement of literature, I acknowledge, is a sufficient compensation, yet when the labour alone is considered it must be acknowledged that the student's life is more irksome than that of either the farmer or the merchant."[74] The goal of the college—and,

STUDENT SOCIETIES IN AMERICAN COLLEGES, 1750-1814 (*cont'd*)

Year	Society	College
1796	Adelphic	Union
1801	Demosthenian	Georgia
1802	Athenaean	Bowdoin
1802	Philolexian	King's
1803	Phi Sigma Nu	Vermont
1805	Peucinian	Bowdoin
1805	Philo	Jefferson
1806	Peithologian	King's
1806	United Brothers	Brown
1807	Philological	Pennsylvania
1813	Philomathean	Pennsylvania
1814	Phoenix	Hamilton
1814	Union	Hamilton

[72] For a lengthy example of this usage see Samuel Miller, *A Brief Retrospect of the Eighteenth Century*, 2 vols. (New York, 1803), II, 384-85, and esp. ch. xxvi, "Nations Lately become Literary."

[73] Abraham Bancker to Anthony Rutgers, 26 November 1816, Rare Book and Manuscript Room, Firestone Library, Princeton.

[74] Joseph Warren Helme to Nathan W. Helme, 2 February 1812, Rare Book and Manuscript Room, Firestone Library.

even more, of the literary society—was to transform the student into a man of letters.

This had not always been the case. Colleges, apparently, only began to be thought of as "literary" institutions in the 1760s. Looking for motives for Princeton's founding, Samuel Blair, Jr., the college's first historian, writing in 1764, concluded that "affairs of state also became embarrassed for want of proper direction, and a competent number of men of letters, to fill the various political offices. The bench, the bar, the seats of legislation, required such accomplishments, as are seldom the spontaneous growth of Nature, unimproved by education."[75] Wrong for the 1740s, Blair's description was accurate about the aims of the 1760s. The "man of letters" he described was meant to fill a lofty role indeed.

The idea of the man of letters originated in the same milieu that saw the rebirth of the myth of the *Choice of Hercules*—Renaissance humanism. It was based squarely on the revival of the Greek and Roman classics, particularly Cicero, and more particularly on Cicero's model of the orator, that ideal civic leader who combined in equal measure eloquence and learning, or, rhetoric and philosophy. For Cicero, as one historian has described it, "wisdom without eloquence was of little use to civic life, eloquence separate from wisdom was often of great harm; only the man who joined the two could bring true benefit to himself and his fellow men."[76] To the Ciceronian model of the orator the humanists added the element of a sincere Christian faith. It was no accident that when Odoardo Cardinal Farnese was called upon to become regent of the family duchy of Parma he ruled successfully as the perfect humanist prince.[77] The Christian and the classical elements of the ideal—as in the Farnese *Choice of Hercules* and the Princeton *Choice of Hercules* are inseparably intertwined.

The passage of the humanist ideal of the man of letters through the 17th and 18th centuries has never been properly charted. By the 18th century the ideal education for the man of letters was thought to be saturation in the study of belles lettres. The ideal—and the very phrase

[75] *An Account of the College of New-Jersey. In which are described the Methods of Government, Modes in Instruction, Manner and Expenses of Living . . .* (Woodbridge, N.J. 1764), 5, 6. The term "literati" itself was in general usage in America at least as early as the 1740s. A newspaper account of Princeton's first commencement, in 1748, reads thus: Harvard and Yale, "one or the other had been the *Alma Mater* of most of the *Literati* then present." *New York Gazette Revived in Weekly Post-Boy*, 21 November 1748.

[76] Jerrold E. Seigel, *Rhetoric and Philosophy in Renaissance Humanism: The Union of Eloquence and Wisdom, Petrarch to Valla* (Princeton 1968), 6.

[77] See Giovanna R. Solari, *The House of Farnese: A Portrait of A Great Family of the Renaissance* (New York 1968), 212-13.

—entered permanently into the English language with the translation from the French in 1734 of Charles Rollin's *De la Maniere d'Enseigner et d'Etudier les Belles Lettres* (Paris 1728). Rollin's work, Wilbur Samuel Howell has written, established the term belles lettres "as a generalized word for an entity made up of languages, poetry, rhetoric, history, moral philosophy and physics." Together with Hugh Blair's 1783 *Lectures on Rhetoric and Belles Lettres*, Rollin's work gave the terms belles lettres and rhetoric "a reference to all the forms of discourse—orations, historical works, philosophical treatises and dialogues, epistles, fiction, pastoral poems, tragedies, and comedies."[78] Both works were widely read by Princeton Whigs. Better than anyone else in America, John Witherspoon implemented the ideal of the man of letters—though he used the older term "orator." "By orator," Howell has observed, Witherspoon meant not only "the parliamentary speaker, the legal speaker, and the preacher, but also the scientific writer, the historian, the controversialist, the writer of epistles and essays and dialogues, and the poet in his minor capacities, and in his epic and dramatic might."[79] It was an ideal which would pervade American colleges for at least a century.

The Princeton Whigs were not the first Americans to feel that the myth of the *Choice of Hercules* perfectly symbolized their ideology and goals. In 1776 John Adams had suggested exactly the same device for the Great Seal of the United States. Adams, along with Benjamin Franklin and Thomas Jefferson, was appointed by Congress to a committee charged with designing a Great Seal for the new nation. "I proposed the Choice of Hercules," Adams reported to his wife,

> as engraved by Gribeline in some Editions of Lord Shaftesburys Works. The Hero resting on his Clubb. Virtue pointing to her rugged Mountain, on one Hand, and perswading him to ascend. Sloth, glancing at her flowery Paths of Pleasure, wantonly reclining on the Ground, displaying the Charms both of her Eloquence and Person, to seduce him into Vice. But his is too complicated a Group for a Seal or Medal, and it is not original.[80]

[78] Howell, *Eighteenth-Century British Logic and Rhetoric*, 533, 535.

[79] Ibid. 676.

[80] John Adams to Abigail Adams, 14 August 1776, in L. H. Butterfield, ed., *Adams Family Correspondence*, 2 vols. (Cambridge 1963), II, 96-97. Every conceivable manner of painting the *Choice of Hercules* was discussed at some length by the Earl of Shaftesbury in his 1713 pamphlet, *A Notion of the Historical Draught or Tablature of the Judgement of Hercules*. . . . The pamphlet was reprinted in Anthony Ashley Cooper, 3d Earl of Shaftesbury, *Characteristicks*, 3 vols. (London 1732), III, 347-91. This work in turn was included in the library of former President Samuel Stanhope Smith which was purchased by the college

Adams was correct: the myth was not original by 1776. The *Choice of Hercules* was a favorite subject among antiquaries of the 18th century.[81] Men of John Adams' time were familiar with it not only from their own reading of the classics or the widely circulated works of Shaftesbury, but from sources such as Johann Sebastian Bach's cantata of 1733, *Hercules auf dem Scheidewege*. The grounds of the country houses of the Whig nobility of England were littered with physical testaments to the attraction of the myth and the ideas it personified. At Stowe, in Buckinghamshire, described by one historian as the "capital seat of . . . the Grand Whiggery," the Temple family and their associates created a whole ideologically determined landscape, replete with a classic *Temple of Ancient Virtue* and a *Temple of Modern Virtue*—the latter built, naturally enough, as a ruin. At Stourhead, in Wiltshire, a Whig magnate erected an enormous *Temple of Virtue* which contained as its centerpiece a large statue of that exemplar of all civic virtues, Hercules.[82] Compared with physical manifestations of the attraction of the myth on such a grand scale, John Adams' suggestions for a seal or the Princeton Whigs' painting seems modest indeed.

In 18th century England and America notions of Virtue and the myth of the *Choice of Hercules* were both associated with a particular intellectual tradition—the "Old Whig," "Commonwealth," or "Country" ideology. As J.G.A. Pocock has described it,

> the Country ideology carried into the eighteenth century . . . a Renaissance pessimism concerning the direction and reversibility of social and historical change. The health of the balanced constitution

for $1250 in 1812. (See MS, "Catalogue of Books in Dr. S. S. Smith's Library," Manuscript Department, Firestone Library.) In other words, the Whigs had access to a detailed and expert discussion of how to go about painting a *Choice of Hercules*. Whether they consulted Shaftesbury or not is uncertain. Important iconographical differences between the Shaftesbury and Princeton versions would suggest that they did not. (I.e., no poet, philosophers, or group of bacchantes appear in the Shaftesbury *Hercules*, while all are present in the Princeton version.) The Gribelin engraving to which John Adams referred is reproduced in Butterfield, *Adams Family Correspondence*, II, following 102. See too the editorial comments, ix-x. For an example of a *Choice of Hercules* which follows Shaftesbury closely, see Benjamin West's 1764 version, reprinted in Grose Evans, *Benjamin West and the Taste of His Times* (Carbondale, Ill. 1952), plate 20.

[81] Edgar Wind, *Pagan Mysteries in the Renaissance*, rev. ed. (London 1967), 81, n.2.

[82] Christopher Hussey, "Stowe, Buckinghamshire: I—The Connection of Georgian Landscape with Whig Politics," *Country Life* 102 (1947), 526-29; Kenneth Woodbridge, *Landscape and Antiquity: Aspects of English Culture at Stourhead, 1718-1858* (London 1970).

lay in the independence of its parts; should a change or disturbance bring one of these into dependence upon another, a degenerative trend would commence which would soon become almost impossible to remedy. Similarly—or indistinguishably—the moral health of the civic individual consisted in his independence from governmental or social superiors, the precondition of his ability to concern himself with the public good, *res publica*, or commonweal. Should he lose the economic foundations of this ability (i.e., independent property), or be demoralized by an exclusive concern with private or group satisfactions, a comparable imbalance or disturbance in the civic and social foundations of moral personality would set in which would also prove irreversible. The name most tellingly used for balance, health, and civic personality was 'virtue,' the name of its loss was 'corruption.' "[83]

The "Country" ideology was the ideology of the American Revolution and of the early American Republic. The Princeton Whigs were the natural heirs of this tradition. However, the Country idea of Virtue was essentially static.[84] Between 1776 and 1819 a gradual change in Americans' attitudes toward Virtue took place. Americans began to shift toward the idea that self-interest and popular consent among the populace could furnish a sufficient and stable foundation for republican government, rather than insisting that such a polity could only be sustained by a "Virtuous" people.[85] However, concern with Virtue and with the myth of the *Choice of Hercules* did not disappear as a consequence. Instead, the notion of Virtue acquired a dynamic element and the application of the myth of the *Choice of Hercules* was narrowed. A reexamination of the emblems of the American Whig Society and the Farnese *Choice of Hercules* will clarify these changes.

The *Choice of Hercules* commissioned by the Whigs in 1819 replaced an earlier device designed by Charles Fenton Mercer of the class of 1797, engraved in 1799-1800 (Fig. 5).[86] Mercer, a brilliant young Virginian (and an uncle of James Mercer Garnett) graduated

[83] Pocock, "Virtue and Commerce in the Eighteenth Century;" 121.

[84] Ibid.; see too Jerrold E. Seigel, "*Virtú* in and since the Renaissance," in the appropriate volume of the "Dictionary of the History of Ideas," forthcoming. I am grateful to Professor Seigel for permitting me to consult a manuscript version of this essay.

[85] John R. Howe, Jr., *The Changing Political Thought of John Adams* (Princeton 1966), 28-58; Gordon S. Wood, *The Creation of the American Republic 1776-1787* (Chapel Hill 1969), 610-11, 48-53, 65-70.

[86] Beam, *American Whig Society*, 113, 59.

first in his class and later became a distinguished congressman and an ardent advocate of the abolition of the slave trade.[87] His device symbolizes perfectly elements of the Country ideology, neoclassical ideas of the basis and aims of education, and of the making of the man of letters.

The main scene of the device is enclosed within an oval cartouche. Supporting the cartouche on the left are a globe and four volumes marked, respectively: Moral Philosophy, Antiquities, Belles Lettres, and Philology. Supporting the cartouche on the right are five volumes, marked: Statutes, Natural Philosophy, Mathematics, Natural History, and Logic. The cartouche is surmounted by an emblem of two hands shaking each other on a bed of clouds. At the center of the scene within the oval the engraving depicts a helmeted Minerva or Pallas (a figure commonly used to symbolize wisdom)[88] guiding a youth who holds a book. The youth faces a choice of two ways: a low and easy one leading to a distant body of water, or a rough and craggy one leading to a mountain—doubtless Parnassus—surmounted by a columned Temple of Virtue. The left side of the picture seems to represent the actual process of education. Five youths stand or sit on the steps of a neoclassical monument, which consists of steps, a plinth, and surmounting the plinth a tablet on which are engraved the names Demosthenes, Xenophon, Homer, Cicero, Tacitus, and Virgil. A standing youth orates, and is watched by a crouching one; one youth sketches the orator; one reads, and another appears to be computing. Though the composition as a whole is naive and overcrowded, it symbolizes the activities and goals of the Whigs of 1799 as well as the *Choice of Hercules* symbolizes the goals of the Whigs of 1819.

The differences between the two pictures are significant. The 1799 device reflects a sunny optimism. There seems no doubt but that the student will follow the rough, narrow way to the fame and distinction of Parnassus, based upon the education his fellows are still pursuing. The broad way is so indistinct as to be almost invisible. Minerva guides all; the youth is barely faced with choice of any sort. The attainment of Virtue will be an essentially static process. A generation later, however, in the *Choice of Hercules* of 1819, no such superficial optimism is present. Hercules does indeed appear to have decided in favor of Virtue, but the temptations of Pleasure/Vice are overwhelmingly apparent. The 1819 device has recognized the temptations of sensuality, perhaps even the forces of the unconscious, in a way the earlier one blithely ignores. The neohumanistic *Choice of Hercules* puts the

[87] For Mercer, see *DAB*, XI, 539.

[88] Guy de Tervarent, *Attributs et Symboles dans l'Art Profane, 1450-1600: Dictionnaire d'un Langue Perdu*, 2 vols. (Geneva 1958), I, 270-71.

individual student face to face with a clear personal, moral decision about the course of his life, a problem which the 1797 device evades. Mercer's composition reflects, perhaps, the sunnier Enlightenment faith in the infinite progress of Reason as well as the static 18th century conception of Virtue. The *Choice of Hercules* of 1819, on the other hand, suggests that the attainment of Virtue will be a dynamic and uncertain process. It presages the moral agonies of the Victorian age, in which, as Walter Houghton has observed, the "Christian life became in literal fact a life of constant struggle—both to resist temptation and to master the desires of the ego."[89]

A last comparison of the iconography of the Princeton *Choice of Hercules* with that of the Farnese *Choice* suggests a dramatic development in notions of the ideal and role of the man of letters between the 16th and the 19th centuries. In the Farnese *Choice* the man of letters —or poet—in the lower left-hand corner plays an important, but subordinate, role. If the hero chooses Virtue, the painting suggests, he will be celebrated and immortalized by the *literati*. Almost precisely the same figure of the poet appears in the Princeton version—on the right-hand side, among a group of scholars. However, in the Princeton *Choice* Virtue does not simply offer literary immortality to the hero if he makes the correct choice: she is, apparently, suggesting to Hercules that the proper role for the hero is *to become* a man of letters. In the Princeton *Choice of Hercules* the 19th century man of letters—not the Virtuous prince—is presented to the students as the culture-shaping hero.

Some early 19th century students, as always, chose Pleasure. Thousands of other youths, molded in the student societies, chose the way of Virtue. They would follow the path of Hercules; they would try, in Cicero's phrase, "to save the world," to do great deeds for mankind. Equipped with a profound faith in the power of oratory, of the pen, and of the printed word, the neohumanistic man of letters of 19th century America saw himself as a culture-shaping hero, bent on the reformation of society according to the ideals transmitted in the student societies and colleges. Some would try to reshape existing institutions according to these ideals, or to embody them in new institutions. Others were among the leaders in the scores of reform movements that characterized the United States of the 1810s, 1820s, and 1830s. Like the humanists of the 16th century, the neohumanistic men of letters of the 19th century often found their efforts misunderstood, their actual effects ambiguous, the grand reformation of society they strove for elusive.

[89] *The Victorian Frame of Mind, 1830-1870* (New Haven 1957), 233.

Vice, Virtue, Hercules—by the end of the Victorian period it would all seem somewhat meaningless to a later student generation. The triad lingers on in a Whig emblem of 1876 (Fig. 2), but it is rather perfunctory. Hercules is a puzzled youth in an ill-fitting bikini, Virtue gestures toward the owl of wisdom, Vice toward the peacock of Vanity. A man of letters dangles like a pendant unrelated to the total composition. The prospective man of letters seems to have been metamorphosed into an aspiring football player.

In the late 19th century the gods fell ill; weakened, they were wounded in World War I and died again. In 1921 the Princeton Whigs retired the *Choice of Hercules* as their main device.[90]

[90] Beam, *American Whig Society*, 114. As a last word, I might note that the Cliosophic Society also had engraved devices dating from the same period. They are now in the PUA.

10

University Reformers and Professorial Scholarship in Germany 1760-1806

by R. Steven Turner

Traditional histories have always regarded the 18th century as an era of institutional and intellectual decline for the German university system. They point out that the century of Aufklärung brought little to the German universities beyond falling enrollments, contracting budgets, and incessant attacks, often well-merited, from critics of every stamp. And while they detect at individual institutions during the later period from 1760 to 1800 marked signs of reform and revitalization, the first true wave of recovery and prosperity nevertheless arrived only during the early 19th century. Occasionally traditional histories have gone further to trace this lingering 18th century malaise into the field of professorial scholarship as well. There they detect primarily pedantry, encyclopedic repetition, and little which could be called original or innovative. Obviously the developments in philology, history, and the sciences pioneered by scholars at the University of Göttingen and many individuals at other institutions constitute important exceptions to this generalization. But traditional histories correctly note that these innovations had found little echo in the university system at large before 1790. For most institutions, although by no means for all, the later 18th century remained a period of relative stagnation for many traditional academic disciplines.

Especially where scholarship is concerned the universities of the later 18th century suffer in any comparison with those of the early 19th. Historians have always regarded the years from 1806 to 1835 as decisive in the renewal of the German university system and in the transformation of the universities' relation to scholarship. Between 1806 and 1818 the Humboldtian educational reforms in Prussia rationalized university administration, modernized and consolidated existing institutions, and founded new universities at Berlin and Bonn. The same period produced a renaissance in German scholarship associated with the names of the brothers Grimm, Karl Lachmann, Franz Bopp, F. C. Savigny, and Barthold Niebuhr.[1] By 1835 most universities in

---

[1] On the development of classical philology in Germany see John Edwin Sandys, *A History of Classical Scholarship* (Cambridge 1908), vol. 3, and Wilamowitz-Moellendorff, *Geschichte der Philologie*, vol. 1 of *Einleitung in die*

northern Germany had already begun to assume, both in rhetoric and in practice, new functions as centers of scholarly and scientific research in addition to their traditional role as professional schools. In defense of this commitment they could point to the "Humboldtian ideology" laid down by Humboldt, Fichte, and Schleiermacher, with its stress on creativity, discovery, research, and a growing, organismic concept of learning.[2] When mature, this "research ethos" would lead to the great university institutes of the late 19th century and to the new model for the organization of science and learning which they embodied. In 1790, however, the university system still afforded few hints of these innovations to come.

By comparison with the glories of the Humboldtian era, the later 18th century appears often as a pale prelude of decay and pedantry.[3] In part this comparison accounts for the darker hues in which historians have often portrayed the intellectual history of the universities in the decades before the reform period. Furthermore, this unfavorable comparison has been carried over into examinations not only of the actual achievements of university scholarship during the 18th century, but also of the attitudes of academics toward scholarship and research. In contrast to the research ethos of the *Vormärz* era, the traditional interpretation insists that before 1800 the universities regarded themselves chiefly as pedagogical institutions whose function was to transmit and to propagate, but not necessarily to expand, existing learning. Only later during the reform era, the interpretation goes on, did the

---

Altertumswissenschaft (Leipzig 1921), 45-61. On modern German historiography see Eduard Fueter, *Geschichte der neueren Historiographie* (Munich 1936), esp. 415-42, 461-96, and George Peabody Gooch, *History and Historians in the Nineteenth Century*, 2d ed. (New York 1935), 18-102. The rise of Germanic philology is treated in Rudolf von Raumer, *Geschichte der germanischen Philologie* (Munich 1870), 292-378.

[2] The major treatises upon this theme by Schelling, Fichte, Schleiermacher, Steffens, and Humboldt are collected in *Die Idee der deutschen Universität*, ed. Ernst Anrich (Darmstadt 1964). For F. A. Wolf's ideas see *Ueber Erziehung, Schule, Universität*, ed. Wilhelm Körte (Leipzig 1835). The German secondary literature upon this new university ideology is immense. See particularly Helmut Schelsky, *Einsamkeit und Freiheit: Idee und Gestalt der deutschen Universität und ihrer Reformen* (Reinbek 1963). An excellent English discussion of the basic categories of the new ideology is found in Fritz K. Ringer, *The Decline of the German Mandarins. The German Academic Community, 1890-1933* (Cambridge 1969), 85-96. Also see Friedrich Paulsen, *Die deutschen Universitäten und das Universitätsstudium*, 2d ed. (Hildesheim 1966), 204-05ff.

[3] Alexander Busch, *Die Geschichte des Privatdozenten* (Stuttgart 1959), 13-14, esp. nn. 29, 30, and 31; also see Paulsen, *The German Universities and University Study*, trans. Frank Thilly (New York 1906), 40.

professor adopt the further duty of expanding scholarship and come to regard research and teaching as linked inseparably to each other.

In contrast to the careful study which has been devoted to the thought of the Humboldtian reformers and to the emergence of the new scholarship, little notice has been taken of the corresponding efforts of 18th century theorists to define the relation of the professoriate to the advance of scholarship. The following essay attempts to evaluate these theoretical efforts, and so to provide a basis for tentatively reevaluating the traditional interpretation of the professoriate's outlook on scholarship. Restricting its scope largely to the University of Göttingen and the universities in Prussia, it asks how German academics of the later 18th century actually did assess the universities' obligation to the advance of scholarship. It points out first how familiar institutional conditions and patterns of recruitment bore upon the professor's attitude toward learning. Second, it samples the opinions of university critics, theorists, and reformers on the subject of professorial publication and scholarship.[4] In some respects the results of this examination confirm the traditional view; yet on a deeper level they also point to fundamental inadequacies in its assumptions. What divided the late 18th and early 19th centuries on the issue of professorial scholarship, this essay will argue, was more than merely different assessments of its desirability within the university context. The difference rather involved widely divergent assumptions about the nature of scholarship, its organization, its method of advancement, and its relation to teaching. Clarifying these two differing visions of scholarship not only explicates important issues affecting German academic life in the later 18th century, but also helps to set in historical context the Humboldtian reforms of the early 19th.

I. THE INSTITUTIONAL SETTING

In the 18th century as in the 19th, few professors escaped the trammels of institutional affiliation to lead the pure life of the mind. The pressures of the institutional setting affected both the scholarship carried out by individual professors and also the effectiveness of individual universities as centers of teaching and academic learning. These pressures seemed especially severe to academics of the later 18th century, for all contemporaries considered this a time of severe crisis for the German university system. Enrollment statistics in particular suggest

---

[4] The sources for such a sampling are readily at hand. The 18th crisis of the universities provoked numerous treatises attacking or defending the universities. On this literature see Rene König's brief but invaluable treatment in *Vom Wesen der deutschen Universität* (Berlin 1935), 34-39.

the dimensions of that crisis. As late as 1720 some 4400 students had matriculated into the various German universities. But from mid-century on the level of matriculation dropped precipitously to 3400 in 1790 and plummeted to 2900 in 1800. Only Göttingen partly escaped the falling enrollments; even Halle, Leipzig, and Jena experienced severe decline, while smaller schools like Erfurt and Rostock suffered crippling losses.[5] Professors, especially those in the arts or philosophical faculties, depended heavily upon student fees to supplement their small government salaries. As this source of income diminished, many teachers found themselves in severe financial straits. For the system as a whole it meant constantly fewer funds with which to attract competent teachers and to modernize a curriculum already widely recognized to be in need of expansion.[6]

The effects of falling enrollment would have been less severe had it not been for Germany's chronic overabundance of universities. In accordance with what Friedrich Paulsen called the "territorial-confessional" principle of university administration, each tiny German state strove to support its own provincial university. Even in periods of high enrollment, therefore, the number of students was divided among an excessive number of schools.[7] Reformers complained that this condition harmed the intellectual as well as the financial life of the institutions. J. D. Michaelis in his 1768 study of the Protestant universities noted that "the number of students is so divided that the number can be only moderate at any university, and then the best and most schol-

[5] Franz Eulenburg, *Die Frequenz der deutschen Universitäten* . . . (Leipzig 1904), 132. The following statistics are reproduced from Eulenburg (132, Fig. 6):

Approximate Total Matriculations in German Universities

Five-Year Intervals 1700-1805					
1700	4180	1740	4400	1780	3500
1705	4300	1745	4000	1785	3700
1710	4200	1750	4370	1790	3400
1715	4300	1755	4000	1795	3180
1720	4400	1760	3670	1800	2920
1725	4070	1765	3700	1805	2980
1730	4200	1770	3400		
1735	4300	1775	3600		

Source: Eulenburg, p. 132, Fig. 6.
Note: For the enrollments of individual universities, see Eulenburg, 164-65.

[6] See Busch, *Privatdozenten*, 14.

[7] The smallest of the institutions, mostly tiny Catholic universities in the south, were hardly universities at all. Although Strassburg and Ingolstadt remained among the best of the second-rank universities, other Catholic institutions like Paderborn, Gratz, and Bamberg lost their university status during the century; see Eulenburg, *Frequenz*, 207.

arly professor must be satisfied if he can fill . . . his few 'bread courses.' " All professors, Michaelis went on, must neglect the teaching of basic scholarship (*grundliche Gelehrsamkeit*) because there are too few students to make advanced or scholarly courses possible.[8] This condition, especially aggravated in smaller institutions, hampered the universities in fulfilling their role as centers of high academic culture.

A few reformers recognized a more insidious threat to the universities in the decay of the philosophical faculties. Heirs to the medieval faculties of arts, the philosophical faculties had originally dispensed a general, propaedeutic education to students who would later enter the upper, professional faculties. Late in the 17th century, however, secondary schools had begun to usurp this traditional propaedeutic function. Students began to matriculate directly into the professional faculties, bypassing or neglecting the lower. After 1700 the philosophical faculties declined in importance and deteriorated to direct preparatory schools dispensing auxiliary learning for professional study.[9] Accordingly both the prestige and the income from chairs in the lower faculty reached their nadir in the 18th century. At Prussia's Frankfurt-an-Oder in 1721 salaries in the philosophical faculty ranged from 100 to 175 thaler yearly, while those in the theological, juridical, and medical faculties amounted respectively to 557-338, 500-200, and 300-100 thaler yearly.[10] Furthermore, although professors in the higher faculties could and invariably did supplement their income by practicing the profession they taught, professors in the philosophical faculty usually had no auxiliary calling open to them except secondary teaching, which was notoriously unprofitable. Frequently chairs in the lower faculty were not considered independent positions at all, but temporary "first posts" in which perseverance would be rewarded by a promotion to a higher faculty. Often a professor from a higher faculty would hold a chair in the lower simultaneously and, of course, draw the salary from both.[11] These practices furthered the decay of the lower faculties throughout the late 18th century.

[8] [J. D. Michaelis], *Raisonnement über die protestantschen Universitäten in Deutschland*, 4 vols. (Frankfurt 1768), I, 209; also see 247ff. This and all subsequent translations from the German are my own unless otherwise indicated.

[9] Eulenburg, *Frequenz*, 138-39.

[10] Conrad Bornhak, *Geschichte der preussischen Universitätsverwaltung bis 1810* (Berlin 1900), 113.

[11] Joseph Engel, "Die deutschen Universitäten und die Geschichtswissenschaft," *Hundert Jahre Historische Zeitschrift, 1859-1959* (Munich 1959), 248-49; A. Tholuck, *Das akademische Leben des siebzehnten Jahrhunderts* (Halle 1853), 57-58; Franz Schnabel, *Sigismund von Reitzenstein, der Begründer des badischen Staates* (Heidelberg 1927), 86; Bornhak, *Universitätsverwaltung*, 23. For a contemporary account see Johann Christoph Hoffbauer, *Geschichte der Universität zu Halle bis zum Jahre 1805* (Halle 1805), 159-60.

This decay proved injurious to the universities for two reasons. First, it strengthened the image of the universities, not as centers of culture and liberal education, but as utilitarian professional schools. This in turn opened the universities to the attacks of critics who claimed that such professional education could better be dispensed within another institutional context. Still more serious, the contraction of the philosophical faculty lessened the number of teachers and scholars in the universities who had a direct, professional interest in the new developments in mathematics, science, and history. Just as these disciplines were entering periods of vigorous expansion late in the 18th century, the universities' ability to absorb these innovations into their traditional structure was becoming more and more feeble. Critics were quick to charge the universities with intellectual obsolescence, an obsolescence which had its institutional basis largely in the decline of the lower faculty.

As the universities never tired of pointing out, many of their troubles were ultimately financial. As income from student fees dwindled, territorial princes hesitated to sink money into their feeble universities. In Prussia state outlay for universities remained constant under Frederick William I and Frederick the Great; only at the succession of Frederick William II in 1787 did the state allot an extra 10,000 thaler yearly for its universities. Even this significant increase brought the annual government outlay to only 43,000 thaler, while it had been 26,000 almost a century before in 1697.[12] Although these figures refer to only one state, Prussia seems to have been typical in its approach to financing its universities. Government expenditures remained static throughout the late 18th century, even as the universities experienced new pressures to expand their curricula and to found medical clinics, libraries, and physical cabinets.

Falling enrollments, the decay of the lower faculty, government neglect—these difficulties expressed institutionally a malaise much deeper and more chronic. All during the 18th century the immense prestige of the universities, the very ideal of university education, had been slipping perceptibly away. One unmistakable sign of this loss lay in the growing number of attacks upon the universities. Critics of the universities were not new to the German scene, nor were they necessarily an unhealthy sign; throughout the century critics' ranks included many academics and administrators who combined criticism with their goal of moderate reform. After 1750, however, a more portentous and more radical critical tradition had come rapidly forward. Throughout

[12] Conrad Varrentrapp, *Johannes Schulze und das höhere preussische Unterrichtswesen in seiner Zeit*, 509; also see Wilhelm Schrader, *Geschichte der Friedrichs-Universität zu Halle*, 2 vols. (Berlin 1894), I, 566-73.

the 18th century Germany had experienced the growth of an urban intelligentsia which possessed few ties to the old academic system. This emerging group included journalists and literati, progressive bureaucrats, academicians, pedagogical theorists, and certain professional groups. Unhampered by loyalties to the older academic culture and fired by the Enlightenment's impatience with what it viewed as anachronistic institutions, representatives of this critical tradition began after 1760 to attack the universities with a vehemence unprecedented in previous decades. They no longer attacked curriculum and methods alone, but also the most basic institutions of the universities: corporate government, the lecture, and the division into faculties. Occasionally critics even impugned the integrity of the professoriate as a professional group and with increasing frequency called for the outright abolition of the universities.[13]

One line of attack adopted by critics alleged a general intellectual obsolescence on the part of the universities and cited in particular their neglect of such subjects as history, science, and modern languages. In the name of Aufklärung critics denounced the universities for their outmoded, medieval constitutions and their pedantic curriculum still mired in Wolffian philosophy, theological dogmatism, and the Latin *imitatis*. "The creation of our universities," wrote Christian G. Salzmann, "occurred in a time when the world was still poor in books, and a man who could read and write was still a rarity. And the universities would also like to be useful today. But now they make as sorry a figure as a fortress built during the crusades in a war in which men use bombs and cannons. . . ."[14] The universities' function as professional schools, other critics wrote, could be better met by dissolving the old universities with their scholastic anachronisms and their corporate intransigence and founding separate academies for professional education. Their function as centers of scholarship, critics pointed out, had already been largely usurped by the academies of arts and sciences like that founded by Leibniz at Berlin (1700), that at Göttingen (1751), and that at Munich (1759).[15] These institutions had been founded to advance and to promulgate learning, and they operated free of corporate restraints and medieval vestiges. At the peak of their

[13] König, *Wesen*, 22-29; also Adolf Stözel, "Die Berliner Mittwochsgesellschaft über Aufhebung oder Reform der Universitäten (1795)," *Forschung zur brandenburgischen und preussischen Geschichte*, II (Leipzig 1889), 201-22.

[14] *Carl von Carlsberg oder über das menschliche Elend* (Carlsruhe 1784), I, 341; also see 168-73, 236-341, and 82-86.

[15] Karl Biedermann, *Deutschland im achtzehnten Jahrhundert*, 2 vols. (Leipzig 1854), II, 661; J. H. Campe, *Allgemeine Revision des gesammten Schul- und Erziehungswesens* (Vienna 1792), XVI, 174-83; Stözel, *Mittwochsgesellschaft*, 201-4, and passim.

confidence and vigor by 1760, the academies had not only become centers for the promulgation of Enlightenment ideas, but also the undisputed leaders of scholarly inquiry into such fields as science, mathematics, and history. The century of Aufklärung had no place for the universities, critics wrote, and had already produced alternative institutions.

Inseparable from the former line of attack was that which criticized the universities for their pedagogical failure. J. H. Pestalozzi had formulated an ideal of education based upon freedom, nature study, and individual observation and discovery. J. B. Basedow and the Philanthropists combined with these ideals an emphasis on utilitarian subjects, modern languages, and physical development. Teaching, both insisted, was an art, a profession which required professionally trained practitioners.[16] Against these new pedagogical ideals stood the universities with their lectures, their stress on rote memorization, their strict segregation of students and professors, their obsession with outmoded dogmas and systems. "This arrogant pedantry, this monologic [teaching method], this declamation *ex auctoritate*, the whole old-Frankish, monkish concept of our universities—that is what annoys me," wrote one Berlin critic in 1795. "This corrupts the professors and can have no good influence on the students. . . . An oral, Socratic teaching method as Herr Maier has advocated is certainly excellent and is not to be found in one of our universities."[17] J. H. Campe, in advocating the abolition of the universities, wrote bitterly, "Here [in the universities] the relationship of educator to pupil cannot take place. The students believe they have outgrown discipline. And why should they not? They are men; they wear daggers. . . . And who should educate them? Certainly not the professors. Who could require that of them? They have not studied the theory of education."[18] The solution, Campe went on, is to abolish the universities, incorporate the philosophical faculties into the larger Latin Schools, and found separate professional academies for law, medicine, and theology.

How widespread among the German intelligentsia such anti-university sentiments as these had become by 1790 can only be inferred. Certainly the number and popularity of these critiques suggests a general public approval of their indictments against the universities. At the very least the critiques indicate a serious waning of the universities' intellectual prestige during the late 18th century. Professors pursued their scholarly and pedagogical functions within an institutional con-

[16] Theobald Ziegler, *Geschichte der Pädagogik* (Munich 1917), 261-75; H. G. Good, *A History of Western Education* (New York 1968), 225-45.

[17] Stözel, *Mittwochsgesellschaft*, 218.

[18] Campe, *Revision*, XVI, 148.

text to which the general public, if not openly hostile, was becoming increasingly disdainful or indifferent. To make matters worse, critics concentrated their heaviest attacks upon the one issue which no German parent could ignore, the volatile issue of student immorality. Totally free of adult supervision, protected legally by the university's corporate privilege of academic jurisdiction, German students in university towns had by 1700 evolved an elaborate, coarse, and often violent student subculture. Long before 1750 the dueling, rioting, and whoring of student life had become open scandals in respectable circles. After 1750 critics directed their bitterest attacks against the rampant violence and immorality in the universities which clashed so strikingly with the moral and ethical ends of education they advocated. In *Carl von Carlsberg oder über das menschliche Elend* Christian G. Salzmann describes a student riot in progress. As Salzmann's protagonist sits in a darkened window he expresses the thoughts of thousands of German parents:

> Dear Aemilie! How sad I am when I think of the wretched state of the academies. Are they not the site of the coarsest barbarism? And out of these raw, coarse houses are to be taken the men to whom we must entrust our body and soul, property and honor? These perverse minds in a few years are to take charge of the Aufklärung, the legal practices and the government of the nation . . . ? Am I to send Ferdinand into these dens of baseness and depravity?[19]

Had contemporaries judged the universities only by the relevance of their scholarly ideal or by the efficiency of their pedagogy, the malaise affecting the institutions would have been neither as profound nor as widespread. But such charges of student immorality found immediate, fervent response in the moral outrage of German society over the conditions of student life. This moral outrage in turn furthered the erosion of public respect for the universities' intellectual function.

By 1790 critics had become so loud and vehement that they tended to obscure the formidable efforts made by various universities throughout the century to modernize themselves and to meet the many pressures of the 18th century crisis. These efforts centered in the Universities of Halle and Göttingen. Halle, founded in 1694, reached the peak of its fame in the 1740s. By then it had introduced into its curriculum such enlightened studies as the doctrine of natural law; pietistic theology; rational philosophy in the system of Christian Wolff; and the elements of the new science, especially in their more utilitarian form. Halle led the university system in introducing major institutional

---

[19] Salzmann, *Carl von Carlsberg*, I, 155-56.

R. Steven Turner

changes: the vernacular lecture, a program for training teachers, and a level of academic freedom in theological matters unequaled in Germany.[20] The force of its example propagated these innovations among other universities.

After 1750, however, Halle gradually ceded to the University of Göttingen its claim to be the first university of Germany and the leader of the reform movement. From its founding in 1734 Göttingen had consciously and assiduously cultivated an atmosphere of aristocratic conservatism, of quiet and warranted superiority. In an age when theology and philosophy ruled the curriculum, Göttingen stressed law, history, politics, mathematics, and the sciences—subjects calculated to appeal to the noble youth destined for a career at court or in the diplomatic service. Through this policy it succeeded in attracting the wealthiest and most international student body in Germany.[21] Better financed and administered than its Prussian rival Halle, Göttingen had by 1770 assembled in its faculty the most prestigious group of scholars in Germany outside the Berlin Academy. Especially in the philosophical faculty, uniformly neglected in other institutions, such men as J. G. Schlözer, C. G. Heyne, and G. C. Lichtenberg pioneered the scholarly methods and approaches to be applied later with great success by

[20] See Schrader, *Halle*, vol. 1, and J. C. Hoffbauer's rather prejudiced account in *Geschichte der Universität zu Halle*, esp. 1-163.

[21] On the history of the University of Göttingen in the eighteenth century see Götz von Selle, *Die Georg-August-Universität zu Göttingen, 1737-1937* (Göttingen 1937), 1-156, and Emil F. Rössler, ed., *Die Gründung der Universität Göttingen* (Göttingen 1855), esp. 257-468. Professor Charles McClelland of the University of Pennsylvania stresses the importance of Göttingen's excellent faculty of law in attracting the sons of the Hannoverian nobility. I am indebted to him for advice and criticism on this and other points. The prosperity and the rapid rise of Göttingen can be seen by comparing its estimated yearly enrollment over five-year periods with that of its rival Halle:

Dates	Göttingen	Halle
1731-35	330	1075
1736-40	416	1116
1741-45	385	1244
1746-50	625	1026
1751-55	600	918
1756-60	521	734
1761-65	427	799
1766-70	653	587
1771-75	805	673
1776-80	855	1021
1781-85	874	1076
1786-90	816	1042
1791-95	726	854

Source: Eulenburg, *Frequenz*, 164-65.

scholars of the early 19th century.[22] Göttingen symbolized throughout the 18th century crisis the continued viability of the traditional university as a center of scholarship and teaching in the face of institutional conditions which militated against both activities. Göttingen theorists took it upon themselves both to lead the counterattack against the universities' critics and also to offer a program of conservative reform.[23] In doing so they attempted to defend the universities against the growing public disdain of their scholarly function and to clarify that function in the eyes of academics themselves.

II. THE MAKING OF THE PROFESSOR

The institutional context of university life greatly affected the general viability of the universities as intellectual and pedagogical centers. Other institutional factors, particularly those related to appointments and promotions, also helped to define the scholarly ideal to which most 18th century academics adhered. A comparison with the modern professorate offers the best approach to these factors.

In most modern university systems, as in the mature German university of the 19th century, the professorial role is characterized chiefly by its peculiar dual nature. The modern professor is a man of two loyalties, one directed toward the local institution of which he is a part, the other directed toward the larger community of specialists in his discipline. These two loyalties impose different and often conflicting sets of academic activities and values. On the one hand the professor's commitment to his institution imposes "collegiate values" which are locally defined. They esteem the man who teaches with competence and versatility, who fits well socially and intellectually with his colleagues, and who identifies with his institution and accepts his share of its tasks. On the other hand the professor's commitment to his academic specialty imposes largely "disciplinary values," values which concern standards of research, publication, and professional interaction. The discipline as a whole and the specialist community in particular define these professorial values, for they govern the struggle for reputation and recognition within the discipline community.

In any progressive university system the requirements imposed upon young academics who seek appointment or promotion define and sustain professorial duties and values. The modern research-oriented university, like the mature German university of the 19th century, im-

[22] Herbert Butterfield, *Man on his Past, the Study of the History of Historical Scholarship*, 2d ed. (Cambridge 1909), 52-61; Friedrich Carl Savigny, "Der zehnte Mai 1788," *Vermischte Schriften*, 5 vols. (Berlin 1850), IV, 195-209, esp. 197-98; Selle, *Göttingen*, 150-56.

[23] For a brief survey of these writings see König, *Wesen*, 34-39.

poses requirements of a characteristic sort. In matters of salary, appointment, and promotion these institutions expressly subordinate university-centered collegiate values to disciplinary values in determining a candidate's fitness for promotion. Ostensibly the modern academic is hired to perform mainly pedagogical and other university-centered functions, but in practice his talents in these areas play only secondary roles in qualifying him for advancement. Instead his success within the local academic world is usually determined chiefly by the prestige which he holds or promises quickly to attain within his broader professional community, prestige gained largely, although by no means exclusively, through research and publication.[24] These criteria for appointment seem to have originated first in Germany during the 19th century and since then have played a major role in sustaining the ethos of research within the modern professoriate.[25]

In the academic world of 18th century Germany, the modern dualistic concept of the professorate had barely begun to form. Academics directed fewer ties of loyalty and identification outward toward disciplinary or professional communities at large. Correspondingly, they felt fewer obligations to pursue scholarly or professional interaction with these groups. Instead the professor's conception of his post and its duties channeled his attention inward toward his local corporate ties. It promoted a strong localism in intellectual and social life which hampered the development of a second, outer-directed loyalty to his disciplinary colleagues at large. Many factors helped to sustain this corporate and collegiate interpretation of the academic post, most of them related to the institutional context of the professorate.

By 1790 the professorial life had become a "career" in the 19th century sense for only a few academics. The financial difficulties of the universities ensured that few single chairs offered sufficient income for the academic and his family, and consequently few academics looked on the professorate as a full-time occupation. J. D. Michaelis of Göttingen reported that not only did professors of medicine, theology, and law commonly maintain private practices, but also that their university salaries were set correspondingly low in the expectation that they would do so. Frequently chairs carried with them the right to a second ecclesiastic or civic post. At Königsberg, for example, chairs in the law faculty entitled their occupants to positions as magistrates in the city government. Even in the philosophical faculties most academics regarded themselves as educators or members of established professions.

[24] See Theodore Caplow and Reece J. McGee, *The Academic Marketplace* (New York 1958), 82-83.

[25] R. Steven Turner, "The Growth of Professorial Research in Prussia, 1818 to 1848—Causes and Context," *Hist. Studies in the Physical Sciences*, III (1971), 167-82.

At Erfurt in 1778 exactly half of the professors in the lower faculty held second posts in the local schools, while another third held other simultaneous chairs in the professional faculties. As the professorate had not become a career, so the professor had not yet become distinguished by any specific scholarly or pedagogical expertise which differentiated him sharply from mere practitioners of the discipline he taught.[26]

Methods of recruitment pointed to the same conclusion. In the 18th and well into the 19th century, professorial recruitment tended to be not only "vertical," through *Privatdozenten* and junior professors working their way up through the professorial hierarchy, but also "horizontal," through men recruited directly from private and professional life. A distinguished doctor, lawyer, or teacher who possessed local ties with a university might be invited into the university corporation. He would then hold his chair as a lucrative and honorific post while maintaining his professional practice. Such men usually joined the corporation directly and did not habilitate themselves like vertically recruited faculty members who joined the university as *Privatdozenten*. Although no good statistics for the 18th century exist, the group of professors who were in no sense career academics seems to have made up a large percentage, if not a majority, of the professoriate. A sample group which will be studied extensively in this essay is the twenty-two teachers in the philosophical faculty at the University of Göttingen, who in the winter semester of 1765-66 announced lectures in the subjects of the philosophical faculty. Of these twenty-two, Johann Meusel in his *Lexikon der vom Jahr 1750 bis 1800 verstorbenen teutschen Schriftsteller* provides biographical material for nineteen.[27] Of this nineteen, six or almost a third had never held the post of *Privatdozent* or comparable positions. Like the local librarians J. A. Dieze and S. C. Hollmann and the local preacher Lüder Kulenkamp, all seem to have been recruited directly from practical life, sometimes because of their local ties to the corporate faculty. Until the careers of larger groups of academics at different universities have been examined, no confident generalizations can be made. Nevertheless it seems reasonable to expect

---

[26] Michaelis, *Raisonnement*, II, 253; Predeek, "Ein verschollener Reorganizationsplan für die Universität Königsberg aus dem Jahre 1725," *Altpreussische Forschungen* 4 (1927), 81; Wilhelm Stieda, *Erfurter Universitätsreformpläne im 18. Jahrhundert* (Erfurt 1934), 134ff. Stieda's work reprints the lengthy, highly detailed reform plan proposed by Wieland in 1778. Also see Tholuck, *Das akademische Leben*, 64.

[27] *Das gelehrte Teutschland oder Lexikon der vom Jahr 1750 bis 1800 verstorbenen teutschen Schriftsteller, angefangen von Georg Christoph Hamberger, fortgesetzt von J. G. Meusel* . . . (Lemgo 1796-1834).

[507]

the comparable percentage of horizontally recruited professors in the philosophical faculties of universities less distinguished than Göttingen to be somewhat greater than a third.[28] Whatever their numbers, for men recruited in this manner the professorate represented no graduated career defined specifically in terms of scholarly expertise. Beyond the local, pedagogical duties of their chair such academics often devoted their attention to the practice of their profession rather than to the pursuit of esoteric scholarship.

In lieu of a definition based upon scholarly or pedagogical expertise, 18th century academics adhered to the traditional corporate conception of the professorial dignity. Membership in the corporate body of full professors conferred certain obligations to the state and the corporation, valuable financial opportunities in salaries and fees, and considerable social distinction. Even as the actual financial position of the local professoriate declined, it continued to enjoy social and financial prerogatives which set it apart as a privileged social group and reinforced the honorific aspect of the position. Although the professors' traditional sumptuary privileges and their frequent monopolies over certain kinds of trade and manufactures were disappearing in Prussia after 1740, their right of censorship, their right of representation in the *Landtag*, and their control over lucrative ecclesiastical posts survived in force. Even at Halle, a relatively new institution, professors enjoyed all these privileges as well as exclusive use of one of the city churches and the right to their own beer and wine cellars.[29] Partly because of these corporate prerogatives, faculty groups tended to be extremely homogeneous, ingrown, and static. Königsberg and Duisburg in particular remained isolated and ingrown until early in the 19th century. Of Königsberg University Chancellor Korff complained in 1768, "The natives do not go out; outsiders do not come in; hence everything here remains slack and complacent."[30] These conditions reinforced the corporate, honorific conception of the professorate and directed the academic's attention inward toward his collegiate obligations.

[28] The use of the percentage of unhabilitated faculty as a parameter in measuring the "professionalization" of the professorial career is introduced and discussed by Christian von Ferber in *Die Entwicklung des Lehrkörpers der deutschen Universitäten und Hochschulen, 1864-1954* (Göttingen 1956), 20, 77 (Table VII). This parameter is inadequate for the period before 1800 when the status of the *Privatdozent* was quite different from that in the 19th century. It remains significant if supplemented with other biographical material like that provided by Meusel.

[29] Schrader, *Halle*, I, 83-89; Tholuck, *Das akademische Leben*, 41; Christoph Meiners, *Geschichte der Entstehung und Entwicklung der hohen Schulen unser Erdtheils*, 4 vols. (Göttingen 1805), IV, 215-16.

[30] Götz von Selle, *Geschichte der Albertus-Universität zu Königsberg in Preussen* (Würzburg 1956), 161.

Extensive legal restrictions on the mobility of students and professors also encouraged the dominant sense of localism in academic life. To the princes of 18th century absolutist states universities existed to fulfill a mercantilistic purpose. The provincial university kept the money and the talents of native sons within the state by obviating the necessity of studying abroad; hopefully it would also lure a few wealthy foreign students. In keeping with this policy the kings of Prussia and especially Frederick the Great issued numerous edicts prohibiting Prussian youth from studying outside the state.[31] In keeping with the same policy Prussia arbitrarily refused to allow prominent professors to resign their Prussian posts in order to accept more lucrative calls elsewhere in Germany. A decree of 1733 imposed on all Prussian academics an oath never to accept any future, foreign call. This prohibition fell particularly hard on natives of Prussia. A Professor Schmauss at Halle was able to accept a call to Göttingen in 1744 only by informing authorities that he had purchased another apartment in Halle, loading up his wagon with household goods, and then driving rapidly across the border.[32] Such prohibitions seem to have been fairly common in Germany, for even liberal Göttingen restricted the right of its professors to resign until late in the 18th century.[33] In practice these regulations were poorly enforced and seem only to have hampered rather than to have eliminated the mobility of the professors and students; nevertheless, to the extent that they were enforced they promoted an intellectual as well as a social localism in the Prussian universities. For as the professor found his right to resign his post restricted, he found his material incentive to work for reputation in the broader academic world limited as well. Even if his labor resulted in a lucrative and prestigious call to another post, there was no guarantee either that he could accept the offer or that he could use the opportunity to better his local position. Limitations on the professor's right to resign his post survived almost to the Humboldtian era.

These legal restrictions combined with the corporate, honorific conception of the professorate itself to inhibit the professor from identifying with disciplinary groups across the university system. The centripetal pulls of collegiate duties, professional practice, and social prerogatives distracted him from actively participating in the larger

[31] Reinhold Koser, "Friedrich der Grosse und die preussischen Universitäten," *Forschungen zur brandenburgischen und preussischen Geschichte,* 17 (1904), 118, 131.

[32] Bornhak, *Universitätsverwaltung,* 119-22.

[33] Ernst Brandes, *Ueber den gegenwärtigen Zustand der Universität Göttingen* (Göttingen 1802), 172-73. Undoubtedly such restrictions had fallen into disuse well before 1802.

world of scholarship, especially the intense, research-oriented scholarship coming rapidly to the fore. Of course, many scholars who held university chairs did pursue extensive scholarly research of all kinds throughout the 18th century. But the popular conception of the professorate implied no such duty intrinsic to the office itself.

Other factors also hampered the formation of a dualistic conception of the academic's obligations. The modern dualistic professorate, and especially the accepted use of predominantly disciplinary criteria in appointments, presupposes several conditions in the larger academic world. In particular it presupposes the existence of well-defined disciplinary communities, the reputation of whose participants can be at least roughly assessed by local administrators as a basis for their decisions about promotions. In 18th century Germany, however, these communities were themselves still in the process of formation. "Discipline community" as used here refers to the inner circle of recognized authorities who actively engage in research in the same subfield or on the same problem. They possess most direct access to research facilities and journals, and they carry out scientific debates largely among themselves. The rise of such disciplinary communities in the later 18th century can be traced in the emergence of self-conscious schools, the propagation of specific research techniques, and the proliferation of specialized journals. Mathematics, for example, had long been an established scholarly discipline within the universities. The consolidation of Germany's first disciplinary community in the field, however, can be traced to Professors Pfaff at Helmstadt and Hindenburg at Leipzig, who founded the combinatorial school of analysis and began Germany's first specialized mathematics journal, the *Archiv der reinen und angewandten Mathematik*. C. G. Heyne at Göttingen and his school broadened the scope of classical philology after 1750 to include a general study of antiquity. Heyne's pupil F. A. Wolf added to this program an emphasis on rigorous critique, and from his seminar at Halle trained a methodologically conscious philological elite whose cadres would dominate chairs of philology in northern Germany after 1800. In chemistry Karl Hufbauer has recently traced the formation of the German chemical community and its consolidation around Lorenz Crell at Helmstadt and his *Chemisches Journal*. In each of these fields an inner circle was gradually distinguishing itself from the larger group of practitioners who were learned in the discipline but who contributed infrequently or who engaged mainly in teaching or applying their knowledge.[34]

[34] On the community of German mathematicians before 1800 see E. Netto, "Kombinatorik," *Vorlesungen über Geschichte der Mathematik*, ed. Moritz Cantor (Leipzig 1908), IV, 201-21, and Wilhelm Lorey, *Das Studium der Mathematik*

Despite their vigorous growth, these new communities remained rather novel during the later 18th century. The ideal of scholarly participation and performance latent in them had not yet become general norms for the larger academic world. In particular the criteria commonly used in academic appointments and promotions suggest that active participation in these communities had become neither obligatory nor universally expected of academics. The emerging young communities had not yet begun to serve as foci for a dualistic conception of the professor's loyalties or for the consistent use of disciplinary criteria in appointments.

In Germany by 1760 authority over academic appointments and promotions had generally become legally invested in the state. By that date the territorial princes had gradually usurped the universities' ancient corporate privilege of self-recruitment, even though a few institutions and individual faculties retained that right throughout the century. Prussian institutions enjoyed somewhat less autonomy than other universities in these matters, for they did not even possess a statutory right to nominate candidates. This did not mean, however, that the local faculties had ceased to exercise power over appointments. Prussia's bureaucratic control of its universities had remained remarkably ineffective throughout the 18th century, and except for short periods of despotic intervention it took little interest in superintending its universities or in exploiting its authority over appointments. Consequently, the local faculties or a few dominant individuals in each one managed, largely by default of the state, to retain considerable influence over professorial appointments. Conrad Bornhak's study of the Prussian university administration before 1810 cites numerous cases preserved in ministerial records in which Prussian universities were called upon to propose candidates for vacant chairs. In the case of Königsberg University, which Berlin administered indirectly through the provincial government, the state left appointments almost entirely in local hands. Bornhak concludes that "the participation of the university in the filling of vacant chairs was in no way extinguished and can be demonstrated during the whole century."[35] Although occasionally the state imposed controversial professors upon a university

---

an den deutschen Universitäten seit Anfang des 19. Jahrhunderts (Berlin 1916), 26-29. For classical philology see Sandys, Classical Scholarship, III, passim. For chemistry see Karl Hufbauer, "The Formation of the German Chemical Community (1700-1795)" Ph.D. diss., Univ. of California at Berkeley (1969); and Hufbauer, "Social Support for Chemistry in Germany during the Eighteenth Century," Hist. Studies in the Physical Sciences 3 (1971), 205-32.

[35] Bornhak, Universitätsverwaltung, 98-129, esp. 99-100; and Selle, Königsberg, 158-61. For a fuller discussion see Turner, "Professorial Research," 158-63.

against its will, on the whole the local corporate faculty successfully set the criteria used in most academic appointments.

The modern professorial system utilizes university appointments and promotions to encourage scholarship and research. This system presupposes that the authorities which control appointments will subordinate to disciplinary criteria the collegiate virtues of effective teaching, versatility, social and intellectual acceptability, and family ties. In 18th century Germany, however, university critics, theorists, and reformers of every ideological hue agreed that collegiate values far outweighed disciplinary values in importance, a condition they attributed to the domination of appointments by the corporate faculties. Although critics generally admitted that such faculty-controlled appointments did promote a desirable solidarity within the university corporation, they invariably condemned these appointments as damaging to scholarship. Faculty jealousies, they insisted, guaranteed the exclusion of the most competent teachers and scholars. Christoph Meiners of the University of Göttingen, where the state closely controlled all professorial appointments, wrote approvingly that "the great Münchhausen granted to our university the right to present and to nominate or to recommend as little as he did the right of free selection, because he knew through experience that although the faculties of universities know always the men who most deserve vacant chairs, they are seldom or never inclined to propose the most capable whom they know."[36] Christoph Martin Wieland wrote of the University of Erfurt that "it would be highly beneficial to the university and to the prevention of many abuses which have taken place, if the right of appointment was vested in the prince in those faculties where the opposite custom now prevails."[37] Without exception, 18th century reformers sought not more academic freedom in matters of appointment, but more state control to prevent what they regarded as open corporate abuses.

Critics also insisted that the great authority vested in the corporate faculties encouraged professorial monopolies and restricted the healthy competition necessary to vigorous intellectual life. J. C. Hoffbauer, in writing of the Prussian universities in 1800, urged that

> every instructor ought to enjoy the fullest independence from every other. . . . In my opinion all relationships which make an instructor dependent on the interests of others in any manner must be banned. . . . I know of cases in which younger instructors have oriented their choice of lectures, however unwillingly, in accordance with the

[36] Meiners, *Entstehung*, 1, 202; also see Bornhak, *Universitätsverwaltung*, 100.
[37] In Stieda, *Universitätsreformpläne*, 154.

wishes of their seniors in order not to displease them, because they hoped either for further advancement through their recommendation or for other sorts of advantages arising from their favor. . . . Everyone who seeks advancement in the university knows that it depends upon whether the faculty will recommend him or not. . . . Often everything hangs upon the will of one individual, to whose vote the other members of the faculty conform more than they should.[38]

The professorial monopolies which restricted competition and innovation, Hoffbauer went on, affected not only younger academics but established full professors as well.

Reformers frequently observed that professorial evaluations ignored a candidate's disciplinary attainment and looked primarily to his social and corporate acceptability. At worst the universities' most bitter critics satirized the institutions as openly and unambiguously corrupt in this respect. In one scene from Salzmann's *Carl von Carlsberg* the young university instructor Ribonius confesses to a colleague that he loves Luise but is too poor to marry. A chair has become vacant at last to which Ribonius is entitled by seniority, but the full professors in charge seem cool toward him. "Indeed," says his friend, "you seem not to know how one gets a chair here in Grünau. . . . We have many pretty professors' daughters. Marry one! What does it matter? Things will go better." The virtuous Ribonius is shocked and replies that since he either has the requisite professorial ability or does not, such a marriage can have no effect. "That is certainly a *syllogismus disjunctivus* if I am not mistaken," laughs his friend. "Propositions are all right for the lecture room . . . , but in everyday life they are worth nothing. You don't yet know how it is." Ribonius soon learns, however, for he marries the daughter of a professor, enters into the dignity of the professorial office, and forsakes Luise, who promptly dies of heartbreak.[39]

Other contemporary critics less hostile to the universities voiced similar conclusions in less outrageous terms. Even Frederick William I had chided his university curators early in the century, noting, "We do not wish to conceal from you our resolution that in the future when professorial posts become vacant you are to recommend to us only such people as have earned fame and renown at other universities and as will make our universities flourish and grow; and you are to ignore matters of kinship, marriage, and the like."[40] Wieland, by far

---

[38] *Ueber die Perioden der Erziehung* (Leipzig 1800), 182-84; also see 185-86. Hoffbauer was Professor of Philosophy at Halle.

[39] Salzmann, *Carl von Carlsberg*, III, 141-42.

[40] Bornhak, *Universitätsverwaltung*, 99.

the bitterest critic of contemporary appointment criteria, complained of his own University of Erfurt that

> all along the philosophical faculty, instead of concentrating at all times and to the best of its ability on the best possible choice, has let itself be led by completely false premises; it has notoriously concerned itself more with its relatives and personal friends, more with religious, fraternal, or collegiate relationships and the like in the selection of its new members than with true learned capability. Out of this practice has arisen not only a mass of quarrels, but also—understandably—the circumstance that it was only a fortunate coincidence when a really skillful man ever found his way to a teaching post.[41]

Always, Wieland wrote elsewhere, "the most essential concerns in the filling of a vacant chair are least discussed; often completely secondary matters predominate, and there is little talk of learnedness, scientific skill, teaching ability, and other necessary abilities and demands."[42]
Appointive criteria based upon "religious, fraternal, or collegiate relationships" discouraged the evaluation of young academics upon their disciplinary attainment. Even when this factor was weighed, the full faculty, dominated by professors of theology and law, usually lacked the ability to judge candidates in specific fields upon disciplinary grounds. It was even less prepared to judge specialized research within these fields, and Wieland used this fact to attack the principle of faculty self-recruitment:

> Because a professor does not teach all the sciences and consequently does not need to understand them, so-called scholars can be guilty of still greater misjudgments about professors. Let us assume, for example, that a university has only one professor of mathematics and that this chair is to be filled. Then among the men who will make the appointment there are no real professional mathematicians; what, then, makes their judgment particularly accurate in comparison with that of others? The same case can occur in many other fields. [Such circumstances promote] . . . only too often the most common personal considerations which in no way further learning.[43]

Reliance on such "common personal considerations" in appointments, Wieland went on, not only restricted the growth of university scholarship, but also blocked the possibility of reforms aimed at promoting

---

[41] In Stieda, *Universitätsreformpläne*, 227.
[42] Ibid., 134.　　　　　　　　　　　　[43] Ibid., 153-54.

more effective teaching, a progressive curriculum, and the gradual improvement of student life and morals.

The programmatic intent of reformers such as Wieland, Hoffbauer, and their colleagues has to be kept in mind in evaluating their writings. Such critics did not undertake impartial assessments of university conditions; instead they wrote reform treatises aimed at exposing the corporate abuses of the university system and at rallying academics and administrators to reform. This reform, as theorists envisioned it, would proceed on many fronts, of which the reform of university scholarship would be only one. With this program in mind, critics usually phrased their complaints over appointment procedures as general indictments of the university system, even though in practice their criticisms applied neither to all appointments nor to all universities. The University of Göttingen constituted the obvious exception to all such generalizations about the 18th century universities, as to a lesser extent did Halle under Freiherr von Zedlitz, and as did individual faculties and universities of other states. Even with this qualification, however, the testimony of reformers provides entrée into important 18th century attitudes toward academic appointments. Clearly these men believed that in a sufficient number of academic appointments to merit a general university reform, social and corporate factors outweighed candidates' disciplinary attainment and even their pedagogical skills. This testimony suggests that the local faculties, which controlled or greatly influenced appointments, still felt little compulsion to subordinate their obvious local interests to the furtherance of an esoteric and specialized scholarship, even though they might regard such work as intrinsically valuable and important. This circumstance, as the next section will argue, did not so much discourage professorial scholarship as channel it into certain areas, away from the specialized research interests rapidly rising in sectors of German scholarship and science. The institutional conditions of late 18th century academia, especially as they expressed themselves in the criteria of academic appointments, had not yet begun to promote on a large scale the modern dualistic conception of the professorate.

III. THE PROFESSOR AS SCHOLAR

University theorists were quick to point out that the institutional circumstances surrounding the appointment and promotion of academics affected the universities' outlook on scholarship, usually for the worse. That argument made, they rarely hesitated to interject their own opinions concerning the professor's duties toward teaching, publication, and discovery. In this sense the reform treatises yield a small cross section of academic opinion regarding the professor's scholarly function.

These discussions, however, ought not to suggest that the improvement of scholarship dominated the concerns of 18th century reformers. On the contrary most writers would have agreed that the demands of scholarship ought to take second place to the more pressing needs to stimulate enrollment and funding, to create a more competent system of state administration, and to improve student life and morals. This issue of reform priorities can be seen in the recurrent debates over the relative importance of teaching versus scholarship to the university's proper function. Two distinct traditions of reform thought emerged with respect to this question, although both shared a wide range of common views.

On the issue of teaching versus scholarship, a few theorists went so far as to argue that the university had no obligation at all to advance scholarship. Others agreed to the more moderate precept that the professor's role as scholar must be strictly subordinated to his role as teacher. This latter argument reached its most extreme form on the brink of the Humboldtian era among the circle of Prussian reformers whose chief representatives were L. H. Jacob and J. C. Hoffbauer. Both men charged that the failure of the traditional university lay in the near-total emphasis upon its role as a professional school to the neglect of its propaedeutic, pedagogical function. "The university is not merely a teaching institute (*Lehrinstitut*)," wrote Hoffbauer, "but rather also an educational institute (*Erziehungsinstitut*), and in a narrower sense is the school proper. The whole organization of the university ought to be referred to this role. . . ." Jacob added that "the surveillance over the students must be made more school-like (*Schulmässig*); otherwise all hope of improvement is lost."[44] As immediate remedies they advocated more rigid discipline of students, Socratic teaching methods, and more elementary courses. This emphasis upon the university's pedagogical function naturally implied that teaching rather than scholarship should be the chief concern in academic appointments. Although both authors honored the necessity of professorial learnedness, both urged that scholarly activity be de-emphasized among academics. Occasionally there emerged a note of near-hostility to the professor-scholar:

> In the future more consideration must be taken of both aspects of the professor's talents in selection of candidates. An orderly, upright man with a well-ordered erudition and a gift for communicating it is more suitable to become a professor than a scholarly monster who labors only for himself and the world or who does little for his stu-

[44] Hoffbauer, *Perioden*, viii; [Ludwig Heinrich Jacob], *Ueber die Universitäten in Deutschland, besonders in den königl. preussischen Staaten* (Berlin 1798), 26.

dents, or a genius who has offensive morals and who does not think it worth the labor to employ diligence on lectures for his students, or a rhapsodic polymath who strews everything together without any connection and has no proper method in instruction.[45]

Sentiments like these certainly imply no hostility to professorial scholarship in general, but they do testify to the primary emphasis upon pedagogy running through many theoretical assessments of the professorate and its requirements.

Against the opinions of the Prussian reformers must be balanced the ultimately more influential tradition emanating from the University of Göttingen. Göttingen theorists, and especially their dean J. D. Michaelis, agreed that the first duty of the university was to instruct the young and that consequently the professor was primarily a teacher. But they insisted upon a loftier concept of teaching than the propaedeutic, methodological instruction envisioned by the Prussian theorists, and they denied that the university was nothing more than a school. Ernst Brandes, in whose treatise the Göttingen tradition culminated, argued vehemently that as university instruction was "more rigorous and systematic" than that of the schools, universities must be sharply distinguished from true pedagogical institutions.[46]

Göttingen's "more rigorous and systematic" concept of university instruction also left more room for professorial scholarship, a theoretical view supported by Göttingen's preeminence in German learning. Later writers in the Göttingen tradition especially stressed the importance of university scholarship. By 1805 theorists like Brandes and Christoph Meiners were ready to attribute to academic reputation an importance almost as great as that of effective teaching itself. Brandes, for example, wrote:

> The distinguished scholar should be a teacher of youth by virtue of his designation as professor. But because . . . [perfection] is not always to be had, so can a few deserving professors, even if they train only a small number of students . . . still make great contributions to the fame of the university through their writings. The double point of view by which we must always consider a university, namely that the professors at the same time are to maintain, disseminate, and enlarge the treasury of human wisdom and are to teach the youth, leads us to the wish that every professor might be a deserving teacher and a distinguished writer. If both are not possible, however, he must be one.[47]

[45] Jacob, *Universitäten*, 254-55.   [46] Brandes, *Göttingen*, 26-27.
[47] Ibid., 188-89; also see Meiners, *Entstehung*, IV, 372-76.

Against these opinions the older but still very influential tract of J. D. Michaelis maintained that the professor had no obligation either to publish or to make discoveries, and that in no case could these activities compensate for poor teaching. Even Brandes agreed that pedagogical fitness ought to govern appointments. The most important criteria in selecting a professor, he wrote, should be (1) his ability as a lecturer and (2) his "systematic embrace of the whole of his science." The professor's learnedness, Brandes went on, should be addressed not to discovery but to judgment and synthesis.[48]

If any consensus emerged from these divergent opinions about the relative merits of teaching and scholarship, it was that the professor's role as scholar ought to be subordinated to his role as teacher at least in determining academic appointments. But the lack of consensus about how exclusively teaching should be emphasized opened the way to detailed discussions of the professor's broader duties as a scholar. The most heated of these discussions involved the relative merits of professorial publication. Did the professor's literary activity interfere with his teaching? Did it make of him a literary hack? These issues were bound to be important, for theorists agreed that the literary works produced by the professors of the local university largely determined the institution's fame abroad, and that fame, in turn affected the prosperity of the local institution in students and income. With a fine disregard for more idealistic or euphemistic justifications of professorial writing, 18th century discussions proceeded directly to the issues of finance and prestige at the heart of the matter.

J. D. Michaelis advanced the view that professors should not strive to be literary figures:

> Must professors in general be writers—famous writers?—This is a new question to which one will expect an answer.
> In fact I do not believe that this is an indispensable characteristic of a good professor; and where it is emphasized too much I suspect that the authorities . . . do so not merely for the effectiveness of the university or the advance of learning, but rather to do something to raise the prestige of the university.[49]

The professor who is both a capable teacher and a noted writer is to be doubly valued, Michaelis went on, but the professor who is only the former has done his duty in full.

Against this view Wieland fervently argued that publication was an auxiliary duty (*Nebenamt*) inherent in the professorate. "The business

[48] Michaelis, *Raisonnement*, I, 92-93 and passim; Brandes, *Göttingen*, 159-61.
[49] Michaelis, *Raisonnement*, II, 225.

of publishing," he wrote, "belongs in and for itself among the activities of a scholar, and it is so much the more suitable to the professor because through it he has the opportunity to make himself known abroad and so promote the honor of the university. In this respect publication by professors ought to be favored in every possible way." But Wieland opposed any attempt to make publication obligatory, noting that "it is not given to everyone to be a writer, although through one's knowledge and other capabilities one may yet be a really good teacher."[50] Although no consensus emerged among theorists concerning the desirability of professorial publication, most writers agreed with Wieland that for the good of his university the professor should publish if he possessed sufficient skill and opportunity.

Reformers and theorists had little to say about the more significant issue of whether any literary production was actually incumbent upon the 18th century academic in virtue of his position. In Prussia, at least, other sources suggest that the state did make a few largely ineffectual attempts to require publication of its professors. Conrad Bornhak records decrees issued to Frankfurt-an-Oder in 1737 and to Halle in 1768 admonishing the local faculties to publish more in order to ensure the reputations of the institutions. In both cases the state made clear that it desired not works of esoteric scholarship but rather widely available works of practical interest to the common man. There is no evidence, however, that Prussia ever enforced literary activity by restricting the salary or advancement of individual professors who neglected to write, even though the administration did take these steps occasionally to discourage pedagogical laxness. Although the state recognized and encouraged professorial publication as important in sustaining the mercantilistic position of the universities, it seemed to maintain no consistent policy for promoting literary activity.[51]

In practice the degree of obligation or incentive to literary production undoubtedly differed greatly from university to university during the late 18th century. In discussing the proper criteria according to which professorial salaries should be allotted, Christoph Meiners, a firm advocate of professorial publication, made the following recommendation:

Most universities were formerly inclined to consider a special talent for the oral lecture as much more worthy of reward than distinctive gifts and fame as a writer. In my opinion smaller universities were correct to think in this manner. At larger universities [however], a widespread literary reputation accompanied by meager . . .

[50] In Stieda, *Universitätsreformpläne*, 176-77.
[51] Bornhak, *Universitätsverwaltung*, 58.

approbation [as a teacher] counterbalances distinctive pedagogical talents which are enhanced by no literary fame. The repute of a good oral lecture promotes in local regions the prosperity and enrollment of universities, while literary fame [acts] in distant lands.[52]

The few cases in which professorial output can be estimated seem to corroborate Meiners' distinction between large and small institutions. Not surprisingly they indicate that literary output varied greatly from academic to academic and that professors at more prestigious schools published significantly more than those at smaller institutions. Wieland reviewed the literary activity of the twenty-two professors in the Erfurt philosophical faculty between 1738 and 1778. Of that twenty-two he found only five who in his opinion had achieved any fame through their writings, five who were completely obscure and ineffectual, and the rest, mediocre. Karl von Prantl in his history of the University of Ingolstadt, forerunner of the University of Munich, reviewed the efforts of the lower faculty there. For the period 1715 to 1746 he discovered that twenty-eight of the forty-one professors maintained no literary activity. In the later period 1746 to 1773 he declared nineteen of the thirty-one professors in the lower faculty to be "without literary significance."[53] These relatively low levels of professorial output at smaller institutions like Erfurt and Ingolstadt suggest that professors there felt little compulsion to publish and experienced no significant pressure to do so from the administrative bureaucracy or their peers.

The prestigious University of Göttingen presented a rather different situation, for its faculty as a whole published extensively during the second half of the 18th century. Johann Meusel's *Lexikon* provides lists of publications for nineteen professors in the philosophical faculty of 1765-66, and his compendium shows that all of these men did publish at least a few works of some description during the course of their careers. Eleven wrote quite extensively, while the works of Samuel Christian Hollmann, Abraham Gottfried Kästner, and J. D. Michaelis could fairly be called encyclopedic in scope and approach. If by 1765 Göttingen could boast of being the most prestigious intellectual center in Germany outside the Berlin Academy, it clearly owed this reputation largely to the publications of its faculty.

Meusel's data also allows the literary activity of each teacher to be

[52] Christoph Meiners, *Ueber die Verfassung und Verwaltung der deutscher Universitäten*, 2 vols. (Göttingen 1801; photocopy repr. Darmstadt 1970), II, 55.

[53] Stieda, *Universitätsreformpläne*, 224; Karl von Prantl, *Geschichte der Ludwig-Maximillians-Universität in Ingolstadt, Landeshut, München*, 2 vols., 2d. ed. (Munich 1968), I, 542, 613.

correlated with the time of his first appointment to the university and his subsequent promotion into its corporate ranks. At the time of their first appointment to the professorship, i.e., as junior professors (*Extraordinarien*) or at comparable ranks, the nineteen academics of the sample had already produced an average of five works each.[54] Around this average, actual figures ranged from no works at all to as many as nine at the time of first appointment. These five works, however, by no means consisted only of scholarly treatises aimed at the larger community. In keeping with the localism of intellectual life they invariably included several academic dissertations, printed disputations, and occasional pieces printed in small numbers primarily for local use. If works of this kind are considered somewhat less important than books and journal articles, and if the significant differences in the number of publications from individual to individual are taken into account, then the literary output of academics prior to their first appointment at Göttingen would not seem to be significantly high. Certainly it permits no inference that any given level of literary output was required for a first appointment.

All but three instructors among the nineteen of the sample later received invitations to join the corporate faculty as full professors (*Ordinarien*). By the date of that promotion the average member of the group had published nine or ten works of some type, an impressive figure, since the percentage of required dissertations seemed to be much lower. Great individual differences remained, however, ranging from a few instructors who had produced only one or two works to the continual outflow of mathematics texts from the pen of A. G. Kästner. Those instructors who fell well below the average form a particularly significant subgroup. At least six professors reached the status of full professor on the strength of five publications or fewer, many of these required dissertations. With some exceptions this group corresponded closely to those academics previously mentioned as having been recruited "horizontally," directly from practical life. They included Gottfried Achenwall and the Becmann brothers who had entered the professoriate from established legal practices and who simultaneously held chairs in both the juridical and philosophical faculties. Others like Ernst Weber, Lüder Kulenkamp, and Georg Hamberger possessed nonacademic entrée into the faculty group through pastoral or literary positions; these collegiate connections clearly smoothed the

---

[54] The *Privatdozentur* conferred only permission to give private lectures under the auspices of the university. In 1765 this permission was relatively easy to obtain and constituted no official appointment or even significant recognition. The *Extraordinariat* or lectureship did constitute an official appointment and usually conferred a salary, although not corporate membership.

way for their initiation into the faculty. Although the size of the sample invites no generalizations, the impressive number of publications behind most academics at the time of their initiation into the university corporation does suggest that sustained literary activity was a professorial norm at Göttingen. On the other hand the frequent exceptions made for men who possessed collegiate or professional entrée indicates that even at Göttingen extensive publication had not yet become the sine qua non of the professorial career.

The most important characteristic of the 18th century's attitude toward university scholarship did not lie in the number of works academics felt obliged to produce or even in assessments of the sheer desirability of professorial erudition. The distinguishing characteristic of the 18th century's attitude lay rather in the purpose for which scholarly works were intended, the form which they took, and the audience toward which they were directed. Again a comparison with the modern, dualistic professorate can bring these characteristics into sharper relief.

Consistent adherence in academic appointments and promotions to disciplinary standards sustains the modern dualistic professorate. This system, however efficient in promoting research, has had great implications for the kinds of scholarship pursued within the academic framework. The appointive criteria previously discussed in connection with the modern professorate do not, in theory, reward scholarship and publication directly. Instead they reward only scholarship which heightens the individual's reputation among his disciplinary peers. This means—or has meant in practice—that incentive accrues only to those forms of scholarly contribution which are of interest to the specialist group. Other forms such as didactic or popular scholarship are likely to be ignored or even disdained. The individual academic accepts the disciplinary community to which he feels allied as the only proper judge of his scholarly capacity. He directs his most important work toward this group and adheres to the problems, methods, and standards which it respects. Much scholarship carried on within this framework, therefore, carries within itself an innate tendency toward specialization. By 1840 this framework had been firmly established in Germany. The literary production of a professor had by then come to mean ideally the results of his original research addressed to the circle of specialists in his field. Conversely his work addressed to a larger audience—textbooks, popular works, belles lettres—had come to have a distinctly different connotation, to be considered as secondary to his principal scholarly activity.

German academics in the later 18th century approached the subject of professorial publication with completely different preassumptions.

The emerging young specialist communities had not yet established themselves as the arbiters of scholarly excellence. The adherence to collegiate criteria in local appointments greatly reduced the significance of scholarly achievement in specialized topics which could be evaluated only by a few specialists. Instead these conditions encouraged scholarship of a broader, more synthetic, and sometimes shallow nature, a scholarship which could be appreciated and evaluated by one's corporate fellows. They placed a special premium upon intellectual breadth and versatility, and they discouraged rigid distinctions between "learned" or "scientific" works on the one hand and pedagogical, popular, or didactic works on the other. Of course, theorists recognized the distinction, but they rarely declared the former to be in any sense "proper" to the professorate or to be intrinsically more desirable than works of a less esoteric nature. As a result the publications of 18th century professors often showed a diversity and diffuseness unrestricted by the later confines of specialized audiences, disciplinary boundaries, or methodological critique. By 1790 the familiar hierarchy of respectability in professorial publications had not yet become clearly established.

This attitude manifested itself in various ways and especially clearly in the "textbook tradition" of professorial scholarship. In keeping with his pedagogical conception of his post and the encyclopedic preferences of his age, the professor devoted much of his publishing activity to handbooks, translations, and works of a pedagogical or encyclopedic nature. When 18th century academics spoke of a professor's scholarly writings through which he won fame and reputation they usually meant these textbooks and compendia, works which by definition were rarely directed at specialized audiences. Even while recognizing its importance for pedagogy, Michaelis gently mocked this textbook tradition, noting that "as often as a new professor gets good, an old compendium goes bad."[55] But most other theorists, especially the pedagogically minded reformers in the Prussian tradition, regarded such production as wholly desirable, as the proper form of professorial literary activity. "I know that many have protested often and emphatically against the too-great accumulation of textbooks," J. C. Hoffbauer wrote in 1800,

> but such protests are wrong. A textbook by a teacher is not written for the great public but for his hearers. One should never seek to discourage a teacher from such activity, for compiling a textbook affords him the best opportunity of ordering his knowledge and working out its individual parts. . . . Nor is one to worry that the

[55] Michaelis, *Raisonnement*, II, 227.

urge to write will lead more to the compiling of textbooks than to other writings. The public, whose demand determines the readiness of the publisher to accept a work, asks less after compendia than other writings. Furthermore, even a mediocre textbook demands more knowledge and diligence in most cases than the treatment of a learned topic in many volumes.

If an instructor lectures from his own text, then one outside the university is in a position to know what one can expect of him, whether he surveys the whole of his science and its parts. . . .

On these grounds it is perhaps to be wished that every instructor lecture only from his own textbook.[56]

The many professors who ascribed to this view did not regard the production of textbooks as an activity wholly distinct from analytic examinations of smaller areas by research or speculation, and they certainly did not regard the former as secondary or inferior. On the contrary, the intellectual abilities associated more with the former than with the latter—the synthetic view, sensitivity to the relationship of the parts to the whole, breadth and clarity in presentation—these were the values which the professor ranked highest among the demands of erudition.

This tolerant, perhaps freewheeling attitude toward professorial publication expressed itself in other ways also. Consider the familiar nineteen professors of the Göttingen philosophical faculty in 1765 and the literary work of each prior to his appointment as full professor. One can hardly review the literary output of these men and fail to be struck by the high percentage of works which the 19th century would never have called *wissenschaftlich*, by 1820 the supreme scholarly accolade. Most of the publications of at least eleven of the nineteen Göttingen academics would have clearly been regarded as "unscientific" by the 19th century; that is, the works made no claim to extending the frontiers of scholarship or were not the result of the methodical, critical methods for which later German scholarship became justly famous. The Becmann brothers published only two or three joint literary works during their careers. Isaak Colom wrote primarily translations of literary works from the French and textbooks of French grammar and stylistics. Johann Dieze the librarian contributed translations from the Spanish and editions of various Spanish works. Georg Hamberger edited the important encyclopedia of German writers continued by Meusel but did little else. Johann Tobias Köler published primarily poems and travel descriptions. Kästner, although he contributed sev-

---

[56] Hoffbauer, *Perioden*, 178-80; also see Rössler, *Gründung*, 473-74.

eral original papers in mathematics, was most famous for his well-known textbooks and for his philosophical and literary writing. Professors Kulenkamp and Weber published frequent collections of sermons. Other professors such as Hollmann and Michaelis, who cannot fairly be listed with this group, nevertheless devoted much of their publication to popular or strictly literary efforts. Before 1790 the range of intellectual endeavors considered proper to the professorate had not narrowed to its 19th century limits, in which the ideal of academic publication would be the announcement to one's fellow specialists of the results of critical research.

Other preassumptions also helped to characterize the 18th century outlook on professorial scholarship. Consider the issue of scholarly performance from a broader perspective. During the Humboldtian era, in which the professorial ethos began first to take on its modern form, reformers urged above all else a rebirth of "creativity" in all phases of university life. Opinions about what studies and activities would actually evince "creativity" among professors varied from reformer to reformer. But despite this initial indecision, within a few decades the German academic world had reached a surprising consensus. Professorial creativity had come to mean—and usually to mean exclusively—the extension of scholarship, discovery. More important, discovery, in the only form considered proper to the professorial endeavor, had come to mean the fruit of original research, usually research of a highly esoteric and specialized nature.

German academics in the later 18th century esteemed professorial creativity no less than did their successors in the age of Ranke and Boeckh, but they perceived creativity in a far wider range of scholarly activities. In particular they refused to equate scholarly creativity with discovery alone; and, as the previous discussion indicated, they never tacitly assumed that publication would ideally embody discovery. On the contrary, theorists persistently bisected their discussions of professorial scholarship into discussions of the academic's proper activity as a writer and his activity as a discoverer of new truths. J. D. Michaelis, for example, found it completely proper to first discuss the professor's duty as a discoverer and then seventy pages later to return to his duties as a writer, with no reference to the former discussion and no suggestion that the two activities bore any necessary relation to each other.[57]

This attitude toward the context of university scholarship led to the occasional debates within the writings of university theorists concerning the professor's responsibility as a "discoverer." The authors did not

[57] Michaelis, *Raisonnement*, II, 134-35.

assume discovery to be coterminous with scholarship, nor did they assume discovery itself necessarily to be the result of research. In this restricted sense nearly all theorists readily acknowledged the ideal of original discovery by professors. Meiners in his history of the German universities of 1805 noted with pride—and considerable exaggeration —that the professors of Halle had made rich contributions to scholarship. And "I can boldly claim," he added, "that [also] among the living Göttingen scholars not a few are to be found who have broadened the horizons of human knowledge, increased the useful spheres of instruction, or improved the species of sciences."[58] Even Michaelis was forced to admit that "the prejudice is certainly common enough which views the professor as a discoverer of new truths by virtue of his office," and he noted that many academics cultivated this view for the sake of their own vanity.[59]

But while many theorists, especially those at Göttingen, acknowledged the ideal of professorial discovery and noted with pride the universities' achievements in this respect, none went so far as to declare discovery to be a duty inherent in the professorial post. Discovery constituted only one of many ways through which the academic could distinguish himself through his scholarship, and it was too rare an achievement to be routinely expected or to be a basis on which to evaluate one's self and one's colleagues. Many would have agreed with Michaelis, who delivered what perhaps approached a representative judgment on the issue of professorial discovery:

> To improve the sciences and to make new discoveries is simply not the duty of a school whether it be high or low. It is rather the duty of a few fortunate geniuses, or, if one wants to have an official institution, of an academy of science. And yet the German universities have achieved so much in this regard, though it was not their obligation, that I need not say in their defense they had no such duty. A man of great genius who has ambition or impatience enough not always merely to repeat his lectures, not to read merely bread courses, not to overburden himself with lecture hours, never to lecture unprepared, and who is motivated by his way of life daily to immerse himself in learning, such a man can hardly fail to discover something new in his science where it is to be discovered. . . . But a school for young people does not have such a duty or purpose. The instruction of the young and the *Parte tueri* in the realm of learning is enough. Whichever of their teachers does more achieves an *opus supererogationis*, and is entitled to double honor and reward.[60]

[58] Meiners, *Entstehung*, IV, 372. [59] Michaelis, *Raisonnement*, II, 134.
[60] Ibid., I, 92-93.

The professor regarded discovery as an academic ideal but not as a duty inherent to his post itself, defined as that post was by largely pedagogical and collegiate criteria.

This outlook received official recognition, for the Prussian government seemed to share it well into the reform era. Although the state encouraged its professors to publish, it never assumed or desired that this publication would contain scholarly discoveries. On the contrary, in a communication to the Berlin Academy of 1770 the ministry insisted that "the ultimate purpose of the universities is the instruction of youth. A professor of a university has fulfilled his office satisfactorily if he thoroughly teaches the youth what is known and discovered in his subject." The academy of science rather than the university, the minister went on, has the responsibility of filling in the lacunae of learning. Geheimer Tribunalrat Steck, whom we have already seen criticizing the Halle professors in 1768 for their failure to publish, asserted in his visitation to Frankfurt-an-Oder in 1770 that the business of the universities is not discovery but the "service of the state and the enlightenment of the nation." Still more pointedly, an 1802 decree to Halle from the government denied that the purpose of the university was the expansion of science as many professors believed; its purpose was rather teaching, which would lead indirectly to discovery.[61]

Both university theorists and the Prussian state could advance excellent reasons for their conviction that discovery could not and should not be a duty of the university. First, the efforts devoted by the professor to discovery would surely distract him from teaching, by common agreement his first responsibility. Second and more important, theorists agreed unanimously that the psychological and intellectual characteristics of the successful discoverer differed so radically from those required of the effective teacher that the two could rarely be combined in one individual. Upon this premise the Berlin academician F.A.M.G. Castillon rested his last-ditch defense of the division of labor between the university, the domain of teaching, and the academy, the center of creative scholarship. The academician, Castillon argued in his *Ueber die Begriffe einer Akademie und einer Universität*, is a creator partaking of the genius; the professor, he hinted, is a mere pedant. Only in the rarest of cases, he concluded, could the same individual belong to both institutions and simultaneously fulfill the contradictory demands of teaching and discovery.[62] Others better disposed toward professorial scholarship than Castillon also shared this opinion, includ-

[61] Bornhak, *Universitätsverwaltung*, 147.

[62] F.A.M.G. Castillon, *Ueber die Begriffe einer Academie und einer Universität. . . . Eine Vorlesung gehalten in der königlichen Academie der Wissenschaften am 26sten October 1809* (Berlin 1809), 36-37.

ing Ernst Brandes in his *Ueber den gegenwärtigen Zustand der Universität Göttingen*. In arguments that prefigure those of the Humboldtian reformers, Brandes urged that the professor is not merely a teacher of youth, but a scholar and a writer as well. But that professorial scholarship should be oriented toward research and discovery Brandes was not ready to admit:

> A few thoughtful men set too high a criterion in judging the worth of an academic; they demand that all professors be among the foremost intellects, that all be distinctive geniuses and discoverers. Aside from the impossibility of this demand, a discoverer in individual branches of learning could be a bad professor. Aside from the gift of lecturing, which minds of this type often lack, the professor ought to embrace and to have worked out the whole of his science. This characteristic is essential; and it is completely different from the perceptiveness (*Scharfblick*), the creative spirit (*Erfindungsgeist*), and it can be combined with them occasionally but not always.
>
> We prefer the more sufficient and in general more useful demand that the professors ought to maintain, disseminate, and where possible enlarge the treasury of human wisdom. The fundamental erudition (*Gelehrsamkeit*) which we demand of professors is not an unsystematic, useless learning which leads to nothing, but rather it must be directed by judgment and order . . . , an erudition which does not dissolve the powers of judgment, an erudition which can be maintained only by the greatest diligence like that which the scholars of Göttingen so excellently exemplify.[63]

In part, theorists' unanimous faith that the intellectual attributes of the successful discoverer must differ radically from those of the teacher reflected their preassumptions about the nature of academic discovery itself. The modern academic tacitly assumes that discovery arises normally from research, that is, from the systematic application of definite scholarly techniques to some limited area of investigation for the purpose of extracting critical knowledge. The 18th century, however, did not tacitly equate academic discovery with the results of research in any formal sense. In fact the very concept of research in its familiar form seems not to have been clearly articulated before 1790, for even university theorists spoke invariably of discoveries (*Entdeckungen*) and emendations (*Verbesserungen*) in the sciences rather than research (*Forschung*). Most theorists viewed discovery as arising from sheer force of intellect, from the penetrating mind which could seize a previously unrecognized relationship, or from the powerful mind

[63] Brandes, *Göttingen*, 159-61.

which could order a mass of learning on a new level of comprehensiveness and so extract the higher generalization. In short, discovery remained the prerogative of genius alone except in the cases when it resulted from sheer chance:

> Finally, the discovery of new truths depends so very much on chance that one can scarcely establish it as someone's duty. Most discoveries are made, not because one seeks them, but rather because chance brings them into our hands, or that with one long known truth another will occur to us at just the right time, out of which a third may be concluded. In only a few cases it is within the power of the greatest genius to discover through mere diligence and continued investigation some unknown truth which one desires to know.[64]

Occasionally theorists combined with this outlook on the nature of academic discovery surprisingly pessimistic views on the very possibility of new discoveries in various academic fields. J. D. Michaelis and Christoph Meiners, at least, regarded large fields of learning as essentially static. In his defense of the academic career in 1776, Meiners contrasted those sciences which are constantly in flux with "those sciences that are static and admit of no change." This distinction seemed to draw upon Michaelis, who in his *Raisonnement* had argued against the expectation of professorial discovery on the grounds that "there are in fact sciences in which one can scarcely expect the discovery of new truths." These sciences by no means included only a few isolated fields, but rather philosophy, law, theology, and by implication, much of history as well. Medicine and the natural sciences lay open to discovery, but only, Michaelis carefully pointed out, to men of innate genius. If the possibility of discovery was so restricted, if it was the mere product of chance or the monopoly of genius, then the average professor could never be a discoverer and the expansion of scholarship could not be a major duty of the university.[65]

IV. CONCLUSION: THE OLD UNIVERSITIES AND THE NEW

As the mood of crisis deepened over the German university system in the decades after 1760, many thoughtful academics sensed the institutions to be approaching a historical crossroads. The sudden outpouring of hostile critiques and reform tracts probed the symptoms of university decline, including the gradual loss of the universities' once

---

[64] Michaelis, *Raisonnement*, II, 132; also see Castillon, *Begriffe*, 29.

[65] Christoph Meiners, "Schutzschrift für den Stand und die Lebensart der Professoren," *Vermischte philosophische Schriften* (Leipzig 1776), III, 141; and Michaelis, *Raisonnement*, II, 124, 129.

preeminent leadership of Germany's intellectual and scholarly life. Critics vaguely sensed that the corporate definition of the professorial career was beginning to hamper the vigor of professorial scholarship. The centripetal, collegiate loyalties which that definition implied gave academics little incentive to participate in the rigorous modes of research and scholarly interaction rapidly emerging in many areas of German learning. Similarly, the use of collegiate and corporate criteria in appointments, so necessary to solidarity and economy, seemed simultaneously to be depriving university scholarship of needed incentive. By 1800 these considerations and many, many others had convinced academics, especially those in Prussia, that a major upheaval was imminent and inevitable. The question was, would it be university abolition or university reform, and if reform, along what lines.

The reformers and theorists who spoke for the universities proved better at diagnosing old ills than in agreeing upon a new ideal of university life. But in spite of many disagreements and differences of emphasis, they approached a consensus on the difficult issue of professorial scholarship. Publication is commendable and beneficial to the university, most agreed, but few advocated it as an absolute criterion for the professorate. Publication itself, they felt, should embrace many different kinds of literary work, including popular or didactic treatises and belles lettres, with a special premium placed on textbooks beneficial to the professor's pedagogical duties. Theorists regarded discovery as the highest, most honored achievement of scholarship; but at the same time they considered it too rare, too illusive, to form a realistic scholarly norm. These convictions set the 18th century attitude toward professorial scholarship apart from the new university ideology soon to arise in Germany in the wake of the Humboldtian reforms.

The preceding discussions give a basis for reevaluating the traditional interpretation of the 18th century universities' outlook on scholarship. That traditional view maintains that the professoriate regarded itself primarily as a teaching body. The individual academic felt no obligation by virtue of his chair to make "discoveries" or to strive for new interpretations. That imperative, the traditional view goes on, arose only in the 19th century largely under the influence of Humboldtian ideology. In support of this interpretation many university spokesmen did claim that the institutions' first duty was to teach, to prepare students for a profession, and some urged this even to the exclusion of university scholarship. No theorist claimed that discovery, as distinct from other forms of scholarly activity, could ever be regarded as a duty intrinsic to the professorate. The great emphasis placed upon creative scholarship at a university like Göttingen shows that the generalization cannot be applied indiscriminately to all institutions; but even at Göttingen a literary reputation had not become an absolute pre-requisite for a chair by 1765. These characteristics do suggest for the university system as a whole a predominantly pedagogical conception of the professorate.

On a deeper level the preceding discussions suggest that the distinc-tion which the traditional interpretation attempts to draw is not so much false as trivial. What distinguished the "old universities" of the later 18th century from the "new universities" of the 19th was not their differing assessments of the professoriate's obligation to learning. It was rather their different visions of scholarship itself, their very differ-ent assessments regarding of what scholarship should ideally consist. By 1835 much professorial learning had narrowed into disciplinary channels oriented toward research, discovery, and specialization. The old universities, however, would never have accepted the 19th cen-tury's tacit assumption that this approach should represent the exclu-sive or ideal form of scholarship. Granted their convictions about the nature of academic discovery and the potential for academic advance, they could only have regarded that assumption as wholly unrealistic and unduly restrictive. Their own vision embraced a more synthetic, more style-oriented, and in many respects more humane approach to learning. Furthermore this vision of scholarship lay deeply rooted in the institutional context of the professorate and the social patterns of scholarly interaction, both of which were to undergo substantial changes only during the early 19th century. To approach the old uni-versities unaware of these distinctions of institutional context and aca-demic vision means to impose upon them 19th century concepts which had no place in German academia before the Humboldtian era.

11

The Sources of German Student Unrest
1815-1848

by Konrad H. Jarausch

Confronted with the student challenge, journalistic and scholarly commentators have tended to interpret campus dissent as intensified generational conflict,[1] deepened identity crisis,[2] or increased protest proneness of individual personalities.[3] But within the process of modernization and industrialization, such socio-psychological explanations raise the historical problem of the breakdown of communal and corporate youth culture and its challenge by a critical counterculture characterized by different values, customs, and organizations. Facilitating the transition from family (dependence) to work (independence) in a variety of group experiences, traditional student associations, such as social fraternities, religious and artistic circles, athletic clubs and intellectual debating societies, socialize the future elite toward adult roles and form a safety valve for sporadic outbursts of violence, sexual license, etc. But at certain junctures, opposition groups arise, based on voluntary participation and anti-authoritarian ideals, propagating a consciousness radically disaffiliated from the mainstream assumptions of the grown-up world. The primary modes of such protest behavior tend to be either cultural—i.e., bohemian life-style rebellion—or political—i.e., radical activism channeled into movements advocating revolution or reaction. In the perspective of 19th century

* An earlier version of this paper was read at the Central European History session of the AHA meeting at New York, 1971. The expansion and revision were made possible through a grant from the University of Missouri Research Council.

[1] S. N. Eisenstadt, *From Generation to Generation* (New York 1956); and *Modernization: Protest and Change* (Englewood Cliffs, N.J. 1966), 26ff. Cf. also Lewis S. Feuer, *The Conflict of Generations: The Character and Significance of Student Movements* (New York 1969) for an attempt to apply this concept to different historical examples, perceptively criticized by Richard Flacks in *J. Social Hist.* 4 (1970), 141ff.

[2] Erik H. Erikson, *Childhood and Society* (New York 1963, 2d ed.), 247ff; *Identity: Youth and Crisis* (New York 1968); and his most recent ideas summarized in "Reflections on the Dissent of Contemporary Youth," *Daedalus* (Winter 1970) 154ff.

[3] Kenneth Keniston, "The Sources of Student Dissent," *J. Social Issues* (1967); *Young Radicals: Notes on Committed Youth* (New York 1968) and for the further development of his concepts cf. *Youth and Dissent: The Rise of a New Opposition* (New York 1971).

Europe, the basic conceptual question must therefore be reformulated: Why does youth suddenly shift from traditional culture to counter-culture and back?[4]

Such a comparative analysis of individual instances of the transition from communal-corporate to modern universalistic youth groups should allow further refinement of present explanations of youthful propensity to act as vanguard of change.[5] The objection that students as transitory beings possess only a vague sense of solidarity but no class consciousness and that protest involves merely a committed minority activating a larger passive constituency need not be fatal, since it is precisely the increase in strength of endemic radicalism and the creation of a receptive audience which needs to be explored. The first modern student movement, the German *Burschenschaft* of the *Vormärz* (pre-1848 revolution era) is an excellent case in point, since it was the ambiguous ancestor of both the volkish protest of Weimar (Nazi) and the extra-parliamentary opposition of Bonn (APO).[6] Because 19th century university archives permit neither the construction of psychological linkages for individuals or groups, nor a satisfactory re-creation of family structures, the present essay will limit itself to analyzing the relative dominance of certain ideological, political, institutional, and social impulses in the development of the German student movement. This inductive investigation of clusters of shifting factors seeks to establish an intermediary historical framework which systematizes the sources of student protest in preindustrial contexts and provides a theoretical counterpoint to explanations of current dissent.[7]

[4] Theodore Roszak, *Counter-Culture* (New York 1969); Frank Parkin, "Adolescent Status and Student Politics," *JCH* 5 (1970), 144ff; and Philip Abrams, "Rites de Passage: The Conflict of Generations in Industrial Society," ibid., 175ff, all emphasize the switch from traditional to counterculture as the critical analytical problem.

[5] Although the authoritative collection edited by S. M. Lipset, in *Daedalus* (1968), called "Students and Politics" (hardcover edition: *Students in Revolt* [New York 1970]), and the special issue of the *Political Science Quart.* of June 1969 dealing with student rebellion stress crosscultural comparison, they drastically slight the problem of time perspective. Historians themselves are to blame for this state of affairs, since most of their contributions such as those collected in *JCH* 5, no. 1 (1970), under the title "Generations in Conflict" are naïve in terms of social science methodology. Cf. Phyllis H. Stock, "Students versus the University in pre-World War One Paris," *FHS* 8 (1971), 93ff, and Jesse G. Lutz, "The Chinese Student Movement of 1945-1949," *J. Asian Studies*, 21 (1971), 89ff.

[6] Jürgen Schwarz, "Die deutsche Studentenschaft in der Zeit von 1918 bis 1923 und ihre Stellung zur Politik," Ph.D. diss., Univ. of Freiburg (1962); and the literature cited by Wolfgang Zorn, "Student Politics in the Weimar Republic," *JCH* 5 (1970), 128ff.

[7] For attempts to develop a historical model of youthful unrest, cf. Richard Flacks, "Social and Cultural Meanings of Student Revolt," in E. E. Sampson and

Although attempting to generalize about the prevailing pattern at all German institutions on the basis of an extensive older Burschenschaft literature this case study will draw most heavily on the documentary sources of Heidelberg and Bonn.[8]

I

Self-conscious and organized student unrest arose first in Central Europe because the peculiar sequence of modernization endowed the mandarin elite with a prestigious influence, duplicated only where change was similarly imported from the outside. Rather than self-generated, as in the West, reform demands were raised by a bureaucratic intelligentsia, imitating foreign models, in a largely traditional society which possessed neither national unity, participatory political structures, nor more than feeble beginnings of industrialization. The collapse of the anachronistic Holy Roman Empire and Napoleon's disastrous defeat of Frederickian Prussia presented the reformers around Baron von Stein with the opportunity to modernize army, state, economy, and social structure with a large transfusion of Liberal ideas. Though neither breaking Hohenzollern absolutism nor Junker dominance, these Prussian reforms facilitated the emergence of a self-conscious *Bildungsbürgertum*, striving for equality with the noblesse of birth through education. With this social purpose, Wilhelm von Humboldt fundamentally restructured German higher learning and replaced the practical Enlightenment encyclopedism with a new ideal of *Bildung* (cultivation) and a revolutionary ethos of *Wissenschaft* (research). In practical terms this departure from tradition to innovation meant abandoning the cameralist preparation of public officials

---

H. A. Korn, eds., *Student Activism and Protest* (San Francisco 1970), 117ff, and John R. Gillis, "Youth and History: An Introduction" unpublished paper, Princeton Univ. (1970). Cf. also Peter Loewenberg, "The Psychohistorical Origins of the Nazi Youth Cohort," *AHR* 76 (1971), 1457ff.

[8] For a comprehensive list of the older scholarship, see W. Erman and E. Horn, *Bibliographie der deutschen Universitäten* (Leipzig and Berlin 1904), 596ff. See also L. Petry, "Deutsche Forschungen nach dem zweiten Weltkrieg zur Geschichte der Universitäten," *Vierteljahrshefte für Sozial- und Wirtschaftsgeschichte* 46 (1959), 145-203; Hermann Haupt, ed., *Quellen und Darstellungen zur Geschichte der Burschenschaft und der deutschen Einheitsbewegung* (Heidelberg 1910), 1ff. The actual history of the Burschenschaft is treated by Paul Wentzcke, *Vor und Frühgeschichte bis zu den Karlsbader Beschlüssen* (Heidelberg 1919), vi; G. Heer, *Die Demagogenzeit: Von den Karlsbader Beschlüssen bis zum Frankfurter Wachensturm, 1820-1833* (Frankfurt 1927), x, and *Die Zeit des Progresses: Von 1833 bis 1859* (Frankfurt 1929), xi, 97ff. Cf. also Paul Wentzcke, ed., *Darstellungen und Quellen zur Geschichte der deutschen Einheitsbewegung im neunzehnten und zwanzigsten Jahrhundert* (Heidelberg 1957), 1ff.

Konrad H. Jarausch

in favor of a neo-hellenistic idealism. The philosophical vision of Fichte, Schleiermacher, and Schelling endowed the intellectual with a new exalted duty: through the pursuit of knowledge the scholar should purify the state into a *Rechts-* and *Kulturstaat*. This conjuncture of the onset of modernization with the rise of the educated bourgeoisie and a heightened academic mission provided fertile soil for the growth of student unrest.[9]

Since the Humboldtian redefinition of university purpose did little to change their actual role, the students formed a movement in 1815 to renew their own life and customs themselves. Because of intermittent adult repression, this Burschenschaft evolved in three fairly discontinuous stages, differing in modes of inspiration, organization, and action. The initial Christian-German *Schwärmer* (visionary enthusiasts) phase largely stemmed from an acute rejection of Restoration values and served as the ideological matrix of subsequent dissent by formulating a countercreed. Those who spontaneously came together at Protestant north-central German universities were members of an age cohort, marked by the generational event of the Napoleonic Wars, in which early defeat tended to weaken the authority of the parents and later victory in turn proved the superiority of national and liberal ideas. As the first age group which had been taught the neo-humanist ideals as well as the patriotic values of the *Nationalpädagogen*, they volunteered in considerable numbers to fight against Napoleon. Matured before their time through being freed from parental supervision and being allowed to act out their heroic dreams, the *Kriegsfreiwillige* on their return gathered together in reading groups or joined Jahn's teutonic *Turner* (gymnasts) in order to steel their minds and bodies for future struggles for the fatherland. More than one-half of the founders of the student movement were sons of the educated bourgeoisie, a higher percentage than in the general student body, and while nobility and commercial middle class constituted approximately the same share in both groups, the lower middle class was underrepresented in

[9] The founding writings are in Ernst Anrich, ed., *Die Idee der deutschen Universität* (Darmstadt 1956); Eduard Spranger, *Wilhelm von Humboldt und die Reform des Bildungswesens* (Tübingen 1910 and 1960); René König, *Vom Wesen der deutschen Universität* (Berlin 1935, 1970). See also Mohammed Rassem, "Die problematische Stellung der Studenten im Humboldtschen System," *Studien und Berichte der katholischen Akademie Bayern* 44 (1968), 15-35. For the social transformation, cf. Hans Gerth, *Die sozialgeschichtliche Lage der bürgerlichen Intelligenz um die Wende des 18. Jahrhunderts* (Frankfurt 1935); W. H. Bruford, *Germany in the Eighteenth Century: The Social Background of the Literary Revival* (London 1935), and the other literature cited in my paper, "*Menschenbildung* as Bourgeois Ideal: The Social Role of the Neo-Humanist Prussian University" (Princeton Univ. 1970).

the Burschenschaft.[10] Although profoundly restorative in their longing for purity and community, these students nevertheless wholeheartedly embraced the modernizing values of the adult reformers and (after the French defeat) clashed sharply with the majority of their elders, who were striving for postwar and counterrevolutionary stability. Inspired by the anti-Napoleonic rhetoric of Schiller, Arndt, Jahn and Körner, the *Urburschenschaft* founded at Jena embraced a liberal constitutionalism and propagated an anti-particularist German nationalism according to the motto "honor, freedom, fatherland." Since the students' impetus was primarily ideological, the constitution of the *Allgemeine deutsche Burschenschaft* (the national organization created in 1818) called for reform by individual change of consciousness through "the christian-germanic training of all spiritual and physical talents for the service of the nation."[11]

On the level of student life and customs, the rejection of tradition was equally decisive. The overriding aim of the movement was to abolish the corporate obscurantism of ancient *Burschenfreiheit*, an informal freedom won from the authorities which had turned to such riotous license that the Prussian king in 1798 had to threaten severe penalties against further excesses. Except for a brief flowering of

---

[10] This characterization of the founding cohort is based on 157 Burschenschaftler at Tübingen, 1815-1817, named by Georg Schmidgall in "Tübinger Burschenschaftslisten, 1816-1936," in P. Wentzke, ed., *Burschenschaftslisten* (Heidelberg 1942) and checked against A. Bürk and W. Wille, eds., *Die Matrikeln der Universität Tübingen* (Tübingen 1953), III, and below, n. 28. Günther Steiger's attempt to quantify the Burschenschaftler of the Wartburgfest in Max Steinmetz, ed., *Geschichte der Universität Jena 1548/58-1958* (Jena 1958), I, 345f, II, 526ff, remains rudimentary. Cf. also F. Gunther Eyck, "The Political Theories and Activities of the German Academic Youth between 1815 and 1819," *JMH* 27 (1955), 26ff. Lewis Feuer's chapter, "Suicidalism and Terrorism in the German Student Movement," in his *Conflict of Generations*, 54f, is a foil for his contemporary phobias and a late fruit of the Luther to Bismarck to Hitler school of German historiography.

[11] P. Wentzcke, *Geschichte der Deutschen Burschenschaft*, vol. I, passim; H. Haupt, "Die Verfassungsurkunde der Jenaischen Burschenschaft vom 12. Juni, 1815," in *Quellen und Darstellungen*, I, 114ff; E. Dietz, "Die Teutonia und die Allgemeine Burschenschaft zu Halle," in ibid., II, 215ff; G. Heer, "Verfassung und Ziele der alten Marburger Burschenschaft," in ibid., I, 211ff, and Eduard Voigt, *Der Anteil der Berliner Studentenschaft an der allgemeinen deutschen Burschenschaft bis zu ihrer ersten Katastrophe* (Berlin 1914). For the evolution of the constitution of the Burschenschaft, cf. G. Heer, "Die ältesten Urkunden zur Geschichte der allgem. dt. Burschenschaft," in *Quellen und Darstellungen* XIII, 61ff, including the famous nineteen points to be adopted by all chapters and the official report of the first *Burschentag*. Since romantic nationalism is the best-known feature of the Burschenschaft in the West, the present essay makes no attempt to belabor the obvious.

[537]

Konrad H. Jarausch

Masonic orders (Enlightenment oriented) and literary societies (their *Sturm und Drang* counterparts), German student sub-culture had been dominated by the drinking and dueling *Comment* (written custom) of the *Landsmannschaften* (ancient regional fraternities). Glorying in an adolescent *Pennalismus* (combining the negative aspects of school rituals) students had developed the types of the gross *Rennomist*, a mixture of boorish bragging and Junker fighting, and the modish aristocratic and frenchified *Stutzer*. Against the authoritarian organization and social exclusiveness of the fraternities—a microcosm of absolutist society—the Burschenschaften proposed a new kind of student association, embracing all "honorable students" without regard to regional origin or social distinction in a model for a future German state, based on the "equality and freedom of the flourishing people." Rejecting whoring, fighting, and running up debts as immature, radical students strove to "maintain and strengthen national custom and power, spiritual and physical justice, honor and equality of rights among all Burschen as long as they uphold Wissenschaft, law, morality, fatherland and especially their estate." Breaking with the feudal and absolutist spirit of the fraternities, this program called for the emancipation of the student from schoolboy to citizen of the academic community, reflecting the larger transition from *Untertan* to *Bürger*. In practical terms, Burschenschaftler strove for chastity and severe restraints against dueling and gambling, i.e., "the moral regeneration of student life." Through gymnastics and fencing, through scientific discussion groups and a less compulsive form of recreation, they sought to offer a positive alternative. Nevertheless, the departure from the past was incomplete, and since many former Landsmannschaftler were founding fathers of the Burschenschaft, a sectarian teutonic, anti-Semitic romanticism colored their life style. Hence the Urburschenschaft was a transitional creature, striving for a democratic form of student association and government but incapable of transcending a century-old tradition in all respects.[12]

Despite flamboyant rhetoric, the practical actions of the Burschenschaftler were less than momentous. The notorious Wartburg Festival of 1817, commemorating both the tricentennial of the Reformation and the Leipzig victory over Napoleon, was largely a fraternal and religious demonstration of the students' "dedication to truth and jus-

[12] G. Heer, "Die ältesten Urkunden zur Geschichte der allgemeinen deutschen Burschenschaft," in *Quellen und Darstellungen* XIII, 61ff. Cf. also the vivid portraits in Friedrich Schulze and Paul Ssymank, *Das deutsche Studententum* (Leipzig 1910), supplemented by such local club histories as Hans Gerhardt, *Hundert Jahre Bonner Corps* (Bonn 1926), and Otto Oppermann, *Die Burschenschaft Alemannia zu Bonn und ihre Vorläufer* (Bonn 1925).

tice" and their patriotic longing for "the unification of Germany" frustrated by the Congress of Vienna. Only the programmatic denunciation of the authorities both with the restoration governments and in the press, turned the Turners' (Jahn's gymnasts') symbolic burning of a Prussian corset, a Hessian wig, and an Austrian corporal's staff, together with the works of the intellectual defenders of the *status quo*, into a controversial political event. The radical manifesto "Principles and Decisions," which was never officially adopted for fear of jeopardizing future bureaucratic careers, urged the study of "morality, politics, and history" rather than direct action in order to achieve the goals of national unity, constitutional government, the true abolition of serfdom, freedom of speech, and the rule of law.[13] Only a small minority of the estimated 1500 Burschen among the more than 5000 students between 1815 and 1820 shared the extreme views of the Blacks or *Unbedingten* (the unconditionally committed) of Giessen, gathered around the charismatic Charles Follen, who agitated for a christian teutonic egalitarian republic. Ironically it was the assassination of the tsarist apologist, and minor poet, Kotzebue by the highstrung and unbalanced Sand, a member of this circle, which provided Metternich with the pretext for launching the Carlsbad Decrees, marking the physical end of the initial phase.[14] Although knowing that "Germany is in no

[13] For the contemporary controversy between the participants of the festival, Maassmann, Kieser, and Fries, and the defenders of the restoration regimes, Kamptz and Stourdza, cf. the articles by Günther Steiger, "Die Theilnehmer des Wartburgfestes von 1817: Erste kritische Ausgabe der sog. Präsenzliste," in *Darstellungen und Quellen* IV, 65ff, and "Das Phantom der Wartburg-Verschwörung," *Student und Nation* (Jena 1966), 183ff. The text of the "Grundsätze und Beschlüsse des 18. Oktobers," the only, albeit unofficial, political document of the Urburschenschaft is reprinted as an appendix by H. Ehrentreich, "Heinrich Luden und sein Einfluss auf die Burschenschaft," in ibid., IV, 48ff. The anonymous article on the "Burschenfest auf der Wartburg," in the *Zeitschrift für Deutschlands Hochschulen*, nos. 26-29 (1845), also stressed the meeting's "*schwärmerische* and therefore unpolitical nature."

[14] Karl Follen, *Beiträge zur Geschichte der teutschen Sammtschulen seit dem Freiheitskriege 1813* (n.p. 1818); Adolf L. Follen, *Freie Stimmen Frischer Jugend* (Jena 1819); K. A. von Müller, *Karl Ludwig Sand* (Munich 1925); and the most recent evaluation by Willi Schröder, "Politische Ansichten und Aktionen der 'Unbedingten' in der Burschenschaft," *Student und Nation*, 223 which plays up the radicals' progressivism. Though ideologically typical, the anti-Semitic clause adopted because of pressure of the Blacks in 1818 and rescinded a decade later, had little practical effect, since less than 3 percent of German students at the time were Jews and it did not apply to those baptized. Cf. also Karl Griewank, "Die Politische Bedeutung der Burschenschaft in den ersten Jahren ihres Bestehens," in *Wissenschaftliche Zeitschrift der Friedrich Schiller Universität Jena* (1952-53), 27ff; Jürgen Schwarz, "Deutsche Studenten und Politik im 19. Jahrhundert," *Geschichte in Wissenschaft und Unterricht* 20 (1969), 72-94; and K. G.

Konrad H. Jarausch

serious danger," the coachman of Europe conjured up the image of a grand conspiracy, led by the political Professors Kieser, Fries, Luden, and Oken, and warned that at the universities "a whole generation of revolutionaries must be formed unless the evil is restrained." By prosecuting students and professors, by strengthening censorship, and by limiting the demands for constitutions to *landständische Verfassungen* (regional estate bodies) the restoration regimes in the German Confederation sought once more to contract the public sphere and to bureaucratize political affairs. But despite its swift suppression, the student movement succeeded in developing an organizational counterform to the fraternity system and an ideological critique of Biedermaier society in a contradictory mixture of volkish-mystical and moral-liberal strains.[15]

II

During the second, *Demagogen*, phase after 1827 the Burschenschaft, politicized more by persecution than volition, transformed itself into a conspiratorial secret society and moved from intellectual agitation to practical political action. Despite the federal Mainz Investigating Commission's vigorous eradication of real radical groups such as the *Jünglingsbund* and imagined conspiracies such as the "geheime Bund," the student movement reemerged locally and nationally on the basis of an oral as well as a written tradition perpetuated in families and secondary schools by its "old boys." But to survive outside the law, counterculture had to jettison its openness and egalitarianism in favor of the more restrictive and elitist forms of corporate groupings such as the division between an inner circle and a wider social following, the *engere Verein* and the *Renoncenschwanz*. The gradual renewal of public debate and the resurgence of literary radicalism produced a schism of the two strains which had combined in uneasy balance, the politically committed *Germanen*, who advocated constitutional reform but resembled fraternities in student affairs, and the moral-scholarly *Arminen*, whose primary aim was the regeneration of student life—

Faber, "Student und Politik in der ersten deutschen Burschenschaft," ibid. 21 (1970), 68ff.

[15] Metternich to Gentz 17 June 1819, in Prince Richard Metternich, ed., *Memoirs of Prince Metternich*, English ed. (New York 1880-82), III, 287. Cf. also Franz Schnabel, *Deutsche Geschichte im neunzehnten Jahrhundert* (Freiburg 1949), II, 234ff; and Maria Wawrykowa, *Ruch Studencke w Niemcech 1815-1825* (Warsaw 1969). For a provocative reevaluation, cf. Enno E. Kraehe's paper, "The Origins of the Carlsbad Decrees," AHA meeting (1971). Cf. also H. Tümmler, "Wartburg, Weimar und Wien," *Historische Zeitschrift* 215 (1972), 49-106, and G. Steiger, *Aufbruch: Urburschenschaft und Wartburgfest* (Leipzig 1967).

such as the abolition of dueling—but who foreswore politics. Conscious that Germany was still "half sleeping, half awake" the former strove to "gain political independence, in order to stand in the waves like a rock in the surf," thus leading the fatherland into a Liberal and National future: "The realization of the principles of our century . . . is at stake." When the French crowned Louis Philippe a bourgeois king, the activists demanded that "for Germany too, the July revolution must herald the dawn of a new age." Hence they omitted the phrase *preparation* from the constitution of the refounded Allgemeine Burschenschaft and now boldly called for "the *realization* of political participation for the German people, ordered and secured by public freedom and justice" (my italics).[16]

Years of repression, combined with the fall of the Restoration regime in Paris, inspired the second cohort of Burschenschaftler with a willingness to act out their rhetoric directed towards a constitutional or republican state. Participating prominently in the mass celebration of the Hambach Fest of 1832, both a demonstration against local absolutism and an attempt to organize radicals on a national scale, the Germanen joined the Liberal *Presseverein* and agitated in favor of the Polish rising. Prodded by the most committed chapter at Heidelberg, the Allgemeine Burschenschaft disregarded the threatening resolutions of the German Confederation and resolved that "the practical political course . . . must be continued, and the revolution must be pursued as the only practical means." This action program made it "the duty of every Burschenschaftler to publicize his political opinion through word and pen, to found political clubs with citizens, to organize press associations, to buy weapons and to exercise in their use." Undeterred by the disavowal of several moderate universities such as Bonn and Breslau, student radicals eagerly followed the call of the *Vaterlandsverein* (the organization of grown-up activists) to Frankfurt in April 1833 and attempted to seize the capital of the Deutsche Bund as a beachhead for a universal uprising. Some 50 radical students, led by several adult intellectuals and artisans, stormed the police headquar-

16 G. Heer, *Geschichte der deutschen Burschenschaft*, II, passim; A. Petzold, "Die Zentral-Untersuchungs-Kommission in Mainz," *Quellen und Darstellungen*, v, 171ff. Two of the most influential pieces of the written tradition were J. L. Haupt's, *Landsmannschaften und Burschenschaft* (Leipzig 1820) and F. Herbst, *Ideale und Irrthümer des academischen Lebens in unserer Zeit* (Stuttgart 1823). For the victory of the Germanen, cf. G. Heer, "Die Allgemeine deutsche Burschenschaft und ihre Burschentage, 1827-1833," in *Quellen und Darstellungen*, IV, 246ff. The impact of the French Revolution is dramatized by the letters in Otto Oppermann, "Burschenschaftlerbriefe aus der Zeit der Julirevolution," *Neue Heidelberger Jahrbücher* 13 (1904), 57-120. See also R. R. Lutz, "The German Revolutionary Student Movement, 1819-1933," *Central European History* 4 (1971), 215-41.

ters of the imperial city in the evening of 3 April 1833, while outside the gates several groups of peasants awaited the signal and between 300 and 400 Poles stood poised to cross the Rhine. "We were all firmly convinced that even if our step should fail and we would perish, we had to take some kind of action," a student afterward described the motivation of the putschists. "We were certain that every spilled drop of blood would bring a thousandfold harvest in the future."

Ridiculed because of its failure to provoke a popular rebellion, the Frankfurt *Wachensturm* was nevertheless the first armed threat in Germany against the restoration system and an important symbolic precursor of the 1848 revolt. A Prussian prosecutor concluded accurately: "The Burschenschaft has become a thoroughly revolutionary organization whose rebellious paper dreams have turned into concrete violence." Direct revolutionary action proved such a disaster that in the ensuing repression 1200 Burschenschaftler were indicted, including even the harmless Arminen, thus destroying many a promising career through imprisonment or emigration. Hence the traditional fraternities, which had transformed themselves from Landsmannschaften into Corps, were tacitly approved by university authorities as wholesome fun, and reasserted their control over student life. A curator could note with considerable satisfaction: "The radicals are getting slowly older and the overwhelming influence of the largely reliable citizenry makes itself felt in favor of stability." The Demagogen phase demonstrated conclusively that by severing their connection with the reformers of student life, the political radicals were unable to overthrow the restoration regimes even with the help of adult minorities.[17]

III

In the least-known third, *Progress*, phase of the 1840s, radical German students turned toward *Gleichheit* (equality) rather than unity and

[17] G. Heer, "Die ältesten Urkunden," in *Quellen und Darstellungen*, XIII, 61ff; and Harry Gerber, "Der Frankfurter Wachensturm vom 3. April, 1833," ibid., XIV, 171ff. Cf. also the printed "Straferkenntnis des Kriminalsenats des kgl. Kammergerichts wider die Theilnehmer an den geheimen burschenschaftlichen Verbindungen an den Universitäten Greifswald und Breslau, Dezember 5 und 12, 1835," in Preussisches Staatsarchiv Coblenz, abt. 403 no. 2428, and the report of the Badensian Ministry of Interior, 15 April, 1836 Generallandesarchiv Karlsruhe 235/431. See further the repeated ministerial efforts to coax universities into enforcing strict suppression of the Burschenschaft, Badensian Ministry of Interior to Heidelberg Senate, 19 January, 1836, Heidelberg Univ. Archive, VIII, 1, no. 233a, Regierungsbevollmächtigter to Ministry of Interior, 7 April, 1836, GLAK 235/430, and Curator Rehfues to Bonn Senate, 20 March, 1837, Bonn Univ. Archive, Rektorat, U 164 and U 166; A. Toepel, *Die Studentenverfolgungen in Bonn von 1819-1852* (Bonn 1918); and Douglas Hale, "The Persecution of the Demagogues," unpublished paper (Stillwater 1972).

freedom, because they were preoccupied with institutional and social concerns. Unlike the Schwärmer and demagogues, the progressive cohort was not marked by a single overpowering generational event, but rather mobilized gradually through the Francophobe Rhine-enthusiasm of 1840 and the disappointment of their hopes in a new era under Frederick William IV. Student dissenters, some of whom were already the second biological generation within the movement, drew on the romanticized Burschenschaft tradition, the criticism of an increasingly uncensored press, the example of the liberal-democratic opposition in the southwestern provincial diets, and on a rather general and diffuse dissatisfaction with the organizational forms of student life. The progressive movement set out "to bring reason into stagnant medieval academic life, to effect through pen, word and deed the abolition of ancient student abuses within the university and to merge with the great people" outside the ivy walls. According to one concerned official the "purpose of these associations is the same as that of the former Burschenschaften; it chiefly consists in enmity against the existing governmental system, agitation for a general constitution in Germany, favoritism toward writers of Young Germany, enthusiastic approval of the ultra-liberal people's party; and especially within the university, in opposition against the Corps and Landsmannschaften decried by them as aristocratic." Now only one part of a larger anti-Metternich movement, the activists sought to revitalize the "spirit of freedom, justice and progress," suppressed by the Frankfurt Commission of Inquiry. Since they were strongly influenced by their reading and discussion of the Young Hegelians, the democratic poets and the French Utopian Socialists, radicals groped for new organizational models, characterized by "the greatest freedom and informality." The failure of demagogic conspiring made them "the most resolute opponents of secrecy," while the degeneration of the Burschenschaften into quasi-Corps (hierarchical structure, dueling, etc.) made them prefer the foundation of completely equal progressive associations "renouncing all external signs, replacing the duel with a court of honor and exclusively dedicated to moral, scholarly and social tasks." Although they were little more than institutionalizations of friendship circles and were therefore often rent by schisms and disputes, these *Progress-Vereine* in their consequential universalism, egalitarianism, and ideological radicalism were the first truly modern student associations on European soil.[18]

[18] G. Heer, *Geschichte der Burschenschaft*, III, passim. Ernst G. Deuerlein, "Zur Geschichte des studentischen Progresses in Erlangen," in *Quellen und Darstellungen*, I, 157ff; H. Gerber, "Vom Bonner Burschenschaftlichen Progress," *Bonner Zeitung*, 6 and 13 July, 1930, and "Die Burschenschaft und der Progress," *Burschen-*

In order to arrive at a more rational form of "social, moral, and scholarly relations in student life," progressive activists had to renew student government as well. Rebelling against the tyranny of the SC (*Senioren Convent*), i.e., the interfraternity council of the Corps and Landsmannschaften, reform associations first formed a counter AC (*Allgemeiner Convent*), representing Burschenschaften, dissenting fraternities, and Progressive groups. But this half-way house was soon superseded everywhere by an *Allgemeine Studentenschaft* led by a committee elected by the entire student body in groups of ten. Advocated by professors like Scheidler in his *Deutscher Studentenspiegel* or assistants like Deinhardt (pseud. E. Anhalt), the demand for democratic student representation was taken up by students like Jahn, Rogge, and Overbeck who coined the slogan: "Down with fraternities and up with people!" During the brief peak of their popularity in 1844-46 such *Allgemeinheiten* comprised often as much as 50 percent of the student body (with the grudging but temporary cooperation of the Corps) and succeeded in greatly reducing duels and excesses because they effectively maximized the force of progressive opinion. Serving as agitational platform for the committed Left, representative student government nevertheless proved ephemeral because it rested on the only passing involvement of independent students, and attempts to institutionalize it in discussion subgroups only led to the resurgence of traditional associations. Moreover the hostile toleration of the authorities refused the *Allgemeinheiten* all power to enforce their reforming program on the recalcitrant SC. Hence, ideological disputes between liberal gradualists and radical revolutionaries, between university reformers and social critics rendered the Kyffhäuser attempt at refounding an Allgemeine Burschenschaft abortive. But the movement published the first significant student newspaper from 1844 to 1846, the *Zeitschrift für Deutschlands Hochschulen*, and formed the consciousness of those activists who fought and died on the barricades two years later. If a value gap between generations and political re-

---

schaftliche Blätter (1935), 231ff; Hermann Haupt, "Die Progressbewegung in Würzburg seit 1840," MS in the Burschenschaftsarchiv in Frankfurt; G. Heer, "Wiederaufleben burschenschaftlicher Bestrebungen seit 1840 und burschenschaftliche Verbindungen bis 1860 an der Universität Marburg," in *Quellen und Darstellungen*, VII, 243ff; G. Juckenberg, "Zur Entstehung der Jenaer studentischen Progressbewegung," in *Student und Nation*, 259ff; Report of the Universitätsamtmann on Student Organizations (September 1843), GLAK 235/30061. The intellectual influence of the Young Hegelians is traced by R. R. Lutz, Jr., in "The 'New Left' of Restoration Germany," *JHI* 21 (1970), 235-52. Since the *Progress* phase is the least-known stage of the German student movement, the bulk of this study will be devoted to its analysis.

pression spurred the first two stages of student dissent, what impulses prompted the renewed radicalism of the 1840s?[19]

Despite all earlier reform efforts, the most immediate issue, galvanizing the third wave of protest in the Vormärz, was the mindless irrelevance of romantic student subculture, immortalized in *The Student Prince*. The successful satire written under the pseudonym August Jäger about a mythical *Felix Schnabel* describes the dominant ideal of a *flotter Bursch*: "The beautiful, colorful caps, leather breeches and jack boots, complete liberty and lack of restraint, frequent dueling and drinking were utterly to [my] taste." One of the alumni later recalled: "In the middle of the everyday world the student had created a universe of his own, the *Burschenwelt*, with peculiar customs and habits, festivals and weapons, songs and melodies, even an independent language." Called a "crass fox" (*Fuchs*), on his arrival the freshman was immediately captured by a Corps (*gekeilt*) and persuaded to join (and share his voucher!) as *Renonce* or *Mitkneipant*. Only through showing his prowess at drinking immense quantities of beer (there were hierarchical beer-states with kaiser, pope, king, dukes, etc. stratified according to amount consumed) and at sword and pistol duels could he become a full member, eventually a *Senior* or *Chargierter*, the formal leaders of the club. This counterpart to Biedermaier philistinism, with its customs of *Landesvater* (a special toast to the local prince) and *Comitat* (a formal cortege for a departing *Altes Haus*) was theoretically apolitical, but practically perpetuated boundless disdain for the independent students, called "savages," "camels," or "finks." In contrast to this atavistic corporatism, the radicals thought of themselves as members of a new, progressive time, in which natural law and critical reason demanded "the transformation of uni-

---

[19] Karl Hermann Scheidler, *Ueber das deutsche Studentenleben und die Notwendigkeit einer innern, von den Studirenden selbst ausgehenden Reform desselben* (Jena 1840); E. Anhalt, *Die Universität: Überblick ihrer Geschichte und Darstellung ihrer gegenwärtigen Aufgabe* (Jena 1846); C. Jahn, *Einige Worte über allgemeine Studentenschaft* (Bonn 1845); Walter Rogge, *Offener Brief an die Bonner Studenten* (Bonn 1846); Johannes Overbeck, *Offener Brief zunächst an die Bonner Studenten* (Bonn 1848). Cf. also the earlier anonymous argument, *Worte eines Studirenden über die Reform der Universitäten, Burschenschaft und Landsmannschaften in ihren Verhältniss unter sich zu der vergangengen und gegenwärtigen Zeit und zu der Reform* (Leipzig 1834). See also the report of the Amtmann of Heidelberg to the Academic Senate, 12 September, 1847, HUA, VIII, 260, and the cursory notes in the Senate protocols of Bonn, BUA, RA VII, 1846. Another excellent source for the ideology and organization of the movement is the *Zeitschrift für Deutschlands Hochschulen* (Z*f*DH), edited by the well-known radical Gustav von Struve between May 1844 and August 1845 and reconstituted by Friedrich Baader as *Akademische Zeitschrift* (*AZ*), November 1845 to March 1846, also published at Heidelberg.

versity life through the free will and the independent effort of its participants" in order to emancipate the students in their own associations as well as in universities and society at large. Hence they most strongly denounced the social exclusiveness and arrogance of these "sons of aristocratic and rich families" since, despite all youthful excesses, "they will only become tools of the bureaucracy and the status quo."[20]

Although not opposed to youthful fun and frolics, the Progressives demanded "the recognition of common student rights, equal votes in all questions, the codification of a *Comment* (custom) in step with the times and the abolition of the ridiculous and senseless laws about drinking beer," which held students in ritualistic infancy. The radicals especially rejected the neo-feudal notions of external honor, embodied in the dueling code. Following a body of professorial criticism (Fichte, Rosenkranz) of the barbarity of such behavior, progressive students considered "the uncouth custom of ostracism" and of "individual combat" one of those medieval legacies which had to be eradicated. Since the *Paukwesen* had degenerated in the 1840s from a defense of individual honor to a quest for the largest number of *Contrahagen* (brawls) without yet having become only athletic exercise, this simplistic form of proving one's mettle was largely responsible for the brutalization of student life. In contrast activists preferred "the judgment of public opinion through an *Ehrengericht* (court of honor) as the sole means" of settling quarrels and disputes. In Heidelberg this central Progressive institution was so successful that during one semester there was no duel, in contrast to hundreds the year before. In order to break corporative consciousness critical students attempted to found reading clubs (*Lesevereine*) which would subscribe to opposition newspapers and provide recent works of liberal, democratic, and socialist writers. As the bigoted Prussian minister of culture Eichhorn observed, these meeting places between professors, intellectuals, and students soon "became a center of political debate and . . . an instigator of illegal actions," and they were therefore immediately prohibited. Though in some instances overdrawn, the progressive indictment of traditional sub-culture persuaded sensitive faculty members in Heidel-

---

[20] August Jäger (?), *Felix Schnabels Universitätsjahre* (Munich 1835), ed. O. J. Bierbaum with selections from the *Burschicose Wörterbuch* (Ragaz 1846) in Berlin, 1907; W. Fabricius, *Die Deutschen Corps* (Frankfurt 1926), 144ff; L[udwig] F[reihardt], "Zur Naturgeschichte des deutschen Studenten," *AZ*, III, 34f; and "Was wir wollen," *Probeblatt* of *ZfDH*, 1f. Polemics with Corps and Burschenschaft proposals for new organization and the reform of student life dominate the pages of the student papers to such an extent that it would be redundant to give anything beyond an illustrative citation, e.g., G. Langreuther, "Die Stellung der Burschenschaft zu ihrer Zeit," *ZfDH*, XXXIV, 317ff, arguing for its self-dissolution.

berg and Bonn to recommend the creation of representative student government, courts of honor, and the abolition of restrictions on organizations since "they were not only unnecessary but harmful." But the stubborn resistance of the corps, the internal disunity of the radicals and the constant fluctuation between ministerial repression and local toleration stalled all student efforts at self-reform, although they could not suppress "individual petrels of revolutionary consciousness."[21]

Their failure to reach more than a minority of their fellow students turned the radicals against the university itself. The gap between the neo-humanist rhetoric of universal *Bildung* and creative *Wissenschaft* and the doctrinaire formalism of turning out bureaucrats triggered a series of critical pamphlets by schoolmen who, like Diesterweg, charged that the system of higher education was elitist, the dominance of classical over modern studies stifling, and the neglect of higher technical training disastrous.[22] Adding their own bill of complaints, the Progressives demanded that the universities be recognized "as vital national institutions," granting a common right of academic citizenship without any territorial barriers to academic mobility. Conscious of "representing intelligence in the state, and of holding the spiritual culture of our people and its position among civilized nations in our hands," the activists stressed that "only a thoroughgoing reform of the universities, only a greater extension of the freedom of teaching" and learning (*Lehr- und Lernfreiheit*) would allow institutions of higher education to live up to Humboldt's exalted ideals. Specific criticism focused on "the timid exclusion of contemporary ideas," the requirement of certain courses, the enforcement of Latin in examinations, "the prevalence of narrow professionalism," the spread of professorial nepotism, the practice of last-minute cramming and the mindless copy-

[21] "An die Studenten Deutschlands," *ZfDH*, III, 25ff; "Ueber das Duell," *ZfDH*, I, 6ff; "Etwas über Ehrengerichte und ihre Zukunft," *AZ*, XIII, 189ff, etc. The establishment and suppression of the *Lesevereine* is evident from correspondences from individual universities, such as Berlin and Bonn, *ZfDH*, II, 20ff. Cf. also Eichhorn to Curators in Prussia, 5 February, 1844, StaKo abt. 403, no. 577. For the professorial reform proposals in Bonn, cf. BUA, U 167 and the Heidelberg Senate recommendations HUA VIII, I, 260 and GLAK 235/626. Some of the most revealing memoirs of former *Progress* students are Carl Schurz, *Lebenserinnerungen* (Berlin 1906), I; A. von Ernsthausen, *Erinnerungen eines Preussischen Beamten* (Bielefeld 1894); Rudolf von Gottschall, *Aus meiner Jugend: Erinnerungen* (Berlin 1890); Friedrich Spielhagen, *Finder und Erfinder: Erinnerungen aus meinem Leben* (Leipzig 1890), I; and J. Jung, *Julius Ficker, 1826-1902: Ein Beitrag zur deutschen Geistesgeschichte* (Innsbruck 1907).

[22] Friedrich Paulsen, *Geschichte des gelehrten Unterrichts auf den deutschen Schulen und Universitäten* (3d ed., Leipzig 1919), II, and H. König, *Gedanken zur Nationalerziehung aus dem Vormärz* (Berlin 1959).

ing of dictation—in short outward compulsion rather than the inner "awakening of patriotism and enthusiasm for intellectual inquiry in young minds." Idolizing younger dissenting professors like Nauwerck in Berlin, Kinkel in Bonn, and Roeth in Heidelberg, student radicals complained about the lukewarmness of even such Liberal lights as Dahlmann and Gervinus, and rather sought their inspiration from Bruno Bauer, Feuerbach, Strauss, Louis Blanc, etc. While the prestigious *Ordinarien* (full professors) controlled the mass lecture courses (lucrative *sinecures* because of their fees), the struggling *Privatdozenten* (unsalaried instructors) were left with ill-attended advanced classes, thereby giving especially students in theology and law little face-to-face contact with those men who controlled the state examinations in their fields. Although the *Rektoren* and *Dekane* looked with self-satisfaction upon the expansion of the German universities in the first decades of the 19th century, a significant number of students found their educational hopes seriously frustrated.[23]

A large number of Progressive complaints sprang from the corporate structure and separate legal jurisdiction of the university. Although aware that "the final cause of the disease must be sought in the governments" student radicals nevertheless only demanded the cessation of excessive interference such as the *Revers*, a hated pledge not to join secret societies. Equating knowledge with freedom they called for the lifting of police supervision and for the same rights of free speech and assembly for which the liberal opposition was fighting in the *Landtage*. Sympathizing with the plight of younger faculty members, the activists decried political censorship over advancement (leading to a number of *causes célèbres* in the *Vormärz*), and the disenfranchisement of the *Privatdozenten* in university decision-making which made it very difficult to innovate against the instinctive conservatism of the full professors in such areas as philosophical radicalism or phrenology. The compromise of bureaucratic political control from without and full professorial power within left students and instructors with the worst of both worlds: "Teachers and students must work closely together" for change.

For the Progressives, another "central cancer of the university" was the system of separate academic justice with its double jeopardy (institutional discipline followed by criminal proceedings), its lack of due process, its punishment on mere suspicion, its condoning of dueling

---

[23] Program of *AZ*, I, 1ff; "Dr. Röth's erste Vorlesung über Schiller und Göthe," *AZ*, II, 13ff; "Der Gelehrte und der Bürger," *AZ*, V, 61ff; "Offenes Sendschreiben eines neuen Philisters an den Senat der Hochschule, welche er als Student zuletzt besucht hat," *AZ*, XIV, 205ff. See also "Andeutungen für die Restauration unserer Hochschulen," *ZfDH*, *Probeblatt*, 4f; I, 1ff; II, 13ff; IV, 36ff, and XI, 120ff.

and debts, and its underlying assumption of student immaturity, requiring special protection. Repeated in petition after petition, the abolition of exempted university jurisdiction with its anachronistic penalties of flogging and incarceration, and the power of exclusion from state employment (by barring from *Staatsexamen*), became a central plank of the movement, since more than one-quarter of all students were at one time or other involved in discipline cases. The traditional excesses of drinking and destroying property (accounting for two-thirds of these), as well as the duels reported to the authorities (making up the rest), produced usually only grave warnings, fines, or temporary confinement since, despite all professorial moralizing, they were considered *Kavaliersdelikte*. On the other hand the rare political offenses such as membership in secret societies, singing of republican songs, and agitation against university or state almost always led to exclusion from further study either by temporary *consilium abeundi* or permanent *Relegation*. Reacting against the "disregard for law, lack of honor, conspiring, dueling, uncouthness and debts" fostered by the existing system, the radicals formulated a new university ideal which would turn passive schoolboys into active students, treated as young adults and committed to self-learning.[24]

IV

As a complement to their institutional critique, the progressive students called for an end to the academics' social isolation as well as their caste status as *Gelehrte* in order to transform them into full citizens. The sharp legal and status "division between cultivated and uncultured" bourgeoisie fueled the arrogance of the Bildungsbürgertum, which considered itself greatly superior to the mundane *Spiessbürger* of the small towns. Radical students accused this closed corporative spirit of "gradually depriving scholars of their national consciousness, making them disinterested in the questions of the day and disdainful as well as oblivious of those not engaged in Wissenschaft." Perpetuated in the universities, "this separation and mutual distrust" fatally divided the thrust of liberal opposition to the absolutist state, since the edu-

---

[24] "Über die Verhältnisse der jungen Lehrer an den dt. Universitäten," *ZfDH*, I, 3ff; "Über die Reform der Universitäten," *ZfDH*, IV, 36ff; "Unterthänigste Petition mehrerer Studirenden von Heidelberg, Revision der akademischen Gesetzgebung betreffend," *ZfDH*, XIX, 189ff; XXXIII, 233ff; "Die akademische Gesetzgebung," *AZ*, X, 145ff; XI, 157ff; XII, 173ff; XIV, 218ff; XV, 221ff. For the practical handling of academic justice, cf. BUA RA VII (Senatsprotokolle), GI (Untersuchungen), A G9/21ff (Disziplinarakten), Kurator E 9 VII (Akademische Gerichtsbarkeit), HUA, VIII, 1, 233a and 260 and GLAK 236/430f, 235/626. For the problems arising from the dual jurisdiction of city police and university law, cf. Dietrich Höroldt, *Stadt und Universität* (Bonn 1969), 74ff.

cated elite was being co-opted into the aristocratic bureaucracy which left the petit bourgeoisie at the mercy of the often contradictory economic self-interest of the laissez-faire oriented *Besitzbürgertum*. As a remedy similar to the abolition of the guilds, the progressives suggested that the universities "should above all be deprived of their corporate character; then the nimbus of the *Herr Professor* would disappear and nothing but a teacher remain" who could make his knowledge accessible to all and participate actively in community self-government. In order to speed the reintegration of the *Akademiker* into the citizenry, radicals suggested the formation of civic clubs, the easing of access to higher education, and the softening of distinctions between practical and scholarly courses. On the student level, the chief culprit appeared once more academic legal exemption, intended "to provide youth with somewhat greater freedom and with a position meshing with the social prejudices of the privileged," since it reinforced the students' feeling of superiority to the reviled *Philister* (adult burgers). Erupting in numerous battles with the *Knoten* (a derisory term for the town artisans, etc.), this superiority of even the last *Hungerstudent* over the working man owed its existence to judicial privileges which in turn made students dependent upon the bureaucratic paternalism of the university. In order to break down this status barrier, Heidelberg students pleaded in the Badensian Landtag that "we see no disadvantage or dishonor but rather the greatest benefit in being completely accountable to the regular courts of law for all our actions."[25]

In the last prerevolutionary years student radicals moved beyond an awareness of their mandarin privileges to a growing understanding of the *soziale Frage* (social problem) of agrarian and artisan pauperism. The graphic descriptions by Friedrich Engels, Lorenz von Stein, and the *Lieder vom Armen Mann*, as well as the grim reality of the famines following a harvest failure and the plight of the weavers, evoked sympathetic concern. Suffering vicariously, a student poet accused the oppressors: "Yet the labor of our hands only clothed *your* skin/ And the fruits of our travail stilled *your* hungering" and prophe-

[25] "Ueber die Privilegien der Studierenden," *ZfDH, Probeblatt*, 2; "Ueber das Verhältniss der Studenten zu den andern Ständen," *ZfDH*, vi, 53ff; ix, 87ff; x, 34ff, and xxxvi, 337ff; L. Freihardt, "Der Gelehrte und der Bürger," *AZ*, iii, 29ff; iv, 45ff; v, 61ff; vii, 94ff; "Die Neueste Petition der Heidelberger Studirenden um Aufhebung der akademischen Gesetze," *AZ*, xii, 173ff. For the wider implications of this question, cf. R. Meyer, "Das Berechtigungswesen in seiner Bedeutung für Schule und Gesellschaft im 19. Jahrhundert," *Zeitschrift für die gesamte Staatswissenschaft*, 124 (1958), 763ff; and Reinhart Koselleck, *Preussen zwischen Reform und Revolution. Allgemeines Landrecht, Verwaltung und soziale Bewegung von 1791 bis 1848* (Stuttgart 1967).

sied: "All the tears which misery shed before your greedy eye/ Must be expunged, and only then will mankind reunite." One practical response was the creation of a *Hilfsverein* with the purpose of "effectively counteracting material wants, primarily by providing the necessary means for work and survival to the poorer burger class of our community in order to save them from physical and moral degradation." A minority of hard-core radicals like Blind, Lasalle, and Liebknecht placed priority upon a revolution to redistribute wealth, by force if need be. Although the novel phrase which entered Burschenschaft constitutions, "the socialist tendency" referred primarily to abolishing the distinction between student subculture and society at large, in the minds of the most advanced activists it meant the struggle for a "social Republic." In Heidelberg the extreme Left, numbering little more than a dozen called the Neckarbund, which debated such iconoclasts as Stirner, Pfitzer, Proudhon, and Fourier, and ridiculed the "halfhearted Liberals," advocated some form of democratic socialism. Gradually this "small group of eccentric heads who sport extreme political views and who even actually participate in our election campaigns and political demonstrations," became a genuine revolutionary force. Because of the increasing misery of artisans and peasants the majority of Progress students slowly realized that the regeneration of their own life and the liberation of the universities was intimately connected with the renewal of the entire social fabric, even if that required some sacrifice of their own status.[26]

V

The social thrust of the radicals' dissent derived less from a guilty consciousness of their caste position than from the social strains within the university.[27] On the basis of both rudimentary contemporary statistics

[26] Although including articles about vegetarianism, phrenology and German Catholicism, the *Zeitschrift für Deutschlands Hochschulen* (e.g., "Umschau," xxi, 213ff) was notably insensitive to the social problem. Only the deterioration of the situation in the second half of the 1840s made pauperism a major issue in *AZ*, iii, 32f; vii, 106f; viii, 111f; ix, 136; ibid., 139f, etc.; Report of Heidelberg Senate, 8 March, 1846 in GLAK 235/626. For the general context cf. the essays collected in W. Conze, ed., *Staat und Gesellschaft im deutschen Vormärz, 1818-1848* (Stuttgart 1962) and his suggestive "Vom 'Pöbel' zum 'Proletariat.' Sozialgeschichtliche Voraussetzungen für den Sozialismus in Deutschland," in H. U. Wehler, ed., *Moderne deutsche Sozialgeschichte* (Cologne 1966), 111ff; and F. D. Marquardt, "Pauperismus in Germany during the *Vormärz*," *Central European History* 2 (1969), 77-88 and the literature discussed there.

[27] Hajo Holborn, "German Idealism in the Light of Social History," repr. in his *Germany and Europe: Historical Essays* (New York 1971); Leonore O'Boyle, "Klassische Bildung und soziale Struktur in Deutschland zwischen 1800 und 1848," *Historische Zeitschrift* 207 (1968), 584ff; Wolfgang Zorn, "Hochschule und höhere

and figures derived from published matriculation lists, the outlines of
the conflicting pressures for entrance into the Bildungsbürgertum are
clear. During the first half of the 19th century the sons of the educated
bourgeoisie gradually lost their absolute majority in the student body,
but remained the single largest bloc, making the academic elite less
inbred but still remarkably self-sufficient. In the fashionable institutions of Berlin and Heidelberg, the children of the propertied bourgeoisie slowly increased to about one-third of the total, constituting the
second major source of Akademiker primarily concentrated in law and
medicine. At Halle and Tübingen where theology played a larger pro-
portionate role the lower middle-class sector maintained its second
rank, congregating also in philosophy, but in all four institutions the
sons of lesser officials, white collar employees, and elementary teachers
began to outnumber or challenge those of the artisans and peasants.
Moreover everywhere the expansion of the 1820s and 1830s drew larger numbers of petit bourgeois children into the university. In Berlin
and Heidelberg they already outnumbered the plutocratic element,
while in Halle and Tübingen they substantially increased their percentage representation. However, the Kleinbürgertum found it universally difficult to compete in the academic recession of the 1840s and
therefore was the first to drop out, while the advance of the Besitz-
bürger was temporarily halted and the Bildungsbürger enjoyed a brief
Indian summer of restored dominance. Hence, after a period of rising
expectations in the 1820s and 1830s, opportunities for upward mobility
into the educated elite were drastically contracting in the 1840s.[28]

Schule in der deutschen Sozialgeschichte der Neuzeit," in Repgen and Skalweit,
eds., *Spiegel der Geschichte* (Münster 1964), 321ff; cf. also K. E. Jeismann,
"Gymnasium, Staat und Gesellschaft in Preussen: Vorbemerkungen zur Unter-
suchung der politischen und sozialen Bedeutung der 'höheren Bildung' im 19.
Jahrhundert," *Geschichte in Wissenschaft und Unterricht* 21 (1970), 435ff; H.
Busshoff, "Die preussische Volksschule als soziales Gebilde und politischer Bildungs-
faktor in der ersten Hälfte des 19. Jahrhunderts," ibid. 22 (1971), 385ff; and P.
Lundgreen, "Technicians and Labor Market in Prussia, 1810-1850," *Annales Cis-
alpines d'Histoire Sociale*, ser. 1, no. 2, 1971 (Pavia 1972), 9-29.
    [28] J. Conrad's pioneering study, *Das Universitätsstudium in Deutschland während
der letzten 50 Jahre* (Jena 1884), provides original figures for Halle, updated in his
essay, "Einige Ergebnisse der deutschen Universitätsstatistik," in *Conrads Jahrbücher für Nationalökonomie*, III (1906), 433ff. For Berlin see the compilation of
Max Lenz's son in his *Geschichte der Königlichen Friedrich Wilhelms-Universität
zu Berlin* (Halle 1910-18), III, 483ff. Cf. Hermann Mitgau, "Soziale Herkunft der
deutschen Studenten bis 1900," in Rössler and Franz, eds., Universität und Ge-
lehrtenstand 1400-1800 (Limburg 1970), 233-68; and A. Rienhardt, *Das Universitätsstudium der Württemberger seit der Reichsgründung* (Tübingen 1918). Unfortunately according to our own analysis of 1776-1817, and especially 1810-15, Rienhardt
seriously underclassifies the *Besitz* category by putting in only self-declared grand

On the basis of both contemporary descriptions and a sample of Heidelberg activists, it seems plausible that within general student stratification, the radicals of the 1840s, like those of the founding cohort of the student movement, derived primarily from families of the Bildungsbürgertum. Time and again critics point to the exclusively aristocratic and plutocratic style and recruitment of the traditional fraternities. At the other extreme institutional pressure on scholarship holders, theologians, and *pauperi*, prevented the poorer elements from opposing the system, since lower middle-class careerists knew that "outside the path provided by the state, there is no chance of advancement." An analysis of the social origin of 200 Heidelberg Burschenschaftler and Progress Students of the 1840s reveals that over 60 percent derived from the Bildungsbürgertum, 27 percent from the Besitzbürgertum, and only 12 percent from the *Mittelstand*, i.e., drastically underrepresenting the lower middle class in favor of the educated elite. If one takes only membership in predominantly progressive groups the comparison with the general student body becomes even clearer: The activists comprise 13.5 percent more sons of university graduates, 10 percent less propertied, 3 percent less petit bourgeois and 12.4 percent less nobles. Although the difficulties of authenticating names and of identifying indisputable radicals as well as other overriding factors (friendship patterns, etc.) blur the picture, this evidence bears out the hypothesis that the radicals largely represented the educated bourgeoisie, challenging the prerogatives of the nobility. Hence the struggle between Corps and Progressive Burschenschaften was largely a conflict not of the poor against the rich, but of two rival segments of the elite between the cultured classes and the aristocratic

---

merchants, great industrialists and estate owners, etc., which depresses the solid middle class into the *Kleinbürgertum*. Readjusted by a factor of 2/5 they form the following picture:

Date		Bildung	Besitz	Alt	Mittelstand Neu	Totals	Proletariat
1810-15	No.	297 (95)	80 (25)	83 (18)	44 (12)	127 (31)	11 (1)
	%	56 (61)	16 (16)	16 (11)	9 (8(	25 (19)	2 (1)
1835-40	No.	368	111	201	135	336	3
	%	45	16	22	16	38	0.5
1871-76	No.	303	116	154	122	276	3
	%	43	13	20	17	37	0.5

Notes: In parentheses is a sample of 157 Burschenschaftler of 1815-17 (founding generation) in Tübingen, roughly 1/3 of ca. 475 students immatriculated 1815-17. For the categorical basis of the graph cf. Table 1. See also James D. Cobb, "Vormärz Bonn Student Organizations: Variety and Homogeneity," M.A. thesis. Univ. of Missouri, Columbia (1973).

Graph 1

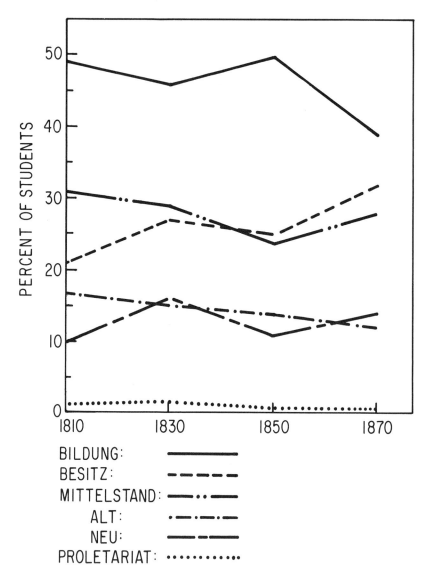

BILDUNG: ————
BESITZ: ————
MITTELSTAND: —··—
ALT: ·—·—·
NEU: ———
PROLETARIAT: ··········

* The *Bildung* figure for 1850 is likely to be too high since it is strongly influenced by an outlier at Halle. For the derivation and content of the categories cf Table Ia.

[554]

as well as plutocratic groups. This social derivation of radical dissent reveals no substantial disparities between leaders and followers and indicates that the student movement was a relatively homogeneous part of a larger emergence of the *Bildungsbürgertum*.[29]

Moreover, in the 1840s, the learned professions within and outside the universities faced a grave crisis which endangered the students' future. This was caused by "a great disproportion between the demand for salaried state officials and the supply" of graduates. Since tuition jumped 50 percent (e.g., at Heidelberg) and living costs for students almost doubled (e.g., at Bonn) from the beginning of the century, curatorial student aid reports indicate that "the number of needy applicants continues to swell" and that "during the last years it grew steadily in far larger proportion than attendance at the university, so that existing funds have proven insufficient at every distribution."[30]

[29] A sample of 200 identifiable student radicals at Heidelberg drawn from HUA and GLAK records as well as the lists in E. Dietz, *Die deutsche Burschenschaft in Heidelberg* (Heidelberg 1895) forms the following picture when compared with the social composition of the entire student body in 1845, based on G. Toepke, ed., *Die Matrikel der Universität Heidelberg* (Heidelberg 1904-7), v-vii:

		Bildung	Besitz	Mittelstand Alt	Mittelstand Neu	Proletariat	No Data
Entire student	No.	254	139	51	27	0	4
body 1844-45	%	53.9	29.5	10.8	5.7		
Entire student	No.	228	125	69	20	0	
body 1850-51	%	51	28	15	4		
Average for							
1844-50	%	52.5	28.7	12.9	4.9	0	
Sample of 210	No.	123	54	17	6	0	10
radicals 1840-49	%	61	27	8.5	3		
Sub-sample of	No.	74	22	11	5	0	
certain pro-	%	66	19.6	9.8	4.4		
gressives							

Note: A count of nobles regardless of profession within the student body of 1844-45 results in a number of 75 among 475 non-Burschenschaft students, i.e., a figure of 15.7%, whereas the entire sample of radicals yields 10 among 210 and the sub-sample only 7 of 112, i.e., 4.7 or 3.3% respectively.

[30] J. G. Hoffmann, *Sammlung kleiner Schriften staatswirthschaftlichen Inhalts* (Berlin 1843). Information on living costs is scattered and impressionistic. At the beginning of the century, 200 Thlr was considered a minimal check (*Wechsel*). In Tübingen the projected constitution of a *Studentenverein* exempted all those under 300 Thlr from contributions, indicating that by the 1840s this was considered the poverty line (*ZfDH*, x, 101ff). D. Höroldt, ed., *Stadt und Universität*, App. 5: "Preise für Wohnung und Verpflegung in Bonn, 1819," 330; Steinmetz, ed., *Jena*, 310ff; Moritz August von Bethmann Hollweg, "Rechenschaftsbericht über den Zustand des Stipendienwesens . . . 1842-44," and for 1845-47, 1848-50, StaKo abt. 403, no. 14045. On the basis of figures from W. Dieterici, *Geschichtliche und stati-*

Konrad H. Jarausch

The overcrowding of the universities in the 1820s and 1830s, prompted
by a post-Napoleonic War deficit of trained personnel, produced a
serious surfeit of qualified academics one decade later.

Contemporary accounts abound with "complaints about the great
number of public servants and aspirants to those positions; every year
the figure of dissatisfied unemployed candidates grows, and despite all
warnings of the government the demand for professional studies continues unabated." The enrollment boom during which the annual student numbers in Germany jumped from 5000 to 15,000 (i.e., from
about 20 to 52.5 per 100,000 inhabitants) produced a glut of professionals who could not be absorbed by business in a still largely preindustrial economy, and led to severe competition for state jobs which
extended the waiting period for administrative trainees up to ten years
before salaried compensation. For the Burschenschaftler, state employment was particularly crucial since out of over 300 Progressives at Tübingen, Giessen, and Greifswald, fully 67 percent entered some sort of bureaucratic office, whereas if the careers of the
members of the Bonn Corps Palatia are representative, one-half of the
wealthier fraternity students sought their fortune in private enterprise.[31] Although attendance fell by almost 5000 in the 1840s (to 34.1
per 100,000 population) allowing Prussian statisticians to argue that
"fear of an excess of present students appear no longer well founded,"
the overproduction of lawyers and theologians continued to be a serious problem since the time lag between graduation and employment
posed a grave hurdle for those less well off. Although the medical faculty increased throughout the period without any demonstrable difficulty (taking up part of the slack from law) and the philosophical
faculty also expanded at an astounding rate to meet the demand for
professionally trained secondary school teachers, the growing number of those seeking to enter a university career created a log jam of
Privatdozenten, often sympathetic to student demands. The unsettled

stische Nachrichten ueber die Universitäten im preussischen Staate (Berlin 1836),
the relative amount of student support per capita has been calculated in App.,
Table 2.

[31] The career data were compiled for the progressive Burschenschaften Walhalla
(Tübingen), Alemannia and Cattia (Giessen), and Kränzchen and Alemannia
(Greifswald) on the basis of P. Wentzscke, *Burschenschaftslisten*, I, 1933ff, II, 83ff,
91ff, 205ff. They yielded a ratio of 212:101 bureaucrats over free professionals with
58 either deceased or lacking career information. The Corps figures are from
"Verzeichnis der Corpsburschen" of the Palatia (n.d. Bonn), 2ff, and produce a
count of 71:69 with 15 people unaccounted for. Part of the boom in higher edu-
cation was also the result of an increased literacy rate. Cf. E. N. Anderson, "The
Prussian *Volksschule* in the 19th century," in G. A. Ritter, ed., *Entstehung und
Wandel der modernen Gesellschaft* (Berlin 1970).

[556]

Graph 2

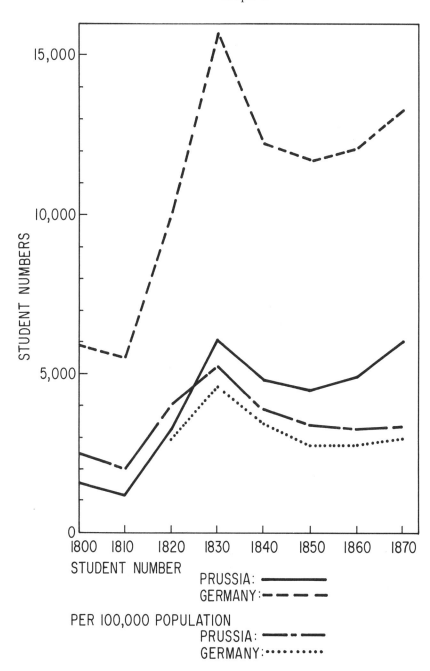

Konrad H. Jarausch

economic prospects and insecure social status of journalists, barristers, and technical professionals added another element of frustration to the career expectations of students. Hence the Progressives felt themselves to be part of a restive academic proletariat blocked in its economic and political aspirations, and formed the potential leadership of a popular revolt.[32]

VI

When the revolution finally came in the heady spring of 1848, Progress students stood in the forefront of the struggle for unity, freedom, and equality, and though only one voice in a chorus of elemental force, played an important role in the overthrow of the Metternich regimes in Vienna, Munich, and Berlin. Göttingen activists congratulated the Austrian *Akademische Legion* on acting out radical student ideas: "Hand in hand with the people who recognize you as friend and bringer of their freedom you daringly confront the bayonets of the enemy, and with one stroke bulwarks of liberty are springing up everywhere." In public assemblies, newly founded newspapers like the *Berliner Volksfreund* and the *Bonner Zeitung*, and in electoral campaigns for the Frankfurt and Berlin parliaments student activists sought to rouse the apathetic to national and social action: "The anarchy which threatens from the suppressed below cannot be prevented by ignoring the social crisis, by leaving the unfortunate to themselves or by repressing them with force, but only if we honestly embrace their cause, thoroughly improve their lot and seek to raise their neglected education." In Heidelberg, a student club proclaimed the principle of "a democratic republic, i.e. that governmental form which embodies freedom, fraternity and equality not only before the law but as much as possible in real life," and encouraged propaganda among the students and the people, in the press, in conversation, and through "exercise in arms as far as physically possible." On the other hand Bonn radicals immedi-

[32] Dieterici, *Geschichtliche und statistische Nachrichten*, 109ff, is the first—if too optimistic—attempt to establish a statistic of supply and demand for academic professions (J. Conrad, *The German Universities for the last Fifty Years* [Glasgow. Cf. also W. Riehl, *Die bürgerliche Gesellschaft* (Stuttgart 1851), 1885], 19ff.). 342ff. In Ermann-Horn, *Bibliographie*, there were eight entries for the first two decades of the 19th century complaining about excessive *Studiersucht*, while in the next two decades eighteen writers warned against studying, and only two in the 1850s and 1860s. Cf. also J. R. Gillis, "Aristocracy and Bureaucracy in Nineteenth-Century Prussia," *Past and Present* 41 (1968), 105ff and *The Prussian Bureaucracy in Crisis, 1840-1860* (Stanford 1971); Leonore O'Boyle, "The Problem of an Excess of Educated Men in Western Europe, 1800-1850," *JMH* 42 (1970), 471ff; Reinhart Koselleck, "Staat und Gesellschaft in Preussen 1815-1848," in Conze, ed., *Vormärz*, 79ff.

[558]

ately went beyond the confines of the campus, and under the leadership of the charismatic professor Kinkel, activists like Schurz became leading figures in the democratic club composed both of burgers and students which so effectively mobilized rural and urban discontent that it captured a mandate to the Berlin parliament. For a brief period the fraternization between students and the peasant-artisans seemed real, as, e.g., when Schlöffel in Berlin led the Borsig workers to the rescue of the fighters on the barricades. Eventually, however, the innate elitism of all but the most radical activists ruptured the alliance between intellectuals and masses. Although volunteering for the Schleswig-Holstein struggle, and participating in the final spasm of the revolt in the southwest, the radicals' role in the actual fighting was minor. Hence the students' primary impact in 1848 lay in their agitation in favor of a sometimes social but mostly democratic consciousness.[33]

Too young to dominate the political stage, Progress students sought to exploit the paralysis of traditional authorities to renew their academic and social life. In order to make the university into "a free state within the state . . . forming a firm phalanx for Germany's unity and freedom" radicals knew that nothing short of "a national reorganization" of its ethos, its relations to the state, its teaching procedures, its student life, and its social role would do. Hence at Pentecost 1848 the Jena activists called a second Wartburg Festival to debate "the future direction of the Deutsche Burschenschaft, its position and participation in the reorganization of our academies and its attitude towards the German fatherland"; but in the new spirit all other "sincere enthusiasts" of change were invited as well. In heated debates between those "who gladly welcomed the revolution and those . . . who would

[33] "Göttinger Adresse an die Wiener Brüder," in the *Deutsche Studentenzeitung* (Göttingen 1848), I, 7 the central revolutionary student newspaper, published in July and August 1848; StaKo abt. 403, no. 6577, 6582, 7332; BUA RA 16a and b (Bewegungen und politische Ereignisse im Jahr 1848); and "Kommilitonen!" radical handbill in HUA, VIII, no. 230. Cf. also GLAK 235/30061 for the printed statutes of the Heidelberg democratic student club and GLAK 235/625 for the confrontation. M. Braubach, *Bonner Professoren und Studenten in den Revolutionsjahren 1848/1849* (Cologne 1967); H. Derwein, "Heidelberg im Vormärz und in der Revolution 1848/49," *Neue Heidelberger Jahrbücher* (1955-56), entire; Karl Obermann, "Die Berliner Universität am Vorabend und während der Revolution von 1848/9," in *Forschen und Wirken* (Berlin 1960), I, 165ff; and R. R. Lutz, Jr., "Fathers and Sons in the Vienna Revolution of 1848," *J. Central European Affairs* 22 (1962), 161ff. Cf. also Griewank, *Deutsche Studenten und Universitäten in der Revolution von 1848* (Weimar 1949), 19ff; Edith H. Altbach, "Vanguard of Revolt: Students and Politics in Central Europe, 1815-1848," in Lipset, ed., *Student Politics*, 451ff; and Priscilla Robertson, "Students on the Barricades: Germany and Austria, 1848," *Political Science Quart.* 84 (1969), 367ff.

rather have undone it" the general student assembly adopted an activist program, demanding that "the universities shall become national institutions" to be supported and administered by a united German state with the limits of "the principle of self-government." As a basic ideological goal, the congress unanimously endorsed "unconditional freedom of teaching and learning," elaborated this to mean that "all division into separate faculties ceases," because of the unity of knowledge, and broadened the access to government office with the provision that "attendance at a university shall not be a prerequisite."

The most acrimonious discussion centered on academic justice, but finally the Left prevailed with "a repudiation of any judicial exemption" in order to "let the student become a general citizen of the state." The Wartburg assembly further sketched the outlines of a federal student government "with equal rights of all," called for the "participation of students in the election of academic administrators and in the appointment of professors" and unanimously demanded the abrogation of the Carlsbad Decrees. A pithy restatement of all major features of the Progressive critique, this petition to the Frankfurt parliament represented the culmination of three and one-half decades of student dissent. The most advanced radicals from Vienna, Berlin, Breslau, and Munich, who had fought on the barricades, turned the festive demonstration of 1500 or so young men into a working session by establishing a student parliament, even more radical than the main assembly. Working out the organizational details of a national student association along the lines of the previous Allgemeinheiten, this self-appointed body added such specifics to the demands as public examinations, the elimination of mandatory Latin, "the abolition of lecture fees and the payment of Dozenten by the state," as well as the unprecedented opening of the university doors "to anyone who wants to educate himself there." Under the lodestars of "political freedom and social equality" the revolutionary students attempted to turn the elitist university into "a true institution of the people."[34]

In the end the students' quest for a renewal of society and university foundered on the same fratricidal division between constitutional Liberals and radical Democrats which doomed the uprising at large. Al-

[34] M. Friedländer and R. Giseke, *Das Wartburgfest der deutschen Studenten in der Pfingstwoche des Jahres 1848* (Leipzig 1848), *passim*; Ernsthausen, *Erinnerungen*, 69ff; Adolph Strodtmann, *Gottfried Kinkel: Wahrheit ohne Dichtung* (Hamburg 1851), II, *passim*. "Der Reichstag der deutschen Studenten in Eisenach," and numerous other articles in the *DStZ*, I, 4ff. For the social radicalism of the most advanced students, cf. P. H. Noyes, *Organization and Revolution: Working Class Associations in the German Revolutions of 1848/9* (Princeton 1966), 108ff.

though parliamentary politics in 1848 were almost exclusively an affair of the Bildungsbürgertum (of the over 800 Frankfurt deputies over 80 percent had attended a university) the educated elite fragmented along professional, geographic, religious, but also generational lines. Impressionistic evidence suggests the hypothesis that of the 100-150 deputies with Burschenschaft connections, the representatives of the Left, since they were younger, generally belonged to the Demagogen phase, while those of the Center-Right, by and large older, harkened back to the ideas of the Urburschenschaft.[35] But although a higher share of vocal sons tended to support the radical democratic cause than their professional fathers, the initial unity of the student body disintegrated at an accelerating pace throughout 1848. In a pattern which was repeated on every German campus, they polarized into a moderately conservative camp, led by the Landsmannschaften, the religious groups, and the adult liberal clubs which endorsed slow gradualism: "Free from political fanaticism, we declare that we love the fatherland above all and consider its unity, power and greatness, yes the freedom of the people, safeguarded only through the full realization of the constitutional principle." In contrast the republican camp, led by the Progress associations, reformist Burschenschaften, independents and local democratic clubs urged radical change: "We want no compromise with the princes, because the people, unified by their own power, will find the right man among the patriots who will become their federal head, not by the grace of God, but freely elected. With one word: we want the Republic." United only in their opposition to absolutist particularism and academic authoritarianism, student dissenters split on the question of the degree of necessary reform, thereby robbing youth of an effective collective voice.[36]

[35] Although L. O'Boyle, "The Democratic Left in Germany, 1848," *JMH* (1962), 374ff, Frank Eyck, *The Frankfurt Parliament, 1848-1849* (London 1968), 94, and John R. Gillis, *Prussian Bureaucracy*, ch. III have made a beginning toward a quantitative analysis of the correlation between age, religion, social background, education, student organization, and political opinion in 1848, suggesting the above hypotheses, they still need systematic prosopographical verification. For the wider context cf. Veit Valentin, *Geschichte der deutschen Revolution 1848-1849* (Berlin 1940-41), II, 557; R. Stadelmann, *Soziale und politische Geschichte der Revolution von 1848/49* (Munich 1948); Jacques Droz, *Les révolutions allemandes de 1848* (Paris, 1957); T. S. Hamerow, *Restoration, Revolution and Reaction: Economics and Politics in Germany 1815-1871* (Princeton 1958).

[36] Friedländer and Giseke, *Wartburgfest*, 47ff; "Die Parteien auf deutschen Universitäten in ihrem Verhältnis zu den Parteien des gesammt-Vaterlandes," *ZfDH*, IX, 85ff; "Wartburger Adressen," and "Die politischen Parteien auf der Wartburg," *DStZ*, I, 4ff; II, 10ff; III, 19ff, and other numerous articles. Cf. also Paul Wentzcke, "Das zweite Wartburgfest, Pfingsten, 1848," in *Quellen und Darstellungen*, XVII, 208ff.

Konrad H. Jarausch

This fundamental political schism deadlocked institutional and subcultural reform as well. The constitutionalists, who were often outmanned in student assemblies, allied with the powerful Liberal professors, while the progressive activists, who were more numerous and vocal during the early stages of the uprising, found sympathy only among the largely democratic *Privatdozenten* and extraordinary professors. A second student parliament in Eisenach in September formulated a new constitution for the German universities, striving to "overthrow the bureaucratic system" and seeking "a correct compromise between academic freedom and the state's right of regulation." Consisting of "teachers and learners" this democratic university would be governed through a committee composed in equal parts of students and professors, which would control the administration, and would be financed by free tuition and state support. All state examinations would be abolished and the unfettered pursuit of Wissenschaft would be allowed, in a vision which combined radical and Humboldtian traditions in a daring blueprint a century ahead of its time. The spirit of drastic change also inspired the instructors and nontenured professors to call for "a reform of their own position" so that their legal and financial security would be increased, their participation in university governance enlarged, and a more rational planning system for the growth of new specialities and appointment be adopted.

Typically, Liberal professors called for "unprejudiced and prudent" changes such as the abolition of the office of government-plenipotentiary (Curator), public scrutiny of administration, the establishment of normal pay scales, the improvement of faculty rights in appointments, wider representation of untenured professors, and the restructuring of academic justice, as well as minor improvements in the examination system. Only very faintly echoing student suggestions, the deliberations of the full professors at Bonn resulted in an even less imaginative blueprint demanding "increased self-government," creating special administrative and disciplinary councils, and allowing extraordinary professors larger rights and token improvements in the position of the instructors. In the negotiations of the Congress of German Professors in Jena, advocates of real change were in the minority (since full professors comprised the bulk of the delegates). Although the assembly was willing to call for greater *"allgemeine Lehrfreiheit"* it refused to vote the cessation of lecture fees, upheld the prerequisite of attendance at some university for state office, and modified the corporate structure of the university by creating a corpus academicum to allow for token instructor and sporadic student representation. Although it extended the scope of civil jurisdiction over students and supported freedom of association, it refused to abolish separate academic justice. The split among students and the status divisions among different levels of faculty led to the shelving of all significant reforms when, under a wave of reaction, another congress convened in 1849 and the elitist, authoritarian *Ordinarienuniversität* escaped unscathed.[37]

On their most immediate level, concerning the quality of student life, the Progressives' quest proved equally barren, and within a few years traditional student culture was completely restored. The second student parliament of Eisenach had formulated a unitary and representative statute of a "deutsche Studentenschaft," an "association for the advancement of general academic interests," based on equal rights and headed by a strong steering committee, locally electing one deputy for each 100 enrolled. But some moderate local chapters such as Halle rejected it as too radical and when the Corps ceased to cooperate, it never got off the ground. In Jena the fraternities met for the first time in their history on the national level to assure that the Student Association would "never intervene in the internal social affairs of the *Verbindungen*" and to voice their public support for "the maintenance of academic justice, lecture fees" and the custom of dueling. Indifference, fear of change, hope for bureaucratic advancement, and elitist arrogance combined to muffle the activists' clamor for the establishment of a Chair of Socialism in Breslau or the appointment of Feuerbach in Heidelberg. When in the winter and spring of 1849 the fate of the revolution at large was in the balance, the true radicals flocked to the southwest German revolutionary armies, while the moderates, sensing the onslaught of reaction, began to shed their progressive views, deprecated in later memoirs as youthful aberrations.

Hence the university authorities had no difficulty restoring discipline by singling out a few exposed individuals who had not emigrated or been killed, while generously overlooking the transgressions of the majority. Although Progressive associations regrouped and attempted to regain the initiative, the general disillusionment with idealistic reformism contributed to the youth's conversion to Rochau's slogan of *Realpolitik*. When radical ideologues like Marx continued to denounce

---

[37] Karl Schurz, *Der Studentencongress zu Eisenach am 25. September 1848* (Bonn 1848); *Lebenserinnerungen*, I, 145ff; III, 32ff. For the programs of the disenfranchised *Privatdozenten* and *Extraordinarien*, the liberal professors and the Senate, cf. BUA RU 172, Protokolle der Berathungen über die Universitätsreform, 23. VI.-25. VII. 1848 and BUA, Kurator, CII "Reform in der Verfassung der Universitäten," and *Officielle Protokolle über die Verhandlungen deutscher Universitätslehrer zur Reform der deutschen Hochschulen* (Jena 1848). For the radical teachers cf. also H. König, *Programme der bürgerlichen Nationalerziehung in der Revolution von 1848/49* and N. Andernach, *Der Einfluss der Parteien auf das Hochschulwesen in Preussen, 1848-1918* (Goettingen 1972).

reactionary politics, they found less echo at the universities, since the establishment of representative bodies like the Prussian Landtag offered some outlet for political action, the abolishment of the Carlsbad Decrees corrected the worst instances of repression, and the takeoff of industrialization offered nonbureaucratic career prospects. In general the age cohort marked by the failure of the revolution generally became less willing to get involved. Nevertheless the radicals' institutional and social critique had shaped the consciousness of the revolutionary generation. A decade later it challenged Prussia once more in the constitutional conflict, and served as ideological and organizational model for later dissent. Prompted by the adult failure to socialize the young into their own roles compromised by servility, hypocrisy and greed, the Progressive's futile quest was a paradigm of the impotence of youth in attempting to change university and society in one bold stroke.[38]

VII

The pervasive emotionalism of youthful protest makes the analytical separation of the underlying sources of student unrest from exalted rhetoric and flamboyant action a complex task. The limited nature of the records does not sustain anything beyond vague psychological speculation, but in terms of social analysis some generalization regarding the emergence and failure of the first modern student movement in the West seems not only possible but imperative. The evolution from corporate Landsmannschaft through intermediary Burschenschaft to universalistic Progressverein in the 19th century Germanies points to the sequential interaction of several clusters of factors, which dominate successive phases of unrest, and though elsewhere differing in relative timing and strength, appear essential to the emergence of sustained student dissent. In a scenario of modernization where indus-

[38] Schurz, *Studentencongress*, 15ff; "Der Corpscongress zu Jena," *DStZ*, vi, 42; "Studentischer Indifferentismus," *DStZ*, vii, 49f; "Zur genaueren Charakteristik der politischen Ansichten der Göttinger Studenten," *DStZ*, viii, 57ff; Ernsthausen, *Erinnerungen*, 76ff; G. Heer, "Die Zeit des Progresses," in *Quellen und Darstellungen*, xi, 151ff. The literature on the resurgence of traditional student culture is much more tentative than that on the student movement. One typical individual fate is that of Heinrich von Treitschke who began as a member of the Bonn Frankonia, then joined a corps in Heidelberg and later denounced the exalted idealism of the Burschenschaft. Some of his letters are reprinted in the *Festschrift* of the Frankonia (Bonn 1969), 219ff, 224ff. Cf. also his *Deutsche Geschichte im 19ten Jahrhundert* (Leipzig 1927), pt. 11, ch. vii, 383ff. According to one foreign observer of the 1860s, "The time when the students were political conspirators has gone by," and romantic irrelevance once again reigned on campus. James Morgan Jart, *German Universities: A Narrative of Personal Experience* (New York 1874), 294ff.

trial technology as well as ideas of progress are imported from the outside (the non-western European pattern), youthful enthusiasm for the new when confronted with the instinctive traditionalism of adults leads to an ideological gap between young and old. The intrusion of rational and critical value patterns, such as French nationalistic and English self-government ideas, undermines the authority of adults and provides youth as a self-conscious vanguard of change with a program of action, justifying generational revolt. Political restriction and repression (Carlsbad Decrees) in preparticipatory and prerepresentative bureaucratic systems, possessing no accepted channels of public criticism and influence on decision-making, apparently fosters the crystallization of a youthful counterelite, which though trained to take over the levers of power, rejects its instrumental role and demands the liberalization of political structures in order to renew their legitimacy. Especially in prenational contexts (such as in East-Central Europe), unification is directed against both external and internal oppression and forms a magnetic, revolutionary goal. In the case of the Burschenschaft this combination of factors was so powerful that it stamped the movement's historical self-consciousness as a secular order upholding *national-liberal* ideology and thereby forged the central core of German academics' political values for the succeeding century.[39]

A perceived malfunction of institutions of higher learning, a tangible manifestation of the insufficiency of traditional values and practices, seems to be another important link in the mobilizing chain, since universities provide the physical setting for protest and assemble a critical mass, capable of concerted action. The clash between the educational rhetoric of molding harmonious, creative, and ethical leadership personalities and the reality of producing timid bureaucrats disillusions students, especially when they measure routine indoctrination against the neo-humanist ideals of Bildung and Wissenschaft. Most directly, the mindless irrelevance of traditional sub-culture, which channels youthful desire for active change into infantile rituals, offends their self-sacrificing idealism. At the same time the prolonged dependence, enforced by a double legal standard, frustrates their desire to escape the moratorium and enter responsible adulthood, since the romantic ideal of *Jugend* provides only aesthetic freedom. Finally, decreasing access to the educated elite in terms of the social composition

[39] L. Krieger, *The German Idea of Freedom* (Boston 1957). For the symbolic reconciliation between Burschenschaft and the Prussian state, cf. Bismarck's "Ansprache an eine Abordnung der deutschen Burschenschaft," April 1, 1890, in which the iron chancellor praised the student movement's contribution to German unification, in *Gesammelte Werke* (Berlin 1930), XIII, 406f. Cf. also Robert M. Berdahl, "New Thoughts on German Nationalism," *AHR* 77 (1972), 65ff.

of the student body, and the crisis of the academic professions during a phase of initial overproduction before an expanding economy can absorb the surplus, appear to add fuel to the fires of unrest. In terms of derivation the student movement by and large represents the leading edge of the challenge of the Bildungsbürgertum against the prerogatives of crown and nobility, rejecting the social fusion of a power elite of birth, wealth, and education which characterizes the regional and social fraternities. Hence the case study of the German Burschenschaft suggests that the switch from traditional to counterculture—i.e., the heightening of generational conflict and the intensification of the identity crisis—derives primarily from a set of intermediary historical factors. Such factors include a value gap, political repression, institutional malfunction, and social frustration, perceived even by the students as parts of an interrelated breakdown of the old order.[40]

This framework of sources of student unrest resolves some of the paradoxes of its general, as well as specifically Central European, traits. Seldom truly innovative and often merely following the vanguard of adult academic and intellectual dissent, student activists nevertheless tend to protest in greater number, force, and determination than their counterparts among the elders. Moreover their rejection of the traditional sub-culture as a tool for grownup conservatism turns the generational struggle into a conflict between different groups of the young. Hence, when in student protest the endemic generational tension surfaces, it is muted by the sympathy and involvement of adult radicals as well as by the opposition of other elements of youth standing for traditional values and practices. Successive age cohorts are mobilized into radical consciousness by different ideological impulses and different generational events, but in organized and sustained dissent, a counter-tradition of protest becomes an important element. Although it is a truism that socially students are part of the elite, this condition does not preclude severe strains within the leading strata in which challenging groups seek an alliance with other disadvantaged classes to gain power. Similarly, modernization has an ironic impact, since it is usually fostered first by bureaucratic governments, and then, emancipating itself from its source, often turns against authoritarian structures in the name of novel values such as liberty and national unity. In terms of numbers, student protest is always the creation of

[40] John R. Frisch, "Youth Culture in America, 1790-1865," Ph.D. diss., Univ. of Missouri, Columbia, Mo. (1970) allows a cross-cultural comparison with an example in which modernization did not produce a student movement. The more recent chapter of that story as well as a perceptive summary of the existing conceptualization on the sources of student dissent is Seymour M. Lipset's, *Rebellion in the University* (Boston 1972).

a minority, which increases in size and determination when the causative factors are operating. Most importantly, these clusters provide a larger sympathetic audience, and in moments of perceived crisis attract the support of as much as 50 percent of the student body. Student movements are therefore more often successful in shaping a critical generational identity than in achieving practical political, social, or institutional aims. Hence, the German *Burschenschaft* formed the political and social consciousness of the progressive segment of the academic elite, which pressed for national unification and liberalization of government. But when the causative factors reversed, the failure of the student movement to reach its reforming goals, largely due to its elitism, contributed heavily to the incompleteness of modernization in Germany.[41]

[41] For the larger perspective cf. F. Ringer's provocative *Decline of the German Mandarins* (Cambridge, Mass. 1969), and F. Lilge, *The Abuse of Learning: The Failure of the German University* (New York 1948). Since Robert Anchor, *Germany Confronts Modernization* (Lexington, Mass. 1972) fails to say as much about society as about culture, the history of German higher education still needs to be examined consistently from the point of view of its social purpose and role.

APPENDIX

TABLE 1

The Social Composition of the Student Body of Three German Universities

		Bildung				*Besitz*			*Mittelstand* *Alt*			*Mittelstand* *Neu*			*Totals*				*Proletariat*[d]		
		BL	HA[a]	HE[b]	TO	BL	HA	HE	TO	HA	HE	TO	HA	HE	TO	BL[c]	HA	HE	TO	HA	HE	TO
1810	No.	213	510	89		113	134	41		179	29		148	10		128	327	39		8	2	
	%	47	48	52	49	25	24	24	21	18	16	17	15	6	10	28	33	32	31	1	1	1
1830	No.	401	601	327		280	271	200		297	73		321	43		203	628	116		26	7	
	%	45	41	51	46	32	18	30	27	20	11	15	26	7	16	23	46	18	29	2	1	1.5
1850	No.	440	759	228		289	223	125		201	69		281	20		198	482	89		15	0	
	%	47	52	51	50	31	15	28	25	14	15	14	19	4	11	21	33	19	24	1	0	0.5
1870	No.	470	799	209		405	527	191		308	55		470	31		361	778	86		22	0	
	%	38	37	43	39	32	25	39	32	14	11	12	22	6	14	29	38	17	28	1	0	0.5
Total	No.	381	654	213		272	289	137		246	56		350	26		222	596	83		18	2	
	%	44	45	49	46	30	18	30	26	16	13	14	20	6	13	25	36	21	28	1	0.5	1

Source: See n. 28.

[a] Since there are no 1810 figures for Halle, the numbers and percentages for the two adjacent entries, 1788-91 and 1820-22 were averaged. For 1830 the figures for 1832-36 are given. The 1850-54 averages are distorted by a gross outlier, since sons of pastors with 414 and 29% are abnormally high, falsifying the general trend. To check the degree of deviation the percentages for 1832 and 1872-76 (for 1870) were averaged, giving 39% for Bildung, 21% for Besitz, 17% for the old and 25% for the new Mittelstand, i.e., together 42% whereas proletarians remained at 1%.

[b] Because the 1830 figures for Heidelberg contain an abnormal proportion of missing data (sons of widowed mothers or those of age) amounting to over 12%, the figures for 1831 were substituted, since they have only 3.5% no information on father's status or profession.

[c] The Berlin information is not broken down into old and new Mittelstand and no entries for servants or workers were given.

[d] The categories are largely based on 19th century German statistics and represent self-defined contemporary social groupings rather than units of modern analysis. Bildung includes all fathers with university or higher education or equivalent status such as officers and court officials. Besitz refers to landed and commercial property and attempts to account for agrarian as well as industrial capitalists, the primarily economic elements of German elites in contrast to the bureaucratic segment based on education. The Mittelstand comprises both the old (Alt) occupations of peasant, artisan, small tradesman etc. and the new (Neu) white-collar professions of petty officialdom, grade and middle-school teachers, clerks and dependent salaried personnel. The Proletariat contains the traditional servant and landless laborer groups as well as the emerging industrial workers. The status vs. professional dichotomy bedevils all attempts at establishing universal classification schemes but the present large divisions, at the risk of some imprecision, give the rough outlines of the social dynamics at issue.

TABLE 2

Student Financial Aid at Prussian Universities Compiled from Figures for First Half of 1830s

University	Greifswld	Königsbg	Halle/Wittenbg	Breslau	Bonn[d]	Berlin	Total
Students	217	431	844	951	828	1,777	5,048
Stipends	1,499 Thl	2,000	1,200 (50)	5,860 (177)	3,000	4,000[c]	17,559
Donations		2,064 (70[a])	2,000 (36)[b]		1,873 (290)	1,732	7,669
Free food	3,036	2,845	4,400 (139)	3,070 (332)	1,200 (55)	2,000	16,551
Support			350 (35)	422 (49)		?	772
Total	4,535	6,909	7,950 (260)	9,352 (558)	6,073 (345)	10,000[c]	44,819
Per Cap.	20.89	16.03	9.41 (10.0+?)	9.83	7.33	5.62	8.87

Notes: Average size of *Stipendium* (state and private): *23.83* Thl; Average size of *Freitisch*: *16.48* Thl; Average size of other aids: *9.19* Thl.

[a] The figures in parentheses indicate the number of stipends etc. granted.

[b] The estimate for Halle's donations (my own) is likely to be low and hence the total per capita support should lie above that of Breslau, since on the basis of contemporary literary evidence it seems to have granted a high amount of support and the large proportion of lower middle-class students bear this out.

[c] The stipend figure for Berlin is again a rough personal estimate, whereas the total is taken from Dieterici's informed guess, since the fragmentary nature of support in the Prussian capital from various different sources makes it difficult to arrive at any clear total.

[d] The Bonn figures for the 1840s are:

	1842-44		1845-57		1848-50	
Students	632		716 (interpol.)		806	
Stipends	9,000		9,000		9,000	
Donations	1,022		743		1,406	
Convictorium	3,600		3,600		3,600	
Extrord. Suppt.	3,685		3,559		3,180	
Total	17,308		16,902		17,186	
Cath.	482	12,383	530	12,515	565	12,991
Prot.	153	4,655	154	4,232	127	3,991
Jew	10	270	6	155	16	385
Total	645		690		708	

I.e., the average size of the stipend declined from *26.83* Thl to *24.24* Thl whereas the per capita amount which had risen to *9.12* Thl fell again to *7.11*.

[569]

12

Economists as Experts: The Rise of an Academic Profession in the United States, 1870-1920

by Robert L. Church

I

Historians have usually described the development of the academic social sciences as a steady progress from concern with reform toward an increasingly exclusive concern with scientific method, with objectivity, and with understanding social organization for the sake of understanding and not application. In the beginning, the story goes, social science, hardly deserving of the name, was moralistic, practical, and therefore biased, but the fields rapidly advanced toward objectivity, disinterest, and scientific abstraction. Social sciences progressed from "lore" to "science," from social reform to social science.[1] A more accurate and revealing point of view, however, is one that pays particular attention to the academic social scientists' continuing desire to make their knowledge influential in the real world and that interprets the various definitions of social science as different strategies adopted at different times to enhance the social scientists' influence outside the academy.

In part the social scientists desired to influence social development in order to impose the values and interests of their social class on society. Because of very restricted access to college and professional academic training in the United States before World War I (probably less restricted than in Europe at the time but much more so than in the contemporary United States), the vast majority of academic social scientists came from the more comfortable classes. Social science attracted them in part because it appeared to offer them a chance to

[1] Two studies which do not subscribe to the progressive view and which are consequently more insightful than most histories of social science disciplines are Bernard Crick, *The American Science of Politics: Its Origins and Conditions* (Berkeley and Los Angeles 1959), and Albert Somit and Joseph Tanenhaus, *The Development of American Political Science: From Burgess to Behavioralism* (Boston 1967). John Madge, *The Origins of Scientific Sociology* (Glencoe, Ill. 1962), ch. 1, views the science toward which sociology has progressed as one "concerned not merely to formulate knowledge but also to do something with it" (p. 3). It is just this view of science that most histories of social science fail to incorporate, a failure that has led them to misconstrue the nature of change in those disciplines.

[571]

Robert L. Church

maintain the values of these classes against challenges from other social groups.[2]

At another level more germane to this essay, the academic social scientist desired to make a difference in order to enhance his sense of
worth and identity and to justify his choice of career. Perhaps this has
been a special problem in the United States where widespread anti-
intellectualism and utilitarianism have forced the academic to justify—
to himself at least—his decision to withdraw from the "real" world and
the competition of the marketplace.[3] To argue that ideas and research
do affect the real world has been a powerful antidote to the criticism
that the academic was isolated, impractical, and irrelevant.

As the social science disciplines organized and professionalized, they
built into each discipline's very structure the justification that careers
in that field "made a difference" in the real world. They came to define contributing to the literature of political science or economics or
sociology as *ipso facto* "making a difference." Socialization to the profession and its internal reward structure has reassured most workers
in the vineyard of their extra-academic influence. Just how knowledge
achieves that influence, they have left to their field's basic theorists and
philosophers. Among those committed to exploring the basic purposes
of social science, those charged with applying its findings, and those
innovators interested in changing a discipline's methods or scope or
focus, however, the problem of relating knowledge and action is always present and often controversial. They are always concerned with
determining what social science "is for" and with defining how it af-
fects the real world that social scientists study. When a social science
discipline is relatively stable, controversy over relating thought and
action is often muted—even though practitioners may disagree fundamentally on the issue. When fields are developing, as in the period
under study here, or facing fundamental challenges over method and
purpose as they are at present, the controversy is open and often
rather heated.[4] In those years before academic social sciences achieved
the stability of purpose and procedures that would ultimately shield

[2] On the social and class values of professionalizing social scientists, see the
suggestive discussions that bear obliquely on the point in Richard Hofstadter,
Anti-Intellectualism in American Life (New York 1963), pt. III, and Robert H.
Wiebe, *The Search for Order, 1877-1920* (New York 1967), chs. 5-7.

[3] On American anti-intellectualism and its relation to the university, see Hofstadter, *Anti-Intellectualism*, pt. IV; on the academics' ambiguous relation to the
"real world," see Laurence R. Veysey, *The Emergence of the American University*
(Chicago 1965), ch. 2, esp. 61-63, and pt. II, passim.

[4] For a survey of opinions on the relation of economic thought to action and of
the cycles of controversy among economists, see T. W. Hutchison, *"Positive"
Economics and Policy Objectives* (London 1964), esp. ch. I.

most practitioners from the problem of defining their work's relevance to the real world, the relation of social science and social action was at the forefront of concern for a great number of academic social scientists. There is a further point. Most academics probably, and surely almost all social scientists, expected—even before such expectations were built into professionally defined roles—their work eventually to contribute to social or individual betterment. The historian of academic disciplines must determine how soon the academic thinks his work will become relevant or meaningful in the real world in order to specify how various scholars define their obligations to society. Those most concerned with seeing their ideas make a difference will expect the shortest time span between their research and its application. Throughout the period under discussion here social scientists continued to expect academic knowledge to have an immediate impact on social action.

The remainder of this essay proposes to test the explanatory power of this point of view by surveying the development of academic economics in the United States between 1870 and 1920.[5] The academic economist first sought to affect social action by teaching popular audiences or public opinion what he thought were correct principles of social and economic organization. He depended on informed public opinion to force officials to effect appropriate policy changes. By 1920 the economist had adopted the role of the expert in which he sought to affect policy by passing his findings, his advice, and his conclusions about public policy directly to public officials who would, he hoped, transform them immediately into policy. Although academic economists basically redefined the strategy they employed for influencing social action between 1870 and 1920, they did not alter their desire to make a difference in the society. The shift from a stress on moralism and reform to a stress on objectivity and science, which the standard histories of social science have identified, is best seen as a shift in strategy designed to enhance the economist's capacity to affect society. In the fifty-year period under survey the introduction of empirical observation and quantitative analysis made economics more complex,

[5] I have chosen to concentrate on economics because the process under discussion occurred more rapidly and clearly in economics than in other social sciences. However, extensive research and reading in the history of political science and sociology does not suggest that the process of development in those fields differed in anything but detail except that the latter disciplines took somewhat longer to professionalize. I have not attempted to apply the viewpoint argued here to psychology and anthropology since neither of these disciplines took the form of a social science—i.e., a focus on the behavior of men in society —in the 19th-century United States.

more sophisticated, more capable of comprehending and accounting for observed social phenomena, which in turn increased economics' applicability in the determination of public policy. The techniques and the rhetoric of science increased the economist's sense of worth by increasing his capacity to make a difference in the real world. What had changed in the fifty years between 1870 and 1920 was the means which academic economists adopted to affect public policy rather than any fundamental change in their attitude toward reform and their duty to encourage it. What also changed as a consequence of the economists' shift in strategy was that university teaching and "making a difference," once tightly entwined, had become separate and unconnected functions.

II

Faculty, administrators, trustees, and donors cooperated to establish social science in the American college and university after the Civil War as part of a wider effort to nurture socially responsible ideas in the nation's present and future leaders. Isolated professors of political economy or of the science of politics or, more typically, of modern history taught in some antebellum colleges, of course, and the courses in moral philosophy that college presidents taught to seniors contained many issues and topics that later became the nucleus of the social science curriculum. But the institution of social science was desultory; the discussion of economic and political issues was something of an afterthought in the moral philosophy course, nearly always subordinate to religious concerns.[6] After the war social scientists, although not possessing quite the glamor of their colleagues in natural science or philology, aggressively sought complete independence from theological restrictions and the limitations of idealist and common-sense epistemology and developed a powerful esprit de corps and a passion for urging expanded teaching of social sciences in colleges and universities. Independent social science departments got underway with

[6] Michael J. L. O'Connor, *Origins of Academic Economics in the United States* (New York 1944); Edwin R. A. Seligman, "The Early Teaching of Economics in the United States," in *Economic Essays: Contributed in Honor of John Bates Clark*, ed. J. H. Hollander (New York 1927), 283-320; Joseph Dorfman, *The Economic Mind in American Civilization, 1606-1865, Volume Two* (New York 1946), chs. xxv and ff; Anna Haddow, *Political Science in American Colleges and Universities, 1636-1900* (New York 1939); Gladys Bryson, "The Emergence of the Social Sciences from Moral Philosophy," *International J. of Ethics* 42 (April 1932), 304-23, and "The Comparable Interests of the Old Moral Philosophy and the Modern Social Sciences," *Social Forces* 11 (October 1932), 19-27; Wilson Smith, *Professors & Public Ethics: Studies of Northern Moral Philosophers before the Civil War* (Ithaca, N.Y. 1956).

Cornell's founding in 1868 and Eliot's elevation at Harvard in 1869 and gained great momentum with Johns Hopkins' founding in 1876 and the establishment of the School of Political Science at Columbia in 1880.[7]

The academic social scientists' expansionist efforts formed part of the larger "mugwump" or "independent" movement in the United States in the last third of the 19th century. The mugwumps had been, or were descended from, members of the social elite before the war; they were largely of eastern birth and residence; they were committed to political independence, especially from the regular Republican machine of the era, and to civil service reform. All identified the years following the war as the scene of a crucial moral battle. They felt their values increasingly menaced by Greenbackers and labor unions who threatened, the independents thought, to expropriate the property of the rich; by what they viewed as the fanaticism or irrationality of Radical Republican reconstruction policy; and by the politicians, too incompetent in both a moral and technical sense to be called statesmen, who ruled the country.[8]

These men also felt threatened from within—by the backsliding from traditional ideals of service and social responsibility among men of their own class and even more frighteningly among the children of their class. Charles Eliot Norton—Boston Brahmin, Harvard's professor of art history, Dante scholar, and a founder of the *Nation*—urged in the midst of his disillusion with the crusade against slavery an im-

[7] Robert L. Church, "The Development of the Social Sciences as Academic Disciplines at Harvard University, 1869-1900," Ph.D. diss., Harvard Univ. (1965), chs. 1-4; Walter P. Rogers, *Andrew D. White and the Modern University* (Ithaca, N.Y. 1942); R. Gordon Hoxie et al., *The History of the Faculty of Political Science, Columbia University* (New York 1955); Hugh Hawkins, *Pioneer: A History of the Johns Hopkins University, 1874-1889* (Ithaca, N.Y. 1960), ch. x (at Hopkins the difference in the rate of development between the social sciences and the hard sciences and the humanistic "sciences" is most clear); John B. Parrish, "Rise of Economics as an Academic Discipline: The Formative Years to 1900," *The Southern Economic J.* 34 (July 1967), 1-15. The disciplines subsumed under the term "social science" in the late 19th century were history, political science, and political economy. Sociology had yet to be formally introduced; psychology remained a part of philosophy, and anthropology essentially a part of archaeology.

[8] Hofstadter, *Anti-Intellectualism*, ch. vii; Geoffrey Blodgett, *The Gentle Reformers: Massachusetts Democrats in the Cleveland Era* (Cambridge, Mass. 1966), and John G. Sproat, *"The Best Men": Liberal Reformers in the Gilded Age* (New York 1968), portray this group of men most insightfully. The general matter in the paragraphs that follow relies on these general works, on my reading of numerous biographies and autobiographies of these men, and on my reading of several collections of their correspondence—especially the Edwin Lawrence Godkin Papers and the Charles Eliot Norton Papers, Houghton Library, Harvard University.

proved education for the children of the elite. They needed education "in its nature moral,—an education in social duties, and in that enlightened self-interest which sees its advantage, not in a selfish accumulation of wealth regardless of the claims of those who assist in its production, but in such a division of profits as should raise the general standard of comfort. . . . Unless the ruling classes, upon whom rests the responsibility for remedial effort, are aroused from their selfish inactivity to a new sense of duty and to new exertions, no prophet is needed to foretell the approaching overthrow of social order."[9]

To ensure the maintenance of social order, the independents launched a large-scale educational campaign directed at the backsliders of their own generation and at all the children of the elite classes. Much of the effort was a journalistic one. It assumed that a mixture of exhortation and explication of how correct principles applied to current disputes would remind backsliders of the traditional values and of their duty to support them. Edwin L. Godkin's New York *Nation* was perhaps the premier effort. Founded in 1865 to support the extension of full citizenship rights to the freedmen, the *Nation* soon turned to defending liberal Republicanism, hard money, free trade, and property rights. Other journalistic efforts included the *North American Review* and *Harper's Weekly* and several daily papers in major eastern cities.[10] The independents, expanding on their Civil War experience in Loyal Publication Societies which distributed pro-Union pamphlets in the northern states and sought to place pro-Union news releases and editorial comment in small newspapers throughout the nation, formed several organizations—David Ames Wells's Society for Political Education was probably the most important—for circulating information about correct social and economic principles and for securing suitable comment in the media.[11] The Liberal Republican campaign in 1872 and the Independent movement of 1884 also should be included among the best men's efforts to educate the public in order to restore their so-

[9] Charles Eliot Norton, "The Poverty of England," *North Am. Rev.*, 109 (July 1869), 153-54. On Norton see Kermit Vanderbilt, *Charles Eliot Norton: Apostle of Culture in a Democracy* (Cambridge, Mass. 1959), esp. 75-100.

[10] On the founding of the *Nation*, see William M. Armstrong, "The Freedmen's Movement and the Founding of the *Nation*," *JAH* 53 (March 1967), 708-26, and the works cited therein.

[11] George Winston Smith, "Broadsides for Freedom: Civil War Propaganda in New England," *NEQ* 21 (September 1948), 291-312; Frank Freidel, "The [New York] Loyal Publication Society: A Pro-Union Propaganda Agency," *Mississippi Valley Hist. Rev.* 26 (December 1939), 359-76; Fred Bunyan Joyner, *David Ames Wells: Champion of Free Trade* (Cedar Rapids, Ia. 1939), ch. IX, esp. 147-50; Irwin Unger, *The Greenback Era: A Social and Political History of American Finance, 1865-1879* (Princeton, N.J. 1964), 136-42.

cial and political values to their rightful ascendency. The independents intended these campaigns, however futile they were as a means of gaining office, to teach politicians that they must abide by such principles if they were to keep the better classes' support.

Enlarging social science's place in the curriculum was another part of this educational effort. The vast majority of social scientists teaching at universities before 1880, at least, counted themselves among those who sought to reestablish classic principles of social and political organization as standards for Americans.[12] They proposed to teach the future elite—and university education then was pretty nearly restricted to the elite—correct principles of political and social organization, the laws governing social and political relations which had to be obeyed if the society were to function properly. Social science taught just those principles and laws through studying the development of English freedoms since Magna Carta (sometimes since village communities emerged in the German forests) and their extension and further safeguarding in the United States; how the constitution protected individual liberties, property, and the rights of minorities (in this case they meant the rights of the rich against the desires of the "mob") and how it limited the powers of democracy; and the laws and principles of classical laissez-faire political economy.[13]

The bond between the defenders of the traditional principles and the development of academic social science is vividly clear in Harvard's efforts to fill two places on the social science faculty in 1869-71— one in political economy and one in medieval history. Four of the five men seriously considered were intimately involved in the liberal journalism of the day. Charles Franklin Dunbar, chosen to profess political economy although he had never studied, taught, or written specifically on the subject, joined Harvard's faculty after an eight-year stint as editor of the Boston *Daily Advertiser*—the independents' newspaper in that city. Eliot's first choice for the position in medieval history was the Englishman Goldwin Smith, whose substantial historical qualifications included a period as Regius Professor of Modern History at Oxford, but even Smith was known primarily as a journalist, having once

[12] Political independence was not, of course, confined to social scientists on college campuses—leading academics in all fields, many students, and a large number of college and university presidents also joined the movement.

[13] On history and political science, see John Higham, *History* (Englewood Cliffs, N.J. 1965), pt. II, ch. 1, and pt. III, chs. 1-2; Edward N. Saveth, *American Historians and European Immigrants, 1875-1925* (New York 1948); on political economy, see Sidney Fine, *Laissez Faire and the General-Welfare State: A Study of Conflict in American Thought, 1865-1901* (Ann Arbor, Mich. 1956), chs. II-III; Joseph Dorfman, *The Economic Mind in American Civilization, Volume Three, 1865-1918* (New York 1949), ch. III.

edited the *Saturday Review* and having established his American reputation as journalistic advocate of the British Liberal Party and the cause of Anglo-American understanding in the 1860s. Eliot also offered the post to Godkin, who had no experience or qualifications as an historian. Godkin finally refused it because Harvard would not let him remain the "responsible" editor of a weekly journal, although Eliot did expect him to continue writing for and taking a "lively" interest in the *Nation*. Henry Adams, who at the urging of his father, a prominent Liberal Republican, finally accepted the position, had made what reputation he possessed at the time not in scholarship but in his journalistic observations of Grant's Washington. The few historical pieces he had done covered only modern history.

Largely self-taught in the school of British Liberal political science and British and German evolutionary thought, Adams learned in Europe not the value of disinterested scholarship but the need to apply learning to the immediate improvement of political and social mores. Ironically, the fifth candidate—largely a self-proclaimed one—was the best qualified as a scholar and medieval historian. But John Fiske, although he shared the others' values and indulged in similar journalistic activities to some extent, took his scholarship a bit too seriously and followed his ideas to the point of proclaiming—so it seemed to the powers at Harvard—an anti-religious doctrine. Thus, he was never a serious candidate.[14]

All the serious candidates appeared to view teaching as another way

[14] For a detailed discussion of these appointments, see Church, "Development of the Social Sciences," ch. 1. President White of Cornell offered social science positions at the same period to Smith, Godkin, and Fiske (Smith accepted). Biographical information on the five candidates is found in Frank William Taussig, "Introduction" to Charles Franklin Dunbar, *Economic Essays*, ed. O.M.W. Sprague (New York 1904), vii-xvii; Elizabeth Wallace, *Goldwin Smith: Victorian Liberal* (Toronto 1957); Sidney Lee in *DNB*, Suppl. 1901-11, s.v. Smith, Goldwin; Rollo Ogden, *Life and Letters of Edwin Lawrence Godkin* (New York 1907); Charles William Eliot to Godkin, 18 July, 23 July, and 27 August 1870, Godkin Papers; Godkin to Eliot, 6 August, 25 August, and 29 August 1870, Charles William Eliot Papers, Harvard Univ. Archives, Harvard Univ.; Ernest Samuels, *The Young Henry Adams* (Cambridge, Mass. 1948); Milton Berman, *John Fiske: The Evolution of a Popularizer* (Cambridge, Mass. 1961); and John Edward Higgins, "The Young John Fiske: 1842-1874," Ph.D. diss., Harvard Univ. (1960). Many have assumed that because Adams set out for Germany in 1858 "to become a scholar," he was prepared to assume a scholarly post in the United States upon his return from Europe. But his German training amounted to but a few, poorly understood lectures. George McKee Elsey, "The First Education of Henry Adams," *NEQ* 14 (December 1941), 684; Samuels, *The Young Henry Adams*, 56.

of reaching the same goals that they had set for themselves as journalists. Godkin once described the Harvard offer as a chance to indulge his "burning longing to help to train up a generation of young men to hate Greeley and [Theodore] Tilton and their ways." Like Godkin, Adams did not see his move to Cambridge as the beginning of a new kind of career; rather, he planned to continue to urge reform of Grant's Washington upon his audience from his professorial chair in Cambridge. After coming to Harvard, Adams informed David A. Wells that "in order not to break entirely from old connections I have become editor of the North American Review, and propose to make it a regular organ of our opinions." Adams accepted the editorship at Harvard's request. It was only fitting that the duties of a professor of history at Harvard in 1870 should include those of the political journalist.[15]

These early university social scientists intended to make a direct difference in the world through their university teaching and their journalism and to make that impact sooner rather than later, immediately rather than gradually. The elite would be immediately reminded of the principles that it was their duty to uphold; their children, upon leaving school, would be prepared to assume responsibility, as public servants and citizens, for returning the country to the path of right policy.

In actuality, of course, the social scientists found that their efforts made little apparent difference. The political and social evils which first moved them to stress social science education burgeoned. Protectionist duties rose higher and higher; ill-informed but strangely popular schemes to undermine government commitments to honor the national debt multiplied; labor unions convinced more and more working men to submerge their precious individual liberties in collectives which would fight for higher wages they did not deserve and which the iron law of wages promised they could not receive. The independents most feared the violence—however caused—that accompanied labor's efforts, most notably in the great railroad strike of 1877. The most corrupt administration in the history of the United States won overwhelming reelection despite the strenuous efforts of the Liberal Republicans. Irresponsible and immoral plutocrats—whom Godkin was among the first to label "robber barons"—remained in the saddle, indifferent to and undeterred by the protests of the "best men" and

---

[15] Godkin to Charles Eliot Norton, 28 July 1870 in Ogden, *Godkin*, II, 62 [I have been unable to locate the original letter]; Adams to Wells, 25 October 1870 in John Eliot Alden, "Henry Adams as Editor: A Group of Unpublished Letters Written to David A. Wells," *NEQ* 11 (March 1938), 148.

their spokesmen in social science departments and liberal journals.[16] A decade and more of teaching aimed at reforming the society by recalling the elite to their responsibilities had accomplished little.

Worse yet, labor, soft money advocates, and self-interested protectionists were finding advocates for their causes in a new generation of social scientists, trained for the most part under the German historical school of economics.[17] By the early 1880s it was clear that academic economists did not speak with a single voice on the great issues of the day. The "new" economists began to write for and support the interests of an audience quite different from the elite one the earlier social scientists represented. For instance, Richard T. Ely, professor of political economy at Johns Hopkins, advocated Christian socialism, the rights of labor, the redistribution of resources in the United States. Such activities only increased popular resistance to the independents' laissez-faire ideas.

In response, social scientists in the older tradition intensified their commitment to popular education. They sought to increase their audience and the popular support for their views and to immunize the masses from the historical school's seductive doctrines. In these efforts they and their journalistic allies increasingly neglected their own previously announced values of moderation, rationality, caution, and calm. Instead their writings became increasingly shrill and emotional, their denunciations of evil increasingly bitter, their analysis and their conclusions increasingly oversimplified. Godkin's development as editor of the *Nation*, as John Sproat has amply demonstrated, followed this pattern.[18] The most appropriate case in point, however, is the career of James Laurence Laughlin, economist at Harvard, Cornell, and Chicago, advocate of banking reforms that finally culminated in the Federal Reserve Act, and militant defender of laissez faire before popular audiences.

[16] The independents' increasing disillusion and mounting fear is evident in reading through the editions of the *Nation* in the 1870s. See also the sources listed in n. 8 for their thought in these years.

[17] On the German historical school and its influence in the United States, see Jurgen Herbst, *The German Historical School in American Scholarship: A Study in the Transfer of Culture* (Ithaca, N.Y. 1965), chs. 6-8; Dorfman, *Economic Mind*, III, 87-98, 160-74; Dorfman, "The Role of the German Historical School in American Economic Thought," *Am. Economic Rev.: Papers & Proc.* 45 (May 1955), 17-28; Daniel M. Fox, *The Discovery of Abundance: Simon N. Patten and the Transformation of Social Theory* (Ithaca, N.Y. 1967), 22-24; Jack C. Myles, "German Historicism and American Economics," Ph.D. diss., Princeton Univ. (1956); Joseph A. Schumpeter, *History of Economic Analysis* (New York 1954), pt. IV, ch. 4. On the best men's reaction to the new school, see Sproat, "*The Best Men*," 155-57.

[18] Sproat, 19.

Laughlin, who received his doctorate in history (1876) under Henry Adams, carried Adams' desire to use scholarship to reform and purify national life with him into the teaching of economics under Dunbar at Harvard from 1878 to 1888 and then into the departments he built first at Cornell (1890-92) and at the University of Chicago (1892-1916). He left a secure and well-paying position as an insurance executive to teach at Cornell because, he explained to a friend, the "salary is good, the position independent, and the chance to influence opinion in favor of sound finance is considerable. As things now appear in the country, I cannot rest quietly without taking my part in the fight for honest money & sound taxation." But where these sentiments had led Adams to a concern with teaching the elite, Laughlin, coming at a later time when such elite-focused efforts appeared less effective, directed his teaching to a wider audience. In 1892 he complained that the "influence of scientific thinking in the United States has little or no authority with the masses of the people," especially in quelling public demand for radical reforms. A growing population swelled by immigration would, he felt, soon exhaust the country's natural resources, and as resources diminish, "labor and capital both get smaller rewards[.] [T]hen," he warned, "unless economically trained, even honest men, finding themselves cramped by barriers of their own creation, but brought into operation by natural laws, will not know what is really happening, and in entire ignorance of the truth may fly in the face of law and wreak signal damage on society as the supposed cause of their evil situation." To avoid this fate, "we must get ready to give economic instruction of a simple and elementary kind in every common school in the country, in such a way that it shall reach the ordinary voter, and influence the thinking of the humblest workman." Only the study of economic principles would train the volatile working class to bear the "iron law of wages" and the law of diminishing returns.[19] Laughlin thus substantially widened the audience and the responsibilities of the reforming social scientist.

[19] Laughlin to Henry Villard 17 May 1890, Henry Villard Papers, Houghton Lib., Harvard Univ.; Laughlin, "The Study of Political Economy in the United States," *J. of Political Economy* 1 (December 1892), 1-6; Laughlin, *The Study of Political Economy: Hints to Students and Teachers* (New York 1885), 44-49. All biographical information on Laughlin in this essay comes from Alfred Bornemann, *J. Laurence Laughlin: Chapters in the Career of an Economist* (Washington, D.C. 1940), unless otherwise noted. Dorfman, *Economic Mind*, III, 274, quotes Laughlin to the effect that he believed his devotion to practical questions had prevented him from making theoretical contributions of "sufficient value to recall." Laughlin was not the only conservative economist of the late 19th and early 20th century interested in mass education. C. J. Bullock of Harvard (1869-1941) and Irving Fisher of Yale (1867-1947) fit the same mold. Dorfman, *Economic Mind*, III, 239, 371.

Laughlin set out to follow his own advice. Between the publication of his doctoral dissertation in 1876 and the publication of his *Principles of Money* in 1903, he wrote almost exclusively to affect general public opinion. Laughlin's appointment at Chicago brought him to the head-quarters city of William H. (Coin) Harvey's silver crusade, a proximity that convinced Laughlin of the desperate need for public education on economic questions. Accordingly, Laughlin composed newspaper columns in 1895, debated Harvey on the same platform, and in 1896 published a weighty volume arguing the hard money case which matched Harvey's popular *Coin's Financial School* cartoon for cartoon. Laughlin later claimed that his articles stopped the sale of Harvey's book,[20] an obvious case of wishful thinking. Wesley Clair Mitchell recalled that at the same time Laughlin was training his students at the University of Chicago to continue the fight against the free-silver agitation.[21] Laughlin remained committed to widespread public education as late as 1911 when he took a two-years' leave of absence in order to chair the executive committee of the National Citizens' League for the Promotion of a Sound Banking System. His purpose, he recalled, was to change "the thinking of a nation on an important public question." The league established offices in forty-five states, spent over $400,000 in two and one-half years of canvassing the nation, and published thousands of pages of propaganda, a large majority of which Laughlin personally edited. This propaganda consisted of "literature for the general reader and for speakers . . . of a sort such that, even though complicated, . . . could not only be easily understood by 'the man in the street,' but also be scientifically sound for editors and writers of important journals."[22] Laughlin clung to the assumption that the social scientist could effect social and political reform by building a large-scale political movement through education. In fact Laughlin's efforts at popular education failed to mobilize enough pressure to modify policy but they did make Laughlin's doctrines so suspect that

[20] Laughlin, *The Federal Reserve Act: Its Origins and Problems* (New York 1933), 3. The book, made up of Laughlin's newspaper articles of 1895, was *Facts About Money: Including the Debate with W. H. Harvey ("Coin")* (Chicago 1895). Laughlin appears in Harvey's *Coin's Financial School* (1894) as the interests' financial apologist whose arguments Coin demolishes. See *Coin's Financial School*, ed. Richard Hofstadter (Cambridge, Mass. 1963), 160-61, 174-75, 185, 190.

[21] W. C. Mitchell, "J. Laurence Laughlin" [rev. of Alfred Bornemann, *J. Laurence Laughlin: Chapters in the Career of an Economist* (Washington 1940)], *J. of Political Economy*, 49 (December 1941), 879-80.

[22] Bornemann, *Laughlin*, 49-53; Laughlin, *Federal Reserve Act*, chs. I-IV [quotations from 70, 90].

policy makers excluded him from their deliberations.[23] As more and more economists came to discover after 1890, a more efficient strategy for relating economic ideas to policy was to adopt the role of the expert who advised policy makers without recourse to public education. This lesson Laughlin never learned.

The historical or "new" economists who rose to prominence in the 1880s agreed with Laughlin on the need for widening the economists' audience although they sought to teach that wider audience a message much different from Laughlin's. Like Godkin or Adams, they believed that changing public opinion was the most effective way of changing policy, but they aimed their messages considerably farther down the social scale than did the traditionalists—at the middle classes that filled Chautauqua tents and university extension classes and the skilled laborers who were organizing the crafts and trades. They understood that their support for labor and state regulation or control of monopolies would appeal to these classes more than to the elites whom Godkin and Adams sought to reach. But they did not hope to inspire a genuine "mass" movement; even at their most radical they appealed constantly to responsible public opinion and for piecemeal reform. They felt that reform required, however, the active support of the broad middle class of the country, both urban and rural, rather than just the support of the elite, and they sought to inspire such support. The historical economists' appeals differed somewhat in tone from those of men like Adams or Godkin. Where the traditionalists affected a certain cool aloofness and a moderate rationality, the historical economists appeared more passionate in their advocacy. Although the "new" economists were no more earnest than the traditionalists, their appeals had a more evangelical cast, reflecting in part the contrast between the younger economists' expectation that public opinion would effect positive changes in society and the traditionalists' desire to mobilize their audience to retard change or to restore a previous order.

The difference in tone also reflected a difference in background. Ely, Simon Nelson Patten, John Rogers Commons, Edmund Janes James, and Henry Carter Adams all came from rural or small-town America,

---

[23] Laughlin, *Federal Reserve Act*, 43-49, 53-61, 63-64, 82-84, 99, 104-37, 184-85, claimed that he greatly influenced the shape of the Act but that his role could not be publicly acknowledged because of political pressures. Carter Glass, *An Adventure in Constructive Finance* (Garden City, N.Y. 1927), and H. Parker Willis, in his review of Laughlin's *Federal Reserve Act, Columbia Law Rev.* 23 (1933), 1281-85, and in a letter to Mitchell, 8 March 1934, W. C. Mitchell Papers, Special Collections, Columbia University Library, emphatically disagree with Laughlin's assessment. Willis advised the committee which drafted the Federal Reserve Act.

the largest proportion from the middle west, and they all partook of the pious, preacherly cast of mind more characteristic of those regions. Indeed, for some a career of leadership as an economist took the place of a career of leadership as a minister, as A. W. Coats has ably demonstrated in the case of Henry Carter Adams. Urged by his pious Congregational parents, Adams entered Andover Theological Seminary in 1875 to prepare for the ministry. Finding the curriculum too rigid and his own faith unsure, he aimed instead for a career in reform journalism. He consulted Godkin about his choice of journalism as his way of improving the world. In 1876 Adams accepted a fellowship from the new Johns Hopkins University, intending to study constitutional law and history to prepare himself better for publishing a political quarterly. At Hopkins, however, he became enamored with political economy and decided to study it for journalistic preparation. Like theological training, the study of political economy, a subject which "comes into daily life—affecting the conditions and happiness of men" more than any other—would prepare him to better the social, political, and moral life of Americans.

While studying in Germany in 1878, he began to fear that political economy might indeed be too narrow, to suspect "that there is not enough chance to preach in" it. He vowed that in time he would move beyond political economy into political philosophy, a subject which touched all facets of social and moral problems and gave its students opportunity to be generalists in reform. Instead, Adams eventually expanded political economy to include political philosophy. He focused his work less on the technical points of economics (although he did significant work on taxation and railroad accounting methods) than on the larger problems of reconciling individual liberty and freedom with collective needs and the public interest. For him the economist's mission resembled the minister's. He committed himself as a teacher to getting his students to recognize "the necessity of thinking of these [social and economic] topics that are now coming to make up my life, indeed to take the place of religion." He also sought to arouse interest in the basic issues beyond the classroom. In the 1890s through his friendship with Felix Adler, head of the Ethical Culture Society, he addressed many ethical culture audiences and helped direct the Plymouth School of Ethics and the *International Journal of Ethics*.[24]

[24] Biographical information in this paragraph comes from A. W. Coats's persuasive account, "Henry Carter Adams: A Case Study in the Emergence of the Social Sciences in the United States, 1850-1900," *J. of Am. Studies* 2 (October 1968), 177-97. The three quotations come from documents quoted in that article —H. C. Adams to his parents, 22 October 1877, 184; Adams to his parents, 29 October 1878, 186; Adams to Herbert Baxter Adams, 13 and 23 April 1883, 188.

Adams sought, then, to affect social, economic, and political policies by teaching correct facts and moral conclusions to a large audience, through preaching to all Americans.

Richard T. Ely is the prime example of an academic economist who combined economics and religious reform and who sought to influence policy through appeal to the "masses." Ely was born into a highly religious Presbyterian family in upstate New York. His father let crops rot in the fields rather than harvest them on Sunday and refused to grow barley—the crop best suited to the soil—because he knew it would be used to make beer. Although the younger Ely did not experience conversion, he shared his father's intense dedication to the eradication of sin and the betterment of mankind. Like Adams he felt that the academic economist fulfilled many of the same functions as the minister. Indeed, he even contemplated becoming a Universalist minister at one point, and his initial goals for graduate study—"to go to Germany to study philosophy and find the 'absolute truth' "—had a distinctly religious ring.[25] In Germany he shifted to the study of political economy and finally received a teaching position at Johns Hopkins in that subject.

He found the United States to which he returned in 1880 sharply divided on many economic and social issues and close to open conflict over the respective rights of capital and labor. He traced the causes of this impending conflict to the public's ignorance and lack of Christian toleration and brotherhood. Ignorance of labor's methods and aims and exaggerated views of its strength made people unnecessarily hostile to its organizing efforts, he recalled in his autobiography. The "ordinary man" had no "clear conception of the labor movement" and "was unaware even of the elementary differences between socialism and anarchism. There were a great many trees all around, but no one could see the forest for the trees." Ely wrote *The Labor Movement in America* (1886) to rectify this situation. "I thought I was doing something very remarkable and making a real contribution to human affairs." Although later he doubted whether he had done the right thing or written a very good book, "at the time I was full of enthusiasm and

For a discussion of Adams' concerns as an economist, see ibid., 195; Dorfman, *Economic Mind*, III, 164-74. Another dicussion of religious themes in late 19th century American economics is John Rutherford Everett, *Religion in Economics: A Study of John Bates Clark, Richard T. Ely, Simon N. Patten* (New York 1946).

[25] Richard T. Ely, *Ground Under Our Feet: An Autobiography* (New York 1938), 34. Biographical information in this and the following paragraphs comes from ibid. and Benjamin Rader, *The Academic Mind and Reform: The Influence of Richard T. Ely in American Life* (Lexington, Ky. 1966).

was fired with the thought that I was fulfilling a mission." "In the words of St. Paul, as I wrote to my mother at the time, 'Woe is me if I preach not this gospel!' "[26] Another book, *Social Aspects of Christianity* (1889), resulted from his belief that the impending conflict contained "an unprecedented, unparalleled opportunity for the church to direct the conflicting forces into such fruitful channels that they might have become powerful for the 'good of man and the glory of God.' " He appealed for "a great religious awakening which shall shake things, going down into the depths of men's lives and modifying their character. This religious reform must infuse a religious spirit into every department of political life."[27]

Ely wrote for the "ordinary man," not the elite. He regretted his inability as a lecturer to hold large crowds and give them the message. Instead, he had to depend on his writings. He wrote the first edition of his textbook for the Chautauqua Literary and Scientific Circle, to whose summer sessions in upstate New York both the educated and the "common people" flocked for information and enlightenment. He was very proud that this text "had a very wide circulation" and that "you could hardly find a hamlet anywhere of any size where somebody had not read this book and where it had not been discussed."[28] Between 1880 and 1900 most of his writing was popular. Besides the accounts of socialism, his text for Chautauqua, and his defense of the labor movement, he published *Problems of Today* (1888), *The Social Law of Service* (1896), and a host of popular magazine articles. At the same time he published only a handful of technical economic studies meant for professionals and policy makers. For seven years he actively participated at Chautauqua meetings and he strongly promoted university extension. All these activities played a part in Ely's effort to use his economic training and knowledge to change American social life for the better by educating the masses to understand economic reality clearly.

Ely also sought to engage the emerging profession of academic economics in the same mass educational effort. Principal founder and publicist for the American Economic Association, he sought to make the academic economists' professional organization a popular platform from which economists who shared his goals could influence public opinion. "One aim of our association," Ely told the audience at the organizational meeting in 1885, "should be the education of public opin-

---

[26] Ely, *Ground*, 71-72.

[27] Ibid., 72-73; Ely is summarizing *Social Aspects of Christianity and Other Essays*, new and enl. ed. (New York 1889), 147-48, but although he indicates that he is quoting directly from it, he is not.

[28] Ely, *Ground*, 81.

ion in regard to economic questions and economic literature." Ely and his supporters modeled the association on the Verein für Sozialpolitik and committed it to the views of the "historical" or inductive school of economists who were seeking to overthrow the classical, laissez-faire ideas advocated by more traditional economists. The historical economists agreed generally that only an activist government—anathema to the classicists—could solve America's social and economic problems. Ely and other members of the historical school organized to press their views on public opinion and to loosen laissez faire's hold on the public and political mind.[29]

At the same time that the association's founders were intent on widening the academic economists' influence on practical affairs, they introduced a significantly new emphasis on research and science. The younger economists, with more than a little justice, denounced their predecessors' failure to do original research. All they did, the charge went, was to ransack the archive of long-codified and universally valid principles and subprinciples of classical theory to find those that best suited the specific situation at issue. The economist applied those principles whole in order to discover the best strategy for that situation— usually to do nothing but allow natural forces to run their course. Historical or inductive economists objected to this reliance on an arsenal of immutable principle. The historical school argued that the classicists' supposedly universally valid principles had been formulated in a specific historical and geographic context and were not necessarily applicable in other periods and places where conditions were different. This point of view naturally suggested a further fragmentation or relativism: because no two economic situations were alike, even within a single historical period, no general rules could apply. Instead of seeking to fit a situation to a general rule, the economist should conduct a thorough empirical investigation of the situation and induce from his findings the wisest policy to follow in that situation.[30]

[29] On the formation of the American Economic Association, see Ely, "Report of the Organization of the American Economic Association," *Publications of the Am. Economic Ass.* 1 (March 1886), 5-32 [the quotation comes from p. 15]; Ely, "The American Economic Association: With Special Reference to Its Origin and Early Development: An Historical Sketch," ibid., 3d ser., 11 (April 1910), 47-92; Ely, *Ground*, ch. iv; A. W. Coats, "The First Two Decades of the American Economic Association," *Am. Economic Rev.* 50 (September 1960), 555-74; Dorfman, *Economic Mind*, iii, ch. ix; Fine, *Laissez Faire and the General-Welfare State*, ch. vii; Fox, *Discovery of Abundance*, 33-43; Rader, *Academic Mind and Reform*, 33-40.

[30] On the historical economists, see, besides the sources listed in n. 17, the discussion of W. J. Ashley in Robert L. Church, "The Economists Study Society: Sociology at Harvard, 1891-1902," in Church et al., *Social Sciences at Harvard*,

Robert L. Church

For all its obvious failings as a doctrine upon which to build anything resembling a theoretical science, the historical school's point of view did stimulate vast quantities of empirical research. The historical economists identified themselves with the new university research effort, as accumulators of "new" knowledge. In investigating each specific economic situation, they discovered never-before-known facts and relations whereas their predecessors had mainly manipulated and reapplied already known knowledge. But in no way was the investigator or empiricist to be an ivory-tower scientist who discovered truth for its own sake. Each new fact also contributed to reform or social betterment. The historical economists required the economist to investigate contemporary economic problems to find the means of directing economic development in the public interest and to educate the popular audience to support the solutions to economic problems that he discovered. Science and reform in no way conflicted in their minds.

III

But Ely's vision of the American Economic Association as an organization of empirical economists bent on discovering solutions to immediate social problems and on generating widespread public support for those solutions did not materialize. Members of both the classical and historical schools came to reject the notion that the economist could serve as both investigator and popular educator. Ely's and Laughlin's commitments to popular education appeared to accentuate division and disagreement among economists. Many economists grew to believe that the public airing of disagreement would hinder their efforts to affect public policy. How could economists expect outsiders to listen to them if they could not agree among themselves as to the conclusions of economic science? In appealing for public support, advocates of various points of view often oversimplified the issues, partly to make their position more understandable and partly to make it more attractive to a large group. Their interest in public education led them to produce more controversy rather than less, to paint the opposite point of view as more evil and more irrational in order to place their own point of view in a better light. Such polarization obscured the wide range of agreement among economists of all schools and hindered rational discussion of the issues.[31]

1860-1920: From Inculcation to the Open Mind (Cambridge, Mass. 1965), 61-78.

[31] Mary O. Furner, "Advocacy and Objectivity: The Professionalization of Social Science, 1865-1905," Ph.D. diss., Northwestern Univ. (1972), ch. v, esp. 120-21, makes this point for a somewhat different purpose in her illuminating discussion of methodological and ideological controversies among academic econ-

Academic economists' efforts to gather public support for particular proposals also invited the public to participate in economic debate, on the same basis as academic economists. When Laughlin agreed to battle Coin Harvey on the latter's terms, he lost whatever authority he might have derived from his superior training and experience. Instead, he behaved as if he were no different from the amateur like Harvey. How could academic economists with their superior research ability and their superior knowledge claim special authority for guiding policy if they sought to affect reform in exactly the same manner as those economic thinkers without such training and knowledge? Academic economists did not clearly recognize this problem as they watched Ely engage in popular reform, for they had yet to develop a sophisticated and self-conscious notion of professionalization. A series of academic freedom cases involving economists—the first, ironically enough, a threat to Ely's promotion at Hopkins in 1886—brought the point home. When trustees, alumni, or administrators challenged the economists' right to hold and express heterodox views, academic economists argued that since they were scientists, they should not be subject to the judgment of those not trained as they had been. Economics was a matter of science, not opinion; of research and investigation, not belief. However, it was difficult to maintain this distinction and to claim immunity from the judgment of noneconomists when academic economists engaged in public debates with amateurs and appealed for popular support.[32] For these reasons a large number of academic economists coming to maturity after 1885 rejected the strategy of attempting to effect reform through popular education because they believed that

omists in the 1880s. I learned a great deal on this point, and on all others relating to the professionalization of academic economics, from a draft of her dissertation which I had the good fortune to read while working on this paper. This valuable study won the Frederick Jackson Turner Prize of the Organization of American Historians in 1973 and is scheduled for publication by the University Press of Kentucky early in 1974. See also, e.g., Taussig to Charles W. Eliot, 17 May 1901, Eliot Papers, and Taussig's sentiments described in Furner, "Advocacy and Objectivity," 257.

[32] Furner, "Advocacy and Objectivity," points out the relation between professionalization and a desire to protect academic freedom throughout—indeed, I believe she emphasizes too much the defensive motives behind professionalization. On the academic freedom cases, see, besides Furner, Richard Hofstadter and Walter P. Metzger, *The Development of Academic Freedom in the United States* (New York 1955), ch. IX; Veysey, *Emergence of the American University*, ch. 7; Elizabeth Donnan, "A Nineteenth-Century Academic Cause Célèbre," *NEQ* 25 (March 1952), 23-46. While economists of almost all shades of opinion flocked to Ely's defense in 1886 and 1887, several wrote privately that Ely brought much of the trouble on himself by concentrating on popular education rather than on scholarly work. See Coats, "First Two Decades," 560, n. 9.

it actually hindered the academic economist's efforts to relate his ideas to public policy.

In 1887 E.R.A. Seligman and Richmond Mayo-Smith of Columbia, Frank Taussig and Dunbar of Harvard, Henry W. Farnum and Arthur T. Hadley of Yale, Frank Fetter and Walter F. Willcox of Cornell, and Ely's erstwhile friends H. C. Adams of Michigan and E. J. James of Pennsylvania began carefully to plot Ely's ouster as the association's leader. In a formal written compact Dunbar, representing the traditional school, agreed to join the association and the others agreed to eliminate all the ideological statements Ely had included in the association's constitution in an effort to exclude traditional economists and to remove Ely from the crucial post of executive secretary. The association dropped the offending wording in 1888 and elected Dunbar president in 1892. In that year Ely stepped down—under some duress —as executive secretary and indeed allowed his membership to lapse for the remainder of the decade.[33]

The group that took control from Ely discarded the American Economic Association's emphasis on religiosity and popular education, but they did not intend to relieve the association or the academic economist of responsibility for using knowledge to affect policies in the real world. Indeed, a substantial portion of the extant association correspondence of the period from 1890 to 1910 is concerned with just how the academic economist was to make his views known and get them written into policy now that the strategy of popular education was discarded. The academic economists and their organization began to turn inward. Where once economists had deliberately sought the larger public's support for various policies, after 1885 they increasingly came to speak to each other. Ely and Laughlin wrote for the popular and semipopular press. Ely persuaded many ministers and supporters of the social gospel to join the American Economic Association; Laughlin included political figures and opinion makers of a more conserva-·tive and secular bent in the rival organization he had founded in

---

[33] The most accurate account of the changes in the leadership of the American Economic Association is found in Furner, "Advocacy and Objectivity," ch. VI; see esp. 135-36 for revealing quotations from Mayo-Smith and Dunbar in letters to H. C. Adams, dated 10 June and 1 July 1887. For additional insight into the shift in power and the motives behind it, see Rader, *Academic Mind and Reform*, 117-22; Joseph Dorfman, ed., "The Seligman Correspondence, I and II," *Political Science Quart.*, 56 (March and June 1941), 107-24, 270-86. In one of his last acts as secretary of the association, Ely scheduled the annual meeting at Chautauqua, much to the consternation of many other economists who wanted to sever their relation with popular education and reform. The resulting furor attested to the changing self-concept among economists, see Furner, "Advocacy and Objectivity," 140-42, and Coats, "First Two Decades," 565, ns. 18-20.

1883.[34] In the late 1880s, however, most academic economists sharply curtailed their semipopular publications and concentrated on the new professional journals that appeared in that decade—Columbia's *Political Science Quarterly* (1886), Harvard's *Quarterly Journal of Economics* (1886), the American Economic Association's *Publications* (1886), and Pennsylvania's *Annals of the American Academy of Political and Social Science* (1890). In a process typical of academic professionalization, the economists quite deliberately developed specialized concerns and jargon and a number of exclusive forums in which they could use their new language to exchange ideas and information about these concerns. In this way they turned away from the emphasis on popular education and the extreme divisiveness, oversimplification, and bitterness which that emphasis seemed to entail.

However, the same leaders who engineered Ely's ouster and who founded exclusive professional journals were not at all happy with the limited audience that the association and its members reached. In 1899 the association invited a long list of officials, businessmen, and men of affairs to join. The association did so, the invitation stated, in the interest of "widening the constituency and increasing the usefulness of the Association." A financial crisis resulting from an absolute decrease in membership in the late 1890s precipitated this effort. But it also reflected a feeling that academic economists were speaking only to each other and not, therefore, exerting their rightful influence on public policy. In the first few years of the new century the association's leaders debated seriously the wisdom of including papers on practical affairs at the annual meetings and the association's responsibility for publishing a journal on practical economic questions. Having men like the President of the Sante Fe Railroad speak at the annual meeting, Taussig wrote in 1904, "adds to the interest and variety of the meetings." The leaders discussed the advisability of electing a businessman president in 1899. H. C. Adams advised Seligman in 1902 that he thought "our annual meetings ought to take up the particular questions of the year, and submit them to a discussion from the point of view of economics." As one example, he suggested that Seligman ask Carroll D. Wright, the Commissioner of the U.S. Bureau of Labor, "to show the meaning of his last bulletin on increasing prices—its meaning for men who live on salaries and for those who live on wages." In the same year Irving Fisher of Yale stated his desire "to see the meetings discuss topics of the day from a more practical point of view than is often taken, and with some regard for influence upon public opinion and

[34] Coats, "First Two Decades," 562 and n. 12; A. W. Coats, "The Political Economy Club: A Neglected Episode in American Economic Thought," *Am. Economic Rev.* 51 (September 1961), 624-37.

legislation." He hoped that practical discussions would increase "the power of the Association as a factor in forming public opinion. . . . it seems to me that economists have altogether too little influence; they are too silent on public questions, and when they do speak their opinion commands less respect than it deserves." In 1909 and 1910 the association, again beset by financial difficulties due to lagging membership growth and still concerned with academic economics' influence on men of affairs, started another membership drive to enroll businessmen and government officials. As the various viewpoints quoted demonstrate, the academic economists found it very difficult to strike the proper balance between scholarly abstraction and practicality. They were never able to define clearly their organization in such a way that it retained both its professional exclusiveness and its influence on men of affairs who had not shared the economist's professional preparation.[35]

Just as the academic economists sought to use their professional organization both to distinguish them from society and to establish their contact with influential men in that society, the economists sought to use economic theory as a badge of professional exclusiveness and a source of authoritative conclusions about policy. In the 1890s academic economists displayed a growing concern with economic theory organized around Alfred Marshall's neoclassicism and the concept of marginal utility and a rapid waning of enthusiasm for the historical viewpoint and for simple empiricism.[36] Economists found theory newly attractive because it helped them distinguish themselves from politicians, men of affairs, and the general public. As part of their effort to professionalize, the academic economists sought to identify a body of knowledge which they could claim as their exclusive possession. The popular educational efforts of the 1870s and 1880s had submerged the distinction between the academically trained economist on the one hand and the average educated person on the other. Yet it was just this distinction that academic economists felt was increasingly necessary after 1890 both to protect their freedom to express opinions and findings without fear of reprisal from powerful amateurs and to support their claim that the public and policy makers should listen to their conclusions with special respect. Mastery of complex, jargonistic, and extended theory and the techniques associated with it came to distin-

[35] Taussig to Walter F. Willcox, c. 13 May 1899, Taussig to Frank A. Fetter, 3 December 1904, H. C. Adams to Seligman, 14 May 1902, Fisher to Seligman, 20 February 1902, all in the Am. Economic Ass. Papers, Special Collections, Northwestern Univ.; Coats, "First Two Decades," 571-72; A. W. Coats, "The American Economic Association: 1904-1929," *Am. Economic Rev.* 54 (June 1964), 263-68.

[36] Dorfman, *Economic Mind*, III, 237-41.

guish the academic economist from the amateur and made his statements about economic affairs and his opinions about economic policy more accurate and authoritative than statements and opinions of those who had not mastered such theory. Any profession's claim to that combination of autonomy vis-à-vis the larger society and authority over certain issues which affect that larger society must rest on a belief that professionals, by dint of their special training, have skills, techniques, and knowledge that the rest of the society does not possess. After 1890 academic economists, only half consciously perhaps, came to believe that elaborate economic theory embodied their claim to professional skill and knowledge.

The economists could professionalize more readily around neoclassical theory than around the doctrines of the historical, inductive school. The historical school's view that economic generalizations were relative and that each economic problem must be approached *de novo* undermined the academic economists' claims that his superior training made his views more authoritative than those of men without that training. Although few members of the historical school advanced the extreme relativist position of which their doctrine was capable, many of that school's American critics identified just this tendency to eschew generalized and widely applicable principles as the inductive approach's great weakness.[37] Without the concept that the trained economist had mastered widely applicable principles and specialized techniques unknown to the general public, the economist could make little claim to authority.

The new theorists of the period after 1890 did not, as their classical predecessors had, conceive of theory as a scientific abstraction divorced from matters of policy and welfare. Since the 1830s classical economists, relying on the methodological formulations of J. S. Mill and Nassau Senior, had sought sharply to divide the scientific from the normative, the "is" from the "ought." In criticizing the historical school's reformist efforts in 1886 Dunbar voiced the traditional view that "economic laws, in strictness, deal with wealth; but the object of legislation is welfare." In 1891 he reminded his readers of

the distinction often insisted upon by economists . . . between economic laws and the application of those laws in practical administration and legislation. The economic law, the deduction of pure science, is simply the statement of a causal relation, usually between a

[37] For a typical critical view of the historical school, see Frank William Taussig, "The Present Position of the Doctrine of Free Trade" [Presidential Address to the Am. Economic Ass. 1904], *Publications of the Am. Economic Ass.*, 3d ser., 6 (February 1905), 56-58.

small number of forces and their joint effect, possibly between a single force and its effect. For the statement of that relation, the case has been freed from every disturbing element, and with the result . . . of giving a proposition which, however important, is only conditionally true. . . . But, when we come to the application of economics to legislation, we enter at once into a region of necessarily confused conditions, and also become conscious of objective ends often having little or no relation to any economic doctrine.[38]

This distinction between the science of wealth and the art of legislation or welfare has always been honored less in practice than in rhetoric, even by those most responsible for its development. It is significant that Dunbar's clear statement of the distinction came only when he was defending the classicists from the charge—advanced by the historical school—that they sought to impose their laissez-faire theory as a perfect and complete guide to policy in all situations. When free of the searching criticisms of the historical school, classical theorists were less prone to recognize the limitations of their work and to act accordingly. It is true, however, that the distinction between wealth and welfare did restrict economic theorists before 1890. They seldom called upon it to guide positive action; generally theory played a negative role. Science was capable of tracing the probable effects of a proposed policy and of warning against evils likely to ensue from its adoption. Thus classicists used Gresham's law to oppose silver coinage. It is also true that the distinction Dunbar cited made classicists largely content with theory as it stood. In studying the principles of political economy they aimed to elaborate details but not to change the theory substantially. They brought theory to bear on facts—for illustrative reasons if nothing else—but they did not study facts in order to modify theory. Theory, after all, was an abstraction and its failure to accord with facts resulted from the action of noneconomic complicating factors rather than from any weakness in the theory.

The new theorists opposed their predecessors on both counts. They sought to change theory from a negative brake on change to a positive guide to change and they sought constantly to test economic theory against facts and to amend theory when it failed to accord with the facts. Wesley Clair Mitchell, for example, gradually elaborated an empirical economic theory by constantly testing its reliability against the

[38] Dunbar, "The Reaction in Political Economy," *Quart. J. of Economics* 1 (October 1886), 7; Dunbar, "The Academic Study of Political Economy," ibid., 5 (July 1891), 409; Hutchison, *"Positive" Economics and Policy Objectives*, 27-41.

occurrences of the real world. Mitchell was very influential in convincing theorists to rely on quantitative analysis of real economic events rather than on logical deduction and speculation. For Mitchell's predecessors theory was an explanation that held only if certain ideal situations obtained—if the value of money or the demand for goods were held constant—and at best, therefore, had an attenuated relation to the real world where such ideal conditions never occurred. After Mitchell and others introduced mathematical analysis, index numbers, procedures for comparative analysis of large numbers of statistical time series of various economic indicators, and other sophisticated tools for handling empirical evidence, economists no longer had to rely on gross simplifications to generalize about the economic order. Mitchell believed that when economists could build their generalizations and principles on the basis of what really happened, economic theory would not simply be an exercise in mental gymnastics; it would be "useful" and practical, a positive guide for policy makers. After 1890 neoclassical theorists in general—whether armed with concepts of marginal utility and procedures for handling large stores of empirical information, or no—deemphasized theory's abstractness and stressed its applicability as a standard for guiding concrete economic policies. Dunbar's successor Taussig put it succinctly in arguing for the applicability of the principle of free trade, an aspect of economic thought not substantially affected by advances in methodology. Taussig began by echoing Dunbar's distinction between the science of wealth and the art of welfare but then drew a parallel between the principle of free trade and that holding "that the use of alcoholic liquors is overwhelmingly harmful." That principle alone would not allow the advocate to decide whether absolute prohibition or government regulation was most appropriate in a given situation, but "if he has the question of principle clearly settled in his mind, he will combat steadfastly popular errors about healthful effects of alcohol, and will welcome every promising device towards checking its use." Similarly, the principle that international trade is preponderantly beneficial because it is a form of the division of labor cannot in itself settle all trade policy problems. "But in considering any question of concrete commercial policy, it is necessary first to know whether a restriction on foreign trade is presumably a cause of gain or loss. Is a protective tariff something to be regretted, for which an offset is to be sought in . . . the way of advantage in other directions, or something which in itself brings an advantage?" The economic principle supplied the answer. "The essence of the doctrine of free trade is that *prima facie* international trade brings a gain, and that restrictions on it presumably bring a loss.

Departure[s] from this principle, though by no means impossible of justification, need to prove their case; . . ."[39] The emphasis had shifted: theory was now presumed applicable until proved otherwise.

Developing an adequate economic theory solved only part of the economists' problem. No matter how accurate, theory could make little difference if economists found no way to apply it in the policy-making process. There remained, of course, the strategy of mobilizing public opinion behind the conclusions obtained when theory was applied to actual problems. However, this strategy threatened to embroil economists in the same discrediting divisiveness and oversimplification that had beset their predecessors. Academic economists did not totally reject popular teaching after 1890, for, like other social scientists, they continued to feel responsibility for public education and for molding public opinion. But few engaged in the kind of public campaigns that Laughlin launched in behalf of his national banking scheme.[40] Instead their appeals were general ones seeking public support for the idea of applying science to government and entrusting authority to scientifically trained administrators rather than party hacks.

Academic economists after 1890 sought to "make a difference" by directly influencing the policy makers. They became "experts" who transmitted the findings of economic investigation directly to policy makers without engaging in popular teaching or preaching. After 1890 large numbers of academic economists began to serve as informal and formal advisers to candidates for public office and to public office holders, as investigators for various branches of government, as drafters of legislation, as members of regulatory bodies, and as government administrators themselves. Academic economists did not invent the idea of the expert (natural scientists had preceded them in this role by some decades) and the process by which they received recognition as

[39] See Mitchell to John Maurice Clark, 9 August 1928, an autobiographical letter reprinted in Lucy Sprague Mitchell, "A Personal Sketch," in Arthur F. Burns, ed. *Wesley Clair Mitchell: The Economic Scientist* (New York 1952), 96-98; Mitchell to Lucy Sprague, 18 October 1911, another autobiographical letter reprinted in ibid., 66-67; Arthur Burns, "Introductory Sketch," ibid., 27 and passim; Frederick C. Mills, "Professional Sketch," ibid., 121-23; Dorfman, "Professional Sketch," ibid., 126-34; Taussig, "Present Position of the Doctrine of Free Trade," 63-65 [which contains the quotation]; Taussig, "Minimum Wages for Women," *Quart. J. of Economics*, 30 (May 1916), 411-12; Dorfman, *Economic Mind in American Civilization, 1918-1933, Volume Four* (New York 1959), 236-47, esp. 238 [Taussig], 360-77, esp. 360-64 [Mitchell].

[40] One exception was the National Tax Association, a group of businessmen, academics, and government officials who sought tax reform. Seligman was its president from 1912 to 1915; C. J. Bullock was one of its most ardent supporters and members in the late teens and the 1920s. See the many letters in the Bullock Papers, Harvard Univ. Archives, Harvard Univ.

experts is far from clear.[41] A number of causes seem to have worked reciprocally to establish the "expert" as a necessary although sometimes unwelcome addition to the governing process. The United States was growing, it had assumed world-wide interests and responsibilities, its population was more heterogeneous than ever, its economy more complex. Increases in size, heterogeneity, and geographic mobility disrupted American society and brought increased conflict among a growing number of interest groups. Labor versus capital was the most obvious of the conflicts, perhaps, but there were hundreds of others—between large businessmen and small, between manufacturers and common carriers, between conservationists and speculators, and so on. The problems that beset the country as a whole influenced rapidly growing urban complexes even more strongly. It was no accident that the expert emerged as an important element in urban government earlier than he did at any other level. In the face of this complexity, reformers called on the government to adopt more efficient and businesslike procedures, including the specialization of function and the use of technical experts. Another cause lay in the change from "social Darwinism" to "reform Darwinism," from the theory of the small, noninterventionist state beloved of laissez-faire advocates to the doctrine of the interventionist, active state characteristic of progressive reform ideas. An active state needed knowledgeable men to direct its work. Academic economists both contributed to and benefited from this

[41] A. Hunter Dupree, *Science in the Federal Government: A History of Policies and Activities to 1940* (Cambridge, Mass. 1957), chs. VIII-XV. Some economists had served as experts before 1890, but they had done so largely on an informal basis and in a manner indistinguishable from that of noneconomists. Nonacademics like Wells and Edward Atkinson had played a larger role as economic "experts" than did the academics of the pre-1890 era (Fine, *Laissez Faire and the General-Welfare State*, 49-51); Carroll D. Wright was the 19th century's most prominent expert and he was not an academic economist at all (except in his last years after he had established his reputation as an expert); his preparation was in law and politics. See James Leiby, *Carroll Wright and Labor Reform: The Origin of Labor Statistics* (Cambridge, Mass. 1960).

On the expert in general see Hofstadter, *Anti-Intellectualism*, ch. 8; Wiebe, *Search for Order*, chs. 5-7; Sidney Kaplan, "Social Engineers as Saviors: Effects of World War I on Some American Liberals," *JHI*, 17 (June 1956), 347-69; Charles Forcey, *The Crossroads of Liberalism: Croly, Weyl, Lippmann, and the Progressive Era, 1908-1925* (New York 1961); Morton White, *Social Thought in America: The Revolt against Formalism*, new ed. (Boston 1957); Samuel Haber, *Efficiency and Uplift: Scientific Management in the Progressive Era, 1890-1920* (Chicago 1964); Jay M. Gould, *The Technical Elite* (New York 1966), ch. III; Barry D. Karl, "Presidential Planning and Social Science Research: Mr. Hoover's Experts," *Perspectives in American History*, III (1969), 345-409; Leonard White, *Trends in Public Administration* (New York 1933), ch. XIX; James Weinstein, *The Corporate Ideal in the Liberal State, 1900-1918* (Boston 1968), esp. 189-213.

change in viewpoint; just how much their support for an active state was consciously or unconsciously tied to their professional self-interest requires further investigation.

The expert appeared also because many in the society came to believe that science—so successful in understanding and manipulating the physical world—ought to be applied to understanding and controlling the social world. The application of science to government was especially attractive to the upper and middle classes of American society because it promised to reduce conflict and restore order. Unaware or unwilling to admit that social conflict could reflect fundamental value disagreements or structural inequities in the society, the more comfortable social classes attributed the conflicts besetting their society to ignorance or emotionalism that blinded the parties involved to their true interests which, when identified, would surely turn out to be mutually harmonious. The social scientific expert, of course, would help discover that truth which would harmonize the competing interests and bring them into accord with those of the society at large.[42] Another reason for the expert's growing importance in the governing process was that economists successfully pressed their claim that they possessed a skill and knowledge that no one without economic training shared. The more successful they were, the more inevitable it became that society would call these specially equipped economists to public service. Monetary, trade, and resource policies were crucial problems for any government; economists claimed that they knew something about these matters that no one else knew; soon others became convinced that economists should help solve those problems.

Academic economists participated as experts in government in many different ways and at all levels. Most commonly in the early years they gave expert testimony before legislative and investigatory bodies. This form of participation was something of a transitional stage in that such testimony was aimed not only at lawmakers but at the general public. Yet the economist's testimony was not likely to be widely heard or regarded; indeed as the government grew, such testimony was buried

[42] By the same token it might be argued further that the reliance on science served the interests of the middle and upper classes. Science was supposed to represent disinterest, neutrality, what was best for all, but the middle and upper classes were the ones that found rationalism and neutrality most congenial to their values and style of thinking. Moreover, the fact that social scientists came overwhelmingly from the middle and upper strata of the society assured those strata of representation and a powerful voice were science to be applied in the process of government. The upper and middling strata of America supported science in government to some degree, I believe, to counter the growing threats to their power coming from organized labor and ethnic bloc voting on the one hand and from the "malefactors of great wealth" on the other.

so deeply in the outpourings of government documents that it reached only those intimately involved in the specific issue. Economists also informally advised candidates or public officials on specifically economic issues (as opposed to the general advice that academics had pressed on presidential candidates for some time). In the new century academic economists served more and more readily as publicly acknowledged expert advisers in the executive branch and on various legislative committees. Many economists advised or served on bodies charged with revamping municipal and state tax structures. Academic economists also played a large role after 1890 in organizing and strengthening the statistical and investigatory work of various government agencies. During World War I, of course, hundreds of academic economists advised or administered government agencies, especially the War Industries Board which was charged with supervising resource allocation within the war effort.[43]

The definition of the expert's function in the governmental process was not well established. Most often economists argued that their purpose was to carry out the wishes of the elected officials for whom they worked, to implement the goals of others. Publicly they claimed little independence or influence on substantive issues. This definition underlay the implementation of the famous Wisconsin Idea, a progressive experiment, according to its critics, in which "professors run the state." The Capitol and the University, at opposite ends of Madison's main thoroughfare, joined forces to serve the popular will. Social scientists from the university formed the Legislative Reference Service complete with a library for legislators' use and access to "experts" from all disciplines ready to use their knowledge to codify any legislator's goals— however agreeable or disagreeable the expert might find those goals— into legislation which would accomplish those aims and meet the test of constitutionality.[44]

Here the expert was defined as faceless and value free—in accord with the notion of social "science's" value neutrality. But the expert's influence on policy was greater than that. It is difficult enough to imagine that in determining what did or did not meet constitutional tests

---

[43] There is no study of the economic "expert" in government. White, *Recent Trends in Public Administration*, 271-72, states that the federal government employed 25 "economic and political science" experts in 1896 (all statisticians) and 848 in the period 1928-31. The trend—and the wide variety of kinds of employment—is clear in reading obituaries and biographies of economists prominent in the early part of the 20th century.

[44] On the Wisconsin Idea, see Charles McCarthy, *The Wisconsin Idea* (New York 1912); Rader, *The Academic Mind and Reform*, 172-81; John R. Commons, *Myself: The Autobiography of John R. Commons* (New York 1934), ch. v.

or accomplish a legislator's goal, the economist could keep his work value free. In Wisconsin and elsewhere, however, the interaction of expert and policy-maker went much further and the distinction between them became severely blurred. In 1904 Governor Robert M. LaFollette asked John Commons, a professor of economics at the university, to draft a state civil service law and then to serve as a commissioner. Commons refused the second invitation, but seven years later he drafted the state's Industrial Commission law—which regulated industrial safety and workmen's compensation, among other things— and then served a two-year term as one of three commissioners. Commons lost much of his advisory role and became instead an administrator and, at least in terms of day-to-day decisions, something of a policy-maker himself.[45] A similar enhancement of the economist's role occurred in the case of Henry Parker Willis, a Laughlin student from Chicago who simultaneously pursued three careers, as professor of finance (at George Washington University and then Columbia), as financial journalist (he finally became Editor-in-chief of the *Journal of Commerce*), and as an expert in banking for the government. Between 1911 and 1913 Willis helped the House Ways and Means Committee draw up the Underwood Tariff Act. In 1912 and 1913 he advised the House Banking and Currency Committee on drawing up the Federal Reserve Act and thus exerted the influence on this legislation that Laughlin had sought to exert in a different manner. In 1914 Willis aided the Joint Committee on Rural Credits in preparing the Federal Farm Loan Act. In addition to helping draft the Federal Reserve Act, Willis joined the committee which organized the Federal Reserve System and also became the board's first secretary (1914-18), where he took an active part in drafting that agency's rules and regulations and in formulating its initial credit policies. From 1918 to 1922 he directed the board's division of analysis and research. In Willis's case the expert was far more than a neutral adviser; the expert played an important role in determining policy.[46]

Another instance of the expert determining policy occurred when President Wilson appointed Taussig as the first Chairman of the Permanent Tariff Commission—a commission for which Taussig had drawn up legislative specifications. An economist had directed the Tariff Board during the Taft Administration, but that body had been temporary and merely advisory. Wilson's commission was permanent and did have ongoing investigatory and administrative as well as ad-

[45] Commons, *Myself*, 100-107, 153-65.

[46] B. H. Beckhart in *DAB*, suppl. 2, s.v. "Willis, Henry Parker"; Dorfman, *Economic Mind*, IV, 314-22.

visory functions. Thus Taussig held a substantially independent position of some power where he could use his special training and his own theoretical conclusions to influence policy.[47]

Academic economists have been very reticent in discussing the power the expert could exert on policy. They have somewhat ritualistically deprecated their government service, arguing that independent scholarly and scientific work freed from the pressures of administration and politics gave them the most satisfaction. They imply that government service was thrust upon them and that they reluctantly accepted it. The historian should accept such rhetoric only in part. Economists did find government service frustrating because political considerations forced them to compromise the elegance of science and theory, and the pressures of time forced them to neglect important basic issues in order to guide day-to-day policies. Nor were economists very successful in effecting more enlightened economic policy since their hard work was often ignored or their findings subordinated to political expediency. The university, where the economist could follow his ideas to their logical end and discuss his results in an atmosphere in which truth rather than expediency governs, had many attractions.

Yet government service continued to attract economists because of their desire to make a difference, to make their knowledge felt beyond the university. Their reticence about acknowledging their motives sprang from the contradiction that lay at the heart of progressivism which simultaneously fostered the experts' elitist claim to authority and power while it sought to enhance the power of the electorate. The problem of justifying why specially trained expert advisers should have such an important role in the governing process without having to earn their right to influence policy by seeking electoral office genuinely disturbed and confused the economists. Like their academic predecessors, they believed in the right of the educated to lead, but the issue was less clear when the educated sought to lead by advising policy-makers privately and by manipulating highly complex technical

[47] Joseph Frederick Kenkel, "The Tariff Commission Movement: The Search for a Nonpartisan Solution of the Tariff Question," Ph.D. diss., Univ. of Maryland (1962); Taussig to David F. Houston (Secretary of Agriculture in Wilson's cabinet), 17 December 1915, Woodrow Wilson Papers, Libr., of Congress, enclosing draft of Taussig's "The Proposal for a Tariff Commission," *North Am. Rev.*, 203 (February 1916), 194-204. Portions of Taussig's draft were incorporated into the Tariff Commission Bill. Taussig also advised the American Commission to Negotiate Peace on matters of international trade and played a part in drafting the third of the Fourteen Points. He served on the Price Fixing Committee of the War Industries Board and took part in Wilson's Second Industrial Conference. Before the World War he had served the Commonwealth of Massachusetts as an expert on taxation.

procedures rather than by leading public opinion openly. In these circumstances academic economists found it very difficult openly to seek nonelective positions of influence or to acknowledge afterward that they had wanted or taken very seriously the positions that they had held.

Frank Taussig, in speculating on the form a tariff commission should take, reflected the combination of reluctance and eagerness, of fear of elitism and hope of accomplishment that characterized many of the academic economists who served the public as experts in the years after 1890. In the 1916 article for the general public, a draft of which the Wilson administration had used in drawing up the Tariff Commission legislation, Taussig immediately sketched the commission's limitations. "No administrative body of any kind can decide for the country whether it is to adopt protection or free trade, to apply more of protection or less, to enact 'a tariff for revenue with incidental protection' or a system of purely fiscal duties. Such questions of principle must be settled by Congress,—that is, by the voters." Nor was hope for "a 'scientific' settlement of the tariff" justified. "There are no scientific laws applicable to economic problems in the same way as the laws of physics are applicable to engineering problems." Some conclusions of economics are "well established"; others "very tentative and provisional." "I believe some things are established concerning the working of protective duties; but I would not for a moment pretend that there is such a consensus of opinion on the subject as to give us a body of principles applicable at once in legislation, or such as to enable us to decide at once a method of procedure."[48]

Despite these disclaimers, Taussig felt that a tariff commission "could be helpful" in many ways. It could substitute "more careful preparation" for the "haphazard" and "rough and ready" means of framing tariff legislation. "It could aid in the accurate, honest, and consistent carrying out of whatever policy Congress,—that is, the party to which the voters had given control of legislation,—might wish to carry out."[49] A permanent commission could, moreover, explain objectively to legislators just what effects suggestions and amendments pressed by special interests would have. Taussig favored a commission whose main duties were administrative and judicial—like those of the Interstate Commerce Commission and the Federal Trade Commission. A commission established solely to advise on legislation would urge un-

[48] Taussig, "Proposal for a Tariff Commission," 194-95. We may note that in this context Taussig is more reticent than usual about the applicability of theory in judging among policy alternatives although we must also note carefully his use of "at once" twice in the above passage.
[49] Ibid., 197.

necessary changes simply to justify its existence. The Tariff Commission should primarily adjudicate conflicts arising from detailed questions of classification and the determination of ad valorem rates and supply Congress and the Executive with statistical information on foreign trade and American production.

Taussig believed that, ideally, highly competent, permanent officials in the executive branch should perform these functions.[50] But he realized that permanent positions paid too poorly to attract competent persons. The incompetents that did occupy them, simply because they were permanent and thus often the only "experienced and well-informed" officials in their section of the executive branch, exercised "great influence in shaping current administrative practice and the details of legislation. It has been said with much truth that the Government of the United States is run by $1,500 clerks. We have sore need in our public service of a body of able, well-paid, permanent officials, whose positions shall not be affected by party changes, who shall not simply follow in mechanical fashion the precedents of their offices as they have found them, who shall be able to give intelligent advice as well as useful information." Since Taussig realized that such a core of permanent, impartial officials was unlikely to develop in the executive branch, he accepted the independent commission as the best alternative for introducing impartial expertise in government.[51]

Taussig again repeated his distinction between advice and policy making, but held wide the door for an independent commission to effect long-run policy improvement.

It does not follow that a tariff board can be of no service whatever in guiding Congress and the country on the larger and more difficult questions of industrial policy. It could undertake investigations on the character and the development of American industries, on the conditions of competition between foreign and domestic industries, on the prospects of growth and development for American industries, which would throw light on disputed questions of industrial policy. Investigations of this sort, however, take time, and are more likely to be carried out with sole regard to the ascertainment of the facts if they are not undertaken with direct reference to any pending legislation or proposals for legislation. They should be conducted slowly, quietly, without any flourish of trumpets. They are more likely to command the respect of Congress and of the public if carried on by a board which had already established its usefulness and

[50] Ibid., 201-2, and see material on 12, 18 of the draft in the Library of Congress which does not appear in the published article.
[51] Ibid., 202-3.

its impartial spirit by routine work more nearly of an administrative sort. The more ambitious and high sounding its regular duties, the less likely is it to be really successful. Let it be given mainly the duty of assisting Congress in the intelligent elaboration of whatever policy the country has decided to follow, and make no pretense of removing the determination of policy from the quarter where in the end it necessarily belongs: Congress and the voters.[52]

The voters were to set policy, Taussig said, but a commission could influence policy making profoundly so long as it kept itself and its findings out of the public spotlight. Taussig could not have been completely unaware of this contradiction. A man who could speculate that low echelon bureaucrats "run" the government must have realized how much power over policy those who administered laws and those who controlled the flow of information to policy makers and administrators exercised. He claimed that powerful role for the economic expert like himself but did so only gingerly since it contradicted so many public beliefs about power in a democracy. "Making a difference" through the exercise of expertise could never be publicly acknowledged in the way that "making a difference" through educating public opinion had been.

The National Bureau of Economic Research was another example of the new strategy with which academic economists sought to relate thought to action. The National Bureau, financed by private and foundation grants, was chartered in 1920 "to encourage, in the broadest and most liberal manner, investigation, research and discovery, and the application of knowledge to the well-being of mankind; and in particular to conduct, or assist in the making of exact and impartial investigations in the field of economic, social and industrial science, and to this end to cooperate with Governments, universities, learned societies, and individuals."[53] That the phrases about "the application of knowledge to the well-being of mankind" and cooperation with other agencies more concerned with policy were more than routine statements of the scholar's faith that his work has some meaning beyond the academy is clear in the careers and interests of two of the bureau's leaders, Edwin F. Gay, its first president, and Wesley Clair Mitchell, its long-time director of research.

Gay, professor of economic history at Harvard, briefly Editor of the New York *Evening Post*, and first Dean of the Harvard Business

[52] Ibid., 204.
[53] "Charter" quoted in [Wesley Clair Mitchell], *Retrospect and Prospect, 1920-1936*, National Bureau of Economic Research (New York 1936), 6. On the founding of the bureau, see Herbert Heaton, *A Scholar in Action—Edwin F. Gay* (Cambridge, Mass. 1952), 196-203; Burns, "Introductory Sketch," 30-35; L. S. Mitchell, "Personal Sketch," 101-3.

School in the years when that school was dedicated to training for public service as well as business, devoted his whole life to mobilizing social science in the service of society. Extensive study in Germany had imbued Gay with Gustav Schmoller's belief that history, economics, political science, sociology, ethics, and psychology must cooperate in finding scientific solutions to the world's problems. To this end he helped found the National Bureau, the Social Science Research Council, and the Council on Foreign Relations. As his editorship of the *Evening Post* suggests, Gay had not completely repudiated the older strategy of educating public opinion as a means of using economic and social scientific knowledge to alter social policy. Between 1910 and 1912 he drafted a new factory inspection bill for a Massachusetts Citizens' Committee and built popular support for it through his work with the American Association for Labor Legislation, the Women's Educational and Industrial Union, and the Boston Chamber of Commerce. At the same time he conducted an educational campaign in behalf of profit-sharing plans. In Washington during the war Gay emerged as more the expert economic administrator than the educator of public opinion. As Director of the Shipping Board's Division of Planning and Statistics, Gay had to devise trade policies that would free the maximum shipping capacity for the war effort. Soon he was heading several different government planning and statistical groups and had become something of a czar in Washington. After the war he sought to influence policy through the private scholarly research agencies. He planned and organized large-scale statistical research projects that served policy makers' immediate needs for information on immigration, philanthropy, recent economic trends, trends in corporate organization, or comparative international wage statistics. The National Bureau was but one agency in which Gay meant to use his training to influence public policy.[54]

Gay's colleague Mitchell had a more theoretical orientation to economics but was always concerned with developing economic theory that was "useful." In 1911 he outlined his "case for economic theory." Theoretical knowledge of causal interconnections had a great practical value in human affairs. "We putter with philanthropy and coquette with reform when we would fain find a definite method of realizing the

---

[54] Heaton, *Gay*, passim. On the early intentions of the Harvard Business School, see the draft report, "School of Business and Public Service," in Taussig's hand in Business School Archives, Baker Library, Harvard University, undated (probably December 1906); Wallace B. Donham and Esty Foster, "The Graduate School of Business Administration, 1908-1929," in *The Development of Harvard University Since the Inauguration of President Eliot, 1869-1929*, ed. Samuel Eliot Morison (Cambridge, Mass. 1930), 533-48.

demand for social justice which is so strong an element in human nature. And tho we are so often discouraged by the futility of our efforts, we stick manfully to our tasks and try to do what little we may to alleviate at retail the suffering and deprivation which our social organization creates at wholesale. What we need as a guide for all this expenditure of energy is sure knowledge of the causal interconnections between social phenomena."[55] Mitchell himself held several government positions which enabled him to apply economists' findings directly.[56]

But Mitchell tempered Gay's enthusiasm for direct involvement by contending that the thinker must stand back somewhat from the day-to-day efforts to patch up and administer the system in order to work out comprehensive explanations of interconnection. The laboratory biologist, not the practicing physician, had made the fundamental discoveries which eased the burden of sickness; so it would be with social issues. The bureau was the laboratory in which economists could elaborate social theory for eventual application to solving social problems. Mitchell thought that eventuality was relatively immediate. Although the early bureau is best known for its long-running projects on business cycles and on the measurement of national income, it also performed (largely at Gay's insistence) much work of a more immediately practical sort—work done for or in cooperation with other agencies concerned with immediate policy issues.[57] The National Bureau's Board

[55] Mitchell to Lucy Sprague, 18 October 1911, loc. cit., 66-67. See also Mitchell, "Statistics and Government," *Publications of the Am. Statistical Ass.*, 16 (March 1919), 223-35; Dorfman, *Economic Mind*, IV, 360-66, 375-76.

[56] Dorfman, "Professional Sketch," 134-36. Mitchell served as chief of the Price Section of the First World War's War Industries Board, he chaired President Hoover's Research Committee on Social Trends, he served on the National Planning Board of the Federal Emergency Administration of Public Works during the thirties, and later as chairman of the Technical Committee which was attached to the President's Committee on the Cost of Living to settle some problems involving index numbers so that war production would not be hampered. On the Committee on Recent Social Trends, see Karl, "Presidential Planning and Social Science Research."

[57] Mitchell to Lucy Sprague, 8 October 1911, loc. cit., 66-67; Heaton, *Gay*, 201. The Bureau researched *Business Cycles and Unemployment* (1923) for President Harding's Conference on Unemployment; for the Committee on Recent Economic Changes it published *Recent Economic Changes*, 2 vols. (1929), *The Planning and Control of Public Works* (1930), *Economic Tendencies in the United States* (1932), *Industrial Profits in the United States* (1934), and *Strategic Factors in Business Cycles* (1934). It published *International Migrations* (1929, 1931) for the Social Science Research Council and International Labour Office; the Carnegie Corporation requested *Trends in Philanthropy* (1928), the Association of Community Chests and Councils, *Corporate Contributions to Organized Community*

of Directors always included men of affairs, in part to ensure that its work spoke to real problems. In 1935 Mitchell, noting that the need for scientific investigation of economic and social problems had not lessened since 1920, reaffirmed his desire to have the bureau's work influence the nation's policies.

> The country's economic record for the last decade is botched by colossal errors of judgment during the boom years, by ineffective efforts to check the depression, and by inspirational attempts to stimulate recovery. That economics has not saved us from these blunders is due partly to the disregard of it by both individuals and officials, but this very disregard is chargeable largely to the uncertainties of economic knowledge. No sensible man supposes that fact finding will put economics upon a strictly scientific basis in short order, or stop wishful thinking. But neither does any sensible man deny that more exact knowledge of economic processes and their interrelations will contribute toward wiser economic behavior in proportion as it is applied to the problems that face us as individuals and as a nation. The need for more exact knowledge grows greater as our economic organization becomes more complex and as proposals for drastic changes multiply.

Proof that the bureau had already had some effect lay in the wide use of its reports in practical affairs and in scientific publications.[58]

The National Bureau did not explicitly define itself as an organization mainly interested in influencing policy makers instead of public opinion, but that is the way it functioned. Its findings reached other researchers, government officials, and men of affairs. It made its findings available to the public, of course, but did nothing to simplify or popularize them. Indeed, Mitchell's introduction of sophisticated quantitative measures effectively prevented all but the most expert laymen— i.e., those businessmen and officials who held key managerial roles in the economy—from understanding the progress of economic research. Quantitative techniques made empirical research in economics as esoteric and exclusive as the most complex and logically rigorous deductive theory. Thus, Mitchell could stress the empirical and the need for minute investigation of specific events without abandoning any of the professional's claim to authority and expertise and therefore avoid the problems that had plagued the inductive economists of an earlier generation.

Welfare Services (1930), and the National Planning Board, *Public Works in Prosperity and Depression* (1935). See [Mitchell], *Retrospect and Prospect*, 11-12.

[58] Ibid., 22.

Robert L. Church

The National Bureau offered academic economists a chance to make a difference in the society according to a new strategy that required them to focus their teachings on a narrow elite of policy makers rather than on the wide audience of "informed" public opinion. The new strategy did not require a total rejection of the older one. Most academic economists, indeed, continued to spend most of their working hours endeavoring to teach the children of the upper strata to become responsible citizens well-informed on economic issues. Even within university teaching, however, the economist's focus shifted increasingly to graduate training, to the creation of more expert economists. Moreover, institutions like the Tariff Commission and the National Bureau succeeded in shifting, psychologically at least, the locus of making a difference from the university to other institutions.[59] Although academic economists continued to try to teach the public to respect the scientific method applied to social problems and to trust experts, they spent little time trying to convince the public of the wisdom of particular policies. As Commons put it in describing his own experience in developing a means of influencing the "real" world around the turn of the century, "I learned . . . that the place of the economist was that of advisor to the leaders, if they wanted him, and not that of propagandist to the masses."[60]

The new definition of the economist's role—as an adviser and teacher who sought to influence policy makers directly—had not lessened his concern with making a difference in the real world. Professionalization and the stress on scientific and quantitative methods had not lessened this overriding concern with using an understanding of economic developments to better the world and soon. Rather, the new definition of the economist's role was but a new strategy for achieving the same basic purpose that underlay the formation of economics as a university discipline. Economists had originally sought to make themselves significant and to make a strong impact on the society by teaching proper economic principles to large segments of the society who would in turn force policy makers to abide by those principles. After 1890 academic economists, discouraged at the slight progress their group had made, sought to achieve a significant impact on the society by working ever more closely with those in power and by influencing their actions directly. In the process they inevitably

[59] Barry D. Karl, "The Power of Intellect and the Politics of Ideas," *Daedalus* 97 (Summer 1968), 1006-7, makes a somewhat similar point about the shift in the academics' focus as the control of research money and professional recognition shifted from the individual university and its president to the national research bodies.

[60] Commons, *Myself*, 88; Weinstein, *Corporate Ideal in the Liberal State*, 189-90.

deemphasized the importance of teaching, in the classroom and in the popular press. This new strategy promised much, both for the economists' professional image and for the harnessing of economic processes to the quest for social justice. But, as the economists themselves recognized, the introduction of the expert and the short-circuiting of popular influence on public policy held grave dangers for a democracy.

13

The New Puritanism: Values and Goals of Freedmen's Education in America

by James M. McPherson

A common theme in histories of Negro education is the importance of "Puritan" values in the establishment of freedmen's schools after the Civil War. "The missionaries from New England who founded the first schools for Negroes in the South," wrote E. Franklin Frazier in his study of the black bourgeoisie, came from a "Puritan background" and did their best to instill the "ideals of Puritan morality" and "the Yankee virtues of industry and thrift" in their students. A white teacher in southern black schools in the early 20th century observed that graduates of colleges founded by the American Missionary Association (AMA), largest and best of the freedmen's education societies, were "called Black Puritans because they were formed in the likeness of the first white New England missionaries." Kelly Miller, a Howard University alumnus, professor, and dean, wrote that the New England founders were "of the Puritan type and spirit" and "sought to make the Negro in their own image and likeness."[1]

None of these commentators makes any systematic effort to define Puritanism, but it is clear that they do not mean a direct reincarnation of 17th century New England theology or polity. Well before 1865 the original creed of New England Calvinism had been largely transmuted into evangelicalism or Unitarianism, which preserved much of the ethics but not the theology of Calvinism. The Second Great Awakening and the recurrent revivals of the 19th century had forged a theology in which God's grace and salvation were open to all who truly repented and sought Christ rather than only to the predestined elect. Inspired by a zealous sense of mission, many 19th century evangelicals strove not only for the conversion of individual sinners but also for the purification of society from such sins as intemperance, prostitution, war, and above all slavery. This was true especially in New England and in areas settled by westward-migrating sons of New England. The army of "New England schoolmarms" who invaded the post-Civil War

---

[1] E. Franklin Frazier, *Black Bourgeoisie*, Collier Books ed. (1962 [1957]), 65, 56; Lura Beam, *He Called Them by the Lightning: A Teacher's Odyssey in the Negro South, 1908-1919* (Indianapolis 1967), 99; Kelly Miller, "The Higher Education of the Negro Is at the Crossroads," *Educational Rev.* 72 (December 1926), 276.

South carried with them not only the Bible and Webster's blue-backed speller but an amalgam of Puritan and Yankee values overlaid by evangelicalism and abolitionism. They were products of the 19th century version of the Puritan commonwealth, a "city on a hill" serving as a model for all the world.[2]

If this 19th century context is kept firmly in mind, the concept of latter-day Puritans seeking to mold the freed slaves in their own image becomes a useful framework for analysis. Despite the absence of precise definition, it is possible to extract three levels of meaning of Puritanism from the discussion by Frazier and the other writers quoted above. (1) *Guilt and conscience*: a sense of duty and responsibility to God and fellow man, an acute consciousness of guilt, a belief in the necessity for repentance and expiation of sins both individual and social, an intense moral earnestness, a highly developed conscience and rigid categories of right and wrong. (2) *Piety and repression*: the layman's definition of Puritanism—especially in the 1920s before such scholars as Perry Miller and Samuel Eliot Morison set to work to modify the image—as excessive piety and moralism, a repressive attitude toward secular pleasures, an attempt by blue-nosed zealots to impose the morality of Protestant fundamentalism on everybody. H. L. Mencken defined this meaning of Puritanism as "the haunting fear that someone, somewhere, may be happy." (3) *The Puritan Ethic*, or as it is more commonly called, the Protestant Ethic: the virtues of industry, thrift, sobriety, reliability, self-discipline, self-reliance, and the postponement of immediate gratifications for the sake of long-range goals.

At all three levels of meaning the concept of Puritanism is helpful for an understanding both of the impulse that sent thousands of northern men and women into the South to establish schools for the freedmen and of the goals and values they tried to instill in their black

---

[2] One of the most perceptive discussions of the attempt by 19th century evangelical reform movements "to sustain the ethics and cultural heritage of an eighteenth-century puritanism" is Bertram Wyatt-Brown, *Lewis Tappan and the Evangelical War Against Slavery* (Cleveland 1969), 243 and passim. Other useful treatments of evangelicalism and reform include Gilbert Hobbs Barnes, *The Anti-Slavery Impulse, 1830-1844* (New York 1933); Timothy L. Smith, *Revivalism and Social Reform* (New York 1957); William B. Gravely, *Gilbert Haven: Methodist Abolitionist* (Nashville 1973); and William G. McLoughlin, ed., *The American Evangelicals, 1800-1900: An Anthology* (New York 1968). Although cynical and hostile toward the evangelicals, Clifford S. Griffin's *Their Brothers' Keepers: Moral Stewardship in the United States, 1800-1865* (New Brunswick, N.J. 1960), is also suggestive. Several of the essays in David B. Davis, ed., *Ante-Bellum Reform* (New York 1967), are valuable. Perry Miller treats the persistence of the Puritan conscience and its diffusion into American society generally in the 19th century in his "The New England Conscience," *Am. Scholar*, 28 (Winter 1958-59), 49-58.

students. This essay will try to describe and illustrate the three levels of Puritanism in the evolution of Negro education.

The traditional identification of abolitionism and the educational mission to the freedmen with New England is substantially correct. This is true not only of the teachers supported by the predominantly Congregational AMA, but of the Methodist, Baptist, and secular societies as well. Even in Quaker schools for freed slaves, New England teachers were noticeably prominent, causing a Philadelphia Quaker to ask plaintively: "Shall all the noble self-sacrifice be accorded to the N[ew] E[ngland] people?"[3] Of 1013 northern teachers (i.e., from non-slave states) in the 1860s whose homes have been located, 520 were from New England and 283 were from Massachusetts alone. Of the 76 white presidents (nearly all of them clergymen) of southern black colleges in the two generations after emancipation whose birthplaces have been identified, 38 had been born in New England and 17 of these were born in Massachusetts. Thus at a time when 15 percent of the *northern* population lived in New England (1870 census; the percentage declined in each subsequent census) that section furnished 51 percent of the northern teachers and 50 percent of the college presidents in these samples; Massachusetts, with 6 percent or less of the northern population, sent 27 percent of the teachers and 22 percent of the college presidents to the South. In addition, many teachers who lived outside New England had been born there. One scholar has estimated that at least 700 of the 1013 teachers in this sample were from New England and areas settled by migrants from New England. The map on p. 614 shows the strong correlation between patterns of migration from New England and the homes of freedmen's teachers.[4]

New England contributed disproportionately to the financing as

[3] James E. Rhoads to Margaret Rhoads, 15 February 1865, Quaker Collection, Haverford Coll. Libr.

[4] For a discussion of the sources on which the data about the homes and birthplaces of teachers and college presidents are based, see the Appendix at the end of this essay. A recent study of sixty-nine AMA teachers from Wisconsin in the years from 1866 to 1876 also emphasizes the importance of a New England cultural heritage in the motivation of teachers from this western state. Six of the thirty-seven Wisconsin teachers whose birthplaces could be determined had been born in New England and eleven others in New York state, many of them in regions settled by emigrants from New England. Seventeen of the forty-five parents of these teachers whose birthplaces could be discovered had been born in New England (and twenty others in New York state). The study concludes that "the Wisconsinites who labored in the South under the sponsorship of the AMA possessed a strong New England religious and cultural heritage." Jacqueline J. Halstead, " 'The Grand Opportunity': Wisconsin Yankees Teach the Freedmen, 1866-1876," unpublished research paper, Univ. of Wisconsin (1971), 3 and Appendix. Cited with permission of the author.

HOME TOWNS OF 1,013 NORTHERN

TEACHER'S IN FREEDMEN'S

SCHOOLS, 1862—1970

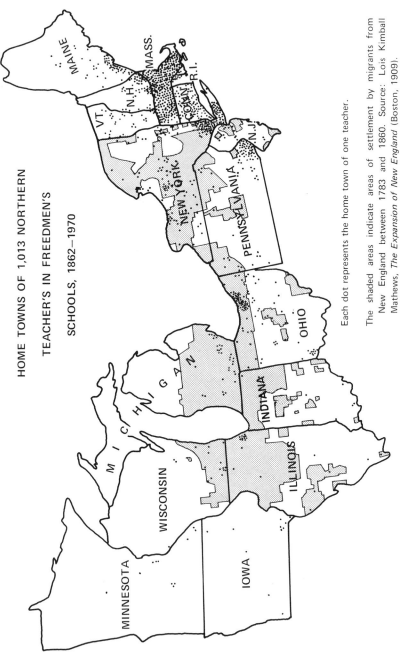

Each dot represents the home town of one teacher.

The shaded areas indicate areas of settlement by migrants from New England between 1783 and 1860. Source: Lois Kimball Mathews, *The Expansion of New England* (Boston, 1909).

This map was prepared by the author's wife, Patricia McPherson. Mr. Lawrence E. Spellman and his staff in the map room of the Firestone Library helped locate the home towns of many of the Northern teachers.

well as the personnel of freedmen's education. Residents of that section provided 60 percent of the AMA's funds from northern sources for randomly selected periods in the 1870s and 1880s. The per capita contributions of the New England conferences to the Methodist Freedmen's Aid Society were consistently at or near the top for the entire Methodist Episcopal Church, and the same was true for the New England collection districts of the American Baptist Home Mission Society. With 1/14 of the membership of the northern Baptist church, Massachusetts provided 1/7 of the amount of individual contributions and 2/5 of the amount of legacies to the Home Mission Society from 1882 to 1902. An analysis of financial data in the Atlanta University archives for randomly selected years in the 1890s and early 1900s reveals that 63 percent of the individual contributors to the school and 53 percent of the money they gave came from New England.[5]

This New England preeminence was no statistical fluke; it was the result of a conscious effort by abolitionists and evangelicals bred in the tradition of latter-day Puritanism to plant their values in the New South. In 1865 the New England Freedmen's Aid Society urged the recruitment of "enough teachers to make a New England of the whole South." Gilbert Haven, the militant Methodist abolitionist from Boston, hailed the first wave of teachers departing for the South as the new "Pilgrim Fathers" sent on a 19th century errand into the wilderness to create "a New South after the Puritan and perfect pattern." An AMA teacher who played a prominent role in the early history of Talladega College conceived of his mission as the founding in Alabama of "a real New England civilization."[6] At Oberlin College, a major outpost of New England religious and social values beyond the Appalachians, students planning to become missionaries to the freedmen were told that "the South must be converted and puritanized" by "men who at

[5] The data on contributions to the AMA are from the monthly or yearly breakdowns by states in the association's journal, *Am. Missionary*, for the following time periods: December 1869, February and September 1870, January, June, and November 1871, October 1872, March and August 1873, April and July 1874, February and September 1875, March 1876, and the entire year from 1 October 1883 to 30 September 1884. Per capita contributions to the Freedmen's Aid Society of the Methodist Episcopal Church were tabulated for each denominational conference in the *Annual Reports* of the society and, after 1889, in its journal the *Christian Educator*. For the Baptists the *Home Mission Monthly* frequently reported the per capita contributions to the Home Mission Society by states: see especially *Home Mission Monthly* 25 (March 1903), 59-60. The data for Atlanta Univ. are from the fiscal years (July 1-June 30) 1893-94, 1898-99, and 1911-12.

[6] *Freedmen's J.*, 1 (January 1865), 3; Gravely, *Gilbert Haven*, 98; George W. Andrews to Erastus M. Cravath, 13 January 1874, AMA Archives, Amistad Research Center, Dillard Univ.

heart hate slavery and oppression." A black graduate of Fisk caught the spirit and in 1876 proclaimed "the necessity for having more of the 'Plymouth Rock' disseminated through the south."[7] The AMA established a black Congregational church in Charleston, the cradle of secession, and perhaps with a retributive sense of irony named it Plymouth Church.

I. GUILT AND CONSCIENCE

An important theme of Puritanism in colonial New England had been the collective as well as individual consciousness of sin and the need for repentance and reformation to avoid the wrath of God.[8] This theme survived the 19th century transformation of Calvinism into evangelicalism and was a powerful motivating factor in the antislavery and freedmen's education movements. The jeremiad sermons of early Puritan ministers imploring a fallen people to repent or suffer divine retribution found echoes in the warnings of evangelical abolitionists during the Civil War. "Our sins have been numerous and flagrant," proclaimed the AMA in 1864. "Intemperance, licentiousness, covetousness, Sabbath desecration, and injustice to the Indians have prevailed for scores of years; but the great sin of the nation has been—as few now deny—SLAVERY." This terrible war had "been brought upon us on account of our national transgressions." Only through "REPENTANCE AND REFORMATION" could the Union be saved. "Until we cease to do evil, until slavery is brought to an end, until the brotherhood of the colored man is recognized," the nation would continue to suffer God's wrath. "Let us not refuse to listen to the awful warnings of the Almighty: 'Now therefore, if ye will obey my voice indeed, and keep my covenant, then ye shall be a peculiar treasure unto me above all people . . . but IF THOU FORSAKE ME I WILL CAST THEE OFF FOREVER.' " Eight years later the AMA still insisted that "slavery was a crime whose expiation must be by suffering and self-denial." The freedmen could be

[7] *Lorain County News*, 20 January 1864, quoted in Robert Samuel Fletcher, *A History of Oberlin College From Its Foundation Through the Civil War*, 2 vols. (Oberlin 1943), II, 917; Quinton B. Neale to Frederick A. Chase, 12 March 1876, AMA Archives.

[8] Winthrop D. Jordan, *White Over Black: American Attitudes Toward the Negro, 1550-1812* (Chapel Hill 1968), 297-300, emphasizes the importance of the sense of collective sin in motivating Puritan antislavery sentiment in the 18th century. For excellent treatments of the Puritan practice of collective self-examination and self-condemnation, see Perry Miller, "Errand into the Wilderness," 1-15 of Miller's collection of essays entitled *Errand into the Wilderness* (Cambridge 1956); Miller, *The New England Mind: The Seventeenth Century* (New York 1939), ch. 16; and Miller, *The New England Mind: From Colony to Province* (Cambridge 1953), ch. 1-3.

redeemed from the consequences of bondage and white America from the sin of slavery only through "self-sacrifice in missionary toil and the giving of money" for black education. "It is not a matter of politics or legislation, but of Christian toil and self-denial."[9]

An intense consciousness of collective guilt and the need for atonement runs through the writings of missionaries and teachers. Richard Rust, Executive Secretary of the Methodist Freedmen's Aid Society and a life-long abolitionist, best expressed this consciousness when he presented the freedmen's claims upon the church and upon white Americans generally. The blacks "have for centuries been wronged by us," wrote Rust. They were "stolen from their homes, sold in the shambles like cattle, degraded by slavery. . . . We have participated in these flagrant crimes, and we are involved in this terrible guilt." New England was no less guilty than the South. Rust, whose ancestors came to Massachusetts in 1635, said that "New England is steeped to the lips in guilt by her participation in bringing Negroes to this country and selling them into perpetual bondage." We can best "atone for our sins," he concluded, by "furnishing schools and the means of improvement for the children, upon whose parents we inflicted such terrible evils."[10] The Secretary of the Presbyterian Board of Missions for Freedmen wrote in 1891 that "the debt we owe the Freedmen has not yet been paid" and probably never could be fully discharged. "We cannot right the wrong we have done them, nor efface the scars which slavery has left . . . but we can help to lift them up from the degradation which two centuries of bondage has entailed."[11]

Related to the concept of guilt and atonement as an impulse for freedmen's education was the doctrine of man's calling to serve God by following a useful vocation. In Puritan tradition, the calling had a social as well as individual dimension; as Cotton Mather wrote, man must have a calling "so he may Glorify God by doing Good for *Others*, and getting of *Good* for himself."[12] From this concept of the calling stemmed much of the New England reform tradition, including aboli-

[9] *Am. Missionary* 8 (April 1864), 90-91; 16 (April 1872), 84-85.

[10] *Fourth Annual Report of the Freedmen's Aid Society of the Methodist Episcopal Church* (Cincinnati 1871), 15; Joseph C. Hartzell, ed., *Christian Educators in Council: Sixty Addresses by American Educators* (New York 1883), 55.

[11] *Church at Home and Abroad* 10 (October 1891), 335.

[12] Miller, *The New England Mind: From Colony to Province*, 40-41, 396-401, 409-16; Sydney E. Ahlstrom, "The Puritan Ethic and the Spirit of American Democracy," in George L. Hunt, ed., *Calvinism and the Political Order* (Philadelphia 1965) 103-4; William G. McLoughlin, *The Meaning of Henry Ward Beecher: An Essay on the Shifting Values of Mid-Victorian America, 1840-1870* (New York 1970), 245; Mather quoted in Carl Degler, *Out of Our Past: The Forces That Shaped Modern America* (New York 1970) 7.

tionism and freedmen's education. In 1865 the *American Missionary*, organ of the AMA, urged the North to obey "the call of God at this crisis" by supplying "education and religious instruction" for the freedman and "full recognition of his rights as a citizen and a child of God." The work of freedmen's missions, declared a Methodist minister in 1873, "is our work, thrust by Providence upon us; and nothing on the face of the earth compares with it in magnitude [and] urgency." A New Hampshire teacher in South Carolina wrote in 1869 that the need for more teachers to make headway against the slavery-bred ignorance of the freedmen was overwhelming. "How any one can lead the idle, useless life, that many do in this world of need, is past my comprehension. What can life be worth to such?"[13]

Ralph Barton Perry's portrayal of the Puritan as a moral athlete resembles the role expected of freedmen's teachers. "The hour demands of Christians," proclaimed the *American Missionary* in 1864, "that they be fully equipped for the great moral warfare now impending." Six years later, commenting on the trials and discouragements faced by teachers, the *American Missionary* stated that "whether the work is easy or difficult, *it must be done*, or woe to this nation."[14] Sophia Packard, founder of Spelman College and a native of New Salem, Massachusetts, recorded in her diary the daily tribulations of teaching in an ill-ventilated, dirty, leaky church basement during the early years of her mission; at the end of one particularly trying day she could find the strength to write only "tired tired tired tired tired tired." In 1870 a teacher at the AMA's secondary school in Savannah deplored the "indolence, degradation and vice" of so many freedmen, but when he recalled that these were faults produced by slavery, an institution for which the white race bore the guilt, he was renewed in his dedication to the great work of regeneration. "It is no time . . . to sit down and cry. The voice we hear today, is Go! work—This people must be educated, and may we rejoice that God permits us to aid in such a work."[15] A visitor to the Baptist Home Mission Society's Shaw University in Raleigh, North Carolina, in 1875 described the teachers as "the scrawniest, severest, primmest, ugliest most forbidding New England

---

[13] *Am. Missionary* 9 (July 1865), 156; *Sixth Annual Report of the Freedmen's Aid Society of the Methodist Episcopal Church* (Cincinnati 1873), 49; letter from Mary A. Hosley, printed in *Freedmen's Record* (February 1869), 7.

[14] *Am. Missionary* 8 (February 1864), 34; 14 (October 1870), 227. See Ralph Barton Perry, *Puritanism and Democracy* (New York 1944), ch. 10, "The Moral Athlete."

[15] Florence Matilda Read, *The Story of Spelman College* (Atlanta 1961), 56; C.C.C. to Dear Friends, 23 May 1870, AMA Archives.

type,—with whom duty—in all matters,—is always a business and never a pleasure." She found such people unpleasant company, "but the truth is that a less cold, obtuse, self-reliant & determined set of people, would be worried & badgered & mortified almost to death, & be driven away in short order." Many years later an AMA teacher from a new generation, a professional educator rather than a missionary, described the first generation of teachers as "prone to sacrifice, more religious and more concentrated in purpose than anyone I now know." She could not completely share her elders' single-minded devotion to duty, but she admired it, as did most of the graduates (whom she called "Black Puritans") of the first generation of freedmen's schools.[16]

Guilt, atonement, calling, and duty—these were the wellsprings of Christian humanitarianism that motivated the moral athletes, three-quarters of them women, half of them from New England, who went South to teach the freedmen. Without this Puritan-evangelical sense of mission, many teachers could not have stayed on the job in the face of southern white hostility, discouragement with the slow progress of the freed slaves, harsh physical conditions, and poverty-level salaries. Their faith gave them a staying power unmatched by other educators or civil rights workers in that era or in our own.

II. PIETY AND REPRESSION

For more than two centuries, higher education in America was associated primarily with the church. The most important single purpose of the founding of Harvard and the New England common schools was the training of clergymen and the education of an intelligent laity able to understand the Bible and Puritan theology. For the Puritans, faith was more than a matter of emotion. "Knowledge is no knowledge without zeal," wrote John Cotton, but "zeale is but a wilde-fire without knowledge." The settlers of Massachusetts Bay founded a college less than a decade after landing in their wilderness Zion mainly because they were "dreading to leave an illiterate Ministry to the Churches, when our present Ministers shall lie in the Dust."[17] Building on this Puritan foundation, every Protestant denomination established academies and colleges in the 18th and 19th centuries in which the inculcation of religiosity was a primary educational objective. Of the 207 col-

[16] Anna E. Dickinson to her mother, 25 April 1875, Anna E. Dickinson Papers, Libr. of Congress; Beam, *He Called Them by the Lightning*, 123.

[17] Perry Miller and Thomas H. Johnson, eds., *The Puritans* (New York 1938), 20-22; Samuel Eliot Morison, *The Founding of Harvard College* (Cambridge 1935), 150-60, 247-48. See also Lawrence A. Cremin, *American Education: The Colonial Experience 1607-1783* (New York 1970), esp. 181, 321.

leges existing in 1860, 180 had been founded by churches, most of them during the 19th century as a part of the great missionary effort to preserve and expand the faith on successive frontiers.[18]

The establishment of freedmen's schools was an extension of this missionary impulse to a new frontier. As with Harvard, the first aim of these schools was the training of an intelligent ministry. "The education of colored preachers is *the one great and crying need* of the Freedmen!" declared a Baptist abolitionist in 1870. "Their preachers have unbounded influence over them." Northern teachers were distressed by what they considered the novel doctrines and emotional excesses of Negro churches and the ignorance and immorality of black preachers. In too many black churches, wrote one northerner, "religion degenerates into mere wild-fire, with as little tendency to transform the character as the heathen rites of their ancestors in their native jungles."[19]

The emphasis on ministerial training as a corrective of this situation was one origin of the "talented tenth" theory of Negro education, by which the masses could best be raised through the efforts of their racial leaders. Many black schools of collegiate or secondary level established theological or Bible departments and offered in-service training to black clergymen. Several Negro colleges evolved out of schools originally founded as Bible Institutes: for example Augusta Institute eventually became Morehouse College, Richmond Institute became Virginia Union University, and the Centenary Biblical Institute became Morgan College. But most ministerial students in these schools, especially before World War I, were at the high school or even grammar school level. As late as 1924, only 38 of 1011 theological students in black seminaries or theological departments were college graduates.[20] Many black preachers, particularly in the Baptist church, received no formal education beyond the sixth or seventh grade. Among some Negro Baptists there was a prejudice against too much education, which was said to rob a preacher of the "spirit" (the same prejudice had existed among several white sects and denominations a generation or more earlier). Ministerial training was a major objective of the missionary schools, but they reached only a fraction of the black

[18] Donald G. Tewksbury, *The Founding of American Colleges and Universities Before the Civil War* (New York 1932).

[19] Charles H. Corey, *A History of the Richmond Theological Seminary, With Reminiscences of Thirty Years' Work Among the Colored People* (Richmond 1894), 112; Gilbert Haven et al., *An Appeal to Our People for Our People* (n.p. 1875), 22.

[20] William A. Daniel, *The Education of Negro Ministers* (New York 1925), 49-53.

clergy. The alleged ignorance and venality of many black ministers continued to be a constant target of criticism not only by northern educators but by black leaders such as W.E.B. Du Bois, Francis J. Grimké, and Booker T. Washington.

The religious purpose of freedmen's education was not confined to the training of the ministers. The need for Christian teachers was regarded as second in importance only to an educated clergy, and in fact most of the graduates of mission schools became teachers (in 1899, 54 percent of the 1252 living black college graduates who reported their occupations were teachers and 17 percent were clergymen).[21] Indeed, whatever an individual's calling, religion and education were considered twin pillars of success and usefulness. In 1869 the Presbyterian General Assembly declared that, with regard to missionary work among the freed slaves, "to organize the church without the school, is to leave the people to the fruitless effort to grow in grace, without the ability to increase in knowledge." Richard Rust outlined the guiding principles of the Methodist Freedmen's Aid Society: "The schoolhouse and the meeting-house . . . are the true emblems of Christian civilization, and should stand side by side, furnishing instruction for a useful life and preparation for a blissful immortality."[22] It was the Congregational AMA that drew a specific analogy between its educational mission and the Puritans. "The heart and conscience" of the freedmen, declared the AMA, "must be quickened with the intellect. . . . The school and the Church must move on together at the South as they started together from Plymouth Rock." Defining the Puritan values that formed the backbone of New England culture as "clear thinking, strong believing, pure living, solemn and earnest acting," the AMA declared that these were precisely the values the freedmen must adopt. "The Puritan church and the Puritan school are a sure and reliable force for this work."[23]

The missionaries' misgivings about the emotional excesses of black church services did not imply an opposition to revivals or to other outward manifestations of intense religious experiences. On the contrary, the Protestant missionary societies were themselves products of the waves of revivalism and reform that had swept over the North in the

[21] W.E.B. Du Bois, *The College-Bred Negro*, Atlanta Univ. Publications, no. 5 (Atlanta 1900), 63-64.

[22] Robert E. Thompkins, "A History of Religious Education Among Negroes in the Presbyterian Church of the United States of America," Ph.D. diss., Univ. of Pittsburgh (1951), 69-70; *Fifth Annual Report of the Freedmen's Aid Society of the Methodist Episcopal Church* (Cincinnati 1872), 6.

[23] *Am. Missionary* 37 (December 1883), 383; 33 (February 1879), 39; 13 (July 1869), 156.

antebellum generation. But these societies sought to impose upon the freedmen the restraints of New England piety and middle-class decorum. Emotional excesses and bizarre behavior had often characterized frontier revivals in the first quarter of the century, but such manifestations of the spirit were frowned upon by evangelical clergy and laymen in older sections of the country. The revivals of 1857-58 (sometimes called the Third Great Awakening) were considerably more restrained than earlier awakenings, and the evangelical atmosphere of Protestant colleges was always more decorous than the camp-meeting variety of revivalism.[24] It was the solemn piety of the mature revivalism of the 1840s and 1850s that missionery teachers, especially those from New England and Congregational or Presbyterian backgrounds, sought to instill in the freedmen. Since solemnity and restraint were not the highest religious values for many Negroes, there was a good deal of misunderstanding and tension between white missionaries and black Christians. Sometimes forgetting that shouting, groaning, falling into trances, and rolling on the floor had characterized earlier frontier revivals among whites, postwar missionaries to the freedmen viewed similar behavior in many black churches as barbarous survivals of African or slave religion which must be cast off if the freedmen were to become respectable middle-class Christians.

The freedmen's teachers tried to introduce into black colleges the religious environment of antebellum Oberlin, Knox, Wesleyan, and other schools from which they had graduated. Chapel services, prayer meetings, Bible study, sermons, and revivals were constant fare at these northern colleges, and became so at the freedmen's schools. A student at Oberlin in the 1850s later recalled that "I was struck with wonder, at the manifest presence of God, everywhere. . . . Before recitation, prayer; before eating, prayer; once a day at chapel, prayer; and so on. . . . At commencements even, we students saw to it that every visitor was warned to flee from the wrath to come, or comforted, by our mutual faith." In the 1870s the religious climate at Atlanta University, where a majority of the faculty were Oberlin alumni, was a carbon copy of Oberlin a generation earlier. "We have texts of scripture, prayers & singing every evening after supper before rising from the table, & a prayer meeting every other thing," wrote the wife of one

[24] Revivals were a major feature of American social history in the two generations before the Civil War. In the words of Perry Miller, "the dominant theme in America from 1800 to 1860 is the invincible persistence of the revival technique. . . . The decades after 1800 were a continuing, even though intermittent, revival" (*The Life of the Mind in America: From the Revolution to the Civil War* [New York 1965], 7). For other treatments of antebellum revivalism, see the works cited in n. 2, above.

Atlanta faculty member (not an Oberlin graduate). "Rather an excess of a good thing, but it helps to keep the pupils occupied & in order & keeps a strong religious influence around them which is important as of course much of their usefulness will depend upon their religious training."[25] In 1886 the Baptist Home Mission Society emphasized that its schools "are decidedly *Christian* Institutions wherein the Bible is a daily textbook . . . and wherein scores of the unconverted are yearly led to the Saviour." Two decades later the society explained that "the supreme object in these schools" was still "soul culture; not merely intellectual training like that given in high schools, academies, and colleges generally."[26] Similar assertions were made by the other mission societies.

A corollary of the middle-class piety which pervaded freedmen's schools was a rigidly enforced code of behavior that came close to H. L. Mencken's definition of Puritanism. Liquor and tobacco were universally proscribed, with expulsion a frequent penalty for violation. Many schools had active temperance societies. Most colleges had rules similar to Fisk University's, which prohibited "profanity, card playing, betting, gambling, dancing, and whatever is immoral or opposed to true culture." In justification of such rules, the *American Missionary* declared that "these regulations are not more rigorous than the moral law; not more radical than is righteousness. . . . Christianity teaches that the body is a temple for the indwelling of the Spirit, and that this temple must not be defiled." Relations between the sexes were a central disciplinary concern of college authorities (twenty-two of the twenty-nine missionary colleges were coeducational, and the remainder included two pairs of coordinate colleges). Social contacts between boys and girls were severely limited. At Howard University in the 1880s, for example, students were forbidden "to take rides, or walks, correspond, or engage in out-of-door games, with those of the other sex without permission from the proper authority." All letters coming to the girls' dormitory were subject to inspection by the matron. A boy who wished to visit a girl in her dormitory at Atlanta University had to present a written application, countersigned by the president or dean, to the matron before he was allowed to spend a maximum of twenty minutes in the parlor with his girl.[27]

[25] W. E. Lincoln to William Goodell Frost, 18 October 1909, William Goodell Frost Papers, Berea Coll. Libr.; Julia Rollins Holt to "My Darling Burtie," 15 March 1875, Holt-Messner Papers, Schlesinger Libr., Radcliffe Coll.

[26] *Home Mission Monthly* 8 (July 1886), 165; 27 (February 1905), 48.

[27] *Am. Missionary*, 47 (May 1893), 158; Rayford W. Logan, *Howard University: The First Hundred Years, 1867-1967* (New York 1969), 102; James Weldon Johnson, *Along This Way* (New York 1933), 68.

James M. McPherson

A major assumption underlying these regulations was the necessity to impress upon a race raised in slavery the connection between religion and morality. The institution of slavery, argued the abolitionist missionaries, had fostered in its victims the vices of licentiousness, dishonesty, cunning, theft, and moral irresponsibility. The indigenous black churches, according to northern teachers, did little to enforce morality; for them, religion was mainly a matter of emotion and shouting (this charge is reminiscent of Puritan complaints against antinomians two centuries earlier). Black ministers were sometimes singled out as the worst sinners, especially against the Seventh Commandment. "The mass of Southern colored churches," declared a northern journalist closely connected with the AMA, were "travesties of Christianity. They must be reformed from without, by planting true churches, whose chief test shall be obedience to the Ten Commandments."[28] Careful supervision of the morals of future teachers, preachers, and leaders of the race during their formative years in school was therefore a vital part of the missionaries' program for the redemption of blacks from the sins of slavery.

The popular identification of repressive codes of behavior with "puritanism" is not entirely wide of the mark. The Puritan concept of a "community of righteousness" led to many "rules, demands, prohibitions, punishments, and other social controls" in colonial New England. For the Puritans every man *was* his brother's keeper and the community or "common wealth" as a collective entity was responsible for enforcing morality among its members. Ralph Barton Perry has defined this collective enforcement of righteousness as a form of benevolent paternalism. On its positive side it "embraced a well-wishing interest in all members of the human family" and was thus "readily assimilated to the broad humanitarian purpose of democracy," but on the negative side it was "an inquisitive, because distrustful kindness, which sought to regulate another's life, rather than to leave that life to the promptings of its own inward impulsions and self-government."[29]

This benign but inquisitive paternalism has characterized much of the American middle-class reform tradition. Perry's words are especially applicable to the attitudes of northern missionary educators toward their black wards. The freed slaves, said the AMA in 1863, "need friends to take them by the hand, to guide, counsel and instruct them in their new life, protect them from the abuses of the wicked, and direct their energies so as to make them useful to themselves, their fami-

[28] *Independent* 27 (6 May 1875), 14.
[29] Perry, *Puritanism and Democracy*, 324, 326. See also Paul H. Conkin, *Puritans and Pragmatists* (New York 1968), 15, 25; and Ahlstrom, "The Puritan Ethic and the Spirit of American Democracy," 97-100.

[624]

lies and their country."[30] In many missionary colleges the faculty lived on campus, ate with the students, and exercised a round-the-clock supervision of their moral and religious as well as intellectual development. An AMA executive described Atlanta University as a home "where teachers & students all live together and form a family," a system which gave the faculty "close & direct" influence over "young men who need to have their whole character and lives moulded anew." The northern Baptist President of Roger Williams University in Nashville wrote that "I have endeavored to be a father unto" the students. A student at Atlanta University in the 1890s recalled that the president welcomed him to the campus "as though he were adopting me into what was his large family. . . . I found the matron even more motherly than the president was fatherly."[31]

This principle of "kind but firm supervision"[32] was not unique to black schools. Required religious observances and extensive parietal regulations were the norm in 19th century American colleges (and during much of the 20th century as well). At Harvard in the 1870s, for example, students could not leave the campus on Sunday without permission. Yale defined the profanation of the Sabbath, disbelief in the Bible's authenticity, and "extravagant expenditures" as formal offenses. In 1885 the Princeton faculty prohibited students from having their laundry done in town and stipulated that such washing "must be done under the supervision of the College Office." The college president in the Victorian era was a benevolent despot (toward faculty as well as students). He took seriously the college's function of *in loco parentis* and felt a direct responsibility for the morals and piety of his students.[33] The paternalism and restrictive rules at both white and black colleges were natural results of Puritan/Victorian views of human nature and of the role of education in shaping behavior and ethics.

In theory these rules were designed to encourage the development of Christian character; in practice they encouraged the development of spying by faculty and students, petty harassment, hypocrisy, student rebelliousness, and ingenious methods of evasion. James Weldon Johnson, song-writer, author, and secretary of the NAACP, recalled that during his student days at Atlanta University in the 1890s he fre-

[30] *Am. Missionary* 7 (June 1863), 130.

[31] Erastus M. Cravath to Oliver O. Howard, 23 September 1873, Oliver O. Howard Papers, Bowdoin Coll. Libr.; *Home Mission Monthly* 10 (November 1888), 283; James Weldon Johnson, *The Autobiography of an Ex-Coloured Man* (Boston 1912), 60-61.

[32] *Congregationalist*, 35 (8 February 1883), 48.

[33] Lawrence R. Veysey, *The Emergence of the American University* (Chicago 1965), 32-34; George P. Schmidt, *The Old Time College President* (New York 1930).

quently sneaked out in the evening with friends to play cards "with the shades drawn, hat over keyhole, crack under door chinked, and muffled voices." Johnson believed that the main effect of the system of obligatory piety and virtue was "to put a premium on hypocrisy or, almost as bad, to substitute for religion a lazy and stupid conformity." Much faculty time and energy were spent in efforts to enforce parietal rules and cope with the consequent student unrest in black as well as white colleges. The atmosphere of piety and repression was laid on more heavily and lasted longer in black schools than in most white institutions, and E. Franklin Frazier was probably right in 1924 when he wrote that the content of missionary education for Negroes had been too much inspiration and too little information, leaving the black elite ill-equipped to meet the demands of an increasingly secular and technological society.[34]

III. THE PURITAN ETHIC

Frazier's indictment was not altogether accurate, however, for there were important secular components in the education of the freedmen. The curriculum of black secondary schools and colleges was derived mainly from that of New England high schools, academies, normal schools, and colleges in the middle third of the 19th century, with an increasing emphasis in some schools on vocational or industrial training in the last two decades of the century. It is not the purpose of this essay to analyze the curriculum of black colleges or to describe the debate over industrial versus academic education. Rather we are concerned here with the values and goals the missionary educators tried to instill in their students. For them the secular counterpart of moral piety was the Puritan Ethic. Described by Ralph Barton Perry as "austerity, reliability, energy, industry, self-control, marital fidelity, frugality, sobriety, thrift, self-reliance, and foresight," the Puritan Ethic had survived almost unchanged into 19th century New England. It formed the core of the values carried South by missionary educators. Indeed, it was the dominant value system of 19th century American society and the basis of reform movements growing out of evangelical Protestantism. As William McLoughlin has pointed out, these reforms were primarily missionary endeavors. Conversion of the poor, the intemperate, the depraved, and deprived would "implant in them the virtues of true Protestantism—industry, sobriety, thrift and piety" which would enable them to become prosperous and useful citizens.[35]

[34] Johnson, *Along This Way*, 77, 80-81; E. Franklin Frazier, "A Note on Negro Education," *Opportunity* 2 (March 1924), 75-77.

[35] Perry, *Puritanism and Democracy*, 302; McLoughlin, ed., *American Evangelicals*, 13.

Abolitionists and some other varieties of reformers tried to combine this emphasis on the Puritan Ethic with efforts to remove environmental constraints upon individual development in a manner that anticipated the social gospel.[36] The freedmen's education movement was in some respects a link between antebellum evangelical reforms and the post-Reconstruction social gospel, although ironically the missionary educators began to place greater stress on the need for freedmen to internalize the Puritan Ethic in order to raise themselves by their own bootstraps at the same time that social Christianity began to move against the external and institutional injustices of urban society. The opposite of the Puritan Ethic virtues were idleness, wastefulness, carelessness, extravagance, dependency, unreliability, infidelity, hedonism, and lack of foresight. These were precisely the vices which abolitionists believed slavery had ingrained in its victims. By 1870 the slaves had been emancipated and granted equal constitutional rights, but this was only half the job of turning them into true Christians and citizens. "We have dwarfed their intellects, enfeebled their physical powers, and taught them vices which nothing but genuine conversion can cure," said the *American Missionary*, "and now we think stealthily to open their prison-doors and invite them to walk out. Never! We must take them by the hand, set them upon their feet . . . and nourish them up to life and manhood, or God is against us."[37] In subsequent years most missionary educators and former abolitionists continued to insist on the government's duty to enforce the Negro's constitutional rights, but increasingly they came to emphasize the need for blacks to learn and apply the values of work, thrift, sobriety, and reliability in order to earn true equality and respectability. Thus the ideology of racial advancement identified most prominently with Booker T. Washington was a logical outgrowth of the missionary viewpoint.

In 1875 John G. Whittier declared that since constitutional amendments and congressional legislation had given the freedmen legal equality with whites, "mainly upon the colored people themselves now depends the question whether, by patient industry, sobriety, and assiduous self-culture, they shall overcome the unchristian prejudice still existing against them, or by indolence, thriftlessness, and moral and physical degradation they shall confirm and strengthen it." Wendell Phillips Garrison, son of the famous abolitionist and assistant editor of the influential *Nation*, wrote in 1879 that "the blacks by good behavior, frugality, sobriety, honesty," and in no other way would win real as

---

[36] For enlightening discussions of the roots of the social gospel in antebellum reform, see Timothy L. Smith, *Revivalism and Social Reform*, ch. 10, and Bertram Wyatt-Brown, *Lewis Tappan and the Evangelical War Against Slavery*, 259-60.

[37] *Am. Missionary* 8 (September 1864), 219-20.

well as legal equality.[38] William W. Patton, President of Howard University and a long-time abolitionist, sounded a common theme in 1880 when he urged Negroes to emulate successful groups, especially New England Yankees and the Jews, who had achieved prosperity through "industry, thrift, wealth, knowledge, culture, morality, and religion." The *Independent*, a large-circulation religious weekly whose editors were closely associated with the AMA, stated in 1890 that blacks and their white allies should of course "make a persistent demand for their political rights, yet we hold that the only ultimate means of success is found in good morals, good education and thrift."[39]

This belief in the Puritan Ethic as the primary means of racial advancement was shared by most black leaders in the generation after Reconstruction, including several who have traditionally symbolized the black opposition to Booker T. Washington. "Our destiny is in our own hands," said Frederick Douglass in 1881. "When we shall possess . . . a class of men noted for enterprise, industry, economy and success, we shall no longer have any trouble in the matter of civil and political rights." T. Thomas Fortune, outspoken editor of the New York *Freeman* (later the *Age*), wrote in 1885 that "the moral, mental and material condition of the race must be properly looked after before we can hope to establish any sort of status in the politics of this country." The reason for the race's poverty, Kelly Miller told the Howard University class of 1898, is that "the Negro does not make provision because he lacks prevision. . . . He can not see beyond the momentary gratification of his desires." In opposing a federal elections bill of 1891 to enforce black voting rights in the South, W.E.B. Du Bois wrote that "a good many of our people . . . are not fit for the responsibility of republican government. When you have the right sort of black voters you will need no election laws. The battle of my people must be a moral one, not a legal or physical one."[40] In a survey of more than seven hundred black college graduates in 1899, Du Bois found that many of them emphasized the gospel of work and thrift as the best solution of the race problem. A couple of sample comments from respondents: The Negro's "future depends upon his own self respect and

[38] John G. Whittier to Dillwyn Parrish, 24 March 1875, printed in the *New York Times*, 4 April 1875; *Nation* 28 (27 February 1879), 147.

[39] From Patton's Baccalaureate address to the Howard University graduating class of 1880, published in the *Independent* 32 (26 August 1880), 8; ibid. 42 (24 April 1890), 554.

[40] Douglass, Fortune, and Du Bois quoted in August Meier, *Negro Thought in America, 1880-1915* (Ann Arbor 1963), 75, 36, 192; Kelly Miller, "The Education of the Negro," in *Report of the Commissioner of Education for the Year 1900-01*, 1 (Washington 1902), 809-10.

thrift"; "Education, refinement, character and money will settle the Negro problem everywhere."[41]

Perhaps one reason why black college graduates stressed this point was that the missionary educators had been driving it home for more than thirty years. The AMA schools made one of their first priorities the lesson that "industry is commendable and indispensable to freedom, and indolence both wicked and degrading." The freedmen were to be turned into ebony Yankees; black students "must be made as nearly as may be like Northern teachers and Northern thinkers. Habits of neatness, system, thrift" must be inculcated. Negroes need "the New England church and school, and whatever has grown out of them, to civilize the people, and beget order, sobriety, purity and faith."[42] In 1902 Thomas J. Morgan, a veteran abolitionist, former commander of black troops in the Civil War, and Secretary of the American Baptist Home Mission Society, summed up the values that the schools he administered tried to teach. The goals of education, wrote Morgan, should be the growth of knowledge, skills, and character, and of these the last was most important. "If a man goes out of the schools depraved in heart and deficient in will power," said Morgan, "all his learning and skill and intellectual qualities may be a curse and not a blessing." Students must "be trained to be honest, truthful and pureminded . . . industrious, thrifty, faithful to the performance of duty, intelligent, moral, progressive, public spirited and self-respecting. . . . Ignorance fosters idleness, thriftlessness, wastefulness and vagabondage; education encourages industry, thrift, frugality and home keeping."[43] There could be no better definition of the Puritan Ethic.

In the era of the self-made man, Horatio Alger, and Social Darwinism this emphasis on hard work, self-denial, foresight, and Yankee enterprise as the best means for a race to lift itself by its own bootstraps is not surprising. And the inculcation of piety, discipline, order, and industry as major educational goals was of course not unique to black schools or to this period of American history. A primary function of the American educational system has been to preserve and perpetuate the middle-class values of the Puritan Ethic. Lawrence A. Cremin has shown that "piety, civility, and learning" in that order were the major themes of colonial education. In setting aside one section of each township to support schools, the Northwest Ordinance of 1787 declared that "religion, morality and knowledge being necessary to good gov-

[41] Du Bois, *The College-Bred Negro*, 91, 93.
[42] *Am. Missionary* 7 (June 1863), 128; 11 (March 1867), 59; 12 (December 1868), 274.
[43] *Home Mission Monthly* 24 (January 1902), 14, 16; (February 1902), 30.

ernment and the happiness of mankind, schools and the means of education shall forever be encouraged." The Massachusetts Commissioner of Education wrote in 1857 that an essential purpose of schooling was "by moral and religious instruction daily given" to "inculcate habits of regularity, punctuality, constancy and industry." A study of leading American educators, especially those of the 19th century, concluded that no purpose "has played a larger role in the thinking and practice of educators than character training" backed by "religious sanctions."[44]

Perhaps the most influential educator of the 19th century (because of the almost universal use of his textbooks) was Noah Webster. Although he is remembered today mainly for his *Dictionary of the English Language*, first published in 1828, Webster was known in his own time as the "Schoolmaster of America" for his famous blue-backed speller (first published in 1783 and reprinted countless times under the title *Elementary Speller* or *Elementary Spelling Book*) and for his *American Reader* and *American Grammar*. These books repeatedly inculcated the maxims of New England piety and the Puritan Ethic (Webster was a Connecticut Yankee); their philosophy bore a close resemblance to that of Benjamin Franklin's Poor Richard. Webster's *Speller* alone was estimated to have sold 100 million copies in the 19th century. "Man has but little time to spare for the gratification of the senses and the imagination," Webster told his young readers. "In selecting books for reading, be careful to choose such as furnish the best helps to improvement in morals, literature, arts and sciences, preferring profit to pleasure, and instruction to amusement. . . . The greatest part of life is to be employed in useful labors, and in various indispensable duties, private, social, and public."[45]

Recent analyses of 19th century and contemporary urban schools have been sharply critical of their efforts to impose a straitjacket of middle-class values upon lower-class children for whom many of these values were alien and useless, if not harmful.[46] Yet for most educators,

[44] Cremin, *American Education: The Colonial Experience*; Michael B. Katz, *The Irony of Early School Reform: Educational Innovation in Mid-Nineteenth Century Massachusetts* (Cambridge, Mass. 1968), 43; Merle Curti, *The Social Ideas of American Educators* (New York 1935), 584. See also Neil G. McCluskey, *Public Schools and Moral Education: The Influence of Horace Mann, William Torrey Harris, and John Dewey* (New York 1958).

[45] Quoted in Alice Felt Tyler, *Freedom's Ferment: Phases of American Social History from the Colonial Period to the Outbreak of the Civil War* (Minneapolis 1944), 264. See also ibid., 231-32; Curti, *The Social Ideas of American Educators*, 17, 32-34; and Henry R. Warfel, *Noah Webster, Schoolmaster to America* (New York 1936).

[46] Katz, *The Irony of Early School Reform*; Eleanor Burke Leacock, *Teaching and Learning in City Schools: A Comparative Study* (New York 1969).

particularly in the 19th century, the formation of the child's character on the basis of religion and moral instruction was a necessary prerequisite for a useful Christian life and for upward social mobility in a competitive, capitalist, democratic society. The crusade of missionary educators to implant New England Christianity and the Puritan Ethic in their black students placed them in the mainstream of American educational development. The missionaries saw their efforts as the only way in which acculturation and assimilation of the freedmen could be accomplished. If they were wrong, their error was the product of a society (and an educational philosophy) whose racial and class biases undermined its Christian and democratic creed.

In addition to several hundred elementary schools, most of which were eventually absorbed into the South's public school system, the Protestant mission-education societies established or supported eighty-five secondary schools and twenty-nine colleges for blacks, including such institutions as Fisk and Atlanta Universities, Spelman and Morehouse Colleges, and Hampton Institute, which are among the best predominantly black colleges in the United States. These institutions were attended mainly by the "talented tenth" of the black community; only rarely did the colleges and secondary schools extend their influence to the semi-literate rural masses. In theory the talented tenth (a phrase probably first used by Henry L. Morehouse, Field Secretary of the American Baptist Home Mission Society[47] and popularized by W.E.B. Du Bois) constituted an educated professional class whose leadership and example would help raise the masses to a higher status. The mission societies frequently affirmed that the theory was working out in practice. In 1892, for example, the Executive Secretary of the AMA spelled out the Negro's progress since emancipation. A generation earlier southern blacks had been forbidden by law to learn to read; now there were 20,000 black schoolteachers. One thousand black ministers had received training beyond the high school level. Twenty-seven years earlier there had been two black newspapers; now there were 154; in 1865 there were two Negro lawyers, now there were 250; then there had been three black physicians, now there were 749. "Verily this is a grand record for one generation, unparalleled in the history of human progress." The leaven of missionary Puritanism was working in the race, giving "old abolitionists" cause for "joy and thanksgiving" and promising to "bear the next generation onward to even greater success."[48]

[47] H. L. Morehouse, "The Talented Tenth," *Independent* 48 (23 April 1896), 541.
[48] *Independent* 44 (16 June 1892), 839; *Am. Missionary* 47 (August 1893), 241.

But on other occasions the missionary educators were less self-congratulatory and more candid. They were aware that while the national percentage of black illiteracy had declined (from 80 percent in 1870 to 45 percent in 1900), the number of illiterate Negroes was the same in 1900 as it had been thirty years earlier and equaled the number of slaves freed in 1865. At times there seemed to be an Alice-in-Wonderland quality to black education—it was necessary to run faster just to stay even. Not until the decade after 1900 did the absolute number as well as percentage of black illiterates decline.[49] The 1000 clergymen in 1892 with some college or theological school training represented only 8 percent of the black ministry. Two decades later, after a considerable expansion of higher and professional education for Negroes, the ratio of black doctors to the total black population was 1 to 3194 compared with 1 to 553 among whites; for lawyers the black ratio was 1 to 12,315 compared with 1 to 718 among whites; for college professors 1 to 40,611 among Negroes and 1 to 5301 among whites; and in the teaching profession generally there was one black teacher for every 334 black persons compared with a ratio of 1 to 145 for whites. In 1909-10 the proportion of black children of school age not attending school was nearly three times the proportion of white children.[50] Nowhere near a tenth of the Negro population benefited from higher education: in 1909 there were approximately 3000 black students in colleges and professional schools and probably not more than 3500 living Negro college graduates in a total black population of nearly 10 million.[51]

In 1909-10 the approximate numbers of black college and professional students and secondary school pupils attending the schools founded or supported by the white Protestant mission societies were

[49] *Northwestern Christian Advocate*, 27 April 1887; *Am. Missionary* 60 (October 1906), 234-35. Detailed statistics on illiteracy can be found in ch. 16 of *Negro Population: 1790-1915*, U.S. Dept. of Commerce, Bureau of the Census (Washington 1918).

[50] Ibid., 510, 385.

[51] W.E.B. Du Bois and Augustus G. Dill, *The College-Bred Negro American*, Atlanta Univ. Publications, no. 15 (Atlanta 1910), 14-15, 45-52. Du Bois and Dill calculated that a total of 3856 known Negroes had graduated from American colleges and universities through 1909. Of these, 3477 had graduated in the three decades since 1880 and most of them were presumably still alive in 1909. Since some northern colleges did not designate students by race in their records, Du Bois and Dill estimated that the true number of black college graduates may have been as high as 5000. This seems too high, but in any case the estimate of 3500 living graduates in 1909 (my estimate) is probably generous. Unfortunately, the U.S. census did not enumerate the number of college graduates in the population until 1940.

respectively 2500 and 9000.[52] This was rather a small leaven to puritanize the masses. Throughout the missionary era of black higher education (which gradually came to an end between 1900 and World War I), northern white teachers and administrators lamented their inability to reach more than a fraction of the black population. Our schools, they declared in a variety of metaphors, are "like a beacon light" sending out "ray[s] of light toward those sitting in the darkness beyond" or "*oases* sparsely planted in the great desert." Most of those who benefited from missionary "education and a pure Gospel" lived up to the Puritan standard of their teachers, but the condition of those in the desert beyond the rays of the beacon light was deplorable: there were millions of Negroes, wrote the AMA's Executive Secretary in 1893, who lived "in density of ignorance, in depths of superstition, poor, thoughtless, mentally and morally weak. . . . [Their] intellectual and moral condition is but little, if any, better than it was in slavery." Of the nearly 7 million southern blacks in 1890, declared the head of the AMA's Women's Bureau, "we think of the few thousands . . . that we have reached, and we must see that there is an immense work to be done among them yet."[53]

Puritanization of lower-class blacks was handicapped not only by the modest resources of the mission societies and the psychological heritage of slavery, but also by an outlook among rural Negroes common to peasant societies throughout the world. The anthropologist George M. Foster has written that "the Anglo-Saxon virtues of hard work and thrift seen as leading to economic success are meaningless in peasant society." Peasants feel themselves powerless to influence the conditions governing their lives, which are seen as subject to natural and supernatural forces beyond their control. When land and power

[52] *The Report of the U.S. Commissioner of Education for the Year 1909-10* (Washington 1911), 1264-75. The unreliability of these government statistics makes precision in the number of students impossible. There was a variety of standards among these schools, and some students reported to be taking college or high school courses should actually be classified at a lower grade, so these figures exaggerate the true number of college and high school students. A more accurate government report of 1916 showed 7773 secondary students and 2517 college and professional students in the mission society schools in 1914-15. See James M. McPherson, "White Liberals and Black Power in Negro Education, 1865-1915," *AHR* 75 (June 1970), 1380-86, Table. Black college and professional school students not in the missionary colleges were in northern schools, black denominational colleges, and southern state-supported black schools.

[53] *Am. Missionary* 45 (October 1891), 355; Isabel C. Barrows, ed., *First Mohonk Conference on the Negro Question . . . June 4, 5, 6, 1890* (Boston 1890), 62-63; *Friends' Rev.* 28 (13 February 1875); *Am. Missionary* 47 (July 1893), 211-14.

are in the hands of others, the practices of self-discipline, self-denial, capital accumulation, and planning for the future seem pointless. A sort of apathy and fatalism characterize all peasant cultures, including that of the freed slaves. Since fate or luck rather than hard work are believed to determine a man's destiny, peasants are inclined toward superstition, gambling, and lotteries rather than toward rational planning and achievement-oriented behavior.[54] This helps to explain the propensity for gambling especially in the form of numbers games among lower-class Negroes. A major reason for the limited success of the puritanization efforts of black education was the cultural gap between the middle-class success ethic of the missionaries and the peasant fatalism of the freedmen. Failure to bridge this gap or even to understand it often led to frustration and disillusionment among missionary educators, and accounts for the frequent note of exasperation in their writings.

On the whole, however, the mission societies more often accentuated the positive than the negative. While deploring the "ignorance and immorality" of the millions not yet under the influence of New England Christianity and the Puritan Ethic, they were proud of the graduates of their schools and optimistic that the masses would yet be redeemed under their leadership. The impact of the missionary schools upon the talented tenth in the two generations after the Civil War was indeed considerable. Some observers, in fact, thought the students had been too successfully molded in the New England image. A white visitor at the Atlanta University commencement in 1905 wondered whether the graduates "should have life made [so] much more serious to them than it [is] to others," although she was aware of "the greater difficulties they will meet than other young people, and the need they will have of a Puritan ability to endure hardness." But H. Paul Douglass, white Secretary of the AMA in the post-missionary era, wrote in 1909 that he found in many black alumni of AMA schools "a gravity of manner, a sobriety of expression, a restraint of religious utterances which I think overdoes the matter." The traditional warmth and spontaneity of black religion were lacking. Because of the type of education in AMA schools, "in this particular our brother has ceased to be a negro and has become a mere Congregationalist. It has been a change for the worse."[55]

In a book entitled *The Mis-Education of the Negro*, published in

[54] George M. Foster, "Peasant Society and the Image of Limited Good," in Jack M. Potter et al., eds., *Peasant Society: A Reader* (Boston 1967), 300-323, esp. 318-19.
[55] Mary White Ovington to W.E.B. Du Bois, 27 June 1905, from the Papers of W.E.B. Du Bois formerly in the custody of Herbert Aptheker; H. Paul Douglass, *Christian Reconstruction in the South* (Boston 1909), 379.

1933, Carter G. Woodson indicted the mission societies for giving blacks a white-oriented education unsuited to their needs. Woodson, founder of the Association for the Study of Negro Life and History and the *Journal of Negro History*, stressed the African cultural heritage of black Americans and the need for Negro education to inculcate racial pride and identity. The missionary colleges, he said, had ignored the black man's heritage, had imposed a New England curriculum and white middle-class values upon the black elite, and had thereby alienated black leaders from the indigenous culture of their people. "The chief difficulty of the education of the Negro," wrote Woodson, "is that it has been largely imitation resulting in the enslavement of his mind" to white viewpoints. It sought to "transform the Negroes, not to develop them." Woodson's criticisms had been anticipated in part nearly half a century earlier by D. Augustus Straker, a black lawyer and educator, who complained that Negro education "has been fundamentally defective" because in spite of gains in literacy and achievement, black youth "yet show a subserviency and a want of aspiration and just pride, arising from the fact that they have been educated in the knowledge of the power and elevation of another race only, and nothing about their own. . . . Why not then teach the Negro child more of himself and less of others. . . . *This* only can produce true pride of race." Woodson's critique was also backed up by Buell Gallagher, white President of Talladega College in the 1930s, who affirmed that the black college "tends to be a respectable copy of the white college. This may serve to give the Negro whatever status comes from being 'just as good' or 'just like' the dominant group; but at the same time it robs him of that subtle and precious ability to estimate himself in terms of his own worth rather than in terms of imitative standards."[56]

These are astute criticisms. The goal of missionary education *was* to acculturate the freed slaves and their children to middle-class white values and institutions, and this acculturation was regarded as a one-way process. The contributions that black culture could have made to the enrichment of American civilization were largely ignored. Fisk University's music department, for example, concentrated on classical European music, the students were encouraged to form a "Mozart Musical Society," and even the spirituals were recast in a formal mold.[57] It was not from Fisk but from the backcountry and the vice

[56] Carter G. Woodson, *The Mis-Education of the Negro* (Washington 1933), 134, 17; D. Augustus Straker, *The New South Investigated* (Detroit 1888), 207; Buell G. Gallagher, *American Caste and the Negro College* (New York 1938), 212-13.

[57] Lucius S. Merriam, *Higher Education in Tennessee*, U.S. Bureau of Education Circular of Information, no. 5 (Washington 1893), 266. For many students at Fisk,

districts of New Orleans and Memphis that blues and jazz emerged. Few courses in black history or the sociology of the black community were offered in Negro colleges before World War I (Du Bois's courses at Atlanta, his Atlanta University Studies, and George Edmund Haynes's Department of Sociology at Fisk were exceptions).[58] The image of Africa imparted to black students was usually that of a benighted continent in need of missionary uplift and westernization.

To the extent that the higher education of black leaders in the two generations after emancipation divorced them from their cultural heritage, it was unfortunate. But in some respects the criticism of Woodson and others tended to overlook the positive contributions of missionary education. Though the number of Negroes in missionary schools was relatively small, many of the 20th century leaders in civil rights movements, black community organizations, and the church were educated in these colleges. "The importance of these New England heirs of the old Puritan-Abolitionist tradition in the molding of Negro leadership over several decades can scarcely be exaggerated," wrote Richard Bardolph in his analysis of the black elite.[59] From W.E.B. Du Bois and Ida Wells-Barnett to Thurgood Marshall and Martin Luther King, these leaders have laid the groundwork for most of the change and progress that have occurred in American race relations during recent decades. The testimony of black alumni to the value of their education cannot be discounted. "In spite of petty regulations and a puritanical zeal," wrote James Weldon Johnson, graduate of Atlanta University, it "was an excellent school. . . . The breadth of the social values that it carried out practically was, perhaps, unequaled. . . . For me there was probably no better school in the United States." W.E.B. Du Bois, a Fisk graduate, was lavish in his praise of New England's educational crusade for the freedmen, "that finest thing in American history." The missionary teachers "came not to keep the Negroes in their place," said Du Bois, "but to raise them out of the defilement of the places where slavery had wallowed them. The colleges they founded were social set-

---

however, their introduction to classical music was one of the most meaningful parts of their education. The Mozart Society became locally famous for its performances of Handel's *Messiah*, Mozart's *Twelfth Mass*, and other 18th century choral masterpieces, and the high point of every Fisk commencement was the singing of the *Hallelujah* chorus. W.E.B. Du Bois joined the Mozart Society, which "did great things for my education. . . . No student ever left Fisk without a deep and abiding appreciation of real music." *The Autobiography of W.E.B. Du Bois* (New York 1968), 123.

[58] John Hope Franklin, "Courses Concerning the Negro in Negro Colleges," *Quart. Rev. of Higher Education Among Negroes* 8 (July 1940), 138-44.

[59] Richard Bardolph, *The Negro Vanguard* (New York 1959), 188.

tlements; homes where the best of the sons of the freedmen came in close and sympathetic touch with the best traditions of New England. . . . In educational power it was supreme."[60] The culture-bound paternalism of the neo-Puritans who founded these schools could not have been all bad if it elicited praise like this.

But what of E. Franklin Frazier's thesis that the missionary colleges were nurseries of the black bourgeoisie, whose imitative customs, crass materialism, conspicuous consumption, and empty achievements Frazier satirized so sharply? Frazier's treatment of this issue was ambivalent. In effect he distinguished between two types of bourgeois values. The first was the Puritan Ethic with its emphasis on piety, morality, hard work, thrift, and responsibility. These were the values of the first generation or two of missionary education, and though Frazier was critical of the disproportionate emphasis on "inspiration" instead of "information" in these generations, he admired the "humanity and idealism" of the "New England schoolmarms." But with the decline of the missionary impulse, the replacement of white teachers with black, the northward migration and urbanization of blacks after 1915, and the consequent secularization of black middle-class values, the colleges underwent a transformation of objectives "from the making of men to the making of money-makers." Middle-class "respectability became less a question of morals and manners and more a matter of the external marks of a high standard of living." Greek-letter societies, dances, and card parties replaced chapel services and prayer meetings as the social centers of college life. Students and faculty were no longer concerned with the state of their souls or their duty to society but with "social status and economic security." The Puritan Ethic had been transformed into bourgeois vulgarity.[61]

This contrast between the heroic age of missionary idealism and the later era of black Babbittry is a major theme in the recollections of several black scholars who graduated from college during the missionary era and taught, often in the same school, from the 1900s to the 1940s. To the extent that such impressionistic evidence can be relied upon, there does appear to have been a generation of "black Puritans" educated in missionary schools who came of age in the years around 1900. But the passing of the missionary era allegedly produced a decline in the moral stamina of Negro education. One black educator, writing in 1939, praised the "great old New Englanders who wrought miracles upon and with crude Negro youths. . . . There is something bordering

[60] Johnson, *Along this Way*, 83-84; Du Bois, *The Souls of Black Folk* (New York 1903), 100.

[61] Frazier, *Black Bourgeoisie*, 56-57, 71-76.

on holiness in the old Fisk and the old Atlanta University where great men and women joined with God in man-making." The achievement of these pioneers was all the more impressive in contrast with the "pathetically empty and shallow, and tragically narrow and cowardly" nature of Negro education in the post-missionary generation. Kelly Miller, Professor and Dean at Howard for more than forty years, lauded the missionary teachers who came out of the abolitionist tradition and "touched the lethargic faculties of the first generation of Negro college youth, as it were with a live coal of fire." But these saints passed from the scene and "left no successors." The northern teachers had been "indoctrinated in the Puritan cult which believed that character could be inspired only through religious consecration and the Christian ideals. As they began to withdraw, this influence began to wane. The Negro colleges were shifted from a Puritan to a pagan basis." Writing in 1933, Miller deplored this change. "Painful observation convinces us that the later crop of college output falls lamentably short of their elder brothers. . . . The inducing process was cut short before the induction had become permanently effective."[62]

Miller's words may sound quaintly old-fashioned today. Contemporary radicals and probably liberals of both races would condemn many aspects of missionary education, especially its paternalism and repression. Some of today's black intelligentsia repudiate "western" or "white" values and are searching for an authentic "black aesthetic" with which to shape a new racial identity and to reinvigorate a genuine Afro-American culture. One of their primary targets is the white-imposed educational system which, in their view, has brainwashed generations of Negroes into carbon copies of "the man." The Puritan Ethic has gone out of style and in many quarters has been replaced by the hedonism of the "expressive life style" of black soul culture or the turned-on existentialism of white youth culture. The missionaries' belief that hard work, thrift, piety, and respectability would win prosperity and respect for the Negro is now considered at best naive and shortsighted, at worst patronizing and racist.

From the viewpoint of 1974 the paternalism and naiveté of missionary educators is undeniable. Yet they were products of their heritage and of their age, and to expect them to have thought or acted differently is to expect the impossible. In their racial attitudes and their efforts for racial progress they were far ahead of most white Americans

---

[62] Lewis K. McMillan, "Negro Higher Education as I Have Known It," *J. of Negro Education* 8 (January 1939), 10-12; Kelly Miller, "The Higher Education of the Negro Is at the Crossroads," *Educational Rev.* 72 (December 1926), 273-74, and "The Past, Present and Future of the Negro College," *J. of Negro Education* 2 (July 1933), 413-14.

of their time. Without them there would have been little college or secondary education for the first two generations of freedmen.

And ironically, the movement that perhaps did the most to inspire black militancy in the 1960s and the individual who symbolizes perhaps better than anyone else the soul culture of the 1970s both subscribe at least as strongly to the Puritan Ethic as did the missionary educators. Black Muslims are enjoined "to live soberly and with dignity, to work hard, to devote themselves to their families' welfare and to deal honestly with all men." Self-reliance and mutual responsibility are the supreme values of Muslim ethics. Black Muslims are expected to pray five times a day. They must attend religious meetings at least twice a week. They are forbidden to use tobacco, liquor, or drugs. Sexual morality is strictly enforced. And James Brown, the rock singer who is known as "Soul Brother number 1," urges blacks to "stay in school, because unless you get a good education you'll never be your own man. Work so you can have your own money. . . . You've got to plan for tomorrow and save, and invest, because unless you have ownership you will never have black power. . . . Be right, be dignified, be cool, be all the things it takes to be a nice person."[63] Cotton Mather would have agreed with this advice, and he would have felt at home with the Black Muslim regimen. So would the New England teachers at black colleges and their students a century ago.

[63] C. Eric Lincoln, *The Black Muslims in America* (Boston 1961), 80-83; Brown quoted in Phillip T. Drotning and Wesley W. South, *Up from the Ghetto* (New York 1970), 83-84. See also Lawrence L. Tyler, "The Protestant Ethic Among the Black Muslims," *Phylon* 27 (Spring 1966), 5-14.

APPENDIX

The data on the homes of teachers cited on p. 613 of this essay are from Appendix III of Henry Lee Swint, *The Northern Teacher in the South, 1862-1870* (Nashville 1941), which lists 1048 teachers whose home towns and/or states Swint was able to determine on the basis of published reports and manuscript records of the Freedmen's Bureau and the freedmen's aid societies. Swint's list includes 24 teachers from slave states and the District of Columbia and eleven from Canada, Hawaii, and England, which have not been included in my sample of northern teachers. Swint's own discussion of the geographical backgrounds of the teachers (pp. 46-47) contains statistics slightly at variance with the data in his tables, apparently the result of faulty tabulation. The estimate of more than 700 teachers from New England plus areas settled by New England emigrants is Swint's (p. 50). Data on the birthplaces of college presidents were obtained from biographical encyclopedias, *Who Was Who in America*, *Who's Who in America*, obituaries, genealogies, and from information in the magazines and published reports of the mission societies. Two of the 76 college presidents were born in the South, four in Canada, and three in the United Kingdom; if these are subtracted from the sample, New England was the birthplace of 57 percent and Massachusetts of 25 percent of the northern-born college presidents whose birthplaces have been identified.

These samples of 1013 teachers and 76 college presidents are neither random nor necessarily representative. The total number of northern white teachers in the South during the 1860s is impossible to state precisely. The best we can do is to make an educated guess based on the number of white teachers in schools (not including Sunday schools) that reported regularly to the Freedmen's Bureau, which probably included all but a handful of the schools supported by the northern societies. From 1867 to 1870 the number of white teachers at any given time averaged 1164, with a high of 1305 reported on 1 July 1868, and a low of 957 on 1 July 1869. See John W. Alvord, Semi-Annual *Reports on Schools for Freedmen, 1867-1870*, U.S. Bureau of Refugees, Freedmen and Abandoned Lands (Washington 1867-70): 1 January 1867, p. 2; 1 July 1867, p. 5; 1 January 1868, pp. 12-13; 1 July 1868, pp. 6-7; 1 January 1869, pp. 6-7; 1 July 1869, pp. 6-7; 1 January 1870, pp. 6-7. The average number of teachers for the four or five years preceding 1867 was lower. There was also a small but undetermined number of northern white teachers in schools that did not report regularly to the Freedman's Bureau. At the same time perhaps as many as 10 percent of the white teachers in both categories of schools were southerners. Taking these factors into account and allowing for an average tenure of three years for northern teachers in freedmen's schools from 1862 to 1870, it is probable that the total number of northern teachers in freedmen's schools during that period was approximately 3000, and Swint's sample therefore represents about one-third of the total. This total and the sample do not include a fairly substantial number of northern ministers and missionaries who founded and conducted freedmen's churches and Sunday schools unless they also taught in functioning day or night schools.

The sample of 1013 teachers whose homes have been located is probably biased in favor of the better-organized and better-financed societies, whose home offices were mostly in the northeastern states. The sample may therefore exaggerate slightly the true proportion of New England teachers. The same may be true of the sample of college presidents, which represents about two-thirds of all white presidents of missionary black colleges during the half century after the Civil War. A disproportionate number of the one-third whose birthplaces have not been located may have come from western states or other regions distant from northeastern communications centers and thus have been less likely to get their names into biographical dictionaries. But even if we had full information on all teachers and presidents it is probable that the percentage of New Englanders would not decline markedly and virtually certain that the thesis of disproportionate New England background would still hold.

Index

Index

Index

Index

Index

Index

Index

Index

Ranke, Leopold von, 525
Rashdall, H., 114
Reading, Oxford students from, 156, 165, 167
Redman, Richard, Bishop, 200
Reformation: Cambridge and, 203, 215; Oxford and, 16, 151, 152, 158, 176; patronage affected by, 148
Reid, Thomas, 426
Renaissance: educational ideas, 24-25; Oxford and, 151-81; in Spain, 377-78, 395
Reynolds, Sir Joshua, 291
Richard II, King of England, 129, 132
Richmond, Virginia Union University, 620
Richmondshire, students from, 201
Rider, Dudley, 55
Robertson, William, 438, 442, 447, 479
Rochau, 563
Rochester, students from, 201
Roeth, Professor, 548
Roger Williams University, 625
Rogge, Walter, 544
Rollin, Charles: *Ancient History*, 478-79; *De la Maniere d'Enseigner et d'Etudier les Belles Lettres*, 489
Rollock, Robert, 426
Roman Catholic Church, 186; Castilian universities and, 357; French clergy in England, 285; German universities, 498n; Tractarian Movement, 309, 317-22, 328; Roman Catholics: at Cambridge, 207-08, 233; emancipation in England, 285; at Oxford, 54; Oxford excludes, 7
Rosenkranz, Professor, 546
Rostock, University, 498
Rouse Ball, Walter William, 248
Rousseau, Jean Jacques, 278, 476
Royal Commission on Oxford (1852), 62-64, 66, 68, 277, 325, 327-35; Hebdomadal Board's reply to, 341-45; Tutors' Association opposed to, 335-41
Ruddiman, Thomas, 431
Rule, Gilbert, 426, 428
Rush, Benjamin, *Medical Inquiries . . . Diseases of the Mind*, 479
Russell, John, Bishop, 143, 147
Russell, Lord John, 328

Rust, Richard, 617, 621
Rutherford, Samuel, 413
Ruthin School, 193
Rutland, students from, 202
Rygge, Robert, 133

St. Bees School, 193, 197
Saint-German, 130
St. Maur monastery, 318
Saint-Pierre, Jacques Bernardin de, *Studies of Nature*, 479
St. Swithin's monastery, Winchester, 153
Salamanca, University, 380, 381, 394n; careers of graduates, 368-70; Colegios Mayores, 383, 385; cost of education, 387n; curriculum, 373-74, 376-77; decline, 376, 389, 390n, 393-94; degrees, 363; enrollment, 400-405; faculty, selection, 382; growth in 16th century, 357-58; monks in, 391; regional distribution of students, 365-67
Salter, H. E., 114, 126
Salzmann, Christian G., 501; *Carl von Carlsberg*, 503, 513
Sand, K. L., 539
Sandys, Edwin, Archbishop, 208
Santiago de Compostela, University, 357, 394n; curriculum, 377; decline, 389; degrees, 363n; growth in 16th century, 358; Jesuits in, 376; regional distribution of students, 365
Saturday Review (British), 578
Savigny, F. C., 495
Savile, John, 52
Scheidler, Karl Hermann, 544
Schelling, Friedrich Wilhelm von, 536
Schiller, Johann Christoph Friedrich von, 537
Schleiermacher, Friedrich, 468, 496, 536
Schlöffel, 559
Schlözer, J. G., 504
Schmoller, Gustav, 605
Schurz, Carl, 559
Scotland: Act of Union (1707), 409, 411, 417, 420; Church of (kirk, Presbyterian), 423-24, 426, 431; economic conditions, 414-16, 420, 442;

Index

Strassburg, University, 498n
Strauss, Professor, 548
Student, The, or the Oxford Monthly Miscellany, 264
Stukeley, William, 51
Stuteville, Sir Martin, 233
Suárez de Figueroa, Christóbal, *El Passagero*, 378-79
Suffolk, students from, 206
Sully, Thomas, *The Choice of Hercules*, 450, 455
Swale, Richard, 208
Swan, William, 137
Swift, Jonathan, 480

Tacitus, 478
Talladega College, 615
Tasso, Torquato, 479
Tatler, 429, 434
Taussig, Frank, 590, 591, 595-96; in Tariff Commission, 600-604
Taylor, Richard, 25
Terence, 478
Thirlwall, Connop, 265, 266
Thomas, Vaughan, 316-17
Thompson, J. C., 60
Tillotson, John, 220
Titmuss, Richard, 116
Toledo, 366, 378
Toledo, University, 393
Tonbridge, Oxford students from, 165-67
Tories at Oxford, 54-55, 320
Tractarian Movement, 309, 317-22, 328
Treaty of Paris (1782), 409
Tübingen, University, 552, 556
Tuckney, Dr., 231
Twyne, Brian, 221

Ullerston, Richard, 133
Undergraduate, The, 264-65
Underwood Tariff Act, 600
Unitarianism, 611
United States: black freedmen's education, 611-42 (*see also* freedmen); economics in government, 598-604; independents (mugwumps) in politics, 575-77; labor movement, 579, 585; Oxford students from, 68; public education, 582-83, 588;

Republican party, 575, 576, 579; Shipping Board, 605; Tariff Commission, 600-604, 608; War Industries Board, 599. *See also under* American
Uppingham School, 193, 202
Urban VI, Pope, 133

Valencia, University, 374, 394
Valladolid: auto-da-fé, 378; *Chancillería*, 386
Valladolid, University, 357, 360, 394n; careers of graduates, 368-70; Colegio Mayor, Santa Cruz, 383; curriculum, 373-74, 376-77; decline and recovery, 389, 393; degrees, 363n; enrollment, 405; faculty, selection, 382; growth in 16th century, 358; Jesuits in, 376; monks in, 391; regional distribution of students, 365, 367
Vaterlandsverein, 541
Vaughan, Bishop, 41
Vaughan, H. H., 333-34
Venn, J. A., 217
Venn, John, 249
Verein für Sozialpolitik, 587
Virgil, 478
Volney, Constantin de Chasseboeuf, Count de, 476
Voltaire, François Marie Arouet, 479

Wakefield Grammar School, 193, 195
Wales, Oxford students from, 35-36, 58, 68-70, 77-81, 199n, 209, 236, 253
Walker, Obadiah, 54
Wallace, George, 433
Wallace, Robert, 437
Wallace, Sir William, 434-35
Walpole, Sir Robert, 435
Warburton, William, 284
Ward, G.R.M., 318
Ward, Samuel, 187, 217, 220, 230
Ward, W. R., 309
Warham, William, Archbishop, 144-45
Warren, Mercy Otis, 479
Wartburg Festival, 538-39; second, 559, 560
Warton, Thomas, the younger, 264
Wase, Christopher, 41

LIBRARY OF CONGRESS CATALOGING IN PUBLICATION DATA

Main entry under title:

The University in society.

Product of a research seminar held at the Shelby Cullom Davis Center for Historical Studies, Princeton University, 1969-1971.

Includes bibliographical references.

CONTENTS: v. 1. Oxford and Cambridge.—v. 2. Europe, Scotland, and the United States.

1. Education, Higher—History—Addresses, essays, lectures. I. Stone, Lawrence, ed. II. Shelby Cullom Davis Center for Historical Studies.

LA183.U54   378   72-14033

ISBN I. 0-691-05213-1

ISBN II. 0-691-05214-X